THE ANGOLAN REVOLUTION:

THE ANATOMY OF AN EXPLOSION (1950–1962)

Map of Angola

THE ANGOLAN REVOLUTION VOLUME 1

THE ANATOMY OF AN EXPLOSION (1950–1962)

John Marcum

THE M.I.T. PRESS
Massachusetts Institute of Technology
Cambridge, Massachusetts, and London, England

Set in Linotype Baskerville. Printed and bound in the United States of America by Port City Press, Inc., Baltimore, Maryland.

Library of Congress catalog card number: 69–11310

FOR ANDREA

PREFACE

Writing of a revolution still in progress may be like exploring the crater of an erupting volcano—one may succeed only in getting burned. Moreover, when, as in this case, the revolution involves persons and ideals that command his personal respect, an author's capacity for objectivity may be sorely tested. This book is being written despite such problems in the hope that it may contribute something to public knowledge and understanding of a little-studied but important colonial conflict soon to enter its ninth year. While it does not presume to break methodological ground, it does attempt an intelligible presentation of data that may be useful for future comparative and theoretical analyses.

The absence of a free press or of conditions favoring the development of modern social science in Portugal has inhibited probing inquiry and research into conditions prevailing in its "Overseas Provinces." Foreign scholars have not been encouraged to fill the resulting knowledge gap, and consequently much of what has been written about Angola, Guinea-Bissau, and Mozambique has been uninformative and propagandistic.

The obstacles to serious research are imposing. All Angolan nationalist movements were illegal and clandestine from their inception. Many were infiltrated and broken up by the police and many of their leaders were jailed. Other nationalists fled into exile where the insecurities and intrigues of exile politics increasingly and understandably inclined them and their goal-frustrated movements to distrust the motives of prying scholars.

Excluded from academic inquiry, of course, are what would surely be some of the richest sources of information, i.e., the files of Portugal's secret police (PIDE) as well as those of the numerous foreign intelligence services that must be presumed to maintain a considerable interest in revolutions like that of Angola. Nevertheless, when pieced together, the disparate data that are available afford a measure of insight into the causes and course of the Angolan conflict. It has been possible to supplement mimeographed publications of nationalist movements, United Nations documents, and a wide assortment of reports, articles, and books published in Europe, Africa, and the United States—all fully cited in footnotes—with interviews and written accounts by exiled Angolan leaders and students. The author is particularly indebted to those Angolan informants for their invaluable assistance, which is also cited throughout. In order to protect persons inside Angola, however, some details and names have been omitted. The author is also responsible for translations from Portuguese and French into English, including attributed quotations.

Except for instances where it appears in direct quotations, Kongo is spelled with a K wherever it refers to the historic kingdom, kingship, or portion of the kingdom now under Portuguese rule, as distinct from the Congo republic of Brazzaville and Léopoldville. Often different words or spellings may be used for the names of persons, ethnic groups, or places in Angola. Some of the alternatives are listed, but one form has been selected for use thereafter on the premise that it seems to be the most common, modern, or simple. The names of some Angolan nationalist movements are given in French rather than Portuguese. This is true in the cases of Congo-based émigré or exile organizations that most commonly use the French form themselves.

Many of the materials used in the study were collected over the past decade during the course of several research trips to Africa—without any expectation that they would serve for more than occasional classroom use. These journeys began with an International Relations Fellowship from the Ford Foundation in 1958–59 and concluded with a Fulbright Hays Grant in 1966–67. Colgate and Lincoln Universities both made possible release time and resources that permitted the pursuit of this interest along with research in the field of African regionalism.

I am grateful to the Center for International Studies, M.I.T., for sponsoring publication of this first volume and for a research grant enabling me to complete the forthcoming second volume. This assistance was made possible by a grant to M.I.T. by the Ford Foundation for teaching and research in international affairs.

The following institutions granted access to relevant material in their libraries, morgues, or archives: the American Committee on

Africa; *Africa Report;* Boston University; Columbia University; Harvard University; the Hoover Institution, Stanford University; the Institut d'Études Politiques, University of Paris, France; the Library of Congress; the Massachusetts Institute of Technology; the University of California at Los Angeles. In addition to the many Angolans whose contributions form such an important part of the study, many others gave generously of their knowledge and advice. They include Professors Ronald Chilcote, James Duffy, and Douglas Wheeler; Bishop Ralph Dodge and Revs. David and James Grenfell, Malcolm McVeigh, Murray McInnes, and Theodore Tucker; Dr. Ian Gilchrist; Messrs. George Houser, Frank Montero, and William Scheinman.

JOHN MARCUM

Lincoln University, Pennsylvania
November 1, 1968

CONTENTS

PROLOGUE TO MODERN NATIONALISM 1

PART I The Rise of Angolan Nationalism: The Decade before the Revolution (1950–1960) 9

CHAPTER ONE

THE LUANDA-MBUNDU SOURCES OF ANGOLAN NATIONALISM 13

The Three Communities of Luanda 16
The Postwar Years 23
The Angolan Communist Party 27
Reaching the Boiling Point 30
The MPLA in Exile 37
Out beyond the Railroad 46

CHAPTER TWO

THE BAKONGO SOURCES OF ANGOLAN NATIONALISM 49

Kingship, Missionaries, and the Rise of Bakongo Nationalism 51
Royal Opposition: The Matadi Group 56
Less Royal Opposition: The Léopoldville Group 60
From UPNA to UPA 64
Trouble in the Congo 70
Simão Toco and the Baptists 76
Prenationalist Protest: From Toco to Assomizo 80
Congolese Independence: The UPA's Head Start 83
Four Other Parties and a Common Front 88
Out of the Front: Into the Fire 96

CHAPTER THREE

THE OVIMBUNDU, CHOKWE, AND RELATED SOURCES OF ANGOLAN NATIONALISM 101

The Ovimbundu Kingdoms 101
Rebels from the Seminary 105
Rebels from the Protestant Schools 108
Down South 112
To the East 115
The Decade of Rising Nationalism: In Summary 120

PART II The Year of Rebellion

CHAPTER FOUR

A SEQUENTIAL EXPLOSION 123

Cotton and Bombs: Maria's War 124
Riots and Vigilantes: Luanda 126
The Fifteenth of March 130
Moving toward Violence 135
A Match to Dry Kindling 140
Retaliation against Protestants 147
PIDE and Prison: Zones of Silence 154

CHAPTER FIVE

FOUR ANGOLAN RESPONSES TO THE NORTHERN REBELLION 159

The MPLA: For Revolution by Coalition 159
Bakongo Moderates: Continuing the Search for Nonviolent Alternatives 164
The Cabindans: A Marginal Reaction 172
The UPA: Adding New Structure—and Surviving 175

CHAPTER SIX

RESPONSES AND REPERCUSSIONS: THE WORLD AND PORTUGAL 181

The American Response 181
Other NATO Allies and Brazil 188
The Portuguese Response: Administrative Reforms 190
The Impact of Rebellion on Portuguese Guinea 193
The Impact of Rebellion on Mozambique 194

CHAPTER SEVEN

THE EMERGING STRUGGLE FOR REVOLUTIONARY LEADERSHIP 200

The MPLA's Autumn Offensive 200
Chetniks and Partisans: The Ferreira Affair 210
The End of the Year: Off to New York 219

PART III A Revolution in Transition

CHAPTER EIGHT

FROM REBELLION TO GUERRILLA WAR AND A GOVERNMENT IN EXILE 227

Inside Rebel Angola 228
Bakongo Moderates and the Revolution 233
The Kassanga-Kassinda Affair 236
The Angolan Revolutionary Government in Exile—GRAE 243
The MPLA: Response and Crisis 249
The GRAE in Quest of African Recognition and Support 255
Agostinho Neto: Last Hope for a Common Front? 263

CHAPTER NINE

AMERICAN, PORTUGUESE, AND COLONIAL RESPONSE TO CONTINUING REVOLUTION 268

The American Retreat 269
Portuguese Tenacity and Treason 277
Moving toward Revolution in Guinea and Mozambique 282

CHAPTER TEN

THE POLITICS OF REVOLUTION: SETTLING IN FOR A LONG STRUGGLE 285

The Bakongo Moderates 285
Multiplying Moderates 290
Micronationalism for Cabinda 295
Merging Streams 296
The MPLA under New Management 299
The GRAE under Roberto 302
Pan-African Perspectives 309

A CONCLUDING NOTE 314

APPENDIX A

PROTESTANTS AND REBELS 320

APPENDIX B

TWO PORTUGUESE DOCUMENTS 333

APPENDIX C

REBELS AND THE KONGOLESE THRONE 339

APPENDIX D

A FORGERY, AN UNPUBLISHED LETTER, AND A LEAFLET 343

APPENDIX E

A PARTIAL LIST OF ANGOLAN NATIONALIST MOVEMENTS—1944–1962 347

NAME INDEX 353

SUBJECT INDEX 361

LIST OF ILLUSTRATIONS

Map of Angola	Frontispiece
Portugal: A Self Portrait	xviii
Major Ethno-Linguistic Communities of Angola	12
Angolan Nationalist Movements and Antecedents	350

THE ANGOLAN REVOLUTION:

THE ANATOMY OF AN EXPLOSION (1950-1962)

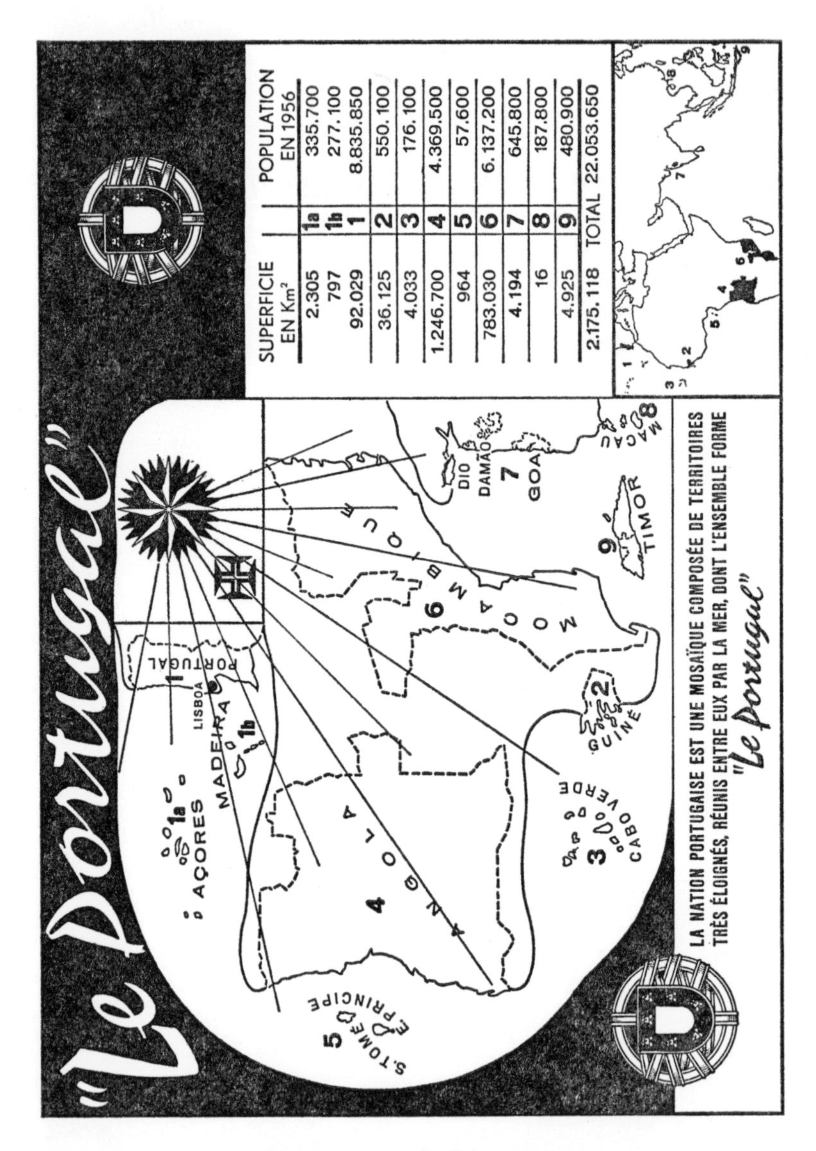

SUPERFICIE EN Km²		POPULATION EN 1956
2.305	1a	335.700
797	1b	277.100
92.029	1	8.835.850
36.125	2	550.100
4.033	3	176.100
1.246.700	4	4.369.500
964	5	57.600
783.030	6	6.137.200
4.194	7	645.800
16	8	187.800
4.925	9	480.900
2.175.118	TOTAL	22.053.650

Portugal: A Self Portrait
Post card map distributed at Portuguese pavilion, World's Fair, Brussels, 1958.

PROLOGUE TO MODERN NATIONALISM

In 1483 one of Portugal's venturesome explorer-navigators, Diogo Cão, dropped anchor in the Congo River estuary and inaugurated a prolonged history of Portuguese penetration into sub-Equatorial Africa. Portugal's King João II commissioned Cão to follow up his initial contact with the Kongo kingdom by making a return trip in 1485 to establish permanent relations. Organized within six somewhat autonomous provinces and bisected by the great Congo River, the kingdom then contained an estimated two and a half million Kikongo-speaking people residing in an area that covered what is present-day northern Angola and the Bakongo regions of the Congo republics of Kinshasa and Brazzaville.[1]

In response to Cão's mission, King Nzinga a Nkuwu, the kingdom's paramount chief or Mani Kongo, agreed to send a small group of his subjects to Portugal for education, and in 1490 he received in return three ships bringing Portuguese priests and skilled workers to evangelize and instruct in his kingdom. As part of this early day "technical assistance," the Europeans baptized the Mani Kongo and rebuilt in stone his capital situated at Mbanza Kongo (São Salvador) in the central province of Mpemba.

Unfortunately, this initially amicable relationship was soon undermined by the multinational slave trade which developed and then continued for some centuries as the principal motive force in Europe's relations with Africa. In the case of the Kongo, slave merchants began operating out of Portugal and the island of São Tomé. They preyed upon the Mani Kongo's kingdom and short-circuited his pleas to Lisbon for protection, teachers, and priests.

After his death in 1506 Nzinga a Nkuwu was succeeded by a son enthroned as Afonso I. The new ruler had been schooled in European culture but had not been taught how to cope with the worldly ravages and intrigues of the likes of the São Tomé adventurers. Nor was he able to control approximately two hundred Portuguese and mulatto clergy and functionaries who maneuvered for power

[1] Roland Oliver and J. D. Fage, *A Short History of Africa* (Baltimore: Penguin Books, 1962), p. 125.

about his throne. These groups undercut his authority and isolated him from the very people whom he wished to assimilate into the Portuguese culture of his training.[2] The result was the collapse of what might have been a pilot project in acculturation.

Convulsed by civil strife, Afonso's kingdom began to disintegrate. Conversely, the slave trade flourished and expanded along the coast from the Kongo port of Mpinda southward, and from 1576 on Luanda developed as a major slave port. Moving inland from the Luanda coastal area, Portuguese forces overwhelmed the Mbundu kingdom of Ndongo, a sometime tributary to the Kongo kingdom, and ensconced themselves permanently in a north-central wedge of what was eventually to become known as Angola. Between 1580 and 1836, when the trade was officially though not yet effectively abolished, some four million Africans were exported to Brazil and elsewhere from the Congo-Angola region, over three million from Angola alone.[3] Whole African communities were decimated. Whereas in 1591 an "enthusiastic official" could assure the Portuguese crown that the densely populated hinterland of Luanda would offer a plentiful supply of slaves "until the end of the world," a century later local authorities "were deploring the serious decline in the population of Angola owing to the internecine wars, excessive forced labor and the ravages of small pox." It reached the point where slave traders "had to travel for three months into the interior before reaching the markets [*pombos*] where slaves were sold." [4]

Only after the long centuries of the slave trade did Portugal gradually occupy the bulk of what constitutes modern-day Angola. Abolition was followed by a program of colonial expansion between 1845 and 1860, which included European colonization schemes, military ventures, and efforts to plant the Portuguese flag over formerly uncontrolled territory in the interior.[5] São Salvador was occupied by Portuguese forces in 1859–60. Disease, distance, and African resistance generally blocked Portuguese efforts to secure authority beyond the coast, however, and a policy of retreat and retrenchment followed from 1861 to 1877. São Salvador was

[2] James Duffy, *Portugal in Africa* (Cambridge, Mass.: Harvard University Press, 1962), pp. 38–43.

[3] *Ibid.*, p. 59.

[4] C. R. Boxer, *Race Relations in the Portuguese Colonial Empire 1415–1825* (Oxford: Clarendon Press, 1963), p. 28.

[5] See Douglas L. Wheeler, "Portuguese Expansion in Angola since 1836: A Re-examination" (Salisbury, Rhodesia: Central African Historical Association), Pamphlet No. 20 (1967), pp. 2–5.

abandoned in 1870. Then near the end of the century Portugal joined in the final burst of European colonial expansion in Africa. In an analysis of the motivation behind this new drive, historian Douglas L. Wheeler has concluded that the determining factor was a desire to shore up Portugal's declining prestige and power in Europe. "Imperialism for the Portuguese, therefore, was less an economic drive than a traditional, nationalistic one." [6]

Portugal's ambitions were somewhat thwarted by bigger colonial powers in the partitioning done at the Berlin Conference of 1884–85 and by its own inability to move with force and speed into the central African interior. Yet by the turn of the century, Portugal had gained international recognition for its nominal sovereignty over an African empire—Angola, Mozambique, Guinea—some twenty-two times its own size. The fact remained that effective occupation was limited to the coast and some adjoining plateau areas, and, in spite of more than 300 years of involvement in Angola, Portugal probably controlled less than one tenth of the territory within the colony's official borders. Saved from the territorial appetites of Europe's major colonial powers, whose jealousies largely checkmated their rival designs on diminutive Portugal's claims, Lisbon nevertheless faced serious African resistance to its widening control up to and even after the First World War.

The insecure, even tentative, character of Portugal's authority in Angola as late as the eve of the First World War was confirmed by negotiations between the Portuguese and the Jewish Territorial Organization of London, which was then looking for a territory within which to establish an "autonomous" Jewish community. Under the auspices of the Lisbon government, the Organization sent a commission to Angola to investigate the possibility of establishing a Jewish colony on the plateau area inland from Benguela in central Angola. Promoters of the scheme openly conjectured that the Portuguese government would feel compelled to cooperate with the project because it did not effectively occupy Angola, because it faced a threat of German encroachment from South West Africa, and because "a Jewish colony in Angola under the Portuguese flag [might] be the only way of keeping the flag flying there." [7] Portu-

[6] *Ibid.*, p. 9.

[7] Statement by Israel Zangwill in introduction to *Report on the Work of the Commission Sent out by the Jewish Territorial Organization under the Auspices of the Portuguese Government to Examine the Territory Proposed for the Purpose of a Jewish Settlement in Angola* (London: ITO Offices, 1913), p. IX.

guese authorities even initiated contact with a branch of the Jewish Territorial Organization in Kiev, and a retired Russian judge and state counselor, Jacob L. Peitel, thereupon visited Lisbon, where he and Jewish leaders from England and Switzerland participated in discussions with government officials and local Jewish circles concerning the Angolan project. It was Peitel's impression that, although Portugal, with at that time only 6.5 million people, was unable to organize massive emigration of its own or to accept settlement by any single non-Portuguese national group, which might produce a conflict of loyalties, it was receptive to promoting settlement in Angola by a multinational Jewish community.[8] By so doing, Portuguese authority might be bolstered at a minimal cost or risk. As a consequence of these initiatives, in June 1912 the Portuguese Chamber of Deputies passed a bill authorizing concessions to Jewish settlers. Its provisions for individual settlement, naturalization, and acculturation did not, however, meet the requirements of the Jewish organization for collective colonization, communal autonomy, and an initial grant of 5000 square miles of land. Furthermore, there was apparently some fear in Lisbon that it would be dangerous to enter into a formal contract with such a strong and well-financed London-based organization. Expression of interest in such an accord from British Foreign Secretary Sir Edward Grey and his ambassador in Lisbon may have contributed to Portuguese suspicion and reticence. In any case, no agreement for the establishment of a Jewish homeland in Angola was reached before the First World War intervened and refocused Jewish attention upon Palestine. (The war, incidentally, also insured Portugal against future German expansion into Angola from the south.)

During Portugal's turbulent life as a democratic republic from 1910 to 1932 European control was secured over all the interior of Angola in spite of violent resistance by Mbundu, Ovimbundu, Cuanhama, and other peoples. The sparsely populated eastern third of the country was the last to come under effective colonial administration—around 1930. The early republican period also saw the continued development of a critical "free press" in Luanda, where in the 1880's a small educated African and *mestiço* elite had already begun to use the printed page as a new instrument for asserting indigenous against colonial interests. This promising

[8] Jacob L. Peitel, *Iz Moei Zhizni* [From My Life], (Paris: Ya Povolotshii and Co., 1925), pp. 215–223.

channel for dialogue and political education was, however, foreclosed by official censorship introduced by the Angolan High Commissioner Norton de Matos in 1922.

With the advent of Dr. António Salazar's conservative and ultranationalist *Estado Novo* in the 1930's, Portugal's overseas territories assumed increased importance as the *sine qua non* of its claim to a place among the world's major powers. Portugal could bask in the "magnificent certainty" of being "the third colonial power in the world." [9] (Within thirty years, of course, it would occupy first place.) Moreover, it translated its belief in a self-appointed "civilizing mission"—pursued with what was at least a relative freedom from color consciousness—into an official policy of assimilation. In 1951 all of Portugal's overseas possessions were officially incorporated into the Portuguese state. The revised Political Constitution of the Portuguese Republic proclaimed that it was "intrinsic in the Portuguese nation to fulfill its historic mission of colonization," and "to diffuse among the populations inhabiting [the Overseas Territories] the benefits of [Portuguese] civilization," since these territories were an "integral part of the Portuguese State." [10] By fiat, then, a small preindustrial state of nine million people with an illiteracy rate of some 40 per cent and a per capita annual income of around 250 dollars, claimed to have done what France, with its much greater resources had, if somewhat half-heartedly, tried and failed to do, i.e., assimilate millions of Africans as black Europeans.

The gap between Portugal's imperial ambitions and its material means was too great. By 1950 at most about 0.75 per cent of the African population of Angola, that is, some 30,000 out of over 4,000,000 Africans, had become *assimilados,* whereas the rest remained "uncivilized" *indígenas* without political or civil rights.[11] Moreover there could be no expectation of a rapid change in this situation, for as late as 1956 only about 1 per cent of the African school-age population was attending school, as compared with a

[9] Jorge Ameal as quoted in James Duffy, *Portuguese Africa* (Cambridge, Mass.: Harvard University Press, 1959), p. 270.

[10] Amendment Law No. 2048, June 11, 1951.

[11] Prof. Gwendolen M. Carter has estimated that even this 1950 figure is swollen by the inclusion of unqualified (less educated) wives of *assimilados,* as well as their children. She concludes that there were "no more than between 8,000 and 10,000 true *assimilados* within Angola" constituting only 0.25 per cent of the African population. Carter, *Independence for Africa* (New York: Frederick A. Praeger, 1960), p. 99.

1958 figure of 11 per cent for neighboring Northern Rhodesia, where the British were not even trying to assimilate Africans.[12]

Lisbon organized a migration of Portuguese settlers following the Second World War, which pushed the white population of Angola up from 80,000 to approximately 200,000 between 1950 and 1961. Yet even that immigration did little in the short run to further the cause of assimilation. Drawn from "the harsh backlands" and urban slums of Portugal, the settlers were largely illiterate and unprepared for multiracial living. They upset the status quo at African expense, by appropriating farm land and preempting semiskilled jobs such as taxi driving. Feeling insecure and threatened by potential competition from young educated Africans, they were the first to take to antiblack vigilante action and to oppose liberal reforms when Africans rebelled.[13]

The government sought to bar or limit any disruptive foreign influences that might undermine its assimilation policy and was particularly exercised by the "danger" of the Protestant missions that had established themselves in several areas of Angola toward the end of the nineteenth century. The government resented Anglo-Saxon and Swiss missionaries for their allegedly systematic refusal "to educate the native for the Portuguese concept of integration," and for their inherent incapacity to believe that Angolans and Mozambicans were Portuguese. Many Protestant missionaries, it was charged, persisted in "preaching self-determination as the only possible solution for problems and difficulties that foreigners and only foreigners [had] raised in the path so far followed by Portuguese policy." [14] In order to secure themselves against the unsettling evangelism and heretical schools of these interlopers, the administration responded with a policy of harassment designed to squeeze them out. This policy was sharply intensified after the armed uprising of 1961, and the number of American missionary personnel fell drastically thereafter from 300 to less than 100. During this period,

[12] Rev. Thomas Okuma, who spent eight years as a Congregational minister and teacher in southern Angola, has further contrasted the educational programs of the British and Portuguese by noting the following comparison: the Northern Rhodesian government was spending approximately four dollars *per capita* on education in 1959, whereas available data indicated that the equivalent figure of expenditure by the Portuguese government was about six cents. Okuma, *Angola in Ferment* (Boston: Beacon Press, 1962), pp. 45–46.

[13] *The New York Times*, March 21, 1961.

[14] Portugal, National Office of Information, *Portugal, An Informative Review*, No. 6 (Nov.-Dec. 1961), p. 379.

the administration continued to operate under a semi "closed-door" religious provision in the 1951 Constitution (Art. 140) which provided that: "The Portuguese Catholic missions overseas and the establishments for training personnel for their service and for those of the *padroado* [patronage] shall, in conformity with the Concordata and other agreements concluded with the Holy See, enjoy juridical personality and shall be protected and assisted by the State as being institutions of education and assistance and instruments of civilization."

In addition to factors of national prestige, power, and "mission," the fact that Angola had become a great economic asset by the 1950's had important implications for Portuguese policy. An estimated half million African *contratados* provided cheap forced labor for Portuguese administrators, traders, and farmers.[15] As of 1959, Angola's annual coffee exports had risen to nearly 50 million dollars and diamonds to over 20 million, and newly discovered petroleum and iron resources, coupled with an influx of West German and other western capital, promised increasing revenue in foreign currency. This Angolan "boom" helped to offset Portugal's own balance-of-payments deficit totaling about 135 million dollars.

Portugal's ability to maintain the colonial status quo, however, weakened in proportion to the growth of African political consciousness and restiveness over the abuses of the conscript labor system. Not only the absence of free ballots, a critical press, or independent courts, but the very permissiveness of article 146 in the Constitution deprived Africans of any protection against systematic exploitation of their labor by local European interests. "The State," said article 146, "may only compel the natives to work on public works of general interest to the community, or tasks of which the finished product will belong to them, in the execution of judicial sentences of a penal character or for the discharge of fiscal liabilities." Accordingly, government administrators needed only to increase local

[15] As late as 1961 a British team investigating the situation relating to Angolan refugees in the Congo reported that within Angola men were still being conscripted for periods up to eighteen months, that women were still being put to work mending roads, and that children from eight years of age and up were known to have been working in the mines and on the coffee plantations. See George Thomas, M.P., and Rev. Eric L. Blakebrough in *Congo-Angola Border Enquiry* (London: Angola Action Group, 1961), p. 12. The British journalist Basil Davidson was among those who had earlier brought international attention to this system. Following a perceptive visit to Angola he wrote an angry article, "Africa's Modern Slavery," *Harper's,* Vol. 209, No. 1250 (July 1954), pp. 56–68.

head taxes to produce more laborers through fiscal liability. In addition to rural resentment against conscript labor, the economic modernization, urbanization, and education, albeit limited, that came along with European settlement induced social ferment within a growing segment of African society.

On the surface Angola remained calm and in 1956 such a sensitive observer of African affairs as Oxford's Thomas Hodgkin wrote of "the apparent non-existence of nationalism in Portuguese Africa." [16] Yet had scholars and journalists been allowed to carry out free inquiry inside Angola, they would surely have come forth with a different assessment. Some literate and literary precursors of modern African nationalism had been protesting as early as the second half of the nineteenth century, and by the early 1950's, though largely unperceived by the outside world, Angolan poets, prophets, peasants, students, functionaries, and émigrés had created a wide assortment of protonationalist movements. Within the decade 1950–1960 Angolan nationalism developed into an important challenge to continued Portuguese rule.

Portugal tried desperately to seal out the wave of political and social change that was sweeping over much of a continent. Yet five centuries after Diogo Cão's first contact with the Kongo kingdom African nationalists were demanding that Portugal restore the kingdom's sovereignty. More were demanding independence for the whole of Angola. Viewing this state of affairs with his customary coolness, Portugal's Dr. Salazar commented in 1961: "A law recognizing citizenship takes minutes to draft and can be made right away; a citizen that is a man fully and consciously integrated into a civilized political society takes centuries to achieve." [17] The Portuguese premier was unprepared to make concessions to the increasingly impatient demands for political reform. Unlike Britain, France, and Belgium, Portugal seemed unwilling to speed up the pace of social and economic change, or to relinquish political power. If it took centuries to produce Salazar's fully civilized man, however, it took a much shorter time to produce a host of consciously unassimilated and rebellious African nationalists.

[16] Thomas Hodgkin, *Nationalism in Colonial Africa* (London: Frederick Muller, 1956), pp. 17–18.
[17] *The New York Times,* May 31, 1961.

PART I

THE RISE OF ANGOLAN NATIONALISM: THE DECADE BEFORE THE REVOLUTION (1950-1960)

It is Angola that has loomed largest in the imperial thinking of Portugal's nationalist politicians, commercial investors, and cultural evangelists. The temperate climate of its central and southern highlands (Amboim, Bié, and Huila), the homelike qualities of its old-establishment coastal towns (Luanda, Benguela, and Moçâmedes), the wealth of its remote diamond fields (replete with company garden town at Dundo), and the remunerative plantation agriculture of its green north (Carmona-Uige)—all these qualities enticed important numbers of Portuguese settlers to Angola, especially after the Second World War. And even more important, these assets excited Portugal's advocates and architects of imperial "mission."

It is also Angola that may claim to have been the first of Portugal's overseas territories to give organized expression to sentiments of modern African nationalism. Political awareness and action developed in a variety of ways and took diverse forms: syncretic religions, movements to restore indigenous kingdoms, ethnic-cultural and mutual-aid societies, and literary, cultural, religious, and youth organizations. All groups suspected of political content were banned. Yet such suppression was only partly effective, as some groups succeeded for a while in dissimulating their political sentiments, more went underground, and still others directed their activity from adjoining sanctuaries in the Congo or Northern Rhodesia and organized among peoples straddling Angola's frontiers. Within Angola the demands of secrecy and the exploits of the police and police informers meant that most groups had only short life spans, small memberships, and isolated impact. In the urban matrix of Luanda, for instance, several clandestine groups apparently operated alongside one another for some time without contact or even knowledge of each other's existence.

In time, as police and military repression intensified, many nationalists fled the country. Once outside where they could communicate freely among themselves, they tended to coalesce or to stand apart according to class and communal loyalties. Reflecting the "elite-versus-masses" dichotomy in Portugal's own social class structure, as well as the polarity that was intrinsic in any colonial system, nationalists from the small multiracial class of educated and semieducated town dwellers found themselves competing with rivals more closely identified with the rural, largely uneducated, black peasantry that constituted the bulk of the country's five million people. At the same time, Angolans also clustered together politically on the basis of strictly precolonial ethnic and regional origins. Taken together, the influence of class and ethnicity resulted in a tripolarity, as reflected in what ultimately developed as the major streams of Angolan nationalism: (1) Luanda-Mbundu, with a predominantly urban, elite leadership, and (2) Bakongo and (3) Ovimbundu plus Chokwe, (2) and (3) with rural, peasant orientations. (See chart in Appendix E.)

In addition to producing a number of small particularist organizations, each of these three streams ultimately gave birth to a major nationalist movement, or alliance of movements, with sufficient following outside its own regional base to give it some grounds for a claim to represent an all-inclusive, all-Angolan nationalism. Gradually these same mainstream movements became locked into positions of bitter antagonism as partisan competition, personal ambitions, and cold-war diplomacy reinforced and added to their communal differences. As newcomers from Angola came to the ranks of nationalist movements outside, they found themselves caught up in rough internecine struggles for which their localized experiences inside the country—where the colonial order was more clearly the principal target—had often not prepared them.

Once in exile, idealistic young men who had left their country hoping to participate in a united campaign to liberate it discovered that, not only social and ethnic divisions, but now considerations of party mythology, political ideology, and foreign aid, ranged them against one another.

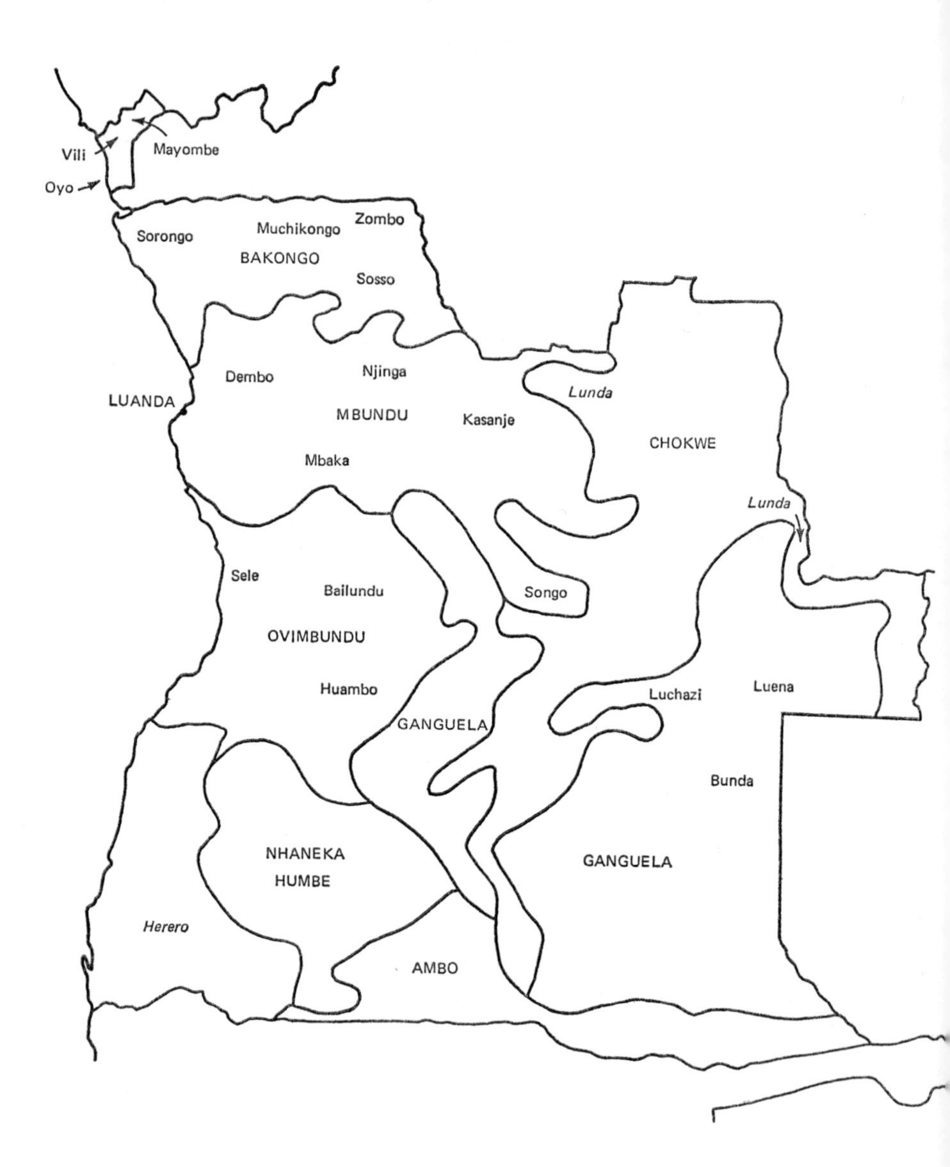

Major Ethno-Linguistic Communities of Angola

CHAPTER ONE

THE LUANDA-MBUNDU SOURCES OF ANGOLAN NATIONALISM

All three major streams of Angolan nationalism derive from or were to some extent influenced by the strong flow of urban and intellectual protest that first developed in Luanda and then spread into its Kimbundu-speaking hinterland. Inhabited by the Mbundu (Ambundu or Kimbundu) people,[1] this area of Angola represents an early and important exception to the general rule that the Portuguese, like other Europeans, did not themselves penetrate in force into the interior of Africa during the period of the slave trade. The Portuguese started like other European powers by confining themselves to coastal areas where they could purchase slaves supplied from wars waged by others. They later began conducting their own military campaigns, however, moving from Luanda up the Kwanza River into the interior in quest of slaves and silver. Beginning on the coast in 1575 and progressing inland by stages during the next century, their forces overwhelmed Mbundu resistance and transformed the Mbundu homeland into what has been called "the first African nation to be subjected to European rule." [2]

When the Portuguese first arrived, the Mbundu were concentrated in a kingdom known as Ndongo, situated along the coastal plain between the Dande and Kwanza Rivers. During the sixteenth century, Ndongo thrived as an intermediary and outlet for the Atlantic slave trade. It was a kingdom in which authority was highly cen-

[1] The Defense Department's *Area Handbook for Angola,* DA PAM No. 550–59, prepared by Allison Butler Herrick, et al., of American University (Washington, D.C.: U.S. Government Printing Office, 1967), uses the collective term Kimbundu. It describes the core of the Kimbundu community as 700,000 Ambundu, Mbaka, and Ndongo people, surrounded by another 500,000 persons belonging to "peripheral tribes" which speak related but distinct dialects (p. 90).

[2] David Birmingham, *The Portuguese Conquest of Angola* (London: Oxford University Press, 1965), p. 1.

tralized and rank was important. Reputedly, commoners were obliged to live in windowless, one-door dwellings and to serve a ruler, or *ngola,* who enjoyed the privilege of two doors and two windows. As Portuguese forces thrust inland, however, they undermined the authority of the *ngola.* In 1629 they imposed a puppet ruler, Ngola Ari, and provoked a major Mbundu migration eastward. Later in the same century, when a resurgent successor, Ngola Ari II, began to manifest troublesome signs of independence, a Portuguese expeditionary force led by Luis Lopes de Sequeira laid siege to the kingdom's rock-fortress capital at Pungu a Ndongo. On November 29, 1671, after an armed contest of some months, the Portuguese entered and sacked the town where they captured hundreds of slaves. They then beheaded Ngola Ari II and sent his son, Dom Philip, to the monastery of Alcobaça in Portugal. The area of Ndongo eventually became known as Angola, after the *ngola* whose kingdom was extinguished with a completeness that left no vestiges of kingship around which a modern, yet traditionalist, opposition might later rally, as it did to the north in the old Kongo kingdom.

To escape European domination, some Mbundu, i.e., the Pende, moved eastward in the seventeenth century, settling outside the boundaries of present-day Angola, as far away as the area around Tshikapa in the Kasai. Others, led by an enemy of Ngola Ari and the Portuguese, a redoubtable woman known as Queen Nzinga Mbande (or Njinga Pande, 1582–1663) moved northeastward and took over a local kingdom called Matamba located on the western side of the Cambo River. From this refugee Mbundu kingdom, Queen Nzinga tried to reconquer Ndongo, for which purpose she allied herself with the Dutch during their brief occupation of Luanda (1641–1648). Though she failed in this mission, her guile and resourceful defiance nonetheless made her "the most important personality in Angola" between 1620 and 1663.[3] Borrowing from the style of roving Imbangala armies that had come from the Lunda empire to the east, she reportedly practiced both ritual cannibalism and infanticide in developing a "hardened corps of followers with a strong religious element in their political association."[4] And though she and Matamba eventually (1656) came to terms with

[3] David Birmingham, *Trade and Conflict in Angola: The Mbundu and their Neighbors under the Influence of the Portuguese 1483–1790* (Oxford: Clarendon Press, 1966), p. 89.

[4] *Ibid.,* p. 101.

and traded with the Portuguese, she is eulogized by contemporary Angolan nationalists as a legendary heroine who led her people in thirty years of warfare against "Portuguese aggressors" and "never accepted Portuguese sovereignty [before her death] at the age of eighty-two." [5]

In sum, the western Mbundu or "Ngolas" of the former kingdom of Ndongo, i.e., those who stayed put as the Europeans advanced, came under considerable Portuguese influence. On the contrary, eastern Mbundu of Matamba, called "Jingas" after Queen Nzinga, maintained into the late nineteenth century an independent kingdom in which European influence was kept at a minimum.

Southeast of Matamba, on the wide plain lying between the upper Kwango River and the Tala Mugongo mountains, another kingdom consisting largely of Mbundu refugees from Ndongo, and known as Kasanje (or Cassange), emerged during the second half of the seventeenth century as an important trade link between the Portuguese and the Lunda empire of the Kasai basin, and for another hundred years "dominated a large part of the westward [slave] trade of Central Africa." [6] This area, long linked to Portuguese commerce but resistant to Portuguese influence, gave rise, not long after its final demise as a kingdom, to prenationalist protest separate and distinct from that produced to the west in the core of the Luanda-Mbundu region, which was under Portuguese rule much longer.

Early in the twentieth century Portuguese influence within the interior of Mbundu country was extended and confirmed by the construction of a railroad linking Luanda to Catete, Dondo, Golungo Alto, and Malange—a communications axis that later served to spread modern political ideas and movements inland from Luanda. Yet opposition persisted, notably within one Mbundu area outside of Luanda that was "more than superficially affected by Portuguese cultural influences," namely, the nearby Dembos hill country to the northeast between the Bengo and Loge Rivers.[7] Bordering on the Bakongo territories of the old Kongo kingdom, to which Dembo chiefs had once paid tribute, the Dembos area, in

[5] MPLA, *Angola in Arms* (Dar es Salaam), No. 1 (Jan. 1967), p. 5. See also Castro Soromenho. "Portrait, Jinga, reine de Ngola et de Matamba," *Présence Africaine* (Paris), No. 42 (1962), pp. 47–53.

[6] Birmingham, *Trade and Conflict in Angola,* p. 99.

[7] C. R. Boxer, *Race Relations in the Portuguese Colonial Empire 1415–1825* (Oxford: Clarendon Press, 1963), p. 36.

spite (or because) of the early presence there of Portuguese traders, missionaries, and advisors to its chiefs, was in a state of revolt during most of the nineteenth century. Its struggle against Portuguese pacification forces from 1907 to 1910 may be said to form an historical link between traditionalist and nationalist resistance to Portuguese rule, for it is still alive in the collective memory of Angola's Kimbundu-speaking community of over 1,100,000 now living in the Dembos and other Mbundu regions that extend north and south of the Luanda-Malange railroad. In 1908, after a costly military campaign at the close of the previous year had failed to secure the area for the Portuguese, a local chief, Dembo Cazuangongo, organized attacks on Europeans working on the railroad. He battled with Portuguese reinforcements, then took to the wooded Dembos hills from whose sanctuary his rebels continued to wage a kind of prenationalist guerrilla warfare for another two years.

Another focal point of African and mulatto discontent was the area around Ambaca (or M'Baka). During much of the nineteenth and early twentieth century, Catholic missions had been especially active in this region, about 100 miles inland from Luanda along the prerailroad trade routes. While some of the local people, or *Ambaquistas,* served as auxiliary soldiers in the Portuguese army, others proved rebellious and gave early support to the proposition that centers of colonial education and acculturation often produced reasoned colonial discontent.

The Three Communities of Luanda

The Angolan center from which all Portuguese power and influence radiated was the city of Luanda. European impact there was so intense as to differ in kind from the Lusitanian imprint on the rest of the colony. The comparatively long and sizable Portuguese "presence" in the colonial capital created a unique urban community composed of three demographic subcommunities, European, mulatto, and African. All three groups contributed to the development of Angolan nationalism in general, but more particularly to the Luanda-Mbundu stream.[8]

[8] Boxer, *ibid.,* p. 39, writes that the slave trade early gave rise to three classes in Luanda: "a powerful slave-owning and slave-trading white class, . . . a detribalized class of Negroes who cooperated in this trade with the Portuguese, and . . . a Mulatto and Mestiço class, some of whom attained important positions in the militia, in the slave-trade, and in the Church."

For centuries Luanda had a small European population (almost exclusively male) which consisted of government officials, military personnel, deported convicts, clergy, and traders. Yet by 1913 the total white population of Angola was only 12,000 and remained dependent upon the metropolitan economy and army. The European population spectacularly mushroomed and diversified after 1930—especially after the Second World War—and in Luanda alone reached a figure in excess of 60,000 by the mid-1960's. Though a few of Luanda's Europeans could then claim to be descendants of several generations of white Angolans, most were but recently from Portugal, for the colony's total European population of approximately 200,000 in 1960 had been only 44,000 as late as 1940.[9]

The social and economic elite that formed the top level of Luanda's heterogeneous white community was relatively cosmopolitan and at the same time insulated from both the African peasantry and those of its own compatriots who settled as farmers, fishermen, and traders in central and southern Angola. It included factions supporting local European autonomy. Such sentiment developed early, encouraged by the antigovernment attitudes of political dissidents exiled to the colony (1860–1890), by the example of and contact with independent Brazil and Brazilians, and by the general feeling among whites known as the "Sons of Angola" that they and not Lisbon understood and spoke for the true interests of Portuguese Angola.

The white community also included Portuguese liberals such as the *Democratas de Angola,* middle-class anti-Salazarists who argued for democratic reform and decentralization under continued Portuguese rule. In Portugal after the collapse of the republic and economy began in the 1920's, however, no virile democratic alternative developed in the form of a Christian or socialist movement capable of seriously challenging the authoritarian, right-wing Salazarist regime. Instead conditions favored the growth of a disciplined and *sub rosa* opposition on the far left. This political polarization was projected into Angola via the European community of Luanda. Thus during the late 1940's and early 1950's a small but active number of anti-Salazarists of Marxist persuasion began to organize and proselytize in the city. They promoted the develop-

[9] Though they included the expeditionary army and possibly reflected wishful official thinking, by 1966 some estimates of Angola's white population went as high as 300,000. See *The New York Times,* May 5, 1966.

ment of both white and nonwhite class and political consciousness. Elitist class rule and antiquated, preindustrial mercantilism rendered the Portuguese government and its economic relationship to Angola particularly susceptible to their Marxist analysis.

Luanda, like the south-coast town of Benguela, has long contained a second politically important minority, a mulatto community that by 1960 numbered in the neighborhood of 15,000 out of a total of probably well over 50,000 mulattoes in the country at large.[10] The Angolan poet Mário António has written of the "Creole islands" of Luanda and Benguela.[11] This minority is a product of the historically long, if sparse, Portuguese "presence" in the colony. According to an early Luandan, António de Oliveira Cadornega, who lived in Angola from 1639 to 1685, Portuguese soldiers, sailors, and civilians, for "lack of white ladies," commonly formed fleeting unions with African women during that period, thus giving birth to a sizable mulatto population.[12] This practice was not short-lived, for as late as 1900 there were only about 100 white women living in Luanda. During the eighteenth century the mulatto population outnumbered Europeans by three or four to one, and it still enjoyed a numerical advantage going into the twentieth century.[13]

In more recent years the numerical expansion of the mulatto population has emerged as a conscious aim of Portuguese policy, a policy designed to de-Africanize and assimilate. Lisbon has embarked upon a last-ditch effort to build and secure the future of European political control on the foundation of an expanded and assimilated mulatto society. Thus in May 1966 Drew Middleton of *The New York Times* reported the unguarded comments of a Portuguese official who told him "bluntly, and probably realistically, that the presence in Angola of 50,000 troops from metropolitan Portugal would increase the birthrate of mulatto children," and who further predicted with approval that these mulattoes would

[10] Óscar Soares Barata, "Aspectos dos condições demográficas de Angola," *Angola, Curso de Extensão Universitária, Ano Lectivo de 1963–1964* (Lisbon: Instituto Superior de Ciências Sociais e Política Ultramarina [1964]), p. 127.

[11] See Gerald M. Moser, "African Literature in Portuguese: The First Written, The Last Discovered," *African Forum*, Vol. 2, No. 4 (Spring 1967), p. 92.

[12] António de Oliveira Cadornega, *História Geral das Guerras Angolanas*, Vol. III (Lisbon, 1942), p. 30.

[13] See Douglas L. Wheeler, "Portuguese Expansion in Angola since 1836: A Re-examination" (Salisbury, Rhodesia: Central Africa Historical Association), Pamphlet No. 20 (1967), p. 13.

"have the future of Angola in their hands." To the same correspondent a "hard-bitten general officer" expressed his hope "that each Portuguese soldier [in Angola] would leave at least six mulatto children behind when he returned home." [14] What future African attitudes would be toward these children of Portuguese policy could only be a matter of somber conjecture.

From the beginning mulattoes both suffered and profited from their vulnerable, caught-in-between position. The Portuguese made military use of them, judging them to be "good material for soldiers, well able to endure the short [rations] and other hardships of tropical warfare in the backlands." [15] They also employed mulattoes as slave dealers and as sailors to man the São Tomé ships carrying "black ivory" [slaves] to whom they were "related by blood." [16] As early as the seventeenth century, then, the Portuguese were using the mulatto to serve colonial interests to the detriment of African interests, and were thereby creating a legacy of mistrust between mulatto and African that has endured into the era of African nationalist politics.

Within Luanda's mulatto community—as within its European and African communities—social stratification based on occupation and education developed and persisted as a divisive, fragmenting force into the middle of the twentieth century. Nevertheless, the founding of a mulatto association, the *Liga Angolana,* in 1913 provided evidence of a degree of mulatto ethnic solidarity.

Relatively privileged access to education and social opportunity led some mulattoes not only to white-collar jobs but to intellectual and even political protest. The difficulties and ambivalences inherent in their position are suggested in the writing of a small mulatto elite that produced a stream of European-style protest as well as proregime literature during what Douglas Wheeler has termed Luanda's " 'free press' era of 1866–1923." [17] Increased Portuguese emigration to Angola in the period of colonial expansion after 1880 had resulted in serious socioeconomic conflict as

[14] *The New York Times,* May 5, 1966.

[15] C. R. Boxer, *Portuguese Society in the Tropics: The Municipal Councils of Goa, Macao, Bahia, and Luanda, 1500–1800* (Madison: University of Wisconsin Press, 1965), p. 129.

[16] Boxer, *Race Relations,* p. 16.

[17] Douglas L. Wheeler, "A Nineteenth Century African Protest in Angola: The Radical Journalism of José de Fontes Pereira (1823–1891)," in Ali Mazrui and Robert *Rotberg, The Traditions of Black Protest in Africa* (Cambridge, Mass.: Harvard University Press, in preparation).

Europeans—often less educated—overturned the local situation in which *mestiços* and a few Africans had come to dominate the services, trades, and civil service. While African grievances still generally found expression in armed rebellion, mulattoes found in the Luanda press a new vehicle for expressing their growing resentment and frustration in the late nineteenth and early twentieth centuries.

The crusading journalism of José de Fontes Pereira (1823–1891) exemplified this form of protest. He belonged to a community that generally considered itself culturally Portuguese and superior to the African peasant. Yet Pereira not only attacked corruption, forced labor, prison brutality, and educational neglect; he went beyond conversion to the republican cause to become "a pioneer in advocating independence for Africans in Angola." [18]

In more recent times, mulattoes confronted by problems of identity—were they primarily European, African, or an elite apart? —were understandably attracted by the political arguments of European Marxists who stressed the importance of class as opposed to racial conflict. Perhaps the principal combined contribution of Luanda's white and mulatto "intellectuals" to the development of Angolan nationalism was their early injection of economic determinism and socialist radicalism into local nationalist thinking.

The third and largest component in Luanda's population has been and is, of course, African. It grew rapidly during the last four decades. The jobs and illusory glamor of the Angolan capital attracted tens of thousands of Africans from all over the territory. They came, settled, coexisted and, to some extent, intermixed, thus forming the nucleus of what was to become a population of some 200,000 African city dwellers, so distinct that a noted ethnologist classified them as a separate ethnic community, the Luandans.[19]

This indigenous community has long included a small black elite that came to view European education as the proper basis for social status, and even as a necessary qualification for political leadership. In the Congo the Belgians built up a broad-based system of primary, trade, and teachers' training schools, which were complemented by a number of Catholic seminaries, and they used vernacular languages as a transition into French-language education. The Portuguese, on the other hand, relied on a narrow-

[18] *Ibid.*

[19] José Redinha, "Ethnic Distribution in the Province of Angola," *Mensário Administrativo* (Luanda), Nos. 167–172 (July–Dec. 1961). (Joint Publications Research Service 28,083, Dec. 31, 1964), p. 6.

based elitist system that placed great stress on the exclusive use of Portuguese as a unifying and assimilating medium of instruction and communication. Though the Portuguese educated fewer Africans, they had by 1958 produced some twenty-three Africans with degrees in higher education, as compared with but eighteen in the Congo two years later.[20] Some of the Africans who were educated and kept safely in Portugal and others who resided in Luanda became aware of and were outraged by the inherent social and economic injustice of the colonial system. They made sporadic, usually cautious, efforts at political protest.

Though numerically weak, the *assimilados* were affected by the same class consciousness and elitism that permeated European and mulatto society. Not only were they expected to break off all association with their country's unworthy traditionalist society—even family—they were further ranked and divided according to the extent of their education and the nature of their occupation. Thus even in protest *assimilados* reflected European values. An early example of *assimilado* protest can be found in the history of a traditionalist leader, Prince Nicolas of the Kongo (1830?–1860). Douglas Wheeler tells us that, following a visit to Lisbon in the years 1845–1847(?), Nicolas studied and worked as a civil servant in Luanda, where republican and Brazilian influences abounded. Possibly influenced by personal ambition, he grew to view European education as vital for Africans assuming positions of traditional authority. When in 1859 an illiterate was enthroned as king of the Kongo (Dom Pedro V), Nicolas charged that the Portuguese were able to exact an oath of loyalty from him precisely because he and his aides lacked the education necessary to protect the kingdom's "national independence."[21]

Assimilados and mulattoes often cooperated in protest action. In 1921 a conservative interterritorial group of educated Africans and mulattoes formed a *Partido Nacional Africano* (PNA) in Lisbon and, in the forum of the First Portuguese Republic, argued that Angola and other overseas territories should be accorded a measure

[20] Clifford Parsons, "The Makings of a Revolt," in *Angola: A Symposium, Views of a Revolt* (London: Oxford University Press, 1962), p. 78 (hereafter cited as *Angola: A Symposium*).

[21] Douglas L. Wheeler, "A Nineteenth Century African Protest: Prince Nicolas of Kongo (1830?–1860)," *Journal of African Historical Studies* (Boston University), Vol. I, No. 1 (1968), pp. 40–59.

of autonomy.[22] Then in 1923, coincident with the pending collapse of the democratic republic, W. E. B. DuBois decided to hold the second session of the Third Pan-African Congress in Lisbon, because, in the words of George Padmore, "He hoped that this gesture would strengthen the agitation of [another] small group of Portuguese African intellectuals then living in Lisbon to achieve some measure of reform in the Portuguese colonies, especially Angola and the cocoa islands of São Tomé and Principe." [23] Through its spokesman, Deputy Megalhães, this second interterritorial group known as the *Liga Africana* described its function as that of petitioning the government "in no ambiguous terms but in a highly dignified manner" for measures designed to "avoid injustice or bring about the repeal of harsh laws." It acted within the bounds of legality "without making any appeal to violence and without leaving constitutional limits."[24]

The coming of the *Estado Novo* brought an end to such legal protest action in Portugal as well as in Angola. Already Luanda's bumptious press had been throttled by censorship imposed by High Commissioner Norton de Matos in 1922, and this clamp-down was perpetuated by the Salazar government after 1926. Along with the press a variety of voluntary associations had developed in Luanda as channels for self-expression. They were also put under tighter control by de Matos and then by the Salazar government, although the latter did sanction some cultural-social organizations such as an essentially mulatto association, the *Grêmio Africano,* later renamed the *Associação Regional dos Naturais de Angola* (Anangola). In 1929 a group of Luandans created another organization, the *Liga Nacional Africana* (LNA), a rebirth of the earlier, more militant *Liga Angolana* founded in 1913. While predominantly mulatto, the LNA offered a few educated Africans an opportunity to gain organizational experience and to press for economic and social reform within the confining limits of the Portuguese political system.

[22] For a detailed and original study of this period, see the forthcoming book by Douglas Wheeler and René Pélissier, *Angola* (London: Pall Mall, in preparation). Wheeler traces the antecedents of the PNA back to the creation of the *Liga Ultramarina,* an African organization founded in Lisbon in 1910 to work for pan-Portuguese African interests.

[23] George Padmore, *Pan-Africanism or Communism? The Coming Struggle for Africa* (New York: Roy Publishers, 1956), p. 141.

[24] *Ibid.*

The Postwar Years

In the decade immediately after the Second World War there was a new flurry of political activity both among liberal and Marxist elements of the growing resident European and mulatto population and within the rapidly expanding population of African city dwellers. Condemned to slum living, Luanda's Africans developed into a volatile black proletariat whose simmering discontent needed only organization and leadership to become a strong political force. A measure of such leadership was eventually provided by (1) rebels from within the European and mulatto elite who were educated in Portugal or at local Catholic schools, and (2) a small but expanding group of assertive young African *assimilados,* some of whom had been exposed to the unsettling pedagogy of Methodist mission schools established at Luanda, Quessua, and other Mbundu centers, and who identified or cast their lot with the uneducated majority.

The victory of the Allied powers—western democracies and the Soviet Union—encouraged some Luandans to believe that the days of Salazar's vintage corporate state, or *Estado Novo,* were numbered. And during the early 1950's there was probably a larger measure of freedom of thought and speech in Angola than in Portugal itself. Foreign publications, notably Brazilian, dealing with the recent war, with fascism, and with national liberation managed to reach Luanda.[25] Nonetheless, Portugal's semi-isolation as a relic of the fascist era continued to limit outside contacts, and legal bans imposed by Lisbon upon most political opposition continued to force secrecy and foster anxiety within all political activity.[26] Inevitably this has made it difficult to reconstruct accurately the obscured events of this formative period in Angolan nationalism.

It seems that a conflict developed within the *Liga Nacional Africana,* pitting an older generation of culturally assimilated Africans, who accepted working in strictly legal collaboration with the colonial administration, against a younger generation of challengers who argued for more radical methods and advocated extension of *Liga* membership and its cultural, social, and political activities to the uneducated masses of Africans. The colonial administration reacted,

[25] Patricia McGowan Pinheiro, "Politics of a Revolt," in *Angola: A Symposium,* p. 107.

[26] Mário de Andrade, "Face à la sauvagerie du colonialisme portugais," *Démocratie nouvelle* (Paris), Vol. 15, No. 7 (July 1961), p. 70.

moved in, and replaced elected *Liga* officials with dutiful administrative commissioners appointed by the governor-general of the colony.[27] Still, as late as 1956 the *Liga* reportedly issued a manifesto lamenting the lot of the African and subsequently declined a government invitation to send a delegation to the United Nations to support the thesis that Angola constituted an overseas province of Portugal.[28] Although emasculated, it continued to work for reduced and realizable goals—such as improving the positions of African civil servants and army personnel in Angola—while avoiding major political issues.[29]

If some of the earliest recorded expressions of nationalist sentiment took the form of protest journalism, in later years some of the most significant protest took the more subtle form of poetry, such as the pieces that appeared in a Luanda literary review *Mensagem,* published under the auspices of the *Associação Regional dos Naturais de Angola* (Anangola). In 1948 Viriato Francisco Clemente da Cruz, a young mulatto born at Kikuvu, near Amboim, on March 25, 1928, and educated in Luanda,[30] helped to organize a literary discussion group among young urbanites in the colonial capital. By 1950 this group[31] had found in *Mensagem* a means to express pent-up resentment against the colonial order. As the editor of *Mensagem,* da Cruz with his associates was able to spread a seminal message of protest that influenced Luanda's *assimilados* and mulattoes well beyond 1950, even though the governor-general closed down the periodical after two issues. Its slogan, *Vamos descobrir Angola,* "discover your human dignity"—or your own Angolan identity—represented a reaction to such developments as the massive recruitment of African labor for the north's booming coffee plantations and the loss of jobs and land to the expanding number of European immigrants.

Through poetry a European dissenter, António Jacinto (born 1932, Luanda), described the conditions of forced labor:

> On this large plantation the rain does not fall
> it is the sweat from my brow that waters the crops;

[27] Mário de Andrade, "Le nationalisme angolais," *Présence Africaine,* No. 42 (1962), pp. 8–10.

[28] See Ronald Chilcote, *Portuguese Africa* (Englewood Cliffs, N.J.: Prentice-Hall, 1967), p. 77. Some observers believe that this may constitute a postdated reference to an earlier (1952) petition to the United Nations. See p. 26.

[29] See Wheeler's forthcoming *Angola.*

[30] Ronald Segal, *Political Africa* (New York: Frederick A. Praeger, 1961), pp. 62–63.

[31] Sometimes referred to as the *Movimento dos Novos Intellectuais de Angola.*

On this large plantation of ripe coffee berries
those cherry red drops
are drops of my blood turned to sap.
The coffee will be roasted,
ground and tortured,
it will turn black, black like the color of the *contratado.*
Black like the color of the *contratado!* [32]

The pages of *Mensagem* fired other literary salvos against forced labor and decried the wanton destruction of traditional African social structures. They featured poetry that not only invoked Angola's African heritage but called upon Angolan poets to create an "Angolan language." In a satirical poem, "Sò Santo," editor da Cruz pointed to the gap between the hopeful reason of his young generation and the fatalistic irrationality of earlier generations.[33] His work reflected what a leading commentator on Portuguese Negro poetry, Alfredo Margarido, has termed a "new awareness of the motives behind the exclusion of the Negro from colonial society." Such poetry produced a new internal freedom that was, Margarido predicted, "bound to be externalized eventually by means of revolt against the established order." [34] da Cruz partially disguised the revolutionary import of his poetry by employing a subtle irony. Yet he clearly meant to make the African aware of himself, his suffering, and the inhuman condition of slavery in which he was kept by the white—all as a step toward revolt and freedom. The struggle of the black man was viewed as a world-wide struggle, as can be seen in da Cruz's "Mamã Negra."

Voices in all of America. Voices in all of Africa.
Voice of all the voices, in the proud voice of Langston,
In the fine voice of Guillén . . .
Generating, forming, announcing
—The time of moisture
THE TIME OF MAN . . .[35]

[32] For the full text of the poem, "Monangamba," in Portuguese see *Présence Africaine,* No. 57 (1966), pp. 438–439.

[33] "Sò Santo" has been republished in a special issue of *Présence Africaine* devoted to African poetry, *ibid.,* p. 447.

[34] Alfredo Margarido, "The Social and Economic Backgrounds of Portuguese Negro Poetry," *Diogenes,* Vol. 37–40 (1962), p. 66. See also Gerald M. Moser, "African Literature in the Portuguese Language," *The Journal of General Education,* Vol. XIII, No. 4 (Jan. 1962), pp. 270–304; and an article on African intellectuals in Portuguese Africa by Virgilio de Lemos in *La Presse du Cameroun* (Douala), Aug. 18, 1964.

[35] As quoted in Moser, "African Literature in the Portuguese Language," pp. 277–278.

Concurrently another form of poetry developed within the crowded *muceques,* the poor African quarters of Luanda. It described the clash between traditional customs and urban conditions and expressed in Kimbundu a revolutionary outlook similar to that of the Portuguese-language poetry of the elite. The poetry of the *muceques* contrasted the low living standards of the African with the higher living standards of the white—and even of the mulatto. Mulattoes and *assimilados* who enjoyed bourgeois comfort were criticized for ignoring the masses, for slavishly imitating the European, and for betraying their race.[36]

In 1950 *Mensagem* and the da Cruz discussion group were banned in conformity with the *Estado Novo's* policy of eliminating all legal channels for political protest. The suppression, of course, encouraged a further radicalization of the political climate. One response to the policy was an effort to obtain intercession by the United Nations. In 1952 a group of more than five hundred Angolans sent a petition from Luanda to United Nations headquarters in New York. They complained of "mistreatment of indigenous inhabitants" by the colonial administration and asked the United Nations "to take steps to end . . . Portuguese rule." [37] Portugal was not admitted to United Nations membership until December 1955, however, and before that time there was little international interest in its colonies. The 1952 petition was therefore fated to a silent reception and eventual retirement to the world organization's archives, without ever having been "made available to anyone, including Delegations of Member States." [38]

Meanwhile conditions inside Angola became increasingly favorable for stepped-up organizational activity by local agents of the small but enterprising Portuguese Communist party. Already by 1948 the latter had reportedly established a secret *Comitê Federal Angolano do Partido Communista Português* in Luanda, and there was a discernible Marxist influence within the city's young intellectual movements, which by then are said to have included two other clandestine groups, the *Comissão de Luta das Juventudes contra o Imperialismo Colónial em Angola* and *Angola Negra.*[39]

[36] Margarido, "Social and Economic Backgrounds," pp. 66–67.

[37] United Nations, General Assembly, *Report of the Sub-Committee on the Situation in Angola.* 16th Session, Supplement No. 16 (A/4978), 1962, p. 42 (cited hereafter as *Report of UN Sub-Committee*).

[38] Letter from I. S. Djermakoye, Under-Secretary-General for Trusteeship and Non-Self-Governing Territories, TR300 PI, New York, Feb. 14, 1968.

[39] Amândio César, *Angola 1961* (Lisbon: Verbo, 1962), p. 97.

Furtive proselytizing by these various groups seems to have promoted political awareness and to have had a catalytic effect upon the development of Angolan political movements, much as the intellectual ferment caused by the *Groupes d'Études Communistes* discussion groups had helped spark political action a few years earlier in the principal cities of French West and Equatorial Africa.[40]

The Angolan Communist Party

According to one of Luanda's angry young poets, Mário de Andrade, when the police in 1950 clamped down on the political-cultural activities begun just two years before, a number of young Angolans—by then "dedicated to Marxist thought"—decided to orient their political action toward "the interests of the popular masses." They had come to recognize that nothing could be accomplished through "old-style legal organizations," and they therefore determined to create "clandestine political organizations of revolutionary character" designed for "the conquest of independence." "It was in this context," according to Andrade, "that the Angolan Communist party (PCA) was born in October 1955." Writing in the official French Communist organ *Démocratie nouvelle* some five years after the creation of the Angolan party, the Luanda intellectual, then an exile in Paris, criticized the early work of the "rigorously clandestine" PCA as having been unrealistic, a shortcoming which he ascribed to "the political inexperience of its young leaders." Nevertheless, he asserted that the PCA had spread widely "the fundamental principles of Marxist doctrine" and had created "hundreds of mobile libraries and clandestine schools" in the African quarters of Luanda.[41] Although his article, destined for French Communist readers, may have overstated the accomplishments of the PCA, it seems to suggest that Portuguese Marxists and their mulatto and African converts were very active during this impres-

[40] See Ruth Schachter Morgenthau, *Political Parties in French-Speaking West Africa* (Oxford: Clarendon Press, 1964), pp. 23–26.

[41] Mário de Andrade, "Et les colonies de Salazar?" *Démocratie nouvelle,* Vol. 14, No. 9 (Sept. 1960), p. 34. In a book entitled *Angola Afire* [*Angola v ogne*] (Moscow: Polizdat, 1961), the Soviet writer V. Sidenko wrote of this same period: "Young people, adherents of Marxism, formed a group of Marxists in October 1955. Working underground, this group was very active in Marxist propaganda among the masses. In particular, it formed hundreds of mobile libraries and underground schools in the African quarters of Luanda." See *The Mizan Newsletter* (London), Vol. 4, No. 5 (Apr. 1962), special issue, "Africa Today: The Soviet View," p. 3.

sionable, incipient period in the development of Angolan nationalism. On the other hand, in the absence of hard evidence to the contrary, it would appear that the PCA itself did not amount to much more than an overseas cell of the Portuguese party, organized by European civil servants, with activities radiating from Luanda up the railroad to Catete and Malange.[42]

Early in 1956, a few months after its creation, the leaders of the *Partido Communista de Angola* reportedly joined in the creation of a nationalist front party, the *Partido da Luta dos Africanos de Angola* (PLUA), "which adopted an action program similar to that of the PCA." [43] Then as other nationalist movements began to form, and, according to Andrade, as "control over" them became "more and more difficult, the young Marxists of the former Angolan Communist party, the leaders of PLUA, and other patriots rapidly founded the *Movimento Popular de Libertação de Angola* (MPLA) in December 1956." [44]

On the one hand, Portuguese writers and, on the other, Soviet and French Communist commentators have affirmed this version of events according to which the MPLA was designed as a broad, encompassing front that could trace its genesis back to the founding of the Angolan Communist party in October 1955 and PLUA in early 1956.[45] Thus according to a Soviet handbook, *Africa Today,* published in 1962, the MPLA was founded in 1956 "on the initiative of the Communist Party and the allied Party of Joint Struggle of the Africans of Angola." [46]

[42] César, *Angola 1961,* p. 99.

[43] Andrade, "Et les colonies de Salazar?" p. 35.

[44] *Ibid.*

[45] For Portuguese sources see César, *Angola 1961;* Artur Maciel, *Angola Heróica* (Lisbon: Livraria Bertrand, 1963), p. 67; and João Baptista Nunes Pereira Neto, "Movimentos subversivos de Angola: Tentativa de esboço sócio-político," in *Angola, Curso de Extensão,* p. 375 (hereafter cited as Neto, "Movimentos subversivos").

[46] From *Africa Today* (translation), as quoted in *The Mizan Newsletter, op. cit.,* p. 2. See also V. Sidenko, "The Last African Colonies: Angola," *New Times* (Moscow), No. 50 (Dec. 1960), p. 20. After mentioning the formation of the Angolan Communist party in October 1955, Sidenko writes: "In 1956 the Communist Party and a number of other organizations merged to form the National Liberation Movement of Angola (sic), which now leads the freedom struggle in the colony." See also *International Affairs* (Moscow), Vol. 7, No. 3 (Mar. 1961), p. 117. The late Soviet specialist on African affairs, Ivan I. Potekhin, published an abridged version of Andrade's Sept. 1960 *Démocratie nouvelle* article in an anthology, *Pravda o Portugal'skikh koloniiakh v Afrike* (Moscow: Institut Afriki, 1961), pp. 32–46. The May 1961 issue of the monthly organ of the Central Committee of the French Communist party, *Cahiers du Com-*

In 1962, two years after his article appeared in *Démocratie nouvelle,* and at a time when he and the MPLA were finding overt Communist associations to be a handicap in terms of international support and united action with other Angolan political movements, Andrade presented a different account of these events in the non-partisan review *Présence Africaine.* There he dated the creation of PLUA as 1953, not 1956, made no mention of the Angolan Communist party (PCA) and noted simply that in December 1956 the leaders of PLUA "and other organizations" appealed in a manifesto for the formation of a vast front, an appeal which coincided with the birth of the MPLA.[47]

Subsequent to this second article, the MPLA has officially maintained that PLUA was formed in 1953 as a result of the need to overcome the dispersion and division of nationalist forces, then made up of "many small organizations spread throughout the country." Portuguese sources indicate that as early as 1952 an effort was made by a Soviet agent, one Feld Matvin, to unite these diverse organizations into a *Conselho de Libertação de Angola.*[48] The MPLA's historians, however, state that it was in 1953, only after a process slowed by the exigencies of clandestine operations, that the number of nationalist groups was both reduced and concentrated within PLUA, another (more obscure) group known as the *Movimento para a Independência de Angola* (MIA or MPIA), and several other groups of "lesser proportions." [49] (Portuguese reports state that members of the MIA later merged with and formed a cell of the MPLA.) [50]

Basing their analyses on Andrade's second account, other observers of Angolan affairs such as Patricia McGowan Pinheiro have also credited PLUA and not the PCA with having been "the first revolutionary political party" in Angola to attempt to build "an illegal mass organization." [51] Generally, European writers sympathetic to

---

munisme (Paris), Vol. 37, No. 5, p. 1041, carried an analysis of "Les événements d'Angola" by Louis Odru, which, like all the aforementioned, further corroborated Andrade's account in *Démocratie nouvelle.*

[47] Andrade, "Le nationalisme angolais," p. 10.

[48] César, *Angola 1961,* p. 97.

[49] MPLA, "Dez Anos de Existência, Dez Anos de Luta em Prol do Povo Angolano" (Dar es Salaam, Feb. 4, 1967, mimeo.), p. 1.

[50] See Maciel, *Angola Heróica,* p. 128; and Neto, "Movimentos subversivos," p. 375.

[51] Pinheiro, in *Angola: A Symposium,* p. 108. Andrade also omits any reference to the Angolan Communist party in his book *Liberté pour l'Angola* (Paris: François Maspero, 1962).

the MPLA—and that has meant most non-Portuguese writers on the subject—have accepted the political sequence set forth in Andrade's second article. They have made no mention of the Angolan Communist party or of the formative role that it was earlier said to have played in creating first PLUA and then the MPLA.[52]

Reaching the Boiling Point

The MPLA manifesto circulated at the time of the movement's founding called for the overthrow of Portuguese rule and the establishment of an independent Angolan state governed by a democratic "coalition of all the forces that fought Portuguese colonialism." It predicted that the latter would not collapse without a "bitter fight" and argued for a "revolutionary struggle" by means of a "single front of all the anti-imperialist forces of Angola," setting aside for this purpose all considerations of political opinion, social status, religious beliefs, or philosophical views. In short, it invoked the need for the broadest sort of popular front to mobilize Angolans for their national liberation.[53]

In order to attract persons with differing interests and of diverse persuasions into a single front, the organizers of the MPLA are said by Andrade to have decided against an effort to amass all Angolan nationalists within a single organization. Instead, he has said, they called for the creation of "thousands and thousands of organizations spread all over the country" and encouraged the creation of separate movements that would accept the program of the MPLA. Andrade has also implied that a separate existence for these movements—including the *Movimento de Libertação de Angola* (MLA), the *Movimento de Independência Nacional de Angola* (MINA) and "many others without specific titles or bearing the names of Angolan patriots in exile"—was decided upon in order to permit coordinated but differentiated appeals to labor, religious, and other special groups.[54]

This suggestion of over-all coordination, however, must be considered in the light of later acknowledgments by the MPLA leader-

[52] For example, Gérard Chaliand in "Problèmes du nationalisme angolais," *Les Temps Modernes* (Paris), No. 231 (Aug. 1965), p. 276; Robert Davezies, *Les angolais* (Paris: Les Éditions de Minuit, 1965); and background reporting in the French press, notably *Le Monde, Le Figaro, Combat, France Observateur,* and *l'Express.*

[53] As quoted in Andrade, "Et les colonies de Salazar?" p. 35.

[54] *Ibid.*

ship that its efforts to organize a front around the MPLA banner, and thus to control a situation within which nationalist movements were proliferating, were not very successful. In particular, Mário de Andrade has blamed the failure to achieve such a united front on the series of massive arrests carried out during this period by the Portuguese secret police.[55] The MINA, which was created in 1957 or 1958, is said to have merged with the MPLA,[56] but the MLA, an underground group of Luanda students and young intellectuals, is reported by former members to have continued its clandestine activities on into the early months of 1961, independently of the MPLA.[57] In addition, during 1960–61 still another group of Luanda students is reported to have formed a secret *Movimento Angolano de Juventude Estudante* (MAJE), which was soon converted into a wider youth movement known as the *Frente Unida de Juventude de Angola* (FUJA). Former militants of FUJA claim, like those of the MLA, that they had no contact with the MPLA or any other nationalist organizations.[58]

In Luanda during this period personal friends often did not dare to confide in one another concerning their respective political activities lest they be betrayed to the police. Therefore some learned of each other's commitments only later in jail or in exile. And in years to follow many found it difficult to accept the premise that other organizations had been engaged in action parallel to their own. It may in fact never be possible to sort out claims and counterclaims of who was responsible for what. Yet one thing is clear. As

[55] In his September 1960 article published by *Démocratie nouvelle,* Andrade implied that the MLA, MINA, etc., were part of a decentralization system under which they had all accepted the program of the MPLA; but writing later during his temporary withdrawal from the MPLA (1963–64), he indicated that the MPLA had not been able to create the united front through which it had hoped to exercise control over these other groups. See *Révolution Africaine* (Algiers), No. 74 (June 27, 1964). The anti-Salazarist, European-led *Frente de Unidade Angolana* (FUA), formed at Benguela in January 1961, later commented in an analysis of this period: "In the first days of March 1959, when some progress towards the achievement of . . . unity seemed at last to have been made, the Portuguese political police—PIDE—embarked on a repressive policy which resulted in the destruction of all organizations existing in the country." *Présence Africaine* (English ed.), Vol. 17, No. 45 (1963), p. 169.

[56] MPLA, *Angola, Exploitation esclavagiste, Résistance nationale* (Dakar: A. Diop, 1961), p. 37.

[57] According to interviews with Leopoldo Trovoada and other Angolan students in Paris, December 1966.

[58] According to former FUJA member Pedro Vaal Hendrik Neto who served later in Kinshasa as an official in the Revolutionary Government of Angola in Exile (GRAE).

police controls tightened, the Luanda groups were increasingly prepared to think in terms of violent action, a development plainly suggested by the name of yet another little-known clandestine group which reportedly functioned at this time, the *Exército de Libertação Angola* (ELA), or Angola Liberation Army.[59]

In conjunction with the political ferment that intensified in the mid- to late 1950's, it should also be noted that an outside catalyst helped to spur the political enthusiasm of Luanda's nationalist intellectuals. In July 1956 a group of Congolese *évolués* in Léopoldville issued their now famous nationalist manifesto, *Conscience Africaine,* which heralded the political awakening of Angola's giant neighbor. This initiative, coincident with their own action, reinforced the belief of opposition elements within the Luanda elite that history was now carrying them on the crest of the wave that would soon thrust all Africa into "the era of national independence." [60]

Apprehension within Portuguese officialdom grew during the years 1957–1959, fanned by the unsettling winds of both a national presidential election and an outbreak of rioting in the Congo. On June 8, 1958, the opposition candidate, General Humberto Delgado, won a quarter of a million votes (22.5 per cent) against the Salazarist candidate for president, Admiral Américo Thomaz. In spite of an harassed campaign and an intimidated electorate, Delgado won nearly 18,000 as against 74,000 votes for Thomaz in the overseas provinces, evidence of appreciable opposition sentiment within the enfranchised European elite of Angola and Mozambique. Then in January 1959 rioting in Léopoldville, triggered by African nationalists of the Abako party, traumatized the Belgian colonial administra-

[59] In 1963 a Portuguese journalist, Artur Maciel, visited Angola and wrote a series of articles for Lisbon's *Diário de Notícias,* which were republished in book form as *Angola Heróica.* On the basis of information from local authorities, he added two more names to the list of clandestine nationalist movements said to have been operating in Luanda, i.e., the *Movimento Nacional de Libertação de Angola* (MLNA), founded in 1959 and whose principal leaders were arrested in August 1960, and the *Frente Unida para a Libertação de Angola* (FULA), created in May 1960 and officially viewed as linked with the MPLA (Maciel, *Angola Heróica,* pp. 125, 127). In a university lecture on "subversive movements" João Neto added still another three names to the profuse list of obscure nationalist organizations said to have had an ephemeral existence in Angola: (1) *Solidariedade Africana para a Independência de Angola* (SAIA); (2) Direco—the *Grupo de Defesa da Região Costeira;* and (3) Comcabi—the *Communidade Cabindense.* Neto, "Movimentos subversivos," p. 380.

[60] Viriato da Cruz, "What Kind of Independence for Angola?" *Révolution* (Paris), Vol. 1, No. 9 (1964), p. 15.

tion, and the shock wave reverberated from the Bakongo regions of the Congo and northern Angola to the *muceques* of Luanda.

By 1957 the Portuguese secret police, the *Polícia Internacional de Defesa de Estado,* or PIDE, had installed itself in Angola and set about infiltrating political opposition movements. On Easter Sunday, March 29, 1959, it conducted a massive arrest of suspected subversives in Luanda. In addition to African and mulatto nationalists, those arrested included European liberals and Marxists operating under the cover of a cultural organization, the *Sociedade Cultural de Angola,* founded in 1943, as well as contributors to the review *Cultura,* which had been set up in 1957 in liaison with the group that had originally produced *Mensagem.*[61] These arrests, followed by more in July,[62] led to three separate sets of indictments, three lists which upon scrutiny reveal that they were grouped along ethnic lines—mulatto, European, African.[63] These indictments led to a

61 Alfredo Margarido, "Portugais des 'provinces d'outre mer' d'Afrique," *Le mois en Afrique* (Paris), No. 12 (Dec. 1966), p. 77; and Marie-Thérèse Maugis, "Entretien avec les 'pieds noirs' angolais," *Partisans* (Paris), No. 7 (Nov.-Dec. 1962), p. 96. It was in 1957 also that Fernando Castro Soromenho wrote a controversial novel, *Viragem* (Lisbon, 1957), in which he described the wanton mistreatment of black Angolans by white officials and their wives.

62 Including Carlos Vieira Dias, André Mingas, and Higino Aires [Alves de Sousa?], cited as "important personalities in the nationalist movement" by the MPLA, "Dez Anos de Existência," p. 3.

63 Luanda's *A Província de Angola,* No. 10,323, Dec. 21, 1959, published the names of three groups of persons indicted for subversive activities under articles 141 and 151 of the penal code. Those indicted were almost all *assimilados,* mulattoes, and Europeans, as evidenced by the striking absence of traditional African (as distinct from Portuguese) names.

The first list was composed of twelve mulattoes and three Africans—reportedly all Catholics, belonging to the small educated class of politically restive Luandans—and three foreigners: Ilidio Tomé Alves Machado (official in the post office, and MPLA president), André Franco de Sousa (bookkeeper), Higino Aires Alves de Sousa (commercial employee), Carlos Aniceto Vieira Dias (bank employee and director of a dance group called *Ngola Ritmo*), Carlos Alberto Pereira dos Santos Van-Dúnem (mechanic), Francisco José Pereira Africano (office clerk), Luis Rafael (typesetter), Amadeu Timoteo Malheiros de Amorim (electrician), Mário António Soares de Campos (oculist), Mário Augusto da Silva (bank accountant), João António Marques Monteiro (bank accountant), Miguel de Oliveira Fernandes (bank employee), Manuel Alves da Cruz (electrician), Matias Miguéis (secretary, then at Pointe Noire, Congo-Brazzaville, charged *in absentia,* later MPLA vice-president), Gabriel Francisco Leitão Pereira (commercial employee), and three sailors, Lawrence Holder (American Negro, charged *in absentia*), Karl Dogbe (Ghanaian, charged *in absentia*), and Francisco Xavier Hernandez (Cuban).

The second list was made up of five Europeans, one mulatto, and one African: António Alexandre Calazans Duarte (electrical engineer), José Luciano Cout Real Vieira Meireles (bookkeeper), António Guilherme de Matos Veloso

celebrated secret "trial of fifty" (1960), in which the colonial government tried and convicted nationalists belonging to the MPLA and other groups, and sentenced them to long terms in jail for political subversion. Anticipating a gross miscarriage of justice, the International Commission of Jurists made several abortive attempts to press for a fair trial for the accused. In May 1960 they managed to send a British M.P., Elwyn Jones, to Luanda, where he expressed the Commission's concern about "due process" to local authorities. But when the Commission tried to send a Lisbon lawyer, Dr. Palma Carlos, to attend and observe the trial of the predominantly European list of seven prisoners scheduled for July, Portuguese authori-

---

(architect), Manuel dos Santos, Jr., African, known as "O Capicúa" (electrician), António José Contreiras da Costa (commercial employee, mulatto), Dr. Maria Julieta Guimarães Gandra (female physician, who reportedly refused to go to prison in the special car sent for her and insisted on riding with arrested Africans), and Helder Guilherme Ferreira Neto (student).

The third, or African, list included only two mulattoes and one European; twenty-one on the list were under arrest and twelve resided abroad in the Congo, Brazil, and elsewhere. This list included thirteen Luandan Protestants (denoted by P): José Manuel Lisboa (mechanic), António Pedro Benge (civil servant), Fernando Pascoal da Costa (P, retired civil servant), Agostinho André Mendes de Carvalho (P, nurse's aid), Sebastião Gaspar Domingos (P, commercial employee), Garcia Lourenço Contreiras (P, nurse), João Lopes Teixeira (mechanic), Belarmino Sabugosa Van-Dúnem (nurse), Joaquim de Figueiredo (P, postal employee), André Rodrigues Mingas, Jr. (civil servant), Pascoal Gomes de Carvalho, Jr. (civil servant), Armando Ferreira da Conceição, Jr. (employee of Portuguese consulate at Léopoldville), Nobre Ferreira Pereira Dias (P, teacher), Noé da Silva Saúde (P, student), Florêncio Gamaliel Gaspar (P, nurse), José Diogo Ventura (P, nurse), Adão Domingos Martins (P, nurse's aide), João Fialho da Costa (P, student nurse), Manuel Bernardo de Sousa (P, student nurse), Manuel Baptista de Sousa (P, typographer), and a sailor named Ferreira from Quibala. Indicted *in absentia* were Manuel Tomás da Costa (better known as Costa Kiolo, of Matadi), João Eduardo Pinok [*sic*], known as "O Pinoca" (a founder of UPNA, of Matadi), António Josias (full name António Jabes Josias, head of first MPLA regional committee, Léopoldville), Manuel Barros Necaca (also spelled Nekaka, president of UPNA, Léopoldville), Onofre, Osusana Milton, or Ruy Ventura (pseudonyms for Holden Roberto, Léopoldville), Inocência Van-Dúnem dos Santos Martins (Léopoldville), and Jorge Mingas (Brazzaville). Two were in Brazil: the European poet, António Jacinto, and a student, Déolinda Rodrigues (also known as Déolinda Rodrigues Francisco de Almeida), who would later head the women's section of the MPLA. The two mulattoes on the list were in Paris: Mário Coelho Pinto de Andrade and Viriato da Cruz. At the bottom of the list was an American journalist, George Barnett, who was also out of the country.

The foregoing information was compiled from *A Província de Angola,* and from an untitled memorandum prepared by the *Democratas de Angola* (Feb. 1960), a pamphlet published by the *Front Révolutionnaire pour l'Indépendance Nationale des Colonies Portugaises* (FRAIN), "Le procès de cinquante" (Antwerp, Belgium, Apr. 1960); and *La Gauche* (Brussels), Mar. 5, 1960.

ties barred him from boarding his plane to Luanda. The secrecy of the trial of these seven and the severity of its sentences—let alone the silence that shrouded the less-known fate of those (Africans and *mestiços*) on the other two lists—bore out the Commission's worst fears.[64]

In February 1960 two Americans visited Luanda, where they met a representative of the European anti-Salazarist and pro-Delgado *Democratas de Angola* who presented them with a statement denouncing the arrests and impending trials as a mockery of justice.[65] The two visitors also met clandestinely with a Catholic priest who passed on to them copies of documents allegedly taken from confidential government files. These documents—dismissed as instructional war-games material by Lisbon—told of propaganda and arms coming into the country from abroad and said that there had already been armed attacks against Portuguese administrators and settlers in the extreme south near South West Africa and in the coffee area of the far North.[66] On March 14 Portugal announced that it was stationing warships along the Angolan coast,[67] just a year after air force units had been installed at Luanda amidst parachute jumps, target bombing, and truculent rhetoric.[68] In late May *The Times* of London reported that Lisbon had secretly sent an additional 2000 men to bring its Angolan forces up to nearly 20,000 (most of whom were, however, still African) in order to counter an expected nationalist effort to infiltrate with both propaganda and agitators.[69]

Fifty-two persons, including Father Joaquim Pinto de Andrade, the brother of Mário de Andrade, and Dr. Agostinho Neto, who later became the MPLA's principal leader in exile, were seized in a

64 *The Guardian* (Manchester), July 25, 1960; World Assembly of Youth, "Report of the WAY Mission on Angola," Document 1984 (Brussels, June 1962, mimeo.), p. 16; working paper for the 10th International Student Conference, "Report on Angola and Mozambique" (Leiden, The Netherlands, 1962), p. 26; and *República* (Lisbon), Aug. 12, 1960. On December 21, 1960, a military court in Luanda handed down prison sentences of from three to ten years each to twenty persons on the third list. See MPLA, "Nouvelles des procès politiques" (Conakry, Feb. 7, 1961, mimeo.).

65 *Democratas de Angola* (Luanda), Untitled memorandum, Feb. 1960, 6 pp.

66 See Appendix B.

67 *The New York Times,* March 15, 1960.

68 See Basil Davidson, "The Time of the Leaflet," *New Statesman,* Vol. LVIII, No. 1497 (Nov. 21, 1959), p. 698.

69 May 27, 1960.

second wave of arrests in June 1960.[70] With their authority to arrest and imprison anyone without charges for consecutive and indefinitely renewable blocks of time (Decree law No. 35,042), the security police (PIDE) were becoming the real core of political power in Angola.

Also arrested during this period was the man whom the MPLA had chosen in December 1956 as its first president, Ilidio Tomé Alves Machado, an Mbundu postal employee born of a former slave mother in 1915 in Luanda. With only a junior secondary school certificate, Machado had managed to become one of the more influential leaders of the old *Liga Nacional Africana* before its emasculation by Portuguese authorities. His leadership of the MPLA was also cut short by Portuguese action when in May 1959, during a visit to Lisbon, he was arrested and returned to Luanda and prison. Held in custody since that time—recently on a remote Cape Verde Island—Machado, in the words of one political observer, "remains one of the most respected of the Angolan leaders," though as "a man of ideas rather than mass appeal." [71]

Soon after its arrival on the scene in 1957, then, PIDE set about decapitating the MPLA and other Angolan nationalist organizations. The MPLA has since said that in December 1959 it was still able to smuggle a document describing the system of forced labor, the absence of collective bargaining, and the exploitative nature of working conditions prevailing in Angola to delegates attending a session of the African Advisory Committee of the International Labor Organization meeting at Luanda.[72] Still, no less an authority than Viriato da Cruz, the party's first secretary-general, later wrote that the "waves of arrests in Luanda, beginning in March 1959," so devastated the MPLA (which he identified with the urban pro-

[70] See James Duffy, *Portugal in Africa* (Cambridge, Mass.: Harvard University Press, 1962), p. 213.

[71] Segal, *Political Africa,* p. 164.

[72] Andrade, "Et les colonies de Salazar?" p. 36. If in fact such a statement was shown surreptitiously to some African delegates, it was never made public. In response to an inquiry concerning this document, said to have been submitted to the First Session of the ILO African Advisory Committee meeting at Luanda from November 30 to December 10, 1959, the Acting Chief of the Central Library and Documentation Branch of the ILO at Geneva reported: "No document of this nature has been brought to the knowledge of the International Labour Office or has been communicated to the African Advisory Committee as such. A careful search of the records and files of the meeting has revealed no trace of the statement. . . ." Letter from G. K. Thompson, ADC 159-1-411, July 17, 1967.

letariat) that it was rendered incapable of transcending its urban origins. According to his reasoning, the MPLA was therefore unable "to lead effectively the armed peasant movement" that ultimately developed as the main challenge to Portuguese rule.[73] Similarly, Mário de Andrade has written that between 1957 and 1960 the fierceness of Portuguese repression in the urban areas was overwhelming, because the MPLA "was not yet in a position to resist effectively." Thus, according to Andrade, it became "necessary to compensate for the breakup of the leadership structure inside" by establishing an external exile organization, an organization that he himself would head for several years.[74]

The MPLA in Exile

The MPLA's exile leadership came for the most part from a student elite that had been in Europe during the period leading up to and immediately following the creation of nationalist movements in Luanda. A small but growing Angolan student contingent had begun arriving at Portuguese universities for the first time in the late 1940's. Most were sons of civil servants. They were from relatively privileged *assimilado* or mulatto families, not from the *muceques*. The government housed most of them together in Lisbon and Coimbra at the *Casas dos Estudantes do Império,* where they were soon caught up in the climate of intellectual radicalism that dominated Portuguese student and anti-Salazar politics. Some functioning under the guise of a cultural group created in 1951, the *Centro dos Estudos Africanos,* applied themselves to a theoretical study of revolution through an examination of the cultural bases of liberation.[75] Two of the three figures destined to be the most prominent leaders of the MPLA in exile were associated with this student elite.

The first, Dr. Agostinho Neto, a soft-spoken Mbundu and the son of a Methodist pastor, was born in the village of Bengo (Catete) on September 17, 1922, and was one of the few Africans to complete his secondary education at the Luanda *Liceu Salvador Correia.* As a youth Neto served for a time as personal secretary to Methodist Bishop Ralph E. Dodge, to whom he is still known by the Christian

[73] da Cruz, "What Kind of Independence," p. 15.

[74] Mário de Andrade, "Angola: Agonie de l'empire et crise du nationalisme," *Remarques Africaines* (Brussels), Vol. 6, No. 14 (July 11, 1964), p. 330.

[75] MPLA, *Vitória ou Morte* (Brazzaville), No. 6 (Aug.–Sept. 1966), p. 3.

name António (see Appendix A). After working in the public health service at Luanda for three years, Neto went to Portugal in 1947 with a Methodist scholarship and began his medical studies, first at the University of Lisbon and then at Coimbra. While studying in Portugal he took an active part in opposition politics and became a member of the central committee of an anti-Salazar youth group, the *Movimento de Unidade Democrática-Juvenil* (MUDJ). For this involvement he was arrested and jailed for a few weeks in 1952. His poems and political views sent him back to jail and then to rustication from February 1955 to June 1957. He was, however, able to complete his medical degree in 1958, and with his Portuguese wife he returned to Angola the next year. At that time, as he began his local medical practice, there were only 203 doctors in all of Angola, a ratio of one doctor for approximately 22,400 Africans, except that most physicians were Europeans and served only European, mulatto, or *assimilado* patients.[76]

After a decade of absence, a politically sensitive Agostinho Neto had returned to find that in Angola "Western Civilization" still meant forced labor.

> Tin sheets nailed to poles
> fixed in the earth
> make a house
>
> Rags complete
> the intimate landscape
>
> The sun penetrating cracks
> awakes each occupant
>
> Afterwards twelve hours of slaving work
>
> Break stone
> cart stone
> break stone
> cart stone
> in the sun
> in the rain
> break stone
> cart stone
>
> old age comes early
> a coarse mat in the dark nights
> suffices for him to die
> grateful
> and of hunger.

[76] See chapter on Agostinho Neto in Peter Benenson, *Persecution 1961* (Harmondsworth, Middlesex: Penguin Books, 1961), pp. 51–62.

Yet there was a new self-awareness, a new tenseness in the policed air of his homeland, a new "Realization."

> Fear in the air!
>
> On each street corner
> Vigilant sentries light incendiary glances
> in each house
> hasty replacement of the old bolts
> of the doors
> and in each conscience
> seethes the fear of listening to itself
>
> History is to be told
> anew
>
> Fear in the air!
>
> It happens that I
> humble man
> still more humble in my black skin
> come back to Africa
> to myself
> with dry eyes.[77]

On June 8, 1960, he was once again arrested, flogged before his family, and taken off to jail. His arrest prompted patients, friends, and supporters from Bengo and the twin village of Icolo to lay plans to go to the administrative center at Catete to demand his release. According to a report that reached London four months later, the district officer learned of this and brought to Catete from Luanda some two hundred soldiers equipped with Sten guns. A week after Neto's arrest, approximately a thousand villagers arrived in Catete to demonstrate peacefully, but the troops fired on them, killing thirty and injuring over two hundred. "On the following day these soldiers went to Icolo and Bengo and killed or arrested everyone who was found in the two villages, which were then set on fire." The villages were "totally destroyed, with not a single soul [left] in them." [78] Nothing of this appeared in the Portuguese press. Two years later Neto is reported to have stated that, at the time of his arrest he was president of the MPLA Steering Committee within Angola. Moreover, in this statement he implied that it was in order to mislead the police and to protect those who were known to have been associated with him that the MPLA in exile subsequently

[77] Poems by Dr. Neto entitled "Western Civilization" and "Realization," as translated into English by Aaron Segal.

[78] Basil Davidson, *Angola, 1961: The Factual Record* (London: Union of Democratic Control, 1962), p. 6.

named him "honorary president"—an action which was justified on the basis of his personal martyrdom and his prison credentials. He has thus suggested that the party discretely dissimulated his original leadership role in the MPLA, a role to which he laid claim publicly only after escaping from Portugal in 1962.[79]

The second of the MPLA's principal exile leaders to have lengthy experience in Europe was Mário Coelho Pinto de Andrade, a mulatto born at Golungo Alto in the Dembos region on August 21, 1928.[80] Upon completing his secondary education in Luanda, Andrade left in 1948 at the age of twenty for Portugal, where he studied philology at the University of Lisbon. After some six years, in 1954, he moved on to the freer political climate of Paris and switched to a social science course at the Sorbonne.[81] While in the French capital he also studied at the *École Pratique des Hautes Études* under sociologist Roger Bastide, a critic of Portuguese African policy.[82] There too he wrote several articles under the pseudonym of Buanga Fele, including a critical piece about the theory of "lusotropicology," the proposition that Portugal's mission in Africa is to pursue racial fusion and Christian conversion so as to produce a new, homogenized civilization like that of Brazil or the Cape Verde Islands.[83] Andrade also contributed to and edited an anthology of Negro poetry in Portuguese.[84]

Andrade's poetry, like that of da Cruz and Neto, cried out against centuries of colonial abuse. In "Song of Sabulu," written originally in the Kimbundu of his Dembos home country, Andrade struck at the hated symbol of São Tomé, long the cocoa island of no return

[79] FNLA, "Entretien FNLA-MPLA le 5 août 1962" (Léopoldville, mimeo.), p. 2.

[80] Though he has been most often described as mulatto, this is an ethnic technicality. Andrade speaks and writes in Kimbundu, is dark complexioned, and might be viewed as an Mbundu *assimilado,* except for the rigorous Portuguese system of categories imposed upon all Angolans.

[81] One disenchanted Portuguese observer described Andrade as "an Angolan educated in Lisbon at the expense of the Portuguese government and head of the embryonic Angolan Communist party since 1956." Hélio Esteves Felgas, *Guerra em Angola* (Lisbon: Livraria Classica Editôra, 1961), p. 54.

[82] See Roger Bastide, "Variations on Negritude," *Présence Africaine* (English ed.), Vol. VIII, No. 36 (1961), pp. 83–92.

[83] Buanga Fele, "Qu'est-ce que le 'luso tropicalismo'?" *Présence Africaine,* No. 4 (Oct.-Nov. 1955), pp. 24–35. The originator and principal proponent of "luso-tropicalism" is the Brazilian sociologist Gilberto Freyre; see his *The Portuguese and the Tropics* (Lisbon: Gráfica Santelmo, 1961).

[84] Mário de Andrade, *Antologia de Poesia Negra de Expressão Portuguêsa* (Paris: P. J. Oswald, 1958).

for countless conscript laborers and political prisoners. He lamented the death of a young man who had been sent to São Tomé simply "because he had no [identity] papers. Aiué!" [85]

Sophisticated and a prolific writer, Andrade moved easily in French intellectual circles, ably articulated the cause of the MPLA of which he became acting president, and contributed much to establishing his party's positive intellectual image in Europe. In 1957 he was one of the principal organizers of a Paris gathering of political exiles from Angola, Portuguese Guinea (members of the *Partido Africano da Independência* led by Amilcar Cabral), Mozambique, the Cape Verde Islands, and São Tomé. The result was the formation of an interterritorial *Movimento Anti-Colonialista* (MAC), which joined the MPLA with other exile groups in an effort to develop a coordinated campaign for independence from Portuguese rule.[86]

The third of the MPLA's main exile leaders was not formed in Europe but on home ground in the Luanda school of politics. Already cited as the editor of *Mensagem,* Viriato da Cruz was a graduate of the Luanda *liceu.* After he was fired from a civil service job in the department of education in 1952 because of his political activities, he worked as a bookkeeper in a Luanda business firm until 1957. The Portuguese secret police installed itself in Angola that year and "succeeded in infiltrating some of its agents into organizations controlled by the MPLA." [87] A founding member and first secretary-general of the MPLA (1956–1962), da Cruz was quickly spotted by PIDE, and a warrant was issued for his arrest. He managed to flee to Portugal and on to France, where he teamed up with Mário de Andrade and other mulatto intellectuals such as Lucio Lara, the son of a wealthy sugar plantation owner (Sousa

[85] "Canção de Sabulu," *Présence Africaine,* No. 57 (1966), p. 443; see also Buanga Fele [Andrade], "Massacres à São Tomé," *Ibid.,* No. 1–2 (Apr.–July 1955), pp. 146–152.

[86] MAC was formed at a meeting in Paris known as the *Réunion de Consultation et d'Étude pour le développement de la lutte des Peuples des Colonies Portugaises.* Conflicting dates have been given for the gathering. According to Mário de Andrade in an official CONCP publication (*La lutte de libération nationale dans les colonies portugaises: La Conférence de Dar Es Salaam* [Algiers: Information CONCP, 1967], p. 36), the meeting took place in December 1957. According to an MPLA periodical (*Vitória ou Morte* [Brazzaville], No. 6, Aug.–Sept. 1966, p. 33), the meeting was held in January 1957. See also Andrade, "Et les colonies de Salazar?" p. 36.

[87] Andrade, "Et les colonies de Salazar?" p. 36; see also Alfredo Margarido, "Les partis politiques en Guinée Portugaise, en Angola et aux Îles du Cap Vert," *Le mois en Afrique,* No. 7 (July 1966), p. 50.

Lara), and together they formed the active nucleus of the MPLA leadership in exile.

In Paris da Cruz joined Andrade in associating with the cultural review *Présence Africaine*. Both helped to organize the Second International Congress of Negro Writers and Artists, held at Rome in March 1959. At the congress da Cruz delivered a paper on "The Responsibilities of the Black Intellectual." [88] Both da Cruz and Andrade became involved in left-wing European politics,[89] developed relationships with French, Soviet, and Chinese Communists,[90] and participated in the Afro-Asian Writers' Conference at Tashkent (October 1958). Andrade in particular contributed a number of articles and interviews to Communist publications.[91]

For some time Andrade, da Cruz, and their associates limited their main lobbying activities to Europe. Thus, although an Afro-Asian Peoples' Conference was held at Cairo in December 1957, and a permanent Afro-Asian Peoples' Solidarity Council was thereupon set up in the Egyptian capital, MPLA leadership seems not to have been involved. Over a year later the Council had apparently not yet been seized with the problem of Portugal's African colonies. As late as February 1959, it adopted a resolution urging that steps be taken "to establish contacts with the freedom forces" of Angola and Mozambique with a view toward helping them.[92] Moreover, neither the MPLA nor the MAC was represented at the First All-African Peoples' Conference held at Accra, Ghana, in December

[88] Viriato da Cruz, "Des responsabilités de l'intellectuel noir," *Présence Africaine,* No. 27–28 (Aug.–Nov. 1959), pp. 321–339.

[89] Building upon the "basic passion" of their own colonial experience, and utilizing European Marxism as a "point of departure," Africans studying in Paris during this period rather generally developed a "world-view" that was increasingly hostile toward the United States. Arguing that because of its "inability to recognize the import of their grievances," the United States was cutting itself off from "fast-changing" nonwestern nations, two American students in Paris wrote up a lengthy interview with a twenty-four-year-old anonymous Angolan pursuing engineering studies there. The latter's perception of political values and issues was then presented in David Ball and Jeremy Larner, "The Mind of an Angolese Revolutionary," *New Politics* (New York), Vol. I, No. 4 (1962), pp. 34–44.

[90] See John K. Cooley, *East Wind over Africa* (New York: Walker and Co., 1965), p. 126; and William E. Griffith, "Africa," *Survey* (London), Jan. 1965, p. 177.

[91] *Démocratie nouvelle,* Vol. 14, No. 9 (Sept. 1960), p. 34; and Vol. 15, No. 7 (July 1961), p. 70; *Turkmenskaya Iskra* (Ashkabad, USSR), Dec. 1, 1960; *Pravda,* Feb. 6, 1961; and *Trud* (Moscow), July 14, 1961.

[92] "Recommendations for Future Work" (No. 5), in *Afro-Asian Bulletin* (Cairo), Vol. 1, No. 10 (Feb. 11–13, 1959), p. 30.

1958. By late 1959, however, the two movements were broadening their range of action.

On December 1, 1959, Lucio Lara and Viriato da Cruz sent a telegram to UN Secretary-General Dag Hammarskjöld in the name of the MAC. They asked Hammarskjöld to use his office to persuade the Portuguese Government to "put an end to constant atrocities and cruel assassinations against the African peoples of Guinea and Angola, set free political prisoners, [and] cease preparations for armed repression."

In January 1960 MPLA leaders participated in the Second All-African Peoples' Conference held at Tunis, where they joined with Amilcar Cabral's Guinean followers in transforming their *Movimento Anti-Colonialista* (MAC) into a hopefully more formidable *Frente Revolucionária Africana para a Independência Nacional* (FRAIN).[93] There they also made an initial attempt to persuade Holden Roberto, leader of a rival movement, the *União das Populações de Angola* (UPA), to join their common front. The importance that they attached to this latter effort stemmed from their assessment that the UPA had "an undeniable following among the forced laborers of [Angola's] northern regions and among Angolan émigrés in the Congo."[94] The best they could obtain, however, was a vague agreement that there was a need to coordinate efforts in the joint fight against Portuguese colonial rule.[95]

In February 1960 the MPLA accepted the hospitality of the militant Sékou Touré government of the newly independent Republic of Guinea and established its main headquarters at Conakry. Reacting to both an intensification of police repression, and an increase in Portuguese military strength in Angola that had come with the approach of Congolese independence, scheduled for June 30, 1960, the Conakry MPLA leadership launched a program to unite all exiled Angolan nationalists into a common front. To this end it undertook to simplify the objectives cited in the MPLA's

[93] Andrade, "Et les colonies de Salazar?" p. 36. For extracts of the MAC's "Rapport sur le colonialisme portugais," presented at the Tunis Conference, see FRAIN, *Le procès de cinquante,* pp. 13–18.

[94] Andrade, "Angola: Agonie de l'empire."

[95] According to the report on political policy presented at the MPLA's First National Conference in 1962, "two MPLA leaders signed an [*sic*] fundamental agreement with the main responsible person from the UPA [at the Tunis Conference, January 1960], establishing the need for coordination of the fight against Portuguese colonialism." MPLA, *First National Conference of the People's Movement for the Liberation of Angola* (Dec. 1962, pamphlet), p. 12.

1956 manifesto, and, as an acceptable common denominator for all, proposed "the conquest of Angolan independence" and forthwith launched an appeal for a single organic front organized around this one goal.[96]

In April, Viriato da Cruz put the MPLA's case before the Second Afro-Asian Solidarity Conference held at Conakry.[97] In May a confrontation between the party's exile leadership and emissaries from inside Angola reportedly revealed an eagerness on the part of those inside for "immediate action." [98] In June the party's Conakry office issued statements charging that Portugal had massed up to 60,000 troops in Angola (20,000 was closer to reality) [99] and warning that Lisbon's persistence in imposing colonial rule was "bound to result" in bloodshed.[100] The June appeal, which argued for round-table negotiations and the withdrawal of Portuguese troops, was promptly answered by Lisbon's authoritative *Diário da Manha* (June 19), which stated that Portugal would never agree to discuss self-determination for her overseas territories.[101] The MPLA in turn publicly charged that, because of its refusal to grant self-government, the Portuguese government would bear full responsibility for the "bloody conflict" that it might therefore provoke.[102]

In August an MPLA delegation led by anonymous "Mona Mundu" visited China as guests of the Chinese Peoples' Institute of Foreign Affairs, and Radio Peking began featuring statements by Viriato da Cruz in its broadcasts to Africa.[103]

The MPLA also carried its external campaign to the United

[96] Andrade, "Et les colonies de Salazar?" p. 37.

[97] For the text of his speech, see *Tam Tam* (Revue des Étudiants Catholiques Africaines, Paris), No. 3–4 (1961), pp. 100–102.

[98] Pinheiro, in *Angola: A Symposium,* p. 110.

[99] *The Times* (London), May 27, 1960.

[100] MPLA, "Statement on War Preparations of the Portuguese Government" by Mário de Andrade and Viriato da Cruz (Conakry, June 12, 1960, mimeo.); and "Statement to the Portuguese Government" by Mário de Andrade, Viriato da Cruz, and Lucio Lara (Conakry, June 13, 1960, mimeo.).

[101] As quoted in Lucio Lara, "The Struggle for Freedom in Angola," *Voice of Africa* (Accra), Vol. 1, No. 11 (Nov. 1961), p. 26.

[102] MPLA, "Déclaration" (Conakry, Oct. 25, 1960, mimeo.).

[103] *The Mizan Newsletter,* Vol. 6, No. 5 (May 1964), p. 6. In a study done for the Library of Congress, Andrew F. Westwood suggests that the Chinese Communists were probably attracted by da Cruz's "Marxist stress on the 'international capitalist conspiracy' led by the United States as the factor behind the repression of the rebels." As an example of this, he cites a Peking broadcast of April 4, 1961. Andrew F. Westwood, "The Politics of Revolt in Portuguese Africa," Library of Congress Legislative Reference Series, DT 760, Apr. 6, 1962.

Nations. In September its Steering Committee urged members of the world body to reject the bogus "integration" of 1951 and to place the issue of Portugal's colonial territories on the agenda of the Fifteenth General Assembly.[104] In order to gain western support for this campaign, it established an office at 374 Gray's Inn Road, London, from which a local representative, João Cabral, an attorney who worked for the Goan League, publicized the MPLA cause.[105] Writing in *The Nation,* Cabral introduced the MPLA to Americans as "a merger of various groups" organized on a "non-racial and non-tribal basis." He said that it could claim "a few white settlers" among its members and a number of university graduates among its leaders.[106]

On November 12, 1960, the Fourth Committee of the United Nations General Assembly adopted a resolution holding that Portugal's overseas territories were in fact non-self-governing within the meaning of the United Nations Charter, and that Lisbon was obliged to submit information about them to the world organization under UN Charter Article 73e. At a Conference of Nationalist Leaders from Portuguese Colonies held on December 6 in London, under the auspices of the Movement for Colonial Freedom, the MPLA hailed this vote by the Fourth Committee as a "moral victory." [107] Attending the conference along with da Cruz and Dr. Américo Boavida, a member of the external affairs committee of the MPLA, Mário de Andrade emphasized his party's desire for a "pacific solution to the colonial problem," but announced that, faced with Portuguese instransigence, the MPLA had decided to move to "direct action." [108] A few days earlier, on November 29, da Cruz had already told the London correspondent of *Agence France Presse* that "Angolan patriots" would "soon launch direct action to win independence." He had also claimed that the MPLA had considerable manpower "organized on a nationwide scale" and

[104] MPLA, "Appeal to the Member States of the UN," by Mário de Andrade and Viriato da Cruz (Conakry, Sept. 13, 1960, mimeo.).

[105] For example, MPLA communiqué, "Massacre in Angola" (London, Oct. 10, 1960, mimeo.).

[106] By way of contrast he described the rival *União das Populações de Angola* (UPA) as "organized on a tribal basis, with anti-white tendencies." João Cabral, "Portugal's Rotting Empire," *The Nation,* Vol. 192, No. 9 (Mar. 4, 1961), p. 182.

[107] Conference of Nationalist Leaders from Portuguese Colonies, "Communiqué" (London, Dec. 6, 1960, mimeo.).

[108] See *Courrier d'Afrique* (Léopoldville), Dec. 8, 1960; and Andrade, *Démocratie nouvelle,* July 1961, p. 71.

that negotiations were in progress among the leaders of "the main Angolan political groups with a view to establishing a revolutionary headquarters" to direct their action. He had added that it was "possible that a liberation army on the pattern of the Algerian National Liberation Army" would be formed "in the near future." [109]

On the heels of the London Conference came another warning, this time from a spokesman of the Portuguese Communist party. In the pages of Moscow's *Kommunist* Abilio da Sousa predicted that the efforts of the MPLA, PAIGC (*Partido Africano da Independência da Guiné e Cabo Verde*), and FRAIN to expand their range of action had finally begun the process of national liberation that had been "somewhat retarded" in the colonies, owing both to the absence of a large industrial proletariat and to the "unbridled terror" of the colonial administration. The way was now open, he predicted, for the national liberation movement to destroy the system of colonial domination in Portuguese Africa, and "no force whatsoever [would] be able to restrain it." [110]

Portuguese authorities were left to decide whether such public warnings constituted bluff or cause for alarm. Retrospectively, the MPLA office in Conakry issued a communiqué which said that Andrade's London statement of December 6 had in fact constituted a *mise en garde* and a signal for MPLA "commandos" to launch an attack upon Luanda's prisons on February 4, 1961.[111]

Out beyond the Railroad

Unrelated to political ferment among the Luandans, a separate challenge to Portuguese rule was developing, by late 1960, deep within the Angolan interior among the rural eastern Mbundu. Off to the east of Malange—the commercial center and district capital at the end of the railroad over two hundred miles inland from Luanda—lies the area of the old kingdom of Kasanje, which had been liquidated only shortly before the First World War. Extending over a wide plain along the Kwango River, the region became known to the Portuguese as the Baixa de Cassange. There and to the north, in areas along the Congolese border, the Portuguese developed a profitable cotton economy.

[109] As quoted in V. Sidenko, "The Last African Colonies," p. 21.

[110] Abilio da Sousa, "Volia kommunistovsil'nee krepostnykh sten," *Kommunist* (Moscow), No. 3 (Feb. 1961), p. 92.

[111] MPLA, Statement (Conakry, July 13, 1961, mimeo.).

Cotton growing was organized on the basis of a manpower raiding system. Africans, including women and children, were hauled out of their villages and obliged to grow cotton on prescribed patches of land. There were no wages, and at the end of the season the villages were forced to sell their product at low prices to Cottonag, a Luso-Belgian firm holding the cotton concession in the area. Uniformed Africans recruited from the army were used to ensure that the conscripted laborers worked their plots and grew only cotton—no family food crops. When the land near their home villages was exhausted (no fertilizer was provided), the villagers were forced to move to land from ten to fifty miles away. Rev. E. Edwin LeMaster, an American Methodist missionary stationed at Quessua near the city of Malange, has described this practice of creating "involuntary migrants" out of African villagers as part of a system of abuses that "made violence inevitable." [112]

Local protest dated back many years. As early as 1927, as part of what was called the *Campanha Nativista,* a small group of politically conscious persons reportedly addressed a letter to the League of Nations seeking international intervention against colonial injustices. Improvidently, they sent their letter by registered mail and it fell into the hands of the police, who with the aid of an informant, a mulatto civil servant, arrested the principals involved. Manuel da Silva Lameira and Pais Brandão were exiled for many years in far-off Timor, while a third protestor, Joaquim Filipe Cardoso (known as Canguia) was sent to prison in Luanda.[113]

In the mid-1930's a movement known as *Moïse Noir* spread through the countryside. According to its message, American Negroes would come to liberate the African from European oppression. Then in the 1950's a son of Joaquim Filipe Cardoso of the earlier *Campanha Nativista* reportedly helped to organize *Baha,* another protest movement, which was built on a system of small secret cells. More important in terms of later events, however, was a syncretic religion known as Kasonzola, which took hold in the region in the 1930's. An outlet for the repressed emotions of a subject people, it was a special blend of Catholic, Protestant, and

[112] Rev. E. Edwin LeMaster, "I Saw the Horror in Angola," *The Saturday Evening Post,* May 12, 1962, p. 54.

[113] According to information provided by Rosário Neto, vice-president of the UPA, the informer was a certain Hemenio Castelbranca; Lameira returned to Angola from Timor after nearly twenty-five years in forced exile only to be rearrested soon after for political opposition and to die in prison.

animist practice. Considered dangerous to public order, it was banned by the administration.

Yet Kasonzola was still lurking beneath the surface in 1959 when a certain António Mariano from Malange moved across the Congo border and took a job as a chauffeur with a local chief, Kizamba dos Maholos, whose Chevrolet he drove on several trips to Léopoldville. In the Congolese capital Mariano came into contact with an Angolan nationalist movement, the *União das Populações de Angola* (UPA). He hauled UPA literature and half-assimilated ideas of nationalism back with him to Kizamba and then on into Angola, where a slump in cotton prices had abruptly intensified local African discontent. Combining his personal charisma, a bit of religious mysticism left over from Kasonzola, and nationalist doctrine from the UPA, António Mariano emerged as leader of a new prophet-protest movement known simply as "Maria." His catechists preached a sort of nationalist evangelism complete with incense, "Maria water," and praise for Lumumba.[114] By December 1960 the cotton region of the district of Malange, like distant Luanda, was clearly headed toward an explosion.

[114] Rosário Neto, "Notas e Impressões do Kwango. A Guerra de Maria," *UPA, A Voz da Revolução* (Kinshasa), No. 1 (1966), p. 9.

CHAPTER TWO

THE BAKONGO SOURCES OF ANGOLAN NATIONALISM

The second mainstream in Angolan nationalism has rural, peasant roots. The northern rolling hill country of the Angolan portion of the old Kongo kingdom produced a brand of nationalism quite separate from that articulated and organized by educated Luanda-Mbundu town dwellers. Though separate in genesis and program, it was not without a certain impact upon Luanda and nearby Dembos, as well as the cotton area of Malange. To the north of Luanda and the old Ndongo kingdom, the Kongo kingdom was the first zone of Angola contacted by the Portuguese and one of the last effectively occupied by them. The Kikongo-speaking people there created Angola's first peasant-based modern nationalist movement.

Having soundly trounced the forces of the Mani Kongo in a battle at Mbwila (Ambuila) in 1665, the Portuguese felt justifiably confident that there would be no more trouble from the devastated north. Bled by the slave trade and fragmented by internecine conflict among its provinces, the Kongo kingdom's political authority or influence over neighboring Mbundu areas (Dembos) to the south had been effectively eliminated. So by the end of the seventeenth century the Portuguese largely withdrew from the territory on both sides of the Congo River.

The 1845–1860 period of Portuguese expansion that followed abolition of the slave trade culminated in a temporary occupation of São Salvador (1859–1870) in order to support the "fragile kingship" of Dom Pedro V. (Kongolese kings assumed the title Dom and a Portuguese Christian name upon accession to the throne.) The kingdom was already heavily dependent upon the Portuguese for trade, arms, and priests. Dom Pedro V was crowned on August 7, 1859, by a European missionary priest in the presence of Portuguese officials and soldiers. At that time he signed an oath of loyalty to the King of Portugal—an oath in Portuguese which he probably could not read. This exaction of fealty was promptly protested by Portuguese-educated Prince Nicolas of the Kongo, a son of the previous king and an employee in the Portuguese civil service. Nicolas publicly argued that the Kongo kingdom was, and should remain, an independent ally and not a vassal state.[1] In truth, however, the king of the Kongo no longer exercised any real authority beyond the environs of São Salvador. When the Portuguese reentered the area in the 1880's—after a nearly total absence during the previous decade and only a very marginal, sporadic contact with the kingdom during the previous two centuries—the Kongo area finally came under direct Portuguese administration. The lateness of this assumption of direct rule, however, meant that the Bakongo region, as compared with the Luanda-Mbundu area to the south, would be relatively less influenced by Portuguese culture and politics as contemporary nationalism took root and grew as a powerful force within the Bakongo community.[2]

The Bakongo people of Angola, estimated at over 500,000 in 1960, have always flowed back and forth across the superimposed colonial border with the Congo, continuing to constitute a single ethnic community with fellow Bakongo ruled by either the French or Belgians. In recent decades thousands of Angolan Bakongo emigrated to the Belgian Congo, drawn by the latter's comparatively attractive educational and economic opportunities. As a result a significant proportion of the Kikongo-speaking people of the Lower Congo living between Kinshasa and the Atlantic are, in fact, émigrés, or children and grandchildren of émigrés, coming from the Congo district of Portuguese Angola.

The Bakongo are divided into some fifteen ethnic subgroups. Two of these, the approximately 150,000 people living in the Mpemba area around the old capital at São Salvador (sometimes known as the Kishikongo, Muxikongo, or Muchikongo, but referred to hereafter simply as Bakongo) and the Bazombo (or simply Zombo), situated to the east around Maquela-Uige, have produced the two

[1] Douglas L. Wheeler, "A Nineteenth Century African Protest in Angola: Prince Nicolas of Kongo (1830?–1860)," *Journal of African Historical Studies* (Boston University), Vol. I, No. 1 (1968), pp. 40–59.

[2] For a Portuguese account of the history of the (Portuguese) Kongo, see Hélio Esteves Felgas, *História do Congo Português* (Carmona, Angola: Empresa Gráfica do Uige, 1958).

most important currents within the northern Angolan stream of modern nationalism. Bakongo resistance to Portuguese rule in the São Salvador area first focused on the local kingship, and developed around this symbol of traditional African authority. On the other hand, the Bazombo, geographically distant and little interested in the restoration of a traditionalist authority to which they had long since ceased to owe any real allegiance, first asserted their unassimilated "Africanness" through religious protest and by means of mutual self-help programs that were supported by a growing class of enterprising Zombo traders, entrepreneurs and white-collar workers spread along both sides of the border from Maquela to Matadi.

Kingship, Missionaries, and the Rise of Bakongo Nationalism

Protestant missionaries entered the scene about the same time that the Portuguese were establishing themselves permanently in the Kongo kingdom. In 1878 Rev. George Grenfell and Thomas Comber of the Baptist Missionary Society (BMS) of London were received by the king Dom Pedro V in the modest capital of São Salvador (known in Kikongo as Kongo dia Ngunga), which was then only a small town of some 200 houses and 1500 to 2000 people. At the invitation of the king they decided to establish a mission station there and by 1887 had formed a full-fledged BMS church. (A list of the Kongo kings is given in the accompanying table.)

KONGO KINGS

(Kivuzi Clan)

1859–1891	Dom Pedro V
1891–1896	Regent, Dom Alvaro d'Aqua Rosada
1896–1901	Dom Henrique Neteyekenge
1901–1912	Dom Pedro VI
1912–1915	Dom Manuel Kiditu
1915–1923	Dom Alvaro Nezingu
1923–1955	Dom Pedro VII
1955–1957	Dom António III
1957–1962	Regent, Dona Isabela da Gama
1962–1962	Dom Pedro VIII

During this same period the Portuguese government used the Catholic Church as a means to secure its secular authority in the Kongo region. In 1884, for instance, a Catholic priest, Father António Barroso, persuaded the illiterate Dom Pedro V to sign a note which he, the king, believed to be an expression of gratitude for the gift of a gold-backed chair. It was instead a new declaration of loyal submission to the king of Portugal, Dom Luis, which was used effectively by the Portuguese government at the Berlin Conference of 1884–85 in support of Portuguese claims to the Kongo area.

Over the next decades the fledgling Protestant church slowly spread out from three centers, São Salvador, Quibocolo, and Bembe. Portuguese authorities meanwhile continued to preserve the institution of Kongo kingship as a useful political control mechanism and employed the king [3] and loyal chiefs as recruiting agents to round up forced labor for the cocoa plantations of Cabinda, São Tomé, and Principe.

Then in December 1913 a chief of the Madimba region, Tulante (Lieutenant) Alvaro Buta, a Catholic who had himself been employed by the Portuguese administration to secure recruits, led a revolt against the then king of the Kongo, Dom Manuel Kiditu, because of the latter's refusal to oppose new labor demands for São Tomé. Beginning on December 10 in Catholic and animist communities, the revolt quickly spread south and east into Protestant areas, and "in the end the whole country was in revolt against the forced recruitment from which all had suffered." [4]

At the request of Portuguese officials, Rev. J. S. Bowskill and Dr. Haldane C. Gilmore, accompanied by a leading African Protestant and interpreter, Miguel Necaca, interceded with Chief Buta and arranged for a "palaver" between him and frightened officials in the now partially burned-out capital of São Salvador. Following these talks Chief Buta withdrew his forces, pending a response to his demands for dismissal and punishment of local colonial officials, deposition of the king, the exile of certain persons, and an end to the practice of "recruiting workmen for private enterprises" and forcing men to work outside their "own language areas." [5]

[3] Dom Pedro V, who unknowingly signed away his kingdom's independence, belonged to the Kivuzi clan, as did all his successors.

[4] From a detailed account by British missionary R. H. Carson Graham, *Under Seven Congo Kings* (London: Carey Press [1930]), p. 137.

[5] *Ibid.*, p. 138.

On January 18, 1914, after posting what appeared to be a favorable response from the governor, Portuguese authorities suddenly moved troops into São Salvador and arrested Miguel Necaca and three others as they were leaving Baptist Sunday services. The four were "locked up in a filthy prison without being told on what charge they were apprehended." [6] As a child, Necaca, separated from his parents, had been acquired by African "owners" whose name he took. They had permitted him to attend a BMS grade school, and as an adult he had become a pillar of the Protestant church and on his own initiative had built a BMS church at the town of Mbwela.[7] His arrest signaled the beginning of a general move against local Protestants. Thus according to one of the British missionaries, Rev. R. H. Carson Graham, only Protestants were arrested, even though Catholics were equally involved, when Buta renewed his attack on January 25 and burned down most of the remaining houses in São Salvador.[8] The Portuguese retaliated by looting and destroying towns that had sided with Buta, and, according to Graham, "wantonly destroyed at least fourteen [Protestant] school-chapels." [9] The damage to the Protestant missions was very severe and laid the foundation for a long and deep conflict between Protestant and Portuguese authorities.

With such faithfuls as Miguel Necaca in jail, those who expected "divine interference" were disillusioned, and many forsook Christianity for the more tangible solace of palm wine. The Protestant Church faced a real danger of being wiped out. This danger grew when on February 10, 1914, Rev. J. S. Bowskill, a Britisher, was arrested and charged with having instigated the rebellion. He later described the charge as a "concoction of absurd falsehoods born of religious jealousy." [10] The British government thereupon dispatched a consular official to Angola to look after the interests of its insecure missionaries.

The rebellion, deprived of the alleged help of Rev. Bowskill, continued unabated until July 1915, when Portuguese authorities used a general amnesty to trick and capture Chief Buta and his

[6] *Ibid.*, p. 139.

[7] For a biographical sketch of Miguel Necaca by Baptist missionary W. David Grenfell, see *The Dawn Breaks* (London: Carey Press, 1948), pp. 68–73.

[8] Graham, *Under Seven Congo Kings*, p. 139.

[9] *Ibid.*, p. 142.

[10] Quoted from a letter to His Excellency, Lt. Col José E. de Carvalho Crates, chief of the cabinet of the Minister for the Colonies from J. S. Bowskill, São Salvador, Aug. 10, 1914. See Appendix A.

lieutenants. He and his men died soon afterward in coastal jails, reportedly of influenza. Meanwhile Miguel Necaca was released, the king Dom Manuel Kiditu was deposed and replaced by Dom Alvaro Nezingu, a respected Catholic who had not been involved in the rebellion, and the colonial administration renewed its pressures to obtain local African manpower. This time it sought Bakongo soldiers and carriers to serve with Portuguese forces in the First World War campaign against the Germans in southern Angola. One of the side effects of this renewed conscription was to provoke a wave of Bakongo emigration north to the Congo.

Later, during the early 1920's, a religious prophet movement in the Congo led by Simon Kimbangu gained followers (Kimbanguists) within the Bakongo population of northern Angola. Responding in customary fashion to this religious channeling of social protest, the Portuguese administration ordered the arrest of scores of "implicated" BMS evangelists. Rev. Graham protested to the authorities, claiming that the detained "were all very badly treated, the men beaten, the women raped and their goods pillaged by the police." [11] The administration soon thereafter issued a decree forbidding Protestant missions to use indigenous languages in their schools and requiring that all teachers possess a certificate of proficiency in Portuguese. According to Graham, "This meant the closing of over two hundred of our little village schools, where the children were being taught to read the Scripture in their native tongue; thus cutting the sinews of this very important branch of our work, and condemning thousands of native children to illiteracy and ignorance; for we could not provide, and the Government would not provide, the towns with Portuguese teachers." [12]

Then with the death of Dom Alvaro Nezingu in 1923, the kingship for the second time within the decade became the focus of a lively dispute with political and religious overtones. Because it had closely associated itself with the colonial administration and enjoyed a near monopoly over education, the Catholic Church inevitably drew fire from those who had become embittered by the colonial system. In 1923, when the administration enthroned as Dom Pedro VII one João Lengo (or Lengho), a renegade Protestant who had fought against Chief Buta and had subsequently joined the Catholic Church, popular reaction was predictably negative. Writing of this incident some thirty-five years later, the prominent Bakongo

[11] Graham, *Under Seven Congo Kings,* p. 237.

[12] *Ibid.,* pp. 194–195. Decree 77 (1921) issued by the High Commissioner, Luanda.

leader, Holden Roberto, charged that in fact the choice of Kongo kings had been surrounded by intrigues since the 1890's. Catholic missionaries, he charged, had interfered "in the internal politics of the country instead of limiting themselves to evangelizing, the aim for which they [had] thronged to the Kongo." In Roberto's view João Lengo had been chosen as a pliable figurehead king in spite of the active opposition of politically aware São Salvadorans who condemned him for being the administration's "principal collaborator" during the 1913–1915 rebellion. "Distinguished for his cruelty towards his racial brothers," said Roberto, João Lengo was "imposed" by the colonial authorities at the insistence of the local Catholic clergy.[13]

In spite of official displeasure, during the reign of Dom Pedro VII (1923–1955) the BMS church grew steadily and acquired what was, at least statistically, the strongest Protestant following anywhere in Angola. Rev. Graham estimated church membership at only 1541 in 1930. The 1950 census, however, listed 35 per cent of the Bakongo as Protestant, as against 13 per cent Protestants in the African population of Angola at large. The São Salvador region itself counted 29,269 Catholics and 15,860 Protestants. This was an alarming proportion, as seen by local Portuguese officials, who came from a country where Protestants formed substantially less than 1 per cent of the population and where it was widely assumed that Protestantism breeds rebellious individualism. Therefore the Portuguese government found it expedient to mount restrictions against any Protestant activity that might conceivably undermine its own authority or the Vatican's prestige.[14]

A natural result of this restrictive religious policy was the tendency for Africans to empathize and identify with British and American missionaries, who were also fighting local officialdom, and to look upon them as potential liberators. When some American Protestants known for their concern with race relations and Africa visited Léopoldville in the 1950's, they were sought out by political leaders of the local émigré Angolan community.[15] Nevertheless, when several of these Bakongo petitioners later set forth their political griev-

[13] Holden Roberto, "La vie en Angola" (Accra, Dec. 1958, unpublished typescript), p. 4.

[14] For an account of Portuguese harassment of Baptist missionaries between 1914 and 1961, see Len Addicott, *Cry Angola!* (London: SCM Press, 1962), pp. 14–15, and *passim.*

[15] Revs. Homer A. Jack (Unitarian) and George M. Houser (Methodist) visited Léopoldville in 1952 and 1954, respectively, and were contacted by Angolan Bakongo leaders.

ances in a letter to an American State Department official, they scored the Portuguese penchant for blaming Protestant outsiders rather than widespread African discontent for all their troubles within Angola. As an illustration of such political escapism, they pointed to the fact that Portuguese officials had accused a Briton, Rev. J. S. Bowskill, of having fomented the 1913–1915 rebellion.[16]

Royal Opposition: The Matadi Group

Dom Pedro VII died on April 17, 1955. Modernist elements that had criticized the deceased king for alleged flabbiness in dealing with the Portuguese promptly seized the occasion to urge the choice of a stronger successor, an educated man who might better represent African interests. The effort to revive the authority of the crown so as to create a political instrument through which to work for economic and social reform was spearheaded by a group of Bakongo royalists then resident in the Congo. This group was led by a gregarious, multilingual (Kikongo, Portuguese, French, English) Protestant, (José) Eduardo Pinock, who was born on March 28, 1905, at São Salvador, where he attended the local BMS school. For many years he had held what was then an unusually responsible post for an African, that of railroad stationmaster at the Congolese port of Matadi.

Eduardo Pinock and an associate, Francisco Borralho Lulendo, who had been at the king's deathbed, threw their support behind the candidacy of a respected community leader and Protestant, Manuel Kiditu, named for his maternal uncle, the former king Dom Manuel Kiditu (1912–1915). While initially seeming to approve of their choice, the local Portuguese administrator Manuel Martins, prodded by an alarmed Catholic clergy, quietly vetoed the reformists' candidate and gave his nod instead to a promisingly weak nonentity, one António José da Gama. da Gama was dutifully elected by an assemblage of elders of the royal Kivuzi clan, guided by Portuguese authorities. Described later by one of his modernist detractors as "an old handyman and printer at the Catholic mission of São Salvador, who suffered from sleeping sick-

[16] Letter to George V. Allen, Assistant Secretary of State, May 20, 1956, signed by Holden Roberto, Manuel Barros Necaca, António Necaca, Eduardo Roberto, and José Eduardo [Pinock].

ness and had only an elementary education," da Gama was crowned on August 16, 1955, in the presence of administrator Manuel Martins and an influential priest, Father Joaquim de Fellette.[17]

The reformists first attempted to block the coronation by means of organized popular protest, but, finding the administration determined to have its pliable king, they altered their strategy. If the king had to be weak, then let him have strong counselors. Thus immediately upon being enthroned as Dom António III, the king was presented with a widely backed demand that he name as his principal advisors Eduardo Pinock as first counselor (seen as potential "prime minister"), Manuel Kiditu as second counselor, and Borralho Lulendo as secretary. The local Catholic mission most strenuously opposed allowing a Protestant to acquire the inside position of king's secretary. But after a day of hesitation and palaver, the king gave in to mobilized public pressure and announced his acceptance of all three advisors through his official spokesman, an uncle, who was thereupon plied with gifts from overjoyed citizens.

Making the best of what they considered to be a "regrettable" turn of events, the Portuguese administration advised Pinock and Lulendo to return to Matadi for one month while things settled down in São Salvador, following which the king would summon them back to assume their new posts. With this understanding, the Matadi group returned home. There they waited in vain for a royal summons, amidst disquieting reports from the capital that the king, under Portuguese influence, had no intention of ever calling for them. After a number of trips from Matadi to São Salvador and confrontations with the king, clergy, and officialdom —all of which produced only circumlocution and stalling—it became apparent to the would-be counselors that they were being outmaneuvered. Their letters of appeal to Luanda, Lisbon, and the Vatican brought no remedy.

Finally Pinock and his supporters decided to overthrow the king. Against the advice of collaborators in Léopoldville, who argued that the effort would only get them arrested, the Matadi royalists decided to turn their annual Christmas holiday journey to São Salvador into a *coup de théâtre*.[18] Forewarned by letters inter-

[17] Roberto, "La vie en Angola," p. 5.

[18] According to Eduardo Pinock, both Holden Roberto and Georges Freitas, who later helped to organize the MPLA in Léopoldville, wrote trying to dissuade him from his project.

cepted en route from the Pinock group to fellow organizers at São Salvador, a nervous Manuel Martins and his incoming replacement as administrator, David Campos, were waiting at the border with a contingent of well-armed soldiers on December 23, 1955, when a twelve-vehicle caravan of several hundred Bakongo descended upon the small Angolan customs post near Songololo. Pinock had been careful to obtain proper authorization for his trip from both Portuguese consular and Belgian colonial officials in Léopoldville. He had given strict orders that no one should carry a knife or weapon of any kind. Waving Portuguese flags and singing the Portuguese national anthem, the caravan docilely delivered itself, complete with guitar orchestra and holiday football team, for painstaking but unrewarding search by the Portuguese border guard. The latter did find a briefcase full of documents in Pinock's lead car and these were immediately impounded for detailed examination by the police. To satisfy his own sense of humor and to give the officials something with which to occupy themselves, however, Pinock had deliberately stuffed his briefcase full of old papers from the railroad station office at Matadi.

The authorities finally allowed the visitors to proceed festively southward. They were hailed along the way by villagers, obviously relieved to see them passing freely. Arriving in São Salvador, however, they found the streets deserted by apprehensive Europeans. They then proceeded to their destination, Pinock's village home, some three kilometers from town. Several days of anxious palaver ensued, during which the king first refused to negotiate with his adversaries and they then refused to talk with him. Scandalized officials tried to avoid a showdown by persuading the aspirant counselors to accept an eleventh-hour royal invitation to come and reside for three months at the court and then (perhaps) assume office.

Meanwhile the African community went ahead with preparations for a massive protest demonstration, which took place on schedule before the king's residence on the morning of December 27. There in the name of the people and in the presence of the king, Eduardo Pinock delivered a destitution proclamation, evicting Dom António III and the whole Kivuzi clan from the Kongo throne (see Appendix C).

A copy of the text was presented to Sr. Martins, who then advised the demonstrators to disperse. Under the impression that they had finally rid themselves of an unpopular king, the crowd cheerfully broke up and repaired to Pinock's home to celebrate, only to have the hero of the day caution them that the battle was far from over. The next day, before departing with his group for the Congo, Pinock went to the administrator's residence. He was well received, obtained promises that there would be no retaliation against the people for the action of the previous day, and was given an escort to accompany him to the Congolese frontier.

The results of Luanda's first inquiries into the affair seemed to suggest that the administration might be prepared to allow the validity of public grievances and the royal destitution. Within a few weeks, however, a military commission arrived in São Salvador. It came to contrary conclusions and prescribed disciplinary action. As a consequence, the police arrested local African leaders indiscriminately and took the most prominent among them off to prison in Luanda and Silva Porto. Among those arrested were Norman Ambrosio Luyanzi, the 83-year-old secretary of the local Baptist church, Rosa Ginga, a 72-year-old businessman, Manuel Kiditu, the earlier unsuccessful aspirant to the throne, and two younger political leaders, Liborio Nefwane (age 43) and Figueira Lello (age 30). These five persons were retained in custody even after the rest of those arrested were freed in July 1956.[19]

Portuguese officials followed up this action with a move designed to seal off São Salvador from further agitation by the Matadi royalists. They had Dom António III, whom they maintained on the faded Kongo throne, issue a proclamation prohibiting any São Salvadorans from returning home from the Belgian Congo after June 30, 1956. Faced with involuntary exile, the royal opposition of Matadi and other émigrés complained that they were being "deprived of their native rights in what constituted a grave infraction of the rights of man," but their protests were ignored.[20]

When on July 11, 1957, a little over a year later, Dom António III suddenly died, wary Portuguese officials decided to leave the throne temporarily vacant rather than immediately begin all over again with the unsettling process of choosing and crowning a king. For some years, therefore, an uneducated queen widow known as Dona Isabela reigned as regent. The administration's inaction concerning the issue of succession, however, heightened African resentment. A thoughtful analysis of the "king palaver" of 1955–56, written by Rev. F. James Grenfell, a British Baptist missionary who served for some years in São Salvador, has concluded that had the

[19] Roberto, "La vie en Angola," p. 6.
[20] Letter to George V. Allen, May 20, 1956.

colonial authorities handled the matter differently, so as to allow the people more say in their own affairs, "some of the conditions in which subversive political organizations flourish would have been avoided." [21] As it was, however, first not allowed to have the king or king's counselors they wanted, then prevented from having a king at all, the Bakongo royalists turned in frustration to the alternative of organizing a *sub rosa* political movement as the only possible means for continuing the quest for political reform.

Less Royal Opposition: The Léopoldville Group

With the total collapse of efforts to transform the Kongo kingship into a modern institution and infuse it with real power, the center of Bakongo political activity shifted from São Salvador and Matadi to Léopoldville. For some years Manuel Barros Necaca, the son of Miguel Necaca of 1914 fame, had been stimulating political consciousness within the Angolan community of the Congolese capital.

Barros Necaca was born on July 28, 1914, at São Salvador where, like Eduardo Pinock, he attended the local BMS grammar school. He then worked for several years at the BMS hospital at São Salvador (1934–1937), studied to become a medical technician during three years at the (Protestant) Currie Institute at Dondi near Nova Lisboa (1937–1940), and then, according to his own account, followed a ten-month in-training program at a hospital in Lisbon (1940–41). It was during Necaca's sojourn in Lisbon that the aging figurehead Dom Pedro VII visited the Portuguese capital and persuaded his talented countryman to serve as his private secretary.

Upon returning to Angola in 1941 Necaca continued to work for the king, who found in his aide someone who shared his rather belated concern for expanding educational opportunity in his realm. While in Portugal Dom Pedro had pleaded for more schools but was told by officials that Catholic authorities in the Kongo had assured them that educational facilities there were adequate. Furthermore these same officials indicated that, before they could consider expanding such facilities, the king would have to enter into certain new contracts with the government. Remembering the fate of his predecessor Dom Manuel Kiditu, who in 1913 had reluctantly signed an agreement providing forced laborers for São Tomé, Dom Pedro shrank from any new commitments. Instead he

[21] F. James Grenfell, "Some Causes of the Revolt in the North of Angola in 1961" (unpublished typescript written during May and June 1961).

decided to prevail upon Necaca, who was once again working at the BMS hospital, to leave São Salvador and go to the Belgian Congo in order to try to mobilize some sort of assistance from outside.

Necaca moved to Léopoldville in March 1942. There his knowledge of both Portuguese and English helped him to obtain a job with the Nogueira trading company, but he found it difficult to arouse local interest in the problems back home in the kingdom. He so reported to Dom Pedro during a visit to São Salvador in August 1948. In one of his more lucid periods—the king had become a heavy drinker while idling in his sinecure—Dom Pedro urged Necaca to redouble his efforts. Accordingly, in 1949 Necaca and a young nephew, Holden Roberto, systematically canvassed and palavered among their compatriots in Léopoldville. That there was still a total ban on African political organization in the Belgian Congo at the time may help to account for the fact that they got a favorable response from only a handful of persons.

In 1952 popular resistance to forced labor led to widespread arrests in the São Salvador region. The same year, leaders of both the Léopoldville and Matadi groups contacted the American consulate in Léopoldville, received a sympathetic hearing, and asked for advice. They were discouraged from expecting much from petitions to the United Nations, for Portugal had not yet been admitted to the world organization. They were encouraged, on the other hand, to believe that, if instead of a Portuguese puppet they could place an effectual, independent-minded person on the Kongo throne, they would stand a better chance of gaining international support for the restoration of Kongolese sovereignty.

When in 1955 Portugal finally gained admission to the United Nations, an unsigned "petition" seemingly written and circulated late that year by these same leaders suggested that salvation might lie in joint American and United Nations action. Their appeal read in part: "The people of the Kongo Kingdom insistently request to be placed under the authority of the United Nations in the form of a Trusteeship of the United States of America. It is unnecessary to stress the preponderant role played by the United States of America on the international scene. If God has given those people Power, Wealth, and Intelligence, it is for the good of humanity, or oppressed peoples." Specifically, the petitioners requested that the United States send a "mission of inquiry" to investigate conditions inside the Kongo and put themselves on record as opposing Communist penetration into their country.[22]

In early 1956 determined efforts led by the Matadi group to enthrone a strong king ended in failure, and those in Léopoldville, like Necaca and Roberto, who had never much believed in the possibility of capturing the throne, now argued for new initiatives at the international level. The views of the Léopoldville group prevailed from this point on. One result was a new approach to the United States. On May 20, 1956, Necaca, Pinock, Roberto, and others sent a letter to an American State Department official, "Monsieur Georg [*sic*] V. Allen," who was then visiting Léopoldville. In it they asserted that historically and legally the Portuguese Kongo constituted a territory separate from Angola, to which it had been unjustly joined in 1884. Overlooking the presence in the colony of more than a million and a half Ovimbundu and many other ethnic communities, they claimed that "in Angola one speaks Kimbundu whereas in the Territory of the Kongo [i.e., the northern sector of Angola] one speaks Kikongo." [23] To them Angola was the Portuguese colony to the south, the conquered Mbundu realm of the *ngola*. In their view the Kongo, unlike Angola, had never really been conquered. Its illiterate king Dom Pedro V had simply been tricked by Father António Barroso into signing something he did not understand. This act did not represent a knowing, legal transfer of sovereignty. In September Necaca repeated these arguments and restated his group's desire to see the Portuguese Kongo placed under a United Nations trusteeship. "We do sincerely wish that the Portuguese may leave our country," he said, "in order to give it to another colonizer, who will be able to civilize us, instead of stopping our needs as it happens for the moment." [24]

In early 1957, according to Necaca, he sent Roberto to Matadi to arrange with Pinock for a general conclave, which reportedly took place that spring at the Catholic mission of Saint Pierre in Léopoldville, a locale chosen in order to manifest the organizers' freedom from religious bias. Several hundred Angolan Bakongo from all over the Lower Congo region are said to have gathered under the cover of the then legal pretext of holding a nonpolitical meeting concerned with ethnocultural matters. Following this meeting a

[22] Translated from French typescript in files of American Committee on Africa, New York.

[23] Letter to George V. Allen.

[24] Letter to George Houser, dated Sept. 12, 1956.

letter was dispatched in June to the United Nations Secretary-General. Sent in the name of the inhabitants of "the Kongo . . . an ex-independent territory with no treaty with Portugal," it condemned forced labor as well as educational and health conditions in the territory and asked for an on-the-spot investigation by the United Nations to bring the facts to light.[25]

Then in July, meeting once again at Léopoldville, the Léopoldville and Matadi groups, whose hard-core militants numbered but twelve and nine persons, respectively, reportedly decided to establish a formal organization, the *União das Populações do Norte de Angola* (UPNA).[26] They named Barros Necaca (Léopoldville group) president and Borralho Lulendo (Matadi group) secretary. It was during that same month, as noted earlier, that Dom António III died. But the UPNA leaders refused to get embroiled in a new struggle over the kingship, for by this time their political hopes lay elsewhere.

In November 1957 a gathering of UPNA leaders at Cattier, a rail stop midway between Léopoldville and Matadi, concluded that the next step should be to send a representative abroad to lobby in Africa, in the United States, and at the United Nations. They felt bottled up in the Congo, where the Belgian administration still proscribed political activity.

Necaca had been in correspondence with the American Commit-

25 Letter to the Secretary-General of the United Nations, São Salvador, June 1957. See also George M. Houser, "Nationalist Organizations and Leaders in Angola: Status of the Revolt," in John A. Davis and James K. Baker (eds.), *Southern Africa in Transition* (New York: Frederick A. Praeger, 1966), pp. 167-168.

26 The approximate date of July 1957 is based on information from interviews with Eduardo Pinock and Barros Necaca. Necaca lost all his political notes when interrogated by Belgian police officials in 1959, and few records were kept of such matters. The 1957 date is some three years after that usually given. According to a "Memorandum Presented by the National Liberation Front to the Commission for the Reconciliation of Angolan Nationalist Movements at Léopoldville," on July 15, 1963, the UPNA was founded on July 10, 1954, by "Angolan émigrés who had taken refuge [in Léopoldville] as a result of the deplorable living conditions prevailing in Angola." A statement by José Gilmore [Roberto] in a "Conférence de presse" (Tunis, Oct. 6, 1960, mimeo.) fixed the day as July 11, 1954, whereas the date of July 7, 1954, was given by Holden Roberto, as reported in an interview with Sylvain Camara in the Dakar weekly *Afrique nouvelle,* No. 740, Oct. 11, 1961, and by the African Catholic student review *Tam Tam* (Paris), No. 3-4, 1961. The Trotskyite journal *L'Internationale* (Paris), Oct. 1962, lists Feb. 7, 1954; and a 1961 report written by Kenny Kaw of the International Student Conference (COSEC) gives Nov. 7, 1954.

tee on Africa since first meeting its executive director, George Houser, at Léopoldville in 1954, and he now found this contact useful in planning for the UPNA's international venture. In January 1958 Houser wrote Necaca, raising general questions about the wisdom of constructing a political program around the idea of resurrecting the old Kongo kingdom and suggesting that it might be difficult to obtain external support for such a scheme.[27] In his reply, Necaca revealed the beginnings of some local doubts on the matter and suggested that consideration of the question of restoring the "Ancient Kingdom of the Congo" could be postponed until "later on when better circumstances will allow it." Meanwhile he said that what mattered most was to change "the conditions now prevailing in Angola." With this latter aim in mind, and indicative of the UPNA's broadening horizons, he wrote Houser: "We have been working for quite a long time with some leaders living in Luanda, because our objectives are in principle the same." [28] He quickly followed up this letter with another asking Houser's opinion about the idea of sending a UPNA representative to newly independent Ghana, where he might make useful international contacts and speak and write freely about the Angolan situation, all of which was still impossible in the Belgian Congo.[29] In response, Houser put Necaca in contact with Kwame Nkrumah's pan-African advisor George Padmore, and the latter wrote Necaca on May 14, 1958, inviting the *União das Populações do Norte de Angola* to participate in the All-African Peoples' Conference to be held later that year in Accra.

From UPNA to UPA

Scattered from Matadi to Léopoldville, the swelling ranks of UPNA members and sympathizers quietly donated funds for the mission to Ghana. Given his position with the Nogueira trading company, Necaca could not leave Léopoldville for a protracted period without arousing Portuguese suspicions and risking complications for his family and the UPNA. So the assignment was given to his nephew and protégé, Holden (Alvaro) Roberto.

Born on January 12, 1923 at São Salvador, Roberto was named after the British Baptist missionary who baptized him, Robert

[27] Letter dated Jan. 25, 1958.
[28] Letter dated Feb. 9, 1958.
[29] Letter dated Feb. 15, 1958.

Holden Carson Graham.[30] His mother, Ana Joana Lala Necaca, was the eldest child of Miguel Necaca; his father, Garcia Roberto, worked at the BMS mission in São Salvador. In 1925 Holden Roberto went to the Congo with an aunt, and his parents followed not long after. He was educated in Léopoldville, where he was graduated from the BMS school in 1940. At this point, according to his uncle, Necaca decided to send him and a younger brother for a stint at the BMS school in São Salvador (1940–41). Roberto had been back only once since leaving at the age of two, and it was time that he rediscover his roots and perfect his Portuguese. Back in the Congo in 1941 he began a service of eight years as an accountant in the Belgian administration. He worked in Léopoldville, Bukavu, and Stanleyville, where he first met Patrice Lumumba at the *Cercle des Évolués.* In 1949, following an aforementioned meeting with Dom Pedro VII at São Salvador, Necaca called Roberto back to Léopoldville, got him a job with the Nogueira company, and enlisted him in the early efforts at political organizing. Roberto also joined his uncle in playing on the local Nomad football team and then went on to play and travel as a member of the Daring club, which was led by a young athlete named Cyrille Adoula.

Roberto has said that it was during a three-week visit to Angola in 1951, at which time he witnessed the brutalization of a helpless old man by a calloused Portuguese *chefe de posto,* that he was shocked into political activism.[31] Following that experience he sent a letter to a former French mentor, Professor Yves Couderc of the BMS school in Léopoldville, who had by then returned to France, asking him in turn to send it on to Secretary-General Trygve Lie at the United Nations. The letter was answered by Wilfrid Benson, Director of the Division of Information for Non-Self-Governing Territories. Though the reply was sympathetic, Roberto has said that he concluded from it and replies to other letters sent to persons, such as A. J. Muste of the pacifist Fellowship of Reconciliation, that Africans would have to count mainly on themselves if they were to succeed in their quest for liberation from colonial rule. It was

[30] See Rev. David Grenfell in *Courrier d'Afrique* (Léopoldville), May 9, 1965. Some of the aliases used by Roberto when traveling incognito in Africa during 1958–1960 were adopted from the name of an Irish missionary, Dr. Haldane C. Gilmore of Dublin. A Luanda court order of December 9, 1959, indicting Roberto *in absentia* for subversion gives his birth date as 11 rather than 12 January 1923, whereas his uncle Barros Necaca recalls it as 12 January.

[31] Pierre A. Moser, *La révolution angolaise* (Tunis: Société l'Action d'Édition et de Presse, 1966), p. 66.

during the same period that Roberto reportedly attended an informal series of discussions on politics conducted secretly for a group of African *évolués* by a resident Belgian.

Following the king palaver of 1955–56, Roberto claims to have made a brief and secret ten-day trip to northern Angola, where he was able to make useful political contacts, and to meet with some Kimbundu-speaking people from the regions of Nambuangongo and Caxito.[32] That same year Necaca advised him to quit the Nogueira firm and to take a less visible job with an insurance company. Then in 1958, primed and eager, he was elected for the mission to Ghana.

Complaining of ill health, in August 1958 Roberto visited the hospital at Kimpese near Thysville and returned to Léopoldville with the report that he had been advised to undergo surgery at the French hospital in Brazzaville. Not even his wife knew of his intended destination when in September he moved unnoticed across the river to Brazzaville. Since the Belgian ban on passports and politics for Africans was still in force, he was armed with only a *carte de séjour* for the French Congo and a vaccination certificate. After contacting friends who advised him that he might be able to obtain a passport in the Cameroon, he proceeded on September 12, 1958, to Pointe Noire, where he managed to persuade the teammate of a cousin who played football to help him board the French liner "Général Mangin" en route for Douala.

Upon arrival in that Cameroonian port two days later, he successfully bluffed his way past security officials with the story that he had come to visit a convalescing sister and was given a one-month visitor's permit. He then made the contact suggested by his Brazzaville friends but was told that a passport was impossible. Instead he was guided on foot by two young Cameroonians past French military patrols operating against the then-active insurgent forces of Um Nyobe's *Union des Populations Camerounaises* (UPC) and across the frontier to Kumba in the British Cameroons. From Kumba he hitchhiked and bussed to Lagos, Nigeria, where he contacted the Ghanaian High Commission. Before he could be issued the various documents required for entry into Ghana, however, he needed an authorization from George Padmore, who was then traveling abroad. Roberto used up his travel funds at the rate of three pounds a day at the Palm Tree Hotel on Apapa Road, waiting for

[32] From interviews with author in New York, Jan. 1963.

word from Accra. He was finally rescued by an old friend of his mother, a Mrs. Caetano, who had earlier lived in Léopoldville, and who now took him into her home and lent him sufficient money so that when the authorization did come from Accra, some three weeks after his arrival in Lagos, he was able to embark on the liner "Mimosa" and arrive in ample time for the Accra Conference.

In late October 1958 George Houser received a letter from Accra dated the 18th and signed Haldane Roberto [*sic*], which began: "Dear Sir: I beg to inform you that I am sent by *União das Populações do Norte de Angola* . . . led by Messrs. Eduardo J. Pinock and Manuel Barros Necaca to attend the Conference of All African Peoples and to continue to United States as you know yourself." [33] In Accra, where he met with George Padmore, Kwame Nkrumah, and Sékou Touré of newly independent Guinea, Roberto found that, in line with Houser's earlier prediction to Necaca, the idea of resurrecting the old Kongo kingdom evoked little enthusiasm. On the contrary, it was criticized as a "tribal anachronism." Given the attitude of West African nationalist leaders, Roberto managed to persuade his home organization—which was counting upon his efforts to obtain outside moral and material support—to accept a more modern and inclusive political platform. By the time the All-African Peoples' Conference opened on December 5, he was circulating a manifesto in the name of the *União das Populações de Angola* (UPA) which called for the national liberation of all Angola.[34] The statutes of the remodeled party subsequently described it as a "political organization formed for all Africans originally from Angola, without discrimination as to sex, age, ethnic origin or domicile," and aimed at installing a "democratic regime for peasants and workers" within an independent Angola.[35]

As "José Gilmore," Roberto made contacts around the fringes of the Conference while continuing to hide his real identity in order that he might protect his family in Léopoldville from possible police reprisals. In particular, he established relationships with a host of young nationalists, including Patrice Lumumba, Kenneth Kaunda, Taieb Slim, Tom Mboya, and Frantz Fanon, relationships

[33] In the letter Roberto reminds Houser that they had talked the year before (summer, 1957) in the company of Necaca and one Thomas Yangha (by this time a student in Los Angeles, California) at the Union Mission House (Protestant), Léopoldville.

[34] UPA, "Drama of Angola" (Accra, Dec. 1958, mimeo.).

[35] UPA, Statutes, Art. 2 (no date, mimeo.).

that were to prove important in the years ahead. At the same time he rejected overtures made to him by a Senegalese Marxist, Majhemout Diop, who suggested to Roberto that he join in an operation to bring Portuguese Communist students from France to Angola where they would set up a political underground in cooperation with Roberto's movement.[36]

In Ghana with what information his colleagues could send him from Léopoldville—including some documents smuggled out of Luanda—Roberto put out a stream of articles. The front page of the *Ghana Times* of November 4, 1958, carried a short interview entitled "The Rape of Angola," granted by a "Mr. O. J. Zantura," an Angolan reportedly en route to France. This was followed by a series of articles in both the *Ghana Times* and *Evening News* signed by one "Rui Ventura." The articles described conditions of "mass slavery in Angola" and spoke of African resistance to the colonial regime, without, however, making mention of the UPA.[37] The articles were militant and befitted the exuberant pan-African spirit of Accra in 1958–59: "The people of Africa did not invite any nation or any government to come and civilize them. The debates in the international arena are spilling a lot of ink while African blood is spilled on their own soil and the land remains arbitrarily divided by the Imperialists."[38]

Roberto stayed on after the conference and worked as a translator at the Ghanaian Bureau of African Affairs under George Padmore. He became a close friend and admirer of Frantz Fanon, the philosopher of the Algerian Revolution (who could trace his Martiniquais lineage on his mother's side back to Angolan slaves) and began to consider seriously the possible need for a revolution in Angola. To a cousin in Léopoldville he wrote of the need to introduce arms into Angola, a question he said "the Ghanaian government [was] going to study." In Fanon style he continued: "Cousin, without bloodshed liberation is not possible. . . ." First, however, it was necessary to see "what result we will obtain [in putting our

[36] Majhemout Diop, an orthodox Marxist-Leninist, was secretary-general of the small opposition *Parti Africain de l'Indépendance* (PAI) in Senegal and author of *Contributions à l'étude des problèmes politiques en Afrique noire* (Paris: Éditions Présence Africaine, 1958).

[37] For example, *Ghana Times* (Accra), Nov. 21, 1958, and Feb. 21, 1959; *Evening News* (Accra), Nov. 25 and 27, 1958.

[38] *Ghana Times,* Mar. 24, 1959.

case] at the United Nations in September or October."[39] In an April letter to Léopoldville he repeated that his forthcoming trip to the United Nations should serve to determine whether force would be necessary. Reflecting the optimistic political thinking then prevailing in Accra, he assured Léopoldville that, if there should be an uprising in Angola or Mozambique, "Portugal will have no support, for its colonial system is known for being the most retrograde."[40]

In mid-1959 Roberto visited Conakry, obtained a Guinean passport, and arranged to be attached to the Guinean delegation at the Fourteenth Session of the General Assembly of the United Nations in New York. On August 4 he attended a Foreign Ministers' Conference of Independent African States at Monrovia, where he was received by Liberian President William S. Tubman. Then in September he flew to New York to put the Angolan case before the world organization.

Still incognito, Roberto worked closely with the Guinean mission to the United Nations. One of the results was a speech by Ismael Touré before the Fourth Committee of the General Assembly, in which he argued that Portugal's African territories were clearly non-self-governing and that Portugal was bound by Article 73 of the Charter to report and answer to the United Nations on the rate of progress being made in preparing them for self-government.[41] On behalf of the UPA Roberto argued the case for United Nations jurisdiction in a lengthy memorandum addressed to delegates of the Fourteenth General Assembly.[42] For the first time the Angolan issue was debated and lobbyists for the nationalist cause were heard in New York. The demands were relatively modest and the results minimal, but they constituted a beginning. At the same time, with the help of the American Committee on Africa, Roberto took advantage of his stay in New York to establish a wide range of American contacts.

[39] Letter from Accra dated Jan. 26, 1959. In the same letter Roberto urged his colleagues to concentrate on organizing inside Angola.

[40] Letter from Accra dated Apr. 19, 1959.

[41] Speech by Ismael Touré, head of the delegation of the Republic of Guinea, Nov. 30, 1959. Roberto's presence on the Guinean delegation seems not to have been known to the Portuguese. Indeed Roberto has said that he overheard members of the Portuguese delegation discussing (in Portuguese) their surprise at how much he, a Guinean, had come to know about Angola.

[42] UPA, Delegation Abroad, [Memorandum] "To the Delegates to the 14th Session of the General Assembly" (New York [1959], mimeo.).

In January 1960 Roberto returned to Africa. After flying to Brazzaville for consultations with UPA leaders, he proceeded to the Second All-African Peoples' Conference at Tunis, where he succeeded in getting himself elected to the Conference Steering Committee. There in the Tunisian capital he met and established what was to be an enduring relationship with President Habib Bourguiba. He also met but refused to merge with the MPLA delegation headed by Viriato da Cruz and Lucio Lara. From Tunis he returned to Ghana, where he renewed his acquaintance with Frantz Fanon, who was representing the Algerian Liberation Front in Accra, and once again met Patrice Lumumba, who invited him to return after independence and to mount his Angolan campaign from the Congo. In April Roberto attended a Positive Action Conference convened by Prime Minister Nkrumah to protest the explosion of a French atomic bomb in the Sahara, to seek a ban on further nuclear testing in Africa, and to promote a program of boycotts and sanctions against the apartheid regime of South Africa.[48] It was during this second sojourn in Ghana, while he impatiently awaited the coming of Congolese independence, that Roberto began to experience serious pressure from Ghanaian political leaders, who urged him to form a united front with the MPLA.

Trouble in the Congo

In October 1958 the Belgian administration finally authorized the formation of African political parties in the Congo. Ethnocultural organizations quickly transformed themselves into overtly political movements, and long pent-up political emotions surfaced dramatically. Even before the opening of the All-African Peoples' Conference in Accra that December, complaints from Roberto to his associates back in the Congo to the effect that he needed more fresh news from Angola for his articles publicizing the Angolan cause had brought back word that the Portuguese had clamped down on all Angolan mail to the politically awakening Congo. Lisbon clearly feared that rising Congolese nationalism might spill over the border and contaminate its own apparently quiescent colony.

Its apprehensions mounted when on January 4, 1959, in the first

[48] Positive Action Conference for Peace and Security in Africa, Accra, Apr. 7–10, 1960. For Roberto's speech to the Conference, see *Africa Weekly* (New York), Vol. VII, No. 19, May 6, 1960.

of a long series of Congolese crises that have had serious ramifications for Angolan nationalists, violent political rioting broke out in Léopoldville. Rampaging Bakongo supporters of the Abako party led by Joseph Kasavubu jarred the very foundations of the Belgian colonial system. The immediate impact on the Angolans was twofold.

First, believing that unemployed Angolan émigrés had played an inflammatory role in the rioting, Belgian police arrested and extradited several hundred Angolans during January and February. Many of these repatriates, who were hustled off by Portuguese officials to work on the booming coffee plantations, went back to Angola influenced by nationalist ideas picked up in the Congo. They were soon spreading the word about higher wages north of the border. Angola was thereby further infected with politico-economic discontent.[44] Later, UPA leadership would credit extradition by the Belgians as having been a real boon to their organizational efforts within Angola, stating that it enabled their militants to infiltrate the colony, and to form "the cells" that were destined "to launch the rebellion of March 15, 1961." [45]

As a second consequence for Angolans, the political explosion in the Congo prompted Lisbon to press Belgian authorities to stamp out all political activity among émigrés living there. They requested the extradition of Eduardo Pinock, a request he learned of during nine days of questioning by a security officer at Matadi. As for Barros Necaca, he was first obliged to sign a document in which he promised to cease all political activity. That was in January. Then at 7 A.M. on April 3 he was taken from his home to the office of a security officer in Léopoldville, where he remained until 10 P.M. for the first of a week-long series of interrogations. Necaca professed not to know the whereabouts of his nephew. Like Pinock he denied any involvement in Congolese politics or in action that could threaten local security. Finally his interrogator, a Monsieur Lahaye, tore up Necaca's notebook of political records and let him off with a warning (similar to one given Pinock) not to use the Congo as a

[44] The well-known Congolese journalist Joseph Ngalula, writing in *Présence Congolaise* (Léopoldville) on February 21, 1959, cited reports that the expelled Angolans were being stripped of all their possessions and "deported by the Portuguese authorities into concentration camps where they are placed under forced labor."

[45] GRAE, Ministry of Information, "Memorandum Presented by the National Liberation Front to the Commission for the Reconciliation of Angolan Nationalist Movements at Léopoldville," July 15, 1963.

base for political activity against the Portuguese regime in Angola.

Trouble with Belgian security officials in early 1959 did not distract UPA leaders from their overriding fear that Portugal, by combining a humanly destructive system of forced labor with a ban on disease-prevention (e.g., yaws) programs by the World Health Organization and UNICEF, was carrying out a calculated program of genocide in Angola.[46] They still desired to see their country (now meaning all Angola) placed under a United Nations trusteeship, preferably administered by the United States, in order to save its people and prepare them for independence. Moreover, with the kind of naïveté that was bound to lead to eventual disillusionment, they were convinced that, after Holden Roberto had presented the facts before the United States and the United Nations, the sympathetic response would be of such magnitude as to force Portugal to accept such an arrangement.[47]

More immediately, the Angolan leaders were concerned by political developments in the Congo. They were frankly worried about the fact that Joseph Kasavubu and his well-organized Abako party were now championing the cause of a resurrected Kongo kingdom, the cause they had so recently abandoned. By pushing the idea of a reunified Kongo kingdom, Abako was appealing to many within the younger generation of Angolans raised and schooled in Léopoldville and the Lower Congo, where they were losing interest in the future of the Portuguese Kongo, or Angola. A lively competition for the political loyalty of what some observers estimated to be as many as 500,000 Angolan émigrés and descendants of émigrés was thus shaping up between the two Bakongo parties, Abako of the Congo and the UPA of Angola.[48] And Abako had the advantage of a legal existence which the Angolans' status as foreigners denied to their movement.

Created in 1950, Abako (the *Association pour le maintien, l'unité et l'expansion de la langue Kikongo*) had worked in its initial period for a cultural renaissance of all the Bakongo people, including

[46] According to the regional representative of UNICEF, Dr. Roland Marti of Switzerland, who was interviewed at Brazzaville, Feb. 1959, Portugal was at that time the only colonial power to exclude UNICEF and WHO from carrying out public health programs, such as inoculations against yaws, within its territories. Lisbon took the position that it was quite capable by itself of meeting the health needs of its colonies.

[47] Barros Necaca, Borralho Lulendo, Eduardo Roberto (UPA representative at Brazzaville), and others interviewed by author, Brazzaville, Feb. 1959.

[48] Amândio César, *Angola 1961* (Lisbon: Verbo, 1962), p. 104.

those living in the French *Moyen Congo* and Portuguese Angola.[49] It had thereby developed considerable support within the Angolan émigré community. As early as 1956 Abako had come out in support of independence from Belgium, but, finding little support among other Congolese ethnocultural groups (political parties were proscribed), it had decided to limit its demands to cover only a restoration of the Kongo kingdom.[50] After the riots of January 1959 and the subsequent banning of Abako, a semisecretive and ephemeral Abako offshoot, the *Mouvement de Regroupement des Populations Congolaises* (MRPC) came forth with a radical manifesto, also calling for the creation of a separate Bakongo state. Just when Angolan Bakongo leaders, under the exigencies of pan-African politics, were extending their political activity across ethnic lines, the MRPC tract of February 26 called for the reunification of all the Bakongo of the Belgian and French Congos, Cabinda, and "Portuguese Kongo," and thereby heightened feelings of ethnic particularism.[51]

Across the river in Brazzaville, the Bakongo leader of the French Congo, Abbé Fulbert Youlou, gave his support to the idea of resurrecting the Kongo kingdom. He was encouraged to do this by would-be kingmakers such as his adviser, former Vichy official Christian Jayle, along with French businessmen interested in the Belgian Inga hydroelectric scheme then planned for the Lower Congo. During February Youlou's Bakongo-based party, the *Union de Défense des Intérêts Africains* (UDDIA), put down a brief insurrection mounted by members of a northern M'Bochi-led opposition party and then spoke openly of allowing the non-Bakongo north to secede and join Ubangi-Shari, thus easing the way for Bakongo reunification.[52]

[49] See Crawford Young, *Politics in the Congo* (Princeton, N.J.: Princeton University Press, 1965), p. 505.

[50] According to the party's official organ, "The Abako was hounded by both the colonialists and all the ethnic groups for having wanted unity; it heard the voice of reason and abandoned this idea." *Notre Kongo* (Léopoldville), Nov. 1, 1959.

[51] The MRPC tract was signed by two known persons, Emmanuel Nzau of Mayumbe and Pierre Nkanu, a former seminarist. The list of fictitious signatories was headed by Floricent Mulopo. See Centre de Recherche et d'Information Socio-Politique, *Congo 1959, Documents belges et africaines* (Brussels: Imprimerie Lielens, 1960), p. 275.

[52] The main support for Youlou's UDDIA came from the Balari (Lari), a Bakongo ethnic subgroup inhabiting the area between Brazzaville and Pointe Noire.

Ubangi-Shari under the leadership of Barthélémy Boganda had become the

Referring to the conflict between Abbé Youlou's UDDIA and the M'Bochi people, the MRPC separatist manifesto of February 26 commented that it was "useless" to try to force people to live together when they have not gotten along together in the past. The sensible approach, it said, was for large ethnic groups to be united, leaving the way open for a future voluntary federation of such ethnic units "when they feel a reciprocal need to unite." [53]

Taking up the theme already sounded by this one-shot February tract, the banned Abako party next spoke out in separatist terms on April 23 through the medium of a new clandestine *Mouvement de Résistance Bakongo.* It rejected Belgian proposals for Congolese unity and argued for partition and immediate independence for a Bakongo state. Renouncing the breakup of the Kongo by the Conference of Berlin (1884) and stressing how difficult it would be to unite people "implacably divided by race, culture or another force" (had it not, they asked, taken the English nearly 1000 years to achieve national unity?) the underground Abako group unequivocally endorsed ethnic nationalism.[54] "We have on the path of progress three centuries of advance over the other ethnic groups of Central Africa. We demand . . . the partition of Belgian Africa." [55] Then in June, when Abako reformed as a legal party, it petitioned the Belgian government for the creation of an autonomous *République du Kongo-Central* to include some three million people of the former Léopoldville Province, and to serve as the nucleus around which to achieve Bakongo reunification.[56] As late as November 1959 the Abako organ *Notre Kongo* was extolling the idea of a new Kongo "empire" and claiming support for it from the UPA. It approvingly cited Abbé Youlou of Brazzaville as having

---

center of a rival, if visionary, unity scheme for regrouping all of French Equatorial Africa, the Cameroons, the Congo, Ruanda-Urundi, Uganda, Spanish Guinea, and Angola within a vast Central African Republic. This proposed Central African union, in turn, was to be a step toward uniting all former French, Belgian, Spanish, and Portuguese colonies, with presumed cultural and religious (Catholic) ties, into a yet more vast United States of Latin Africa. (See *Afrique nouvelle,* No. 595, Jan. 2, 1959.) As things turned out, however, Ubangi-Shari was renamed Central African Republic without even the addition of the M'Bochi territory that Youlou, at one stage, seemed prepared to sacrifice for the sake of Bakongo unity.

[53] *Interafrique presse* (Paris), No. 183–184, Mar. 20–27, 1959.

[54] *Congo 1959,* p. 75.

[55] Young, *Politics in the Congo,* p. 507.

[56] *Congo 1959,* pp. 81–86.

given his endorsement of Kongo reunification with the words: "Tout ce qui se ressemble, se rassemble." [57]

The pace at which Belgium pushed the Congo toward self-government and independence following the January rioting was, however, too rapid for the Bakongo secessionists. Their schemes were trampled in the rush. By late 1959 Abako had altered its position and was prepared to accept a measure of Bakongo autonomy within a federal Congo, foregoing reunification with other parts of the old Kongo kingdom. For his part, Abbé Youlou expediently became a convert to and champion of the cause of French Equatorial African unity following the death of its first architect and his political rival, Barthélémy Boganda of Ubangi-Shari, in March 1959. At one point in early 1960 Abako professed to view Youlou's project for an Equatorial *Union des Républiques de l'Afrique Centrale* (URAC) as a possible basis for a broad union within which the Bakongo might ultimately be reunited. If all the colonies into which they had been divided could now unite within a single Union of Central African Republics, it reasoned, then the Bakongo might be able to obtain local autonomy as a single subunit regrouped within "the boundaries of the Ancient Kingdom of Kongo." [58]

More and more, however, as the date for Congolese independence approached, Abako's pan-Kongo sentiments gave way to preoccupations with strictly Congolese politics and elections. The party concentrated upon consolidating its power in the Lower Congo. At the same time, ethnocentrists within Abako displayed considerable hostility toward the UPA, which they viewed as somewhat traitorous, for having earlier moved away from its Kongo-centeredness as the UPNA, toward a more inclusive Angolan and distinctly non-Congolese nationalism. Dependent upon thousands of emigrants in the Lower Congo for finances, manpower, and organizational structure, and faced with a colonial adversary far more resolute than the Belgians had proved to be, the UPA found itself in a difficult position. As an exile organization, it had to compete with the locally dominant Abako party for support within the latter's own ethnic community. Because of this, the position of the UPA in the Lower Congo was and would remain precarious and complicated in the years ahead, torn by the conflicting pulls of ethnic

[57] *Notre Kongo,* Nov. 19, 1959.
[58] *Ibid.,* Jan. 17, 1960.

solidarity, on the one hand, and the rival demands of Congolese and Angolan nationalism on the other.

Simão Toco and the Baptists

The UPA was not the only Angolan movement operating in Léopoldville and the Lower Congo in 1959–60. There was another, a Bazombo mutual-aid association, Assomizo, founded in 1956. It was the product of a separate current within the development of Bakongo nationalism, a current sufficiently distinct to warrant detailed consideration of its origins and special characteristics.

A subgroup of the Bakongo, the Bazombo, who number in excess of 100,000, inhabit the area east of São Salvador around Maquela-Uige and have long enjoyed a reputation for being an especially competitive and enterprising community. When British Protestant missionaries operating out of their initial base at São Salvador first tried to penetrate the Maquela region, the Bazombo rebuffed them. Resentful of the submission of the king of the Kongo and his followers to the Portuguese, they rejected anything coming from São Salvador. By 1899, however, the missionaries were able to establish a station at Quibocolo (or Kibokolo), a town of about 5000 people (as compared with about 1500 to 2000 people at São Salvador), and five decades later the administrative district of Quibocolo, with a total population of over 61,000, counted some 30,000 Protestants as against 16,000 Catholics.[59] With 10,000 members, the BMS church of Quibocolo was by 1950 the largest congregation in what was one of Protestantism's firmest strongholds in Angola. That the preaching of the Protestant ethic and the teaching of the mission schools made an impact is suggested by the manner in which Bazombo aspirations and grievances first took on the form of religious protest before developing politically as modern nationalism.

Modern Bazombo politics can be traced back to a product of the Quibocolo mission station school, one Simão Gonçalves Toco. Born on February 24, 1918, at Sadi, a small town on the Maquela-Quimbata road, Toco attended the Quibocolo mission school from 1926 to 1933.[60] Rev. David Grenfell, who began his many years of service

[59] Another 16,000 were animists. Statistics from Protestant mission sources.

[60] Padre Carlos Estermann, "O Tocoísmo como fenómeno religioso," *Garcia de Orta. Revista da Junta de Investigações do Ultramar* (Lisbon), Vol. 13, No. 3 (1965), pp. 325–342 (cited hereafter as Estermann, "O Tocoísmo").

at Quibocolo during Simão Toco's last school year, found the latter to be a "very bright scholar" and "far ahead of the rest of the boys" in his school work.[61] In 1933 the BMS staff sent Toco to the *Liceu Salvador Correia* in Luanda where he studied for three years at mission expense.

Upon his return to Quibocolo in 1937 Toco first taught at the mission school where he organized an evening course for adults, and was then placed in charge of educational work at the sister mission to the south at Bembe.[62] After working "steadily and well" and exercising "a great influence for good amongst the boys and young men of the district" for nearly five years, Toco, according to David Grenfell, "grew discontented with his work" and in 1943 left the mission without permission.[63] Quarrels with Portuguese members of the BMS staff over a salary that he viewed as incommensurate with his status as the first African teacher in the north to have studied in Luanda may have been at the root of his disaffection.[64] In any case, preparations were under way for his marriage at Quibocolo, when, because of demands that he first settle a debt to the mission, he departed for Léopoldville where he could seek help from family and friends in the émigré Bazombo community. It was, in fact, common for the Bazombo to go to Léopoldville in order to make purchases and arrangements for wedding celebrations to take place back inside Angola.[65] But Toco was soon involved in activities that were destined to delay and finally eclipse his marriage plans.

In Léopoldville Toco revealed an artistic talent. He produced and sold paintings with religious motifs and formed a highly successful choral group known as the Protestant Choir of Quibocolo

61 From Rev. W. David Grenfell's unpublished "Statement Concerning the Affairs of Simão Gonçalves Toco" (Quibocolo, Feb. 11, 1950, typescript).

62 The third of the BMS centers, Bembe (district), had a population of 60,436 as of 1950, of which in excess of 50,000 were Protestants, though the BMS church at Bembe claimed no more than 2000 members.

63 Grenfell, "Statement." Writing in the Catholic daily *Courrier d'Afrique* of July 13, 1962, Antoine Matumona attributed Simão Toco's discontent to the "many difficulties" that he encountered from the Baptist missionaries "who feared his competition."

64 This is the view of Toco's one-time associate Emmanuel Kunzika. See also Estermann, "O Tocoísmo," p. 327.

65 See Alfredo Margarido, "L'Église Toko et le Mouvement de Libération de l'Angola," *Le mois en Afrique,* No. 5 (May 1966), p. 84. Baptist sources maintained that Toco had rather inexplicably and abruptly left for Léopoldville after selling the wedding gown that the church had ordered from England for the occasion.

which competed with a São Salvadoran choir led by Barros Necaca. He also became active in organizing a mutual-aid group and educational activities among the Bazombo.[66] In 1944 he grouped Bazombo of diverse religious backgrounds into a voluntary association known as *Nkutu a Nsimbani (Solidarité),* with the declared aim of promoting the construction of schools and hospitals in Angola.[67] In 1946 he met a number of foreign church and lay leaders, including Mrs. Paul Robeson, who were attending a missionary conference held at Léopoldville. Grenfell later wrote of Toco's encounter with Mrs. Robeson: "What her business was, I do not know, but she had conversations with Toco and with some of our leading African Christians." As for Toco, Grenfell concluded, these conversations apparently "turned his head." [68]

Simão Toco also made contact with the Kimbanguist sect in Léopoldville and read and translated into Kikongo religious literature published in Portuguese and sent from Brazil by an American fundamentalist sect, the Watch Tower *(Torre de Vigia)* movement.[69] The Watch Tower's emphasis on salvation through the second coming of Christ and its denunciation of all existing political kingdoms of the world rendered it potentially dangerous to the colonial order. In Grenfell's words, it was easy for "race antagonism and politics [to] enter into the [Watch Tower] Movement." [70]

Toco reportedly received and declined job offers designed to divert him from his "dangerous" activities. These offers are said to have included the posts of headmaster of the Protestant (BMS) school and clerk at the Portuguese consulate in Léopoldville. Instead he led his choir in singing of a "new world coming," declined Belgian suggestions that he move to Kalina (the European quarter of Léopoldville) where his movements could be better observed, and

[66] Rev. Grenfell has commented on this period in Toco's career: "Strong efforts were made by the mission to persuade Toco to return to work in the school, but all were in vain. He lived in Léopoldville, but did no work, and was evidently supported by friends. After a time, he formed a very successful choir, and he lived in greater comfort by the gifts of the members. He also became the secretary of various mutual-aid societies, which goes to prove that he was a trusted member of the community. He was never employed by the BMS in Leo." Grenfell, "Statement." According to Emmanuel Kunzika, Toco was in fact the founder and leader of the one and only Bazombo association in Léopoldville, *Nkutu a Nsimbani,* and lived during this period in very humble circumstances.

[67] The author is indebted to Emmanuel Kunzika for much of the information concerning Simão Toco's activities in the Congo.

[68] Grenfell, "Statement."

[69] Known as Kitawala in the Congo.

[70] Grenfell, "Statement."

attracted a following throughout the Lower Congo among Kimbanguists whose own religion was officially banned.

In July 1949 Simão Toco journeyed back to Angola to attend celebrations of the fiftieth anniversary of the founding of the BMS mission at Quibocolo. For the occasion he organized and transported a contingent of some three hundred Bazombo from the Congo, including his choir.[71] His ties to the Baptists had become increasingly tenuous, however, and his choir had gradually taken on many of the organizational and doctrinal qualities of a separate syncretic religious movement. Northern Angola had had such sects, which served as outlets for African protest against European domination, since the time of an Antonian heresy in the eighteenth century. Among the more recent of such phenomena had been a movement which spread in the Maquela region in 1941 known as Kidista.[72]

It was reportedly on July 25, 1949, following Simão Toco's return from the ceremonies at Quibocolo, that he formally launched his own religious movement. He later told an interviewer that he was praying that night with some members of his choir when a wind began to blow and some of his group began to tremble, speaking "strange tongues" as they quoted certain passages from the Bible, particularly those of the Acts of the Apostles, Chapters 1 and 2. "The Holy Ghost had descended upon them." [73]

By proselytizing for their new faith, Toco and his disciples threatened to undercut missionary work in northern Angola and the Congo. It is alleged that some missionaries therefore "denounced him to the authorities of the Belgian Congo as a 'political figure.' " [74] At the very least, one may assume that, if asked their opinion, some missionaries might have described him as an irresponsible and disruptive figure. In any case, on November 22, 1949, he and many of his followers were arrested, and on January 10, 1950, they were turned over to Portuguese authorities near Noqui on the Angolan border.

[71] *Ibid.*, and letter from Rev. Grenfell to author, Jan. 1, 1966.

[72] Referred to as N-tonche by Margarido, "L'Église Toko," p. 81. In Kikongo the correct appellation would be *Nzambi a tosi*—a drop of water indicating acceptance of Christ (*Kidista*).

[73] Toco interviewed by Silva Cunha while under restriction in southern Angola, 1955, as recounted in Estermann, "O Tocoísmo," p. 328. Also Margarido, "L'Église Toko," p. 84.

[74] Margarido, "L'Église Toko."

Prenationalist Protest: From Toco to Assomizo

After some hesitation about what they should do with them, Portuguese officials sent the Tocoistas who were unskilled to Vale de Loge to make a road and sent the skilled (office clerks, tradesmen, house boys, etc.), to a camp near Luanda. The latter were given work in Luanda at half pay but were obliged to return to the camp at night. As detainees, they remained defiant, and when the authorities demanded that they pay taxes they refused on the grounds that they were earning only half pay.[75] Young Marxists of the Viriato da Cruz intellectual circle, who were already active in Luanda at this time, promptly contacted the Tocoistas but found them unprepared to project their religious heresy into organized political protest. Simão Toco's Bazombo disciples spoke Kikongo, little Portuguese, and no Kimbundu, and even more to the point, they spoke the language of a dislocated, rural peasantry, not that of a politically sophisticated urban intelligentsia.[76] The contacts bore no fruit. Eventually many of the leaders, including Toco himself, were sent south to a desert prison at the Ponta Albina lighthouse below Porto Alexandre. There they were surrounded by sea and sand, with no one to proselytize—though Toco maintained a lively correspondence.

By initially splitting them up and moving them from one place of detention to another, the Portuguese government had permitted the repatriated Tocoistas to spread their cult beyond the Bazombo community. Nevertheless, it was principally in the north that the movement remained troublesome, especially at Bembe, where Toco had taught, and in the region between Maquela and São Salvador. To cope with the movement once and for all, the government finally banned all Tocoista meetings.

Tocoism had borrowed from the Baptists, Kimbanguists, Watch Tower, and, in the view of Rev. Grenfell, "the dark depths of heathenism." [77] Like the Baptists, but in a departure from tradi-

[75] Rev. Grenfell twice visited this camp and described the detainees as showing "great courage by having no respect whatsoever for the civil authorities." Letter of Jan. 1, 1966.

[76] Margarido, "L'Église Toko," pp. 89–90.

[77] Rev. Grenfell has reported that the enterprising Tocoistas even "tried to convert us." On one occasion at Quibocolo he had to break up a dancing session in front of his house and to take "one young man up to the *Posto* who was roaming around our house in the nude." Letter to the author, Feb. 1, 1966. See also Artur Maciel, *Angola Heróica* (Lisbon: Livraria Bertrand, 1963), pp. 105–109.

tional Bazombo custom, it upheld monogamy and a prominent role for women in church councils. Like the Kimbanguists, it attributed to its prophet messianic power, including the power to forgive sins. Members prayed to the Father, Simão Toco, and the Holy Spirit. Like the Watch Tower movement, it prophesied that Christ would return to earth, but this time to liberate black men. It imposed a set of clear-cut rules covering food, dress, and behavior: no pork, alcohol, or smoking; no jewelry, except a red star medallion for identification; short hair and white clothes for women; no killing, stealing, or adultery, and respect for secular authority in its proper realm. The rebellion of Tocoism was thus limited to religious matters, broadly interpreted.

There were nonetheless latent elements of racial and political protest, which account in the final analysis for the movement's broader historical significance. By creating and perpetuating an entirely African organization from which Europeans could be and were excluded, the Tocoistas demonstrated the possibilities for developing disciplined black power. And by embracing certain practices and prophesies, they revealed evidence of a deep and probably widespread African distrust of white motives, Portuguese, Catholic, or British Baptist. For example, the Tocoistas adopted a practice of praying to God with head held back and eyes wide open. This was interpreted by some observers as evidence that Tocoistas were convinced that whites had trained blacks to pray with their heads bowed and eyes closed so as "to prevent them from seeing the Holy Ghost and thereby acquiring the wisdom indispensable to overcome their inferior status." [78] In fact, according to African sources, the practice seems to have represented simply a distinctly independent response to Psalm 121 of the Bible: "I will lift up mine eyes unto the mountains; from whence shall my help come? My help cometh from Jehova, Who made heaven and earth." As for their prophesies, Tocoistas predicted a bit of divine rearranging: all whites would become black and all Tocoistas would become white, foreign rule would end, exploitation of the African would cease, and the African would finally rule his own land.[79]

Toco's influence on the development of nationalism was, if indirect, no less real. Within Angola, Tocoism offered an outlet for

[78] Margarido, "L'Église Toko," p. 92.
[79] Grenfell, "Statement."

the frustrations of the peasant whose land had been expropriated by European coffee planters or whose labor had been commandeered for the latter's profit, and in March 1957 a group of Portuguese businessmen of the district of Carmona-Uige reportedly sent a memorandum to the governor-general complaining of the Tocoistas' systematic refusal to be recruited for agricultural work.[80] Tocoistas sought work of a different order. Alfredo Margarido writes that as of 1958 the Tocoistas had a congregation numbering 118 in Luanda and that about 100 of these worked in bakeries or factories or at the Luanda hospital. Though their schooling was rudimentary, they sought out specific job training in order to qualify for work normally held by whites, so as to gain a semblance of economic independence.[81]

Similarly, within the Bazombo émigré community in the Congo, Toco and Tocoism reinforced already-existing tendencies toward assertive, self-reliant behavior. Toco preached communal solidarity and elevated the discipline of work and the learning of skills into important virtues as well. An impressive number of Bazombo moved up the ladder from manual and domestic labor into jobs as skilled workers, tailors, nurses' aides, journalists, and office employees. Following Toco's extradition in 1950, and for fear of suffering a fate akin to his, those who admired and wished to emulate him prudently desisted from creating any formal movement, but continued to channel their collective energy into a restless quest for educational and economic advance. Often blocked as émigrés from attending regular government or even mission schools, they sought out schools that would accept Angolans. They poured into the Salvation Army's school at Léopoldville. They answered newspaper advertisements and followed mail-order courses offered by the Rosicrucian cult and by a variety of correspondence schools in France. Some managed to attend the Protestant (BMS) school in Léopoldville where they (along with Holden Roberto) were influenced by the sympathy and independent thinking of the French educator Professor Couderc. Then finally, on December 23, 1956, after the Toco affair had quieted down and Belgian policy had begun to loosen a little, they formally organized an ethnic mutual-aid society known as Assomizo, the *Association Mutuelle des Ressortissants de Zombo*.

[80] Margarido, "L'Église Toko," p. 89.
[81] *Ibid.*, p. 88.

Assomizo was launched cautiously. For their own protection, its leaders chose the principal Belgian administrator responsible for African associations (Monsieur Duvivier) as their official advisor. And because it was felt that his early association and identification with Simão Toco might alarm officialdom, Emmanuel Kunzika, one of Assomizo's principal organizers and its most forceful personality, declined election to its presidency in favor of an older, mild-mannered Bazombo leader, André Massaki, who took the initiative in forming the association. Massaki simultaneously edited a Léopoldville monthly, the Protestant journal *Sikama* [Wake Up], which guardedly urged its readers on to greater social consciousness.

Functioning as a legal organization, Assomizo was able to serve the economic and educational interests of the Bazombo community. On the other hand, legality entailed certain disadvantages as well. In late 1958 the extralegal UPNA had no problem in making a timely shift from a parochial, monarchist platform to a broader nationalist one (as UPA) and thereby greatly enhanced its potential international appeal. As a legal organization, barred by its Angolan identity from converting (like Abako) into a political party, Assomizo was constrained by its very legality to wait out the period before Congolese independence, trapped within the narrow limits of its official ethnicity. Though Assomizo remained on the margins of burgeoning Angolan political activity, however, a number of its leaders, financial backers, and rank and file contributed funds for the UPA's 1958–59 mission to Ghana and the United Nations and thus kept their political options open.[82]

Congolese Independence: The UPA's Head Start

As of February 1960, according to Barros Necaca, the UPA was marking time, waiting for the Congo's impending independence before launching upon a new phase of expanded action.[83] Even so, it had been busy. The previous November a popular Léopoldville weekly, *Présence Congolaise,* had reported that, in spite of "rigorous police measures" taken by Portuguese authorities, the UPA, a "vast Angolan movement," had "considerably intensified" its political

[82] Henri Larcier, a Belgian journalist, noted in "The Union of the Angolese Populations," *Présence Africaine* (English ed.), No. 42–43 (1962), p. 37: "Eduardo Pinock was responsible for collecting the money needed for this voyage among the Bazombo tribe. . . ."

[83] George Houser, personal notes, Léopoldville, Feb. 1960.

activity and had "managed to cover the whole of Angola from the North to the South with tracts, placards and posters calling for immediate independence." [84] Such reports, though exaggerated, added to growing tensions inside Angola.

With the coming of Congolese independence the UPA opened an office on a busy artery traversing Léopoldville's African quarter (74 rue Dodoma) and began turning out a torrent of mimeographed tracts in French, Portuguese, and the major vernacular languages of Angola.[85] These materials were smuggled into Angola through UPA branch offices, principally Matadi and for a brief time Elizabethville, before the latter office was closed down following Katanga's mid-July secession. Indicative of the party's resolve to transcend its ethnic origins, the person chosen to open and run the new Léopoldville office and to conduct the UPA's first legal (post-independence) political campaigning among Angolan émigrés in outlying towns and villages of the Lower Congo was not one of its senior Bakongo, but Rosário Neto, a newly arrived Mbundu refugee, whose first contact with the UPA had been in Luanda. A practicing Catholic from Malange, Neto was also put in charge of organizing the UPA's reception for its returning emissary abroad, a Baptist from São Salvador.

Holden Roberto got in a final round of international political activity before making his reentry into the newly charged atmosphere of Angolan politics in the Congo. He once again visited Tunis, where he held a press conference, appealed to Portugal and international opinion to heed nationalist demands for political reform, and warned that his party was determined to fight for an end to colonial oppression and for the free development of the "Angolan personality." [86] He also traveled to Addis Ababa to lobby as an "observer" at the Second Conference of Independent African States (June 14–24, 1960).[87] Then in mid-July, after nearly two years of absence and two weeks of Congolese independence, he returned to Léopoldville to be welcomed like a victorious general by a politically excited Angolan community.

President André Massaki and the executive council of Assomizo

[84] No. 45, Nov. 7, 1959.
[85] Kikongo, Kimbundu, Chokwe, Umbundu.
[86] *Le Monde* (Paris), June 12, 1960.
[87] See José Gilmore, "Intervention de M. J. Gilmore, délégué de l'Union des Populations de l'Angola à la Conférence des États Indépendants d'Afrique tenue à Addis Ababa du 14 au 24 juin 1960" (Addis Ababa [?], 1960, mimeo.).

gave a dinner in Roberto's honor and used the occasion to urge him to use his new prestige to bring all Angolans and Angolan organizations together into a united movement under his leadership. But Roberto was more interested in building the UPA into an all-Angolan mass movement and made this publicly clear. Subsequent efforts, including a visit to Roberto's home by Massaki, Emmanuel Kunzika, and Ferdinand Dombele to negotiate an organizational merger between Assomizo and the UPA, only prompted Roberto to invite them to join and accept posts within the UPA on an individual basis. The three Assomizo leaders refused, though others, including prominent members of their organization, did not, and the UPA registered a rapid growth in membership and dynamism. On the other hand, after the initial rush toward unity no existing political groups dissolved, whereas several more were formed, and by the end of the year there were no less than five Angolan parties operating in Léopoldville, not counting a movement for the independence of Cabinda.

The most thriving was the UPA. A party organizational meeting in July apparently left the choice of permanent leadership (to replace that of the superseded UPNA) for a later date, leaving the movement to function temporarily under the collegiate guidance of a provisional twenty-man steering committee. At the same time, whereas Barros Necaca and other veteran political personalities felt constrained by both family and party requirements not to abandon hard-won income-producing jobs, Roberto was free to devote himself full time to the direction of party work. This advantage, along with his careful cultivation of Congolese political leaders, helped materially to further Roberto's personal political fortune.

To work with him, he chose among others a childhood friend, José Kiasonga Manuel Peterson, born at Matadi on March 18, 1925, of São Salvador parents and related to Eduardo Pinock.[88] According to Peterson, after a short career as a teacher at Matadi and as an accountant with a Belgian firm (SEDEC) at Léopoldville, he "returned" in 1953 to his parental homeland, Angola. There, he has said, he quickly learned Portuguese from a Portuguese secretary, gained *assimilado* status, and worked for the Portuguese administration at Luanda and a number of northern towns. Then at the end of April 1960 he fled to the Congo on a tip that he was about to be arrested. Upon his arrival in Léopoldville, UPA

[88] Peterson's maternal grandfather was Pinock's brother.

officials advised him to wait out the weeks before independence across the river in the security of Brazzaville. In July Roberto brought him back to Léopoldville into the UPA structure, gave him the title of administrative secretary responsible for internal party organization, and assigned him the task of opening local offices in and near such centers as Moerbeke, Thysville, Mayumbe (Tshela area), Matadi, and Boma.[89] From that time on, Peterson served as one of Roberto's closest, toughest, most trusted, and most controversial lieutenants.

During the summer months of 1960 Congolese Premier Patrice Lumumba enabled Roberto to stimulate wider political awareness in Angola by authorizing a series of weekly UPA broadcasts over Radio Léopoldville. In his first broadcast on August 3 Roberto warned that Portugal could not "live outside history" and demanded negotiations to end colonial rule and to define "new [Portuguese-African] relationships which would no longer be those of slave and master." He hailed the role of Afro-Asian states in bringing about the condemnation of Portuguese colonialism by the Fourteenth General Assembly and promised that continued political suppression and military reinforcements would only provoke the UPA into organizing a campaign "to render life impossible" for the Portuguese in Angola. In his broadcast of August 30 Roberto claimed that the UPA had received reports that his initial broadcast had caused "panic" among Portuguese settlers and prompted numbers of them to leave areas near the Congo frontier and to seek army protection in central Angola. They had, Roberto said, correctly understood African resolve to make "the supreme sacrifice" if necessary in order to obtain "national independence."

In terms calculated to divide, sow distrust among, and undermine the morale of the Portuguese, Roberto repeatedly distinguished between Salazar's "forces of repression" and those settlers and officials who, he said, had shown signs of wishing to change their comportment. He cited the case of a policeman in Lobito who had assertedly made his sympathy for the nationalist cause known to a local UPA leader. "We assure all those who support us that our people are not motivated by hatred for the Portuguese."

Roberto's broadcasts also stressed the dangers of ethnic disunity among Angolans. There were, he said, no "inferior or superior

[89] Interview with Peterson taped at Ngunda (near Buela) in northern Angola, Jan. 16, 1962.

tribes." Small ethnic parties only "dispersed nationalist forces to the great pleasure of the enemy." Angola was not "a composite of tribes" but "one nation."[90] Translated into all major Angolan languages, these messages were mimeographed and smuggled into Angola for clandestine distribution. Many of the exhortatory scripts were simultaneously published in *Congo,* the city's Lumumbist daily.[91] Then in September the UPA leader launched his own "bimonthly" party organ, *A Voz da Nação Angolana,* edited by himself, Eduardo Pinock's son Johnny, and Anibal de Melo, who was one of the few mulattoes in UPA leadership ranks. de Melo came from a prominent and wealthy (coffee) family in Luanda, from where he had reportedly fled earlier in the year.[92] de Melo had been writing for the daily *O Comércio* at Luanda.

In October Roberto flew to New York for his second rendezvous with the United Nations. There he distributed an English-language pamphlet issued by the UPA steering committee which set forth the party's aims and affirmed its dedication to nonviolent action: "Angolan people have always given proof of absolute pacifism, not out of moral weakness, but because of their firm belief that between men there is always the possibility of pacific solution to any problem." Expressing the UPA's continued hopes for United Nations action, the pamphlet called upon "all international organizations and bodies . . . to bring pressure on Portugal so that the regime of exploitation and willful genocide in Angola shall cease, and that the territory shall recover its independence of ancient days."[93] Following up this plea for international intervention, the Léopoldville organization sent a telegram to the United Nations secretary-general demanding that the Angolan issue be resolved by means of free elections under the world body's supervision.[94] Finally adding to the record of appeals, Roberto, acting on behalf of the steering committee, distributed a memorandum to all the delegates of the Fifteenth General Assembly. In it he lamented political and economic conditions in Angola, asked Afro-Asian and Latin American states to mount pressure against Portugal, and urged that "the

[90] Quote from broadcast of Sept. 6, 1960.

[91] Edited by Philippe Kanza, e.g., see issues of Sept. 1 and 9, 1960.

[92] According to some reports, de Melo had belonged to the *Movimento de Libertação de Angola* (MLA) in Luanda.

[93] UPA Steering Committee, *The Struggle for the Independence of Angola* (1960), pp. 17–18.

[94] *Courrier d'Afrique,* Oct. 23, 1960.

question of Portuguese colonialism" be placed upon the agenda of the General Assembly, a move which he said would be appreciated by the Angolan people "whose revolt against colonial methods risks manifesting itself in an explosive manner." [95]

Four Other Parties and a Common Front

After the UPA refused merger, Assomizo decided to compete. Counting on its wide following among Bazombo, scattered from their home bailiwick in a northeast section of Angola to the Congo River estuary, it transformed itself into a political party. Renamed the *Alliance des Ressortissants de Zombo,* or Aliazo, but still under the presidency of André Massaki, it established an office and permanent secretariat in Léopoldville's Quartier Foncobel.[96] Its three principal personalities, André Massaki (president), Emmanuel Kunzika (first vice-president), and Ferdinand Dombele (secretary-general), were good examples of Bazombo enterprise.

André Massaki was born at Kikaka (post of Banza-Pinda), near Maquela, Angola, on February 25, 1923, attended the Swedish Protestant school at Matadi (1932–1937) and the BMS school at Ngombe-Lutete, near Thysville (1937–1939), and then worked as a school teacher and clerk for the Léopoldville-Matadi railroad. He later moved into journalism, became the editor of *Sikama,* and in 1962 followed a course in journalism at Kitwe, Northern Rhodesia.

Kunzika was born in the village of Kintoto near Maquela, Angola, on June 14, 1925. His parents, who had worked on Angolan coffee plantations, emigrated to the Congo when he was eleven. There he began his schooling in the Salvation Army school of Léopoldville and continued at the Athenée Royal and Collège Albert Ier. He became an admirer of Simão Toco during those formative school years. Later, while holding a managerial post in a local commercial firm, he took courses at the *Institut d'Études Politiques* and studied philosophy and science by a correspondence course with the *École de Science et Art* of Paris. This variety of

[95] Holden Roberto, "Memorandum on the Situation Regarding Angola and the Portuguese Colonies Presented by the Union of Populations of Angola to the Delegates to the 15th General Assembly of the United Nations" (New York, autumn 1960, mimeo.).

[96] *Courrier d'Afrique,* Sept. 21, 1960.

educational experience reflected and reinforced an intense faith in education as a liberating political and social force.

Ferdinand Dombele (or Ndombele) was born at Mbanza Zunzu-Kibokolo in March 1928 and after two years of primary school left Angola in 1937 in order to avoid being caught up in the net of contract labor. He was thus able to continue his education at a Swedish mission school in the Congo, where he subsequently worked as a teacher at Matadi and ultimately trained as an accountant with the huge OTRACO transport organization and then worked for a commercial firm, Amato Frères. Dombele was one of those who followed the Rosicrucian correspondence course from Paris, a two-year program in "metaphysics." At the same time, he, Kunzika, and Massaki remained active Protestants.

In general, Aliazo was nonviolent and conciliatory in tone and reflected the Christian training and middle-class values of its leadership. Still avowedly ethnic, and thus more provincial than either the UPA or MPLA, it was slow to make international contacts and depended exclusively upon internal resources. Its rank and file, which represented its source of financial support, included a growing number of businessmen, teachers, civil servants, and journalists, many of whom were imbued with a tradition of communal self-help and self-determination, a tradition that Simão Toco had done much to foster. As of late 1960 the aim of Aliazo was to win self-government within an independent Angola.[97] Never much attracted to proposals for the restoration or secession of the old Kongo kingdom, the party leadership declared a preference for local Bazombo autonomy within a federated but not partitioned Angola. And though northern and Kikongo-speaking, Aliazo's top men increasingly viewed their political role as that of a leaven or balance of power between the UPA and MPLA, both of whom were much better known to the world outside.

The third Congo-based party developed as a negative reaction to the options and actions of those who created the UPNA and then transformed it into the UPA. Its founders included members of the "deposed" Kivuzi clan in particular and Catholic royalists in general, many of whom opposed the royal pretensions of Protestant forces led by Eduardo Pinock. In due course these elements

[97] Like other Angolan émigré movements, Aliazo was in a state of flux during late 1960, and along with the UPA it first scheduled (for November 20) and then canceled a general party meeting. *Ibid.*, Nov. 19–20, 1960.

were joined by Protestant royalists who could not accept the "Accra decision" of 1958 to abandon the kingdom and embrace the (Angolan) colony. The die-hard royalists grouped themselves within an ethnic mutual-aid society, which in February 1960 they converted into a political party, the *Ngwizani a Kongo* or Ngwizako.[98] Undeterred by past experience—some of them had been arrested for their part in the king palaver of 1955–56—they sought to persuade Portugal to restore the Kongo kingdom and permit Ngwizako to name the next monarch.

As one of several efforts during the summer of 1960 to achieve greater unity among Angolan émigrés and thus maximize political opportunities deriving from Congolese independence, merger talks were held from August 5 to 10 between the executive committees of Ngwizako and Aliazo.[99] According to Emmanuel Kunzika, Aliazo asked whether Ngwizako envisaged making the kingship elective and open to all, including the Bazombo. Ngwizako president José dos Santos Kasakanga, himself a Kivuzi and a pretender to the throne, replied that the king must come from the royal Kivuzi line. Aliazo seized upon this response as further evidence of the outmoded thinking that lay behind the whole idea of reconstituting the Kongo kingdom and tried in vain to persuade Ngwizako to join it, Aliazo, in common-front discussions with the UPA and AREC (a Cabindan group, see below).

Using Bakongo-first arguments, Ngwizako leaders indicated that by keeping the scope of their political action within the limits of the Kongo, "the most miserable of all countries," they might hope to render their goal of independence for that territory less difficult.[100] They apparently considered that Lisbon would be more likely to make concessions to African demands if these were restricted to the modest area of the Kongo and were put in terms of honoring a

[98] Subtitled the *Associação dos Conguenses de Expressão Portuguêsa* [the Association of Portuguese-Speaking Congolese].

[99] Antoine Matumona, "Angolan Disunity," in *Angola: A Symposium, Views of a Revolt* (London: Oxford University Press, 1962), pp. 127–128.

[100] A statement by Ngwizako in the *Courrier d'Afrique,* Aug. 6–7, 1960, put it this way: "Certainly, the Kongo has inherited nothing from the presence of Europeans, unless it is the complete stagnation of the people, illiteracy, oppression, deportations, forced labor, unemployment, destruction of property, lack of hospitals, the extermination of human lives, etc. It is understandable then that the organization of such a territory whose standards are still primitive, is not easy. Therefore, to wish to extend the range of such organization beyond the natural limits of its soil will only render the task of its leaders more difficult and contrary to what is desired, will disadvantage the people of the Kongo."

special historical relationship with Portugal. In early October 1960 Kasakanga implied that some progress was being made when he announced that an Ngwizako delegation had met with Portuguese officials in Angola for a "fruitful" exchange of views touching upon the eventual succession to the Kongo's throne left vacant, or more precisely, in the care of regent Queen Dona Isabela since the death of Dom António III in 1957.[101] On November 23 another Ngwizako delegation reportedly met with a representative of the Portuguese governor-general at São Salvador and then six days later with the inspector-general of the Portuguese overseas territories.[102]

On December 26 Kasakanga addressed a letter to the Catholic and BMS missions at São Salvador. There was great concern, he said, that many years had passed since the death of the king, or *ntotela,* and no one had been named to succeed him. For this reason the sons of the Kongo were ready to return to São Salvador to "plan with [their] elders" in order to choose a new king. "This," he wrote, "is to tell you that on February 17, 1961, we shall start off from here [Léopoldville] where we live, so that you may receive us, for you are our teachers," and then added, "our government, too," has been informed "of that date." [103] On January 2 the Ngwizako central committee announced that, as a result of its negotiations with "the Portuguese nation" and in accord with the king's council, February 17 had been chosen as the day for the nomination of a new king. The party executive went on to say that it was organizing a trip to Mbanza Kongo for the occasion and that all persons interested in coming along should contact Ngwizako headquarters in Léopoldville, Matadi, or Boma to arrange for visas and to reserve their places at the modest price of six hundred francs each.[104]

On February 17 the Ngwizako expedition arrived on schedule at the Angolan border town of Luvo. The administrator from São Salvador, Eduardo Matoso Pio, was there to greet them and to inform them officially that, since the Portuguese government would itself decide what constituted an "opportune" date for the election

[101] *Courrier d'Afrique,* Oct. 5, 1960.

[102] Ngwizako communiqué in *L'Homme nouveau* (Brazzaville), No. 122, May 13, 1962.

[103] Letter written in Kikongo, Ref. PG/018/12/60, dated Dec. 12, 1960, Léopoldville.

[104] *Courrier d'Afrique,* Jan. 2, 1961.

of a new king, they were not to be permitted to enter the country.[105]

Ngwizako enjoyed rather more cooperation on the Congo side of the border, where its leaders conferred several times after independence with Joseph Kasavubu, the president of both Abako and the Congolese republic. Sharing Ngwizako's antipathy for the UPA, Abako helped the royalists on the local level. Thus, for example, an eight-man Ngwizako team, sent on a recruiting mission to the Kimpese area of the Lower Congo in early November 1960, was permitted to sell party cards and to hold a public meeting at the local Abako headquarters. The Ngwizako recruiters in turn publicly thanked Kasavubu's party and its youth wing Jabako for the welcome extended to them.[106] By way of contrast, UPA organizers suffered frequent harassment at the hands of local Abako officials. A hint of just how touch and go UPA-Abako relations really were came in December with a brief announcement by Abako that the UPA's office at Matadi had just been reopened on the advice of Abako leaders, after having been closed for an unspecified length of time by Matadi (Abako) officials "as the consequence of a false interpretation of the party's intentions."[107]

As noted earlier, over the years Abako had received considerable financial support from the Angolan community in the Congo.[108] With the advent of Congolese independence and the party's abandonment of the pan-Kongo cause, however, these contributors tended to divert their assistance to parties concerned directly with Angola. To avoid losing this support to Angolan political parties (UPA, Aliazo, and Ngwizako), Abako decided to create an Angolan auxiliary of its own. Thus two prominent Abako leaders, Georges Mansianga and Antoine Kingotolo, reportedly approached an elderly Bazombo notable, Maurice Kiala Bonga, who had been a major contributor in the past, and proposed that he organize such a subsidiary. Bonga agreed to support the project but suggested

[105] "Declaração" by Eduardo Matoso Pio, Luvo, Feb. 17, 1961. The text translated from the Portuguese reads: "Having been requested to do so, I declare that the members of Ngwizako should return to the Republic of the Congo on my advice not to go to São Salvador do Congo to attend the election of the king of the Kongo because it is the Portuguese government which will set the date for elections when it finds it opportune to do so."

[106] *Courrier d'Afrique,* Nov. 3, 1960.

[107] *Ibid.,* Dec. 10–11, 1960.

[108] The figure of two million escudos is cited in *La Fédération Congolaise* (Apr. 8, 1965), as quoted in Emmanuel Kunzika, "La Révolution angolaise et ses trames" (Léopoldville, July 30, 1965, press conference, mimeo.).

that a younger man with more energy and popular appeal be given the operational assignment. The task was thereupon delegated to a recently arrived Mbundu refugee from Malange, an ambitious and educated young man named José Bernardo Domingos. After a brief association with the UPA, Domingos had found a job teaching at Madimba, where he became acquainted with the Abako leader Georges Mansianga and convinced Mansianga that he qualified for the job of heading its Angolan branch. Viewed as an "outsider" by the Bakongo émigré community, however, Domingos was unable to muster local support for himself and the project and soon abandoned the effort.[109]

Nevertheless *Nto-Bako Angola* was finally formed in Léopoldville on December 8, 1960. In the opinion of an outspoken Angolan journalist, Antoine Matumona, as well as other Angolan nationalists, it was merely the creation of "certain leaders of Abako who had designs on the northern part of Angola." [110] Whether or not they had territorial as well as financial aims, the Abako backers of Nto-Bako had learned the lesson of the earlier false start. This time they chose a Bakongo to launch the movement. They picked Angelino Alberto, a pliable political aspirant from Damba, northern Angola, who was known to Maurice Kiala Bonga. He had worked for a time as a bus attendant in Léopoldville and would later work as a collaborator with the Portuguese police in Angola.

As for José Bernardo Domingos, he became vice-president of a local committee established by yet another Angolan party, the MPLA, which maintained its central office in distant Conakry, Guinea. The MPLA wished to establish a new operational base closer to Angola. Domingos's cousin, Rosário Neto, has said that shortly after his arrival in the Congo in June 1960 he turned down an offer from Mário de Andrade to assume responsibilities there for the MPLA. Yet in the same way that the UPA's effort to build a broader national (extra-Bakongo) image was helped by the ability to elevate someone with Neto's credentials—a Catholic Mbundu from Malange—into the ranks of party leadership, so was it also important for the MPLA to establish itself within the local Bakongo community. With this in mind, the MPLA named one of Holden Roberto's former associates from São Salvador, António Jabes Josias, as president of its Congo committee. The committee

[109] This account of the formation of Nto-Bako is based upon interviews with Angolan nationalists in Léopoldville, notably E. Kunzika and F. Dombele.

[110] *Courrier d'Afrique,* Oct. 18, 1961.

also included Georges (or Jorge) M. Freitas,[111] earlier connected with Barros Necaca's group in Léopoldville. Thus the MPLA's leadership, seasoned in Luanda, Lisbon, and Paris, undertook to give its organization a new Congolese dimension. And as one of its first initiatives, when W. Averell Harriman visited Léopoldville in September 1960 on a fact-finding trip for Democratic presidential candidate John F. Kennedy, the local MPLA leadership tried in vain to obtain an audience in order to tell him of the "deplorable tragedy" facing all Angolans.[112]

Recognizing that they risked being isolated as an ethnic movement with their influence confined to a small sector of Angola, Aliazo's leaders labored to achieve a single united front with other movements. Under António Josias, the MPLA's Léopoldville committee welcomed the idea of such a front as completely consonant with its parent party's endorsement of common action in "the conquest of Angolan independence." [113] As Bakongo separatists, of course, Ngwizako and Nto-Bako were not interested. There remained the question of the UPA.

In early 1959, during his long stay in Accra, Roberto had received a letter from Léopoldville suggesting that he contact Andrade in Paris and da Cruz in Brussels with the idea of teaming up with them and possibly obtaining financial assistance through them.[114] Writing a few weeks earlier to a cousin in Léopoldville, however, Roberto had already expressed concern over reports that Andrade was a Communist, though he said that by roundabout means he would try to contact da Cruz, for whom he had an address in Frankfurt, Germany.[115] When Roberto did meet with da Cruz and other members of the MPLA delegation at Tunis in January 1960, however, he parried their efforts to get him to join a united front. He similarly side-stepped common-front pressures brought to bear by the Ghanaian and Guinean governments and thereby compromised the support that he had heretofore received from the Nkrumah and Touré regimes. Writing of these first common-front discussions of early 1960, Andrade later blamed their failure on two factors: (1) foreign (meaning western) influence within the UPA,

[111] Freitas was married to Josias' sister.

[112] The request for a meeting with Governor Harriman was contained in a letter of Sept. 8, 1960, signed by Jordão d'Aguiar, António J. Josias, and Jorge M. Freitas and sent to the American embassy.

[113] See pp. 43–44.

[114] Letter dated Feb. 22, 1959.

[115] Letter from Accra dated Jan. 26, 1959.

whose leaders he claimed sought exclusively western associations; and (2) miscalculations by both movements, each of which overestimated the breadth of its Angolan support.[116]

Nonetheless in late 1960, while Roberto was in New York lobbying at the United Nations, this very front that he had warily avoided and the MPLA had long promoted, became a short-lived reality. On November 1 representatives of the UPA, MPLA, Aliazo, and a small Cabindan movement, the *Association des Ressortissants de l'Enclave de Cabinda* (AREC),[117] met at the Carrera Bar in Léopoldville. Agreeing that no single party could succeed without the support of the others, they reached an *accord de principe* for the formal creation of a cartel, or common front, which would fall short of full merger and would not entail the dissolution of existing parties but would closely coordinate their activities.[118] The front's existence became known when representatives of the UPA, MPLA, and Aliazo (but not AREC) wrote in an open letter, predated October 31, to the president of the United Nations General Assembly congratulating that body for the recent vote in which it had held Portugal responsible for furnishing information on its colonies under Article 73e of the Charter. The letter also condemned Lisbon for its alleged intention to send a delegation of Angolan collabora-

[116] Mário de Andrade, "Agonie de l'empire et crise du nationalisme," *Remarques Africaines,* Vol. 6, No. 14 (July 11, 1964), p. 333.

[117] Shortly thereafter AREC changed its name to the *Mouvement de Libération de l'Enclave de Cabinda* (MLEC). It did not become a full member of the common front.

[118] *Courrier d'Afrique,* Nov. 3, 1960. See also Michel Luwau, *Angola, Martyre des Portugais* (Léopoldville: Imprimerie Nouvelle, [1960]). In an undated communiqué (Léopoldville, mimeo.), Aliazo commented as follows on the establishment of the new front: "Aliazo, an ethnic party created for the union and defense of the interests of the Zombo, but whose spirit is complemented by a broader nationalism, is delighted to see its desire—shared by other parties—of arriving at a national understanding within the framework of a mutual respect for the opinions of each party thereby avoiding useless discussions which might be prejudicial to the goal sought by all—the conquest of independence and human dignity for the Angolan people.

"However, in order to avoid any possible confusion, the Central Committee of Aliazo draws to the attention of its members and sympathisers the fact that the formation of a Common Front of Angolan parties can in no way lead to the dissolution of Aliazo, or any other party, nor to a change in its action program. It thus warns against any maneuvers by any other party that might try to profit from the understanding reached in order to mislead public opinion by peddling baseless stories for the sole purpose of proselytizing or, worse yet, recruiting members from other parties. Such maneuvers would be contrary to the spirit of this *accord de principe* and thus prejudicial to the understanding to be realized."

tors to present Portugal's case before the world organization.[119] It was sent in the name of all three parties as combined within a *Front Commun des Partis Politiques de l'Angola.*[120]

This coalition commitment on the part of the UPA organization in Léopoldville was made, it later turned out, without consulting Roberto in New York. As a result, it brought the unresolved UPA leadership issue to a head and triggered an upheaval that profoundly altered the nature of the party.

Out of the Front: Into the Fire

During a tumultuous sequence in September 1960 President Kasavubu dismissed Patrice Lumumba from the premiership. With the backing of Col. Joseph Mobutu and the army, he also suspended the Congolese parliament. The well-known Portuguese writer on Angolan affairs, Hélio Felgas, later observed with approval that, after the fall of Lumumba, the Kasavubu government reduced Congolese help to the UPA for fear that the UPA would "establish Communism in neighboring Angola." [121] Generally considered as being close to the fallen premier,[122] Roberto spent the nights of mid-September hidden in Léopoldville embassies, notably the Tunisian. He later told a gathering of African heads of state that at that time he feared arrest as a "Communist" and therefore fled to Ghana "to seek refuge" and financial assistance from the secretariat of the All-African Peoples' Conference. As already noted, he had been elected to the Conference Steering Committee in January of that year. In Accra he suffered a political blow that marked the end of his close ties with Nkrumah's Ghana when he received the following response from the Conference secretariat: "The government of Ghana has given orders that we must not help you because you are in the pay of America." [123]

[119] They cited three persons as slated for this delegation: Manuel Pereira de Nascimento, an accountant, president of the *Liga Nacional Africana,* and allegedly a member of PIDE, Angelino de Castro Paiva, a civil servant, and Alfredo Furtado Antas, a former administrative secretary, at the time unemployed.

[120] For text see *Courrier d'Afrique,* Nov. 8, 1960. The letter claimed that among them the three parties had offices in Paris, London, Liège, Hamburg, Illinois, Rio de Janeiro, São Paulo, Tunis, Conakry, and both Congo republics.

[121] Hélio Felgas, *Guerra em Angola* (Lisbon: Livraria Classica Editôra, 1961), p. 57.

[122] Roberto, like Frantz Fanon, was privately critical of Lumumba's tendency toward impetuousness, given the weakness of his political organization, the *Mouvement National Congolais.*

[123] Holden Roberto, Speech before the Organization of African Unity, Assembly of Heads of State and Government, Cairo, July 21, 1964.

Some weeks later, on November 18, during a private interview at Léopoldville, Barros Necaca spoke expansively of progress made by the UPA, claiming that it then possessed seventeen branch offices and three cars and had one hundred volunteers working inside Angola, where it was collecting funds but not distributing membership cards because of police surveillance. Necaca also indicated that he had recently been chosen president of the UPA.[124] As for his nephew, he said that, though Roberto was a member of the party executive, he was looked upon by the Congolese as having Communist sympathies because of his past associations with Lumumba and was therefore obliged to "take it easy." Necaca went on to report approvingly of the common front that was being formed among the principal Angolan movements.[125]

Interviewed at about the same time in New York, to which he had flown from Accra via Tunis [126] to attend the Fifteenth General Assembly of the U. N., Roberto revealed no awareness of the common-front negotiations and said that he was exercising party leadership as head of a ten-man UPA political bureau whose members formed the core of the party's twenty-man steering committee.[127] Roberto later said that, when he did learn of the common-front rapprochement initiated during his absence, he predicted that it would fail because he knew the ideas of some of those who wished to establish the front.[128] To help his prediction along, he then hastened back to Léopoldville, opposed implementation of the tripartite agreement, and argued that the UPA, free from encumbering alliances, should prepare a program of its own design for militant

[124] George Houser, personal travel notes, Léopoldville, Nov. 18, 1960. Curiously, the Léopoldville press carried an announcement on Nov. 2 saying that a UPA General Assembly would convene four days hence in order to elect a "definitive" Central Committee. All "members and sympathizers of the UPA" were invited to take part in the elections to be held at the Maison des Combattants Congolais at Dendale-Léopoldville "in order to elect the leaders of their choice" (*Courrier d'Afrique*, Nov. 2, 1960). Then abruptly, on November 4, the election was put off to "a future date to be announced at an opportune time" (*Ibid.*, Nov. 4, 1960). Nevertheless, a provisional executive headed by Barros Necaca does seem to have been chosen at about this time.

[125] Houser, personal notes.

[126] Roberto (Gilmore) issued a press statement in Tunis that laid out the achievements of the UPA and passed over the Congolese crises in silence. "Conférence de presse" (Tunis, Oct. 6, 1960, mimeo.).

[127] Roberto also claimed, contrary to what Necaca had said, that the UPA had distributed membership cards, 40,000 in the Luanda area, 10,000 in northern Angola, and 15,000 in the Congo. Interview with author, Nov. 10, 1960.

[128] See "Réunion du 10 mai 1962 avec le ministre Kamitatu" (Léopoldville, mimeo.).

action inside Angola. In the power struggle that ensued within the party, Roberto won the day and the UPA withdrew from the front.

Roberto also gained the acceptance of his demands for a more aggressive UPA program, but at the expense of a rash of resignations among party "moderates." These latter, who had apparently been involved in a move to hold party elections in November while he was away in New York, subsequently claimed that in the showdown with Roberto seventeen out of twenty members resigned from the party steering committee, including Barros Necaca, whom they described as the "founding president of the UPA." Many of the more prominent defectors were Bazombo who had left Assomizo to join the UPA in a rush of enthusiasm the summer before. These included Albert Matundu, listed as UPA first vice-president, Jean Pierre M'Bala, secretary-general, and Simon Diallo Mingiedi, president of the UPA youth (JUPA).[129] UPA loyalists quickly countered with charges that the dissidents, whom they denounced as ambitious Bakongo separatists, had simply been foiled in an attempt to grab power for which purpose they had created a fraudulent UPA executive committee.[130]

From out of all this confusion came a few clear facts. Roberto assumed the presidency of the UPA. Necaca remained a member of the party but without office. Matundu, M'Bala, and other "moderates," who later said they had fought for a UPA policy of negotiation as against a policy of violence, and who enjoyed open support from Portuguese commercial and embassy sources in Léopoldville, left the UPA. Then after initiating abortive talks with Aliazo,[131] on January 22, 1961, they founded a new, predominantly Bazombo, pacifist party, the *Mouvement de Défense des Intérêts de l'Angola* (MDIA).[132]

A year and a half later, during a discussion on unity at a round-

[129] MDIA, "Le Problème angolais. Textes et documents" (Léopoldville, July 29, 1962, mimeo.), p. 2. Also *Courrier d'Afrique,* Mar. 1, 1961.

[130] *Courrier d'Afrique,* Mar. 2, 1961, and *A Voz da Nação Angolana,* Vol. 2, No. 4, Mar. 16, 1961.

[131] According to Emmanuel Kunzika these talks failed because of the UPA defectors' demands that they and Aliazo form an entirely new movement. His explanation thus contradicts that of Antoine Matumona, who reported that the impasse stemmed from exhorbitant demands by the defectors for heavy representation on Aliazo's central committee. Matumona, in *Angola: A Symposium,* p. 122.

[132] The choice of a name for this movement suggests some inspiration from Abbé Fulbert Youlou and his Bakongo party, the *Union de Défense des Intérêts Africains* (UDDIA) in Brazzaville.

table meeting of Angolan nationalists, Roberto cited the MDIA exodus of December 1960 as dramatic proof of his contention that a clear sense of common purpose is necessary for the internal cohesion of any political organization. He said that the danger of such defections constituted an argument against creating catch-all fronts or parties, and stressed that any unity not based upon a real consensus was inherently weak and not likely to last. Defending his decision to pull the UPA out of the *Front Commun des Partis Politiques de l'Angola* because the latter was composed of "incompatible" elements, he noted that, when the MDIA faction within his own party had lost confidence in UPA leadership and had attacked him "as an assassin and a Communist," it had been quite natural, indeed logical, for the faction to quit the UPA and form its own separate party.[133]

The fact remained that the architects of the common front reflected a widely held view that a united coalition of Angolan nationalists would present a more formidable challenge to Portuguese rule. In December they had sent a second joint letter to the president of the United Nations General Assembly detailing their grievances against colonial rule and calling for Portugal to organize a referendum "under UN supervision" on the issue of independence.[134] According to enthusiastically pro-front Aliazo leaders, the ephemeral coalition progressed through a considerable number of organizational meetings—five in November, one in December, and a final session in January—before being killed. It was following this last meeting on January 14 that the UPA pulled out.[135]

In spite of the UPA's withdrawal, the MPLA and Aliazo maintained the *Front Commun* as a two-party coalition until February 1961. At that time the MPLA head office in Conakry sent two party officials, Drs. Hugo de Menezes and Eduardo dos Santos, to Léopoldville, where they charged the local MPLA committee with having exceeded its authority in negotiating the front. They declared the front null and void and proposed instead to create a

[133] "Réunion du 10 mai."

[134] Front Commun des Partis Politiques de l'Angola, "Monsieur le Président de l'Assemblée Générale de l'Organisation de Nations-Unies" (Léopoldville, Dec. 13, 1960, mimeo.), p. 3.

[135] According to Aliazo sources their representatives met together with those of the UPA and MPLA on Nov. 1 (also AREC); Nov. 4 (also AREC and Ngwizako; Nto-Bako declined); (Nov. 12, Aliazo met alone with members of the newly formed JUPA); Nov. 17 (also AREC); Nov. 26; Nov. 29; Dec. 3; and Jan. 14 (also MLEC [ex-AREC, see ftn. 117]).

different front, patterned along the lines of statutes prepared in Conakry.[136]

By the beginning of 1961 in the Angolan Bakongo sector, then, it was every party for itself. Ngwizako and Nto-Bako sought their goals through secession and through collaboration, with Lisbon or Abako. Aliazo remained dedicated to the proposition that Angolan (subsuming Bazombo) independence could be achieved by nonviolent means through political persuasion and diplomatic pressure. The UPA moved away from nonviolence and, like its principal rival the MPLA, opted in favor of a policy of "direct," meaning military, action. And military action it was to be—though sooner and on a larger scale than any of these parties anticipated at the end of 1960.

[136] The local MPLA committee and its president António Josias thus stood repudiated and the party's local prestige undermined. See Parti Démocrate de l'Angola, "Conférence de presse" (Léopoldville, Apr. 12, 1962, mimeo.).

CHAPTER THREE

THE OVIMBUNDU, CHOKWE, AND RELATED SOURCES OF ANGOLAN NATIONALISM

The third stream of Angolan nationalism sprang primarily from the Ovimbundu people of central Angola and, to a lesser extent, from among the smaller ethnic communities such as the Chokwe, Lwena (sub-group of the Ganguela), and Cuanhama, deeper within the interior or farther to the south. In general, much less is or can now be known of this third stream than of the two previously discussed. Its activists have not enjoyed access to the outside world through a major urban communications center like Luanda or Léopoldville. Few had the opportunity to study in Europe. And most were too distant from friendly frontiers to have recourse to massive emigration. What was to distinguish the nationalism of the southern half of Angola, then, was precisely the absence of an early and sizable regrouping abroad of political activists, students, and émigrés within a separately identifiable stream of nationalism. For a considerable period the few external representatives of nationalist currents within the Ovimbundu, Chokwe, and related areas tended to ally themselves with the rural peasant nationalists of the northern Bakongo stream. Only considerably later (1964–65), as their numbers grew and divergent interests separated them from the northerners, would they emerge as an institutionalized third force in Angolan nationalist politics.

The Ovimbundu Kingdoms

The Umbundu-speaking Ovimbundu, totaling over a million and a half and concentrated in the central Angolan highland districts of Huambo and Bié, constitute the largest ethnic group in the territory, equaling in size the Mbundu and Bakongo communities combined.[1] Thus in spite of their relative isolation from ideas and persons outside Angola and the modest scale of modern nationalist movements that first developed among them, the Ovimbundu, to the extent that they are ethnically cohesive, remain potentially the most important political force in Angola. Historically, however, they divided this potential among a baker's dozen of kingdoms, no one of which was able to establish its hegemony over the others.[2] No Ochimbundu [3] ruler succeeded in welding together as extensive a realm as that of the Mani Kongo's Kongo.

The quest for slaves and minerals enticed the Portuguese to the area via the coast—Porto Amboim by about 1584, Benguela by 1617. By the late seventeenth century they were penetrating the plateau country inland from Benguela, where simultaneously the Ovimbundu kingdoms were in the process of formation.[4] Founded by Imbangala invaders from the northeast who implanted themselves among the indigenous pastoral people of the highlands, these kingdoms generally resisted Portuguese occupation but were quickly ensnared in the slave trade. The Ovimbundu, according to a familiar pattern, obtained captives to sell to European slave dealers by conducting "razzias against their southern neighbors or among themselves." [5] At the same time, the kingdoms were penetrated by Portuguese "backwoodsmen" traders (*sertanejos*) from whom, historian Jan Vansina suggests, "the Ovimbundu acquired the taste for the pursuit of wealth and for their entrepreneurship, which characterized them in the nineteenth century." [6]

In spite of transitory military occupation by Portuguese forces (notably the campaign of 1774–1776), the more important kingdoms

[1] For background on the Ovimbundu, see Gladwyn M. Childs, *Umbundu Kinship and Character* (London: Oxford University Press, 1949); Adrian C. Edwards, *The Ovimbundu under Two Sovereignties* (London: Oxford University Press, 1962); and John T. Tucker, *Angola, the Land of the Blacksmith Prince* (London: World Dominion Press, 1933).

[2] Among the more important, with approximate dates of their founding, were: Bailundu (1700), Bié (1750), Huambo (early 1600's), Kakonda (1760), Ndulu (1671), and Tchiyaka (1650).

[3] Singular of Ovimbundu. The adjective as well as the language is Umbundu. The Ovimbundu are quite distinct from the Mbundu to the north, and the languages of the two peoples are not intelligible to each other.

[4] See Ronald H. Chilcote, *Portuguese Africa* (Englewood Cliffs, N. J.: Prentice-Hall, 1967), pp. 71–74.

[5] Jan M. Vansina, *Kingdoms of the Savanna* (Madison: University of Wisconsin Press, 1966), p. 199.

[6] *Ibid.*

retained their independence while forging commercial alliances with the Portuguese, whom they furnished with slaves, ivory, and wax. As one means of assuring a superior power position, the Portuguese employed the classic strategy of divide and rule. They did not discourage the internecine wars of the slave trade; instead, in 1853 for example, they encouraged the Bailundu and Huambo (or Wambo) kingdoms to attack and plunder their coastal neighbors to the northwest, the Sele. The latter had been molesting European traders, and the governor of Benguela, Coelho do Amaral, concluded that the situation required exploitation of the "inherent and lamentable warlike tendencies of the natives." [7]

By the middle of the nineteenth century the Bailundu (population 450,000) and Bié kingdoms survived as the most powerful African agents in a trading system that had provoked widespread warfare and undermined traditional social and economic life throughout the Ovimbundu area. The slave trade finally closed down some time around 1880, and during the reign of Bailundu's forceful King Ekuikui II (1876–1893) disintegrative trends were even reversed for a time. The Bailundu monarch pushed the development of a new trade in rubber and tried to revive local agriculture and artisanry. The independent mindedness of leaders like Ekuikui and King Tchiyuka of Bié, however, brought on a new Portuguese military assault and occupation by 1890. This was followed by an influx of Portuguese settlers and traders with their inevitable demands for land and labor, which in turn produced a general uprising in 1902, led by the Bailundu king Mutu-ya-Kevela. Although Portuguese polemicists have long portrayed the Bailundu people [8] as loyal pillars of the colonial regime, it required a major military effort known as the Bailundu Campaign before the kingdom could be fully subdued in 1904.

Though they were not exposed to the influence of a dominant cultural and governmental center like Luanda, or to the attraction of political and economic opportunity in a contiguous colonial area like the Lower Congo (Léopoldville), the Ovimbundu, situated as they were in the heart of Angola, were nonetheless affected by a variety of disruptive modernizing forces from outside. Ovimbundu traders traveled widely throughout central Africa, making

[7] Ralph Delgado, *Ao Sul do Cuanza,* Vol. 2 (Lisbon, 1944), p. 388.

[8] The Portuguese have confused matters somewhat by using the term Bailundu generally to refer to the Ovimbundu as a whole and even to all central and southern Angolans.

Umbundu an important trading language well beyond the Nebraska-sized (75,000 sq. mi.) confines of Umbundu country. Then the construction of the Benguela railroad (1903–1929) spread Ovimbundu settlements in a sort of diaspora along the rail line through the Angolan district of Moxico and into contact with the developing mineral economies and changing societies of Katanga and Northern Rhodesia. Within Angola the favorable climate on the highlands attracted thousands of Portuguese farmers and traders, who settled in a necklace of towns and farms along the railroad from the port of Lobito and its twin city Benguela, inland to Nova Lisboa, Silva Porto (formerly Bié), Vila Luso, and Teixeira de Sousa.[9] Between 1940 and 1950 the second and third largest cities of Angola, Nova Lisboa and Lobito, increased 73 and 75 per cent, respectively, to a total of 28,000 and 24,000 persons each. These European towns and their outlying farms needed, recruited, and exploited African labor. At the same time they admitted a few Africans as well as mulattoes into their Catholic schools and even into their army and thereby created a small "assimilated" black elite.

How this elite was used to perpetuate an oppressive social order is plain from the testimony of a Baptist missionary nurse who visited the town of Chitembo of Bié district in October 1959. On approaching the administrative post, she wrote, "we heard the sounds of blows and screaming. We passed into the building and through an open door saw an African lying on the floor being beaten by a *cipaio* [African policeman]. The administrator sat behind his desk watching." Onlookers explained that the reason for the beating was that "the man, a village chief, had been unable to collect enough men for contract labour." [10]

In 1955 popular resentment against this system reportedly found expression in an anti-assimilationist religious cult that developed in and spread out from the railroad town of Bela Vista near Nova Lisboa. Its leaders, or "saints," prophesied that great rains would come and wash the whites out of their country. Suppressed by administrative action, it was symptomatic of a growing social malaise.[11]

Beginning in the 1880's Protestant missions served as catalysts of

[9] The Benguela highlands were the areas considered for colonization by the Jewish Territorial Organization in 1912–13. See pp. 3–4.

[10] Len Addicott, *Cry Angola!* (London: SCM Press, 1962), pp. 120–121.

[11] See Edwards, *The Ovimbundu under Two Sovereignties,* p. 161; and *O Apostolado* (Luanda), Oct. 27, 1956.

change. Among the most important accomplishments of some twenty mission stations in the area was the creation of an educational center at Dondi near Silva Porto. There the United Church of Christ (Congregational) and United Church of Canada undertook to train a Christian leadership cadre, including teachers, pastors, and nurses. As of 1950 some 15 per cent or 232,000 of the Ovimbundu were considered to be Protestants, approximately the same proportion as in Angola at large.

Rebels from the Seminary

The religious roots of Ovimbundu protest have been Catholic as well as Protestant. Although information concerning them is incomplete and even fragmentary, several small, local, and often ephemeral nationalist groups developed independently and spontaneously in the southern half of Angola after the Second World War. At least one could trace its origins to a Catholic seminary. Beginning in 1950 a number of senior African students attending Christ the King Seminary at Nova Lisboa, who normally spent their annual vacation period in leisure at a rural mission, decided to use this time to organize a program of general education for people living in nearby villages located outside the Bailundu town of Luimbale.[12] There they taught everything from the Bible to public hygiene and threw in discussions on the principles of racial equality for good measure. The popularity as well as the content of their program inevitably aroused suspicion among Europeans living in the area. The latter brought pressure to bear on the *chefe de posto* at Luimbale, and in 1953 the African seminarians were obliged to discontinue their imaginative experiment in mass education. Already a general discontentment had been growing among them because of what they had considered to be a number of arbitrary expulsions from the seminary in the years just past. With the banning of their prototype Peace Corps, a number of them quit the seminary in disgust. Their protest did not end there, however, for during the visit of Portuguese President Craveiro Lopes to Nova Lisboa in June 1954 these former seminarians composed the bulk of a group of some twenty young men who distributed anti-Salazar leaflets throughout the city. They also scrawled slogans on the walls

[12] João Chisseva, "Ngau, Ngau, Ngau! O'Sino da Liberdade Tocou" (Apr. 1966, unpublished typescript).

and houses of Nova Lisboa condemning colonialism and demanding political freedom.

At first the police suspected that an officially sanctioned regional organization, the *Associação Africana do Sul de Angola* (AASA) might be behind this mischief. A social organization founded by employees of the Benguela railroad at Nova Lisboa, the AASA admitted a select number of Africans, mainly traders, and gave them the opportunity to acquire a bit of organizational experience, to undergo some mind stretching within the limits of the colonial system, and to pay dues. In this instance, however, the unquestioned loyalty of the AASA's president, António Burity da Silva, was enough to protect the regional association from major difficulties with the police.

It seems that the AASA did in fact harbor a few rebellious young Africans in 1954, including some of the ex-seminarians. On the other hand, it was dominated by a mulatto elite that was favored by government authorities and resented by the Africans. Tensions mounted during 1954 between blacks and mulattoes and by the year's end a group of fourteen Africans had withdrawn from the association because, as one of them explained later, it was run by "mulattoes of the South of Angola [who] are more racist than the Europeans." [13]

Next, with the backing of one German and two African priests, nine of these same young men, including five who had left both the AASA and the seminary, joined four kindred spirits to form a secret society known as the *Juventude Cristã de Angola* (JCA). Using the United Nations Declaration of Human Rights as their theme, these Young Christians undertook to organize a program of religious and political education among youths in and about Nova Lisboa. Short on funds and obliged to work clandestinely, their organization functioned for only about eight months before it collapsed, its president having been arrested and two other principal leaders forced to move, one to Luanda and the other to Dundo, in search of jobs.

It was the JCA's vice-president João da Cruz Chisseva Kalutheho who obtained a job as a teacher at Dundo, the Angolan diamond-mining center near the Kasai border. By 1958 he had a new JCA "section" functioning there among his fellow teachers and other literate Africans in the area. A Bailundu who was born April 10,

[13] *Ibid.*

1929, in the village of Kawala near the post of Chiumbo, and who claimed the prestigious King Ekuikui II as his great-grandfather, Chisseva had nine years of training at the Nova Lisboa seminary before leaving it in the collective exodus of 1954. Under his direction the Dundo JCA put increased emphasis on political as against religious activity. It made contacts across the border and in March 1959 at a secret meeting some twenty-seven JCA members listened to three Chokwe from Tshikapa, Kasai, describe the Léopoldville riots of the previous January. During the year they also heard from Congolese informants about the activities of Patrice Lumumba, Joseph Kasavubu, and other Congolese nationalists. Then on December 24, 1959, a Muluba refugee coming from Luluabourg via Sakalamba told the Dundo JCA about the existence of an Angolan nationalist movement called UPNA, which was said to be led by a certain Eduardo Pinock.

The increasing influx of political refugees from the Congo into Dundo inevitably drew the attention of the Portuguese police (PIDE). After looking things over carefully, they arrested Chisseva and two of his associates on January 11, 1960. Once again the repeated efforts of rebellious Young Christians to sustain an organized nationalist movement had been quashed. Yet each effort had left behind an increment of political awareness and bitterness, and each defeat was followed by renewed and bolder action.

Thus in June 1960, after spending five months in a Luanda prison, Chisseva joined the former secretary-general of the original Nova Lisboa JCA, and together they contacted other earlier JCA members then working in Luanda. Before long they had assembled a new group of young conspirators. Their reconstructed JCA was soon larger than its predecessors, and, though located in Luanda, it was composed primarily of young Ovimbundu from Nova Lisboa, Benguela, and Lobito, as well as southerners from Sá da Bandeira and the Cuanhama country of the far south.

The JCA tried to contact other clandestine political groups already operating in Luanda, though this was difficult and risky, given the severity of PIDE and its network of African informers. The Young Christians did manage to exchange views with the local Tocoistas, through one of Simão Toco's former aides whom Chisseva had met in the Luanda prison. Toco's disciples, however, though they accepted the Bible, rejected the appellation "Christian." Moreover they maintained that there could be no question of joining a political movement such as the Young Christians without first consulting their own prophet, and he was being held in isolated detention on the extreme south coast of the country.

Then early in 1961 the JCA got hold of some underground publications of the UPA, including two issues of *A Voz da Nação Angolana.* Its leadership was impressed with the UPA's nationalist goals, and after Chisseva had met with two UPA agents[14] the group collected fees and sent them to Eduardo Pinock in Matadi for UPA membership cards. These had not yet arrived when Luanda exploded on 4 February.

Rebels from the Protestant Schools

Students enrolled in Protestant mission schools also contributed to the growth of nationalism among central and southern Angolans. In particular, these students found a channel for the exchange of ideas in the *grupo avante,* a kind of social-cultural club that was formed in a number of Ovimbundu centers. On the margins of the recreational and cultural activities permitted these groups, youthful daring and idealism led some members into the prohibited and dangerous, yet for those reasons irresistible, realm of politics. From 1953 to 1957, when PIDE began cracking down on them, the *Grupo Avante* of Bié (at Silva Porto), the *Grupo Ohio* of Lobito, and the *Olongende* of Bailundu served as forums for the genesis, dissemination, and popularization of nationalist sentiments.

In 1953 at the busy port of Lobito an older age group formed an association for continuing education known as the *Organização Cultural dos Angolanos* (OCA). Led by two prominent young Protestants, Julio Afonso and José Belo Chipenda,[15] but open to Catholics, the Angolan Cultural Organization received periodicals from Brazil, Portugal, and West Africa, notably Ghana. It organized searching discussions on western culture as well as on the problems of tradition versus modernization in African society. Though officially apolitical, the organization exposed young adults to outside ideas and the process of free inquiry, always dangerous in

[14] Luis Inglês and José César Correira Mekuiza (or Mekwyza) both of whom subsequently worked for the UPA as exiles in the Congo.

[15] Born Oct. 9, 1929, the son of an African pastor, José Chipenda served for some time as co-pastor of an interracial church in Lobito. He completed his seventh year of *liceu* and a course at the Presbyterian seminary in Portugal. Later he went to the United States where he studied at the Hartford Seminary in Connecticut and Pace College, New York, and in 1965 was elected president of the exile *União Nacional dos Estudantes Angolanos* (UNEA).

a closed society. Instinctively, Portuguese officialdom became apprehensive, and in 1957 Julio Afonso was arrested by PIDE while visiting Luanda, where he was detected making contact with two Ghanaian teachers who were attending an international conference on education.[16] With an automatic lurch of the administrative machine, the *Organização Cultural dos Angolanos* was banned.

If the severity of PIDE prevented the growth of an extensive, well-organized political movement in the Lobito-Nova Lisboa area, it could not prevent Africans from watching the approaching independence of the Congo with keen anticipation. Every day France's powerful Radio Brazzaville beamed news in Portuguese southward toward Angola and Mozambique while the "bush telegraph" carried in the Congo story, undeterred by official censorship.

Aware of the sharp interest that had been aroused by the Belgian Congo's accession to sovereignty on June 30, 1960, Portuguese officialdom decided to organize mass demonstrations that would confirm African loyalty to Portugal. One such meeting was held at Nova Lisboa on November 14. The administration recruited hundreds of villagers for the occasion and began moving them toward the city as early as November 10. In the words of one African recruit: "The government had provided free transport to bring people from distant towns and villages. Nova Lisboa had never seen so many people." On the day of the demonstration, African teachers and students from the local *liceu* "were obliged to deliver speeches that had been written by Portuguese officials." They dutifully proclaimed themselves to be "blood and soul" Portuguese and denounced African "nationalist exploiters" who were bent upon destroying Portuguese civilization.[17] Just as the proceedings were about to get under way, however, it began to rain. Elated African "volunteers" hailed this as a sign of God's judgment on what ensued.

The very well-known and prosperous symbol of *assimilado* collaboration within the colonial order, a long-time official of the *Associação Africana do Sul de Angola* (AASA) and rubber-stamp

[16] Held under the auspices of the Commission for Technical Cooperation in Africa South of the Sahara (CCTA). Also said to have been arrested in the wake of this meeting were: Issaias Kamutuke, a Sr. Cunha, Alfredo Benga, Loureiro João Sequeira, and members of their families. See UPA Delegation Abroad, "Memorandum to the Fourteenth General Assembly" (New York [1959], mimeo.), p. 9.

[17] Luciano Kassoma, "The Outbreak of the Angolan Revolution in the South" (Lincoln University, 1965, unpublished typescript).

African deputy in the one-party Portuguese National Assembly, António Burity da Silva, was one of the main speakers at the November 14 rally. His address was widely believed to have been written for him by one of the organizers of the mass meeting, a Portuguese named Serafim Molar. Incensed by what they considered to be his humiliating sellout, a group of *liceu* students decided to organize an assault upon the African deputy's home. When they arrived at his house after the rally, however, they discovered themselves thwarted by a cordon of alerted police, an indication that Portuguese officials had not accepted everything said at the rally concerning African loyalty.

Some students, notably a group at the Protestant mission's educational center at Dondi, refused to attend the demonstration in Nova Lisboa. For this act of defiance, their leader, David Chambassuko Severino, was arrested and apparently executed. This overreaction by a fearful and insecure administration only intensified the alienation of precisely that young African elite that Portuguese policy was supposed to be assimilating.[18]

The November 14 demonstration of "loyalty" may have served as a psychological catharsis for anxious Europeans. For the Africans the rhetorical denunciations of Congolese independence, Patrice Lumumba, and other external evils stimulated the curiosity of heretofore politically unaware people who had not questioned their colonial status. "When the manifestation was over, [these people] returned home with new ideas. The good fortune of the Congo was discussed widely and frequently. The name of Lumumba, made familiar . . . [by] Portuguese denunciation of him, was widely commented upon." And so Africans asked: "Is there any way in which we might become free?" They asked why the Portuguese administration feared the Congo's independence, why they criticized Americans, and what they meant when they charged that some Africans who had left the country during the past years were now trying to cause trouble inside Angola. "People pondered these questions. Their emotions were aroused. They became aware of new realities. Some of the younger people began to organize and mobilize the masses for political action." [19]

[18] Severino was reportedly executed on May 18, 1961. Rev. Gaspar de Almeida of the Dondi Institute, allegedly implicated in the student boycott, was imprisoned. *Ibid.*

[19] *Ibid.* American and Canadian missionaries have reported hearing of local Lumumbist religious cults developing in central Angola during late 1960.

One of those who felt it was time for political action was a former student at the Dondi Institute and active member of the *Grupo Avante* of Bié, Julio Chinovola Cacunda. He was an impetuous young man from Balombo (or Vila Norton de Matos). Inducted into the army in 1960, he began promoting political activity among African soldiers. Some Protestant missionaries who knew him, considered him "unstable." On the other hand, Cacunda has been depicted by African associates of that period as having feigned psychological illness in order to obtain an early army discharge and to pursue his political activities unmolested. Whatever the truth, in January 1961, with the aid of a student leader, Arão Cunga, at the Nova Lisboa *liceu,* as well as the help of Abreu Moises Kayaya and Luciano Kassoma, both of Lobito, Cacunda is said to have succeeded in organizing clandestine political groups at Nova Lisboa, Lobito, Luanda, Sá da Bandeira, and a number of smaller centers in the Bailundu area. Student enthusiasts at the *liceu* pledged fifty escudos, something over a dollar, every three months from their meager allowances.[20]

Cacunda and colleagues in this nameless, scarcely structured underground of students, teachers, and soldiers were inspired by conversations with Ghanaian and other African sailors shipping in and out of Lobito. They decided somewhat improbably to launch a general insurrection in southern Angola, proposed to organize a team of contract laborers (*contratados*) as their initial strike force, and set April 2, 1961, as the date for the uprising.

Thus by the end of 1960 the seminaries and schools of Umbundu country had incubated a determined lot of young nationalists, those of the *Juventude Cristã de Angola,* Julio Cacunda's movement, and probably others whose stories are still to be told. Furthermore, an external nationalist leadership was by now in the process of formation. In September 1958 the Protestant missions had sent an initial group of Ovimbundu students, most of them from peasant families, to Portugal for advanced studies. Like the Luandan elite in Lisbon and Paris and the Bakongo émigré leadership in Léopoldville before them, this small contingent of Ovimbundu was exposed to a variety of broadening educational experience. Its ranks were gradually augmented by compatriots forced into exile by increasing police repression in Angola. Together these young people constituted the

20 Information based on accounts by student participants, notably Jeremias K. Chitunda and Luciano Kassoma.

nucleus of an exile political leadership that ultimately gravitated into a political movement led by Jonas M. Savimbi,[21] one of the young Ovimbundu Protestants who sailed to Lisbon in September 1958.

Down South

Directly to the south of Umbundu country and its principal foyers of embryonic nationalism, Nova Lisboa and Lobito, live a number of scattered ethnic communities culturally related to the Ovimbundu. Noteworthy among these are the Nhaneka-Humbe peoples of the Huila Plateau, a region that also supports a substantial Portuguese settlement. The fact that the 200,000 strongly traditionalist Nhaneka-Humbe did not, unlike their Ovimbundu cousins, become innovators of modern nationalism is at least partly attributable to the fact that the Portuguese ejected them from the plateau's good agricultural land and rusticated them to the backlands at the turn of the century.[22] A group of some 300 Boer trekkers from South Africa had moved into the area in 1880. Lisbon reacted quickly, recruited metropolitan families of poor peasants and laborers, sent them to settle in what was a climatically attractive area, and warded off the threat of a South African challenge to Portuguese rule. Already by 1913 an estimated 2500 Portuguese were residing in the vicinity of Sá da Bandeira (formerly Lubango), and the Huila Plateau with its small cereal and tobacco farms, replicas of those of Portugal and the Madeira Islands, was on its way to becoming what James Duffy has termed "the most Portuguese region of Angola." [23]

Precisely because it became an intensely Portuguese town, Sá da Bandeira was considered a salutary cultural environment for the schooling of selected Africans. A number of Ovimbundu (e.g., Jonas Savimbi) and other African students were sent there to complete advanced courses in secondary education that were not yet offered at Nova Lisboa. Furthermore, with the theateningly popu-

[21] Savimbi ended a three-year association with Holden Roberto and the UPA in July 1964 and formed his own political party, the *União Nacional para a Independência Total de Angola* (UNITA) in Mar. 1966.

[22] See Padre Carlos Estermann, *Etnografia do Sudoeste de Angola.* Vol. 2, *Grupo Etnico Nhaneca-Humbe,* 2nd. ed. (Lisbon: Junta de Investigações do Ultramar, 1960).

[23] James Duffy, *Portugal in Africa* (Cambridge, Mass.: Harvard University Press, 1962), p. 144.

lous Nhaneka-Humbe set apart and protected from the nefarious influences of modern education, Sá da Bandeira seemed a secure place for a bit of lusotropicalizing. Thus an admixture of Goans, mulattoes, and even Africans from safely distant areas was permitted into the settlement, and by 1950 Sá da Bandeira contained some 12,000 people, at least a few of whom were by then growing restive under the thumb of colonial administrators.

According to some plausible if unverifiable accounts, it was about this time (1950) that a group of politically conscious Sá da Bandeirans organized a local reform movement.[24] They were reportedly struck by the rapidity with which the administration had smashed an uprising in 1948 led by a Chief Kassela of the Humbe region, and they concluded that it was time to develop a more effective form of political opposition.[25] The ideas came from a local Goan lawyer, but the organizational work was carried out by a mulatto pharmacist, Eduardo Vitório Pereira. The son of a Portuguese soldier and an African chief's daughter, Pereira had worked earlier at the hospital in Moçâmedes, a fishing port connected by rail with Sá da Bandeira. In addition to organizing in these two towns, his movement, known as the *União dos Naturais de Angola* (UNATA), is said to have managed in 1956 to convene a secret meeting at Benguela, a commercial and transportation hub where the coming and going of people was little noted. Then in 1958 members of UNATA reportedly sent an unsigned memorandum to Portuguese authorities in which they demanded political reforms. The identity of some of those who drafted the petition, including minor government functionaries and members of the local branch of the *Associação Africana do Sul de Angola* (AASA), leaked to the increasingly active secret police. The UNATA opposition then collapsed as those implicated were arrested and rusticated to a remote area near Katanga. Eduardo Pereira reportedly had already traveled to Lisbon with the aim of persuading Portuguese officials to liberalize their Angolan regime.

[24] See testimony of Marcos Kassanga before the Special Committee on the Situation with Regard to the Implementation of the Declaration on the Granting of Independence to Colonial Countries and Peoples. United Nations, General Assembly, Document A/Ac109/ SR 387, Sept. 22, 1965, pp. 10–11. Additional details derive from interviews with the author (1966).

[25] In a paper dated March 1965 (which is at variance in some aspects with his later testimony before the United Nations) Kassanga claimed that the 1948 uprising was "organized under the direction" of UNATA, that it resulted in 10,000 casualties, and that its leader, Commander Carlos Mbwangungu, was deported to Portugal, never to be heard of again. Kassanga, "Aspecto real do problema angolano" (Léopoldville, Mar. 15, 1965, unpublished typescript).

For his temerity, he was arrested as well. Yet at least one young African (a Ganguela) who would later figure prominently in the military-political history of the Angolan revolution, Marcos Xavier Kassanga, has said that he was deeply influenced by his association with UNATA as a student at Sá da Bandeira.[26]

To the southeast of the Huila Plateau, the cattle-raising Cuanhama (a subgroup of the Ambo or Ovambo) proved especially resistant to Portuguese penetration into their remote semidesert domains near the Cunene River. In 1904 a single battle at Pembe cost the lives of some 120 Portuguese soldiers. A Portuguese expeditionary force of about 2000 men managed to crush Cuanhama resistance by 1906. Then during the First World War the German regime in South West Africa cultivated Cuanhama chiefs and gave them arms, and once again the Cuanhama went into action against the Portuguese (1914–15).

To cope with such strong-willed people, the colonial administration adopted a policy similar to that used to neutralize the Nhaneka-Humbe, i.e., a policy of enforced isolation. Thus the one large area of Angola in which all Protestant evangelical, and therefore educational, activity was prohibited over a long period (1914–1960) was the Cuanhama territory (Baixo Cunene-Cuamato administrative areas). Only a few individual Cuanhama managed to break through this screen and establish contact with modern life and education in places such as Sá da Bandeira.

As it turned out, it was more densely populated Ovamboland across the border in South West Africa that would produce the initial leadership of a contemporary Cuanhama, or Ovambo, nationalism. The 250,000 Cuanhama-speaking Ovambo of sparsely populated South West Africa provided the only available labor pool for its European farms, mines, ports, and railroads. A few Ovambo workers even found their way to jobs and (more rarely) education in South Africa proper. Exposed to the relatively liberal political climate of postwar Cape Town, some Ovambo launched an Ovamboland People's Organization (OPO) in 1959, which was later expanded into a multiethnic South West Africa People's Organization (SWAPO).

By 1960 SWAPO was operating with quasi legality both in urban centers like Windhoek and within Ovamboland. SWAPO's Ovam-

[26] Kassanga has said that the late UPA military commander, João Batista Traves Pereira (a Cuanhama), was also associated with UNATA.

boland leaders, such as Toivo Hermann ja Toivo, however, were prohibited from organizing among some 65,000 Cuanhama kinsmen living on the other side of the Angolan frontier in the area around Onjiva (or Vila Pereira de Eça). The South African police, while keeping a watchful eye and a heavy hand on SWAPO activity on its side of the border, cooperated with PIDE in seeking to prevent any nationalist contamination of Portuguese soil. Nevertheless, there was constant contact between the related peoples on the two sides of the colonial line, and it may be reasonable to assume that SWAPO and its nationalist doctrine became known to the Cuanhama of Angola. Indeed Portuguese sources have credited SWAPO with a Cuanhama following in the Onjiva region.[27] It also seems relevant to note that after 1960, as the South African police tightened controls over South West African nationalist activity, an exiled SWAPO leadership headed by a former Ovambo town dweller (Windhoek), Sam Nujoma, established a cooperative relationship, first with Holden Roberto's UPA and later with the more southern-oriented Angolan movement founded by the Ochimbundu, Jonas Savimbi.[28]

To the East

By 1795 Ovimbundu long-distance traders and Portuguese *sertanejos* had reached Lwena country in eastern Angola, whence they moved on to introduce their slave, ivory, wax, and rubber trade to other peoples of central Africa, notably the Chokwe (known to the Portuguese as Quioco). The Chokwe rose suddenly in the second half of the nineteenth century to topple the great Lunda empire from which they had come. Beginning around 1850 the hunting and trading Chokwe burst out from their base area on the upper reaches of the Kasai River, southeast of Kasanje, and proceeded to infiltrate and culturally to assimilate indigenous peoples spread over wide areas of eastern Angola, Kasai, and Katanga.[29] Today in Angola alone the Chokwe number some 360,000, extending in a southward wedge from their principal bailiwick in the Lunda district (bordering Kasai) down through the Moxico district to a point south of Vila Serpa Pinto.

Except at the diamond mines of Dundo near the Kasai frontier,

[27] Artur Maciel, *Angola Heróica* (Lisbon: Livraria Bertrand, 1963), p. 132.
[28] See ftn. 21 above.
[29] See Vansina, *Kingdoms,* pp. 200–201 and 216–227.

the Portuguese did almost nothing to develop the eastern portion of Angola, much of which they did not occupy until as late as 1930. In the absence of economic and educational development, some of the more enterprising of the mobile Chokwe reacted like the Bakongo in the north and emigrated to the Congo. Over the years, Angolan Chokwe also migrated to Northern Rhodesia, where many found jobs on the Copperbelt at places like Chingola. In due course, others began to send their children to Northern Rhodesia to live with relatives and to attend schools in the northwestern towns of Balovale, Kabompo, and Mwinilunga.[30] Whereas those who went to the Congo could quickly melt into the Chokwe community already there, in Northern Rhodesia the Chokwe, numbering around 25,000, were foreigners. As such they not only maintained strong in-group sentiments but continued to identify with Angola and to venerate the memory of chiefs such as Kalendende and Mwachimbundu of São Limbo-Moxico, who had earlier led resistance to Portuguese rule. In addition, they organized a Chokwe self-help association.

The initiative to found such an organization was taken by a Chokwe trader living in Lusaka, John Kajila. In April 1956 Kajila befriended an ailing sixteen-year-old Angolan boy from Lumbala, Cuando district, who had arrived in Lusaka as one of a contingent of Angolans recruited for farm work in Southern Rhodesia and South Africa. Far from home and family, the boy died in the Lusaka hospital.[31] Kajila then collected money for his burial, only to find that the authorities had already had him buried by local prisoners. When another Chokwe recruit, fourteen years of age, soon after arrived from the same area, Kajila took him into his home and began to urge his compatriots to consider creating an association to deal with such cases.

In June 1956 Kajila visited the Copperbelt and explained his idea to friends there. Then in October, following a gestation period

[30] A good example is Kaimbo Sakaimbo, born in 1941 at Leua along the Benguela railroad in the Moxico district. Having learned through relatives living there of the educational opportunities in Northern Rhodesia, his parents took him as a very young boy to live with an uncle and attend school at Kabompo. Yet by the time he had completed standard six and then a two-year course in teacher's training, his parents back in Angola had died, rebellion had broken out in the territory, and he could not return. Continuing to consider himself an Angolan, Sakaimbo became active in Angolan nationalist politics in Zambia and a member of the UNITA party (see ftn. 21 above).

[31] His name was Muchima Saitala.

of several months, he organized a Copperbelt meeting of about fifty Chokwe representatives who gathered at Kansuswa African township, Mufulira. They founded a self-help association, the *Ukwashi Wa Chokwe,* and elected John Kajila as its first president.[32] During the discussions at Kansuswa a proposal was made for a constitutional provision stating that if funds collected should exceed those needed for normal mutual-aid purposes, they should be used for a political struggle in Angola. Though the proposal was rejected as likely to get the association into trouble with local authorities, it reflected a latent Angolan-Chokwe nationalist sentiment. Restricting itself to nonpolitical functions, thc *Ukwashi Wa Chokwe* undertook to pay school fees, assist widows and orphans, and promote business enterprises within the Rhodesian Chokwe community. While doing these things it also maintained good relations with Chokwe chiefs resident in Northern Rhodesia's North Western Province so as not to create enemies among these traditional authorities. The new organization registered with the district commissioner's office at Kitwe and was soon organizing among Chokwe as far afield as Broken Hill, Livingstone, and even Salisbury, Southern Rhodesia.

In 1958 word reached the Copperbelt that a separate Chokwe organization, the *Association des Tshokwe du Congo de l'Angola et de la Rhodésie* (ATCAR), had been established at Elizabethville in the Congo. ATCAR was founded by a Katanga businessman, Ambroise Muhunga, who was thought by the *Ukwashi Wa Chokwe* leadership to have stolen the idea for his movement from them. He had visited Northern Rhodesia in August 1956 (selling jackets and women's clothes), just at the time that plans were under discussion for the creation of a Chokwe association there. In April 1958 Muhunga visited Chingola on the Copperbelt, where ATCAR was building up a following among Chokwe who had emigrated there from the Congo. Alarmed by this intrusion into their territory, Kajila and the executive committee of *Ukwashi Wa Chokwe* hastened to Chingola to confront Muhunga and a key local ATCAR organizer named Sankumbi. Muhunga assured his anxious interrogators that their two organizations were really but one and invited them to be his guests at a big unity palaver in Elizabethville.

Kajila and his associates accepted and made the trip that September, but nothing was solved. For although Muhunga enter-

[32] The principal other officers were Maurice Chimbalanga, deputy president, Lackson Lijimu, secretary, Pedro Makina, deputy secretary, and Bennet Njapayu, treasurer.

tained them lavishly with cultural festivities and plays, he also convinced his visitors that he was excessively ambitious. They were especially upset by his references to himself as the Mwachisenge, or paramount chief of all the Chokwe. As such he seemed to expect that one day he would rule over an independent Chokwe state from the Mwachisenge's old capital at Saurimo (now Henrique de Carvalho) in Angola. Arguing that ATCAR's constitution did not but should conform with theirs, and that Muhunga had no valid claim to Chokwe leadership, the visitors returned home to report to their constituents that no progress had been made in the effort to reach an understanding with Katanga-based ATCAR.

Misunderstandings concerning the use of association funds during the trip to Katanga subsequently resulted in a debilitating internal crisis within the *Ukwashi Wa Chokwe.* This was not resolved until October 1959 when a new president, Smart Chata, was elected during a second meeting at Kansuswa township. A self-employed furniture maker at Mufulira, who had been born in August 1934 at Kamonongi (also known as Mbulusaku or Buçaco) in Angola, Chata had drafted the association's constitution in 1956 but had eschewed office at that time.[33] Under his leadership the *Ukwashi Wa Chokwe* during the next few years progressively took on the character of an Angolan political movement.

Meanwhile self-help associations were organized among two other Angolan émigré communities in Northern Rhodesia, the Lwena (or Luena) and Luchazi. The Lwena, like the Chokwe, broke away from the Lunda empire, and during the late nineteenth century expanded at Lunda expense over a wide area of the upper Zambezi basin of eastern Angola and a western (Balovale) corner of Northern Rhodesia. Together with the Luchazi and Bunda, who inhabit regions just west of Northern Rhodesia, the Lwena form part of the heterogeneous people known as Ganguela (or Nganguela). Some 330,000 Ganguela are sprinkled in a wide swath through eastern and southeastern Angola.

Beginning around 1920 a wave of Luchazi migrated into Barotseland and on north into the Balovale regions, where they intermingled and sometimes intermarried with the Lwena. Combined, the two groups were estimated to number something in excess of 10,000 by the mid-1960's.[34] It was in 1958, following the Chokwe

[33] Interview with author, Lusaka, May 12, 1967.

[34] Estimate by former district commissioner, C. M. N. White, interviewed at Lusaka, May 2, 1967. See also White's "The Balovale Peoples and Their His-

precedent, that they each formed their own self-help association. The Lwena (known locally as Luvale) created the *Chijilochalimbo* association at Kitwe and chose a "hawker" (trader) by the name of Dickson Mukuma as its first president. The Luchazi formed the *Vilinga Va Kambungo* and elected as its president, James Muwema, an Ndola (Twapia African township) businessman.

There were some sporadic efforts to bring the three ethnic associations together. Though there was a general agreement that unity was a desirable goal, there was no similar agreement on procedural questions such as who should become president. In the view of Smart Chata, at least, there was some defensiveness on the part of the two newer groups, who feared being dominated by 2000 well-organized and assertive members of the Chokwe association.[35] Therefore the three groups were still separate when the Congo gained its independence on June 30, 1960.

In the Congo, ATCAR was blocked from political power in breakaway Katanga by Moise Tshombe and his Lunda-based CONAKAT party.[36] Chata urged ATCAR leaders to try to save their position by working within the system (for example, he advised against boycotting the provincial parliament where CONAKAT had only a precariously small majority). In spite of his advice, after secession such ATCAR personalities as Mayele Chilembe fled to Northern Rhodesia. The dictates of ethnic solidarity then temporarily absorbed the *Ukwashi Wa Chokwe* in ministering to the needs of Congolese brothers in distress.

In general, the remote, outnumbered, economically and educationally neglected and more traditionalist Chokwe, Lwena, and Luchazi (as well as Nhaneka-Humbe and Cuanhama) peoples were at a great disadvantage within the evolving picture of Angolan nationalism. As in so many other African colonies, social and economic change accompanying European penetration into Angola

torical Background," *Rhodes-Livingstone Journal,* No. 8 (1949), pp. 26–41; and "The Ethno-History of the Upper Zambezi," *African Studies* (Johannesburg), Vol. XXI (1962), pp. 10–27.

35 There were no formal unity negotiations. These groups later came together, though, first within a local branch of the UPA (1964) and then as basic constituents of UNITA (1966).

36 The Lunda of Katanga tended to project their traditional antipathy toward the Chokwe into a general and convenient hostility toward all Angolan nationalist movements (witness Moise Tshombe's collaboration with the Portuguese and harassment of Angolan nationalists as head of the Katangan and then the central Congolese governments).

had created the basis for an imbalance of power in favor of the coastal and highland communities, which had been subjected to the first and strongest (if grossly inadequate) dose of western education and technology. The ultimate correction rather than the abuse of this imbalance was precisely the concern of the Angolan ethnic associations in Northern Rhodesia. Along with the progressive integration rather than the further separation of the main ethnic streams of Angolan nationalism, it was clearly essential if Angola was to achieve nationhood.

THE DECADE OF RISING NATIONALISM: IN SUMMARY

As of the end of 1960 neither the vast, thinly populated areas of eastern Angola nor the Angolan ethnic associations formed in Northern Rhodesia posed any immediate threat to Portugal. But a major storm was brewing among the underground forces and exile movements produced by the more populous and fortunately located Luanda-Mbundu, Bakongo, and Ovimbundu regions of Angola. And though the sorcerer's apprentice, PIDE, did its best to smash all nationalist organizations, they only multiplied like invisible brooms, hovering in the basement or plotting outside the house, sometimes quarreling, sometimes cooperating, but always watching and working for the day when they might sweep into power. Had Portuguese observers been adequately informed about or sensitive to the extent and intensity of African nationalism in Angola at the end of 1960, they might easily have predicted that 1961 would be a year of rebellion.

When it came, the rebellion was, in the words of Marxist Viriato da Cruz, "the result of the irreversible blow dealt to traditional African structures by the market economy introduced under the Portuguese colonial administration." According to his estimates, some 2,000,000 Africans had been torn from their "social and geographic surroundings": 800,000 were subject to rural forced labor; 350,000 faced underemployment and joblessness in urban areas; and "about 1,000,000 Angolan émigrés" were laboring in the Congo, the Rhodesias, and South Africa.[37] In sum, the disintegration of traditional society and the injustice of colonial society had led to widespread disorientation, despair, and repression, and to preparations for violent protest.

[37] *World Outlook* (Paris), Vol. 2, No. 9 (Feb. 28, 1964), p. 21.

PART II

THE YEAR OF REBELLION

CHAPTER FOUR

A SEQUENTIAL EXPLOSION

By the beginning of 1961 Angola was a black powder keg with a ready fuse. What would finally ignite it was the syndrome of new aspirations and restiveness developing among the 6 per cent of its population who were town dwellers by 1955, the secondary school students, and the uneducated plantation workers. They had begun to question whether there was no alternative to continued rule by foreigners who could expropriate their land, requisition their labor, swindle their traders and consumers, and arrest and dispose of their persons at will.

External evidence increasingly suggested that a nationalist alternative was indeed feasible. In December 1960, for instance, the General Assembly of the United Nations tackled the issue of Portuguese colonialism and voted two resolutions, one specifically holding Portugal accountable under Article 73e of the Charter for the transmittal of information concerning its administration of overseas territories,[1] and another calling on all colonial powers to take "immediate steps . . . to transfer all powers to the peoples" of dependent territories.[2] Closer at hand there was the suggestive example set unintentionally by the Belgians, who during 1960 fled precipitately before ill-organized forces of a nascent Congolese nationalism that lacked sufficient cohesion to hold the Congo together after independence and had to be rescued by the intervention of the United Nations.

At the outset of 1961 Angola was experiencing an economic recession. This was occasioned in large measure by a fall in the world price of coffee, the commodity upon which the colony, or more

[1] United Nations, General Assembly Resolution 1541 (XV), Dec. 15, 1960.

[2] This was the precedent-shattering Declaration on the Granting of Independence to Colonial Countries and Peoples. United Nations, General Assembly Resolution 1514 (XV), Dec. 14, 1960.

accurately its European community, had built its rising prosperity. Coffee that had been earning twenty dollars a sack brought only five dollars in 1959–60.[3] The coffee slump in the north, coupled with a bad year for Malange cotton and for the fishing industry of the south coast, brought on a wave of unemployment and wage cuts just at a time when an increasing trickle of young Africans was graduating from local schools and seeking economic advancement.[4]

Cotton and Bombs: Maria's War

Trouble first broke out in the cotton-growing country of Kasanje (Cassange). From an enforced distance, Methodist missionaries located near the town of Malange watched events unfold in sequential tragedy. A fall in cotton prices was followed by failure to pay African growers, then strikes, retaliatory beatings and arrests, and finally, by mid-February, mayhem and destruction throughout the countryside.[5] Writing in his diary on February 14 at Quessua, Rev. Malcolm McVeigh recorded that word had come to the mission of attacks on property and livestock in outlying areas by members of a sect called Maria, which some thought might refer to the Virgin Mary. Fleeing before the rampaging cultists, he added, Europeans from the cotton zone had been seeking refuge in the town of Malange.

According to Angolan nationalist accounts, this chain of events began in early January when the followers of Maria, in actuality António Mariano, embarked on a campaign against European authority and the whole system of enforced cotton growing.[6] Janu-

[3] At the coffee center of Bembe in the north, there were reports that only two of forty-one Portuguese commercial houses showed a profit for the 1959–60 fiscal year. See report on "Angola" in *The Atlantic,* Vol. 209, No. 3 (Mar. 1962), p. 26.

[4] A former missionary in Angola (1940–1959), and Associate Foreign Secretary of the Baptist Missionary Society (London), Rev. Clifford J. Parsons has presented an informative analysis of the underlying and immediate causes of the Angolan rebellion of 1961 in "The Torment of Angola," *Africa South in Exile* (London), Vol. 5, No. 4 (July–Sept. 1961), pp. 72–80.

[5] "In January and February of 1961, cotton workers in the Cassange Valley, in central Angola, went on strike. Cotton prices had gone down; the workers weren't being paid, and they refused to work." Rev. E. Edwin LeMaster, "I Saw the Horror in Angola," *The Saturday Evening Post,* May 12, 1962, p. 54. See also two articles by Rev. Malcolm McVeigh, "The Bullets of Civilization," *Africa Today,* Vol. 8, No. 7 (Sept. 1961), pp. 5–8, and "Labor in Chains," *ibid.,* Vol. 8, No. 8 (Oct. 1961), pp. 9–11.

[6] Rosário Neto, "Notas e Impressões do Kwango. A Guerra de Maria," *UPA, A Voz da Revolução,* No. 1 (Kinshasa, 1966, mimeo.).

ary was planting time. Instead of sowing this year, however, many burned their seed, heaped their farm tools at roadsides, and, while singing their militant hymns to Lumumba, Pinock, and Maria, launched a religious crusade for "independence." They destroyed barges at Cambo, Lui, and Kwango (or Cuango) river crossings, barricaded roads, slaughtered livestock, broke into stores and Catholic missions, and chased away Europeans. This was characterized by African nationalists as "pacific protest," since African *catanas* (cutting tools) and *canhangulos* (vintage muzzle-loader hunting guns) were not used to attack persons but only to level property and kill cattle.

As Maria's War gained momentum and spread from remote border areas, which seem to have enjoyed some weeks of "independence," into the heart of Malange district, the administration sounded the alarm. Portuguese planes and troops were rushed in to firebomb and strafe villages and to crush all opposition. Maria's crusaders downed bridges and ambushed a few Portuguese soldiers but were outclassed and overwhelmed in short order. Portuguese authority was restored in the area, though at a cost of hundreds, perhaps thousands, of African lives.[7]

As for Mariano, in March he and an allied chief, Kula-Xingu, were captured near Luremo (district of Lunda), allegedly having been betrayed by two latter-day Judases for a reward of 1000 escudos and a bicycle each.[8] From Luremo the prisoners were taken to a Catholic mission at Mussuco (less than twenty miles from the Congolese border), which had been converted into a Portuguese command post. There at his Calvary, Mariano was reportedly interrogated and mutilated before the authorities finally had him tied in a sack and trucked to Malange and prison. When, a few days after his arrival at Malange, his mother, Catarina Pimenta of Canâmbua, a nearby African township, brought food for him, she was told not to bother any more. This was the customary if indirect way of informing relatives or friends of an African prisoner's death.

Many of Mariano's followers fled from Kasanje to the Congo. Coming from the administrative areas of Cahombo, Camaxilo,

[7] UPA sources claim that 7,000 Africans were killed. Portuguese military action reportedly extended over a triangular area from Quela and Xandel (east of Malange) in the south up to the Congolese border from the vicinity of Marimba a Tembo on the west to Camaxilo on the east. *Ibid.*

[8] The informers were reportedly a tailor named Magalhães and a catechist, José Kitumbi. *Ibid.*

Bondo, Bângalas, and Malange, they brought with them a few arms captured from the Portuguese, some of which were subsequently handed over to the UPA by the Angolan chief of Marimba a Tembo.[9] The Angolan refugees settled in the region around Kizamba, for whose chief Mariano had worked earlier as a chauffeur. Upward of 10,000 of them eventually settled there in the Panzi district of the Congo's Kwango Province, forming what would later become a revolutionary support base for UPA military operations back into Kasanje.

Not a word about the strikes, insurrection, or retaliation appeared in the press, though Portuguese sources have subsequently referred to a January strike by cotton workers.[10] African pastors reported on the "clean-up" operations to Methodist headquarters at Malange, where American missionaries witnessed the overflight of bombers and the passage of troops destined for the afflicted area.[11] But no outsiders were permitted to enter the Kasanje region, and the government continued to portray its "overseas province" of Angola as a model of communal harmony. Indicative of the spontaneous and localized nature of the uprising, no African nationalist movement claimed credit for it or publicized it at the time.[12]

Riots and Vigilantes: Luanda

The second eruption of violence in early 1961 coincided with rumors that an anti-Salazar crusader, Captain Henrique Galvão, and a rebel crew that had on January 22 hijacked the Portuguese luxury

[9] *Ibid.*, and interview with author.

[10] Artur Maciel, *Angola Heróica* (Lisbon: Livraria Bertrand, 1963), pp. 66–67; and João Baptista Nuna Pereira Neto, "Movimentos subversivos de Angola: Tentativa de esboço sócio-político," in *Angola, Curso de Extensão Universitária, Ano Lectivo de 1963–1964* (Lisbon: Instituto Superior de Ciências Sociais e Política Ultramarina [1964?]), p. 363.

[11] Rev. David Grenfell's interviews with Angolan refugees in the Congo have produced reports of Portuguese military action against Africans as early as Jan. 1961. See, for example, Grenfell, *Notes*, No. 10 (Kibentele, Mar. 8, 1965, mimeo.).

[12] Mário de Andrade subsequently claimed that the revolt of the plantation workers of the Cassange Valley had been organized by several MPLA nationalists who escaped there from Luanda after the rioting on Feb. 4–6 in the capital. See Andrade, "Le nationalisme angolais," *Présence Africaine*, No. 42 (1962), p. 21. The official MPLA organ, *Unidade Angolana*, edited by Matias Miguéis in Léopoldville (Feb. 4, 1962), claimed only that a few MPLA militants had escaped from Luanda after the February rioting and police retaliation and had moved into the interior (Dembos, Quanza Norte, Quanza Sul, and Malange) in order to organize plantation workers for revolutionary activity—presumably too late to have been centrally involved in the *Guerra de Maria* in Kasanje.

liner "Santa Maria" were sailing toward Luanda, where they might hope to precipitate a *coup* and take over the territory for the Portuguese democratic opposition.[13] Luanda was consequently full of expectant foreign journalists allowed in by a confident colonial administration. The presence of these journalists provided Angolan nationalists with an unusual chance to publicize their cause through some form of dramatic action. It has even been suggested since that such action was originally planned to coincide with the arrival of the "Santa Maria." Accordingly, the late Portuguese opposition leader, General Humberto Delgado is reported to have professed sometime later that there had been "some coordination" between his Iberian Revolutionary Directorate and the MPLA in the "Santa Maria"-Luanda sequence.[14] On the other hand, Captain Galvão, the commander of the twenty-four men who captured and held the "Santa Maria" for eleven days before abandoning it at Recife, Brazil, certainly had no intention of cooperating with what he considered to be "anti-Portuguese" independence movements in Angola.[15] He was a rebel and a democrat, but he was also a Portuguese nationalist. During the unexecuted "second phase" of his operation, he had planned to sail to Fernando Po, seize that Spanish island in a surprise commando attack, and then move swiftly on with captured gun boats and volunteer "native forces" to take (Spanish) Rio Muni on the mainland. Finally, "in very fast, surprise operations taking a maximum of three days," and with the aid of "two, possibly three, airplanes obtained on the island and on the continent" he hoped to attack and capture Luanda with the assistance of "local rebel forces"—presumably local Portuguese democrats. Galvão aimed to liberate "a portion of Portuguese territory," to place it under a new Portuguese—not African—government, and then, with the aid of "concurrent uprisings" in Mozambique and Portugal itself, "to unleash a war against the Salazar regime." [16]

A leading member of the MPLA, Rev. Domingos da Silva, has subsequently said that militant action in Luanda had originally

[13] See Henrique Galvão, *Santa Maria: My Crusade for Portugal* (New York: The World Publishing Company, 1961). James Duffy has described the "Santa Maria" affair as "the symbolic beginning of the end for Portugal in Africa." Duffy, *Portugal in Africa* (Cambridge, Mass.: Harvard University Press, 1962), p. 214.

[14] John K. Cooley, *East Wind over Africa* (New York: Walker and Co., 1965), p. 125.

[15] Galvão, *Santa Maria,* pp. 224–226.

[16] *Ibid.,* pp. 113–114.

been scheduled for January 1, well before the hijacking, and had been postponed only because the police had discovered and confiscated dynamite with which local insurgents had hoped to storm their objectives.[17] Still other sources have suggested that action was timed and initiated by members of the *Movimento de Libertação de Angola* (MLA), who were intent upon releasing from prison, among others, one of their leaders, a public health officer named António Pedro Benge.[18]

In any case, in the predawn hours of February 4, 1961, several hundred Africans armed with knives and clubs mounted an attack on Luanda's main political prison. Clearly, they hoped to free political prisoners who were rumored to be slated for imminent transfer to Portugal. Such transfers were often occasions for prisoners to disappear permanently, and, at the very least, their rumored physical removal threatened to preclude any chance for maintaining contact between arrested leaders and the developing nationalist struggle in Angola.[19]

The results of the first day's assault were reportedly seven Portuguese police killed, about forty Africans machine-gunned, and none of the prisoners freed. The MPLA later charged that the treason of some Africans who were working for the Portuguese militated against the success of nationalist action.[20] On the morning of February 5 armed European civilians leaving funeral services for the seven policemen turned on African bystanders, whom they suspected of having been involved in the prison attacks, chased them into a sawmill, and shot them down. Rioting broke out again; an African mob tried and failed to storm the main prison;

[17] Robert Davezies, *Les angolais* (Paris: Les Éditions de Minuit, 1965), p. 222.

[18] Interview with Leopoldo Trovoada, secretary-general of the National Union of Angolan Students (UNEA), Paris, Dec. 1966. A GRAE communiqué of Sept. 24, 1962 (Léopoldville, mimeo.) announced that Benge, described as a pioneer "militant of the UPA," arrested on March (Easter) 29, 1959, had been "assassinated" on Sept. 13, 1962, by Portuguese authorities.

[19] An anonymous article by an Angolan refugee student in the COSEC journal, *The Student* (Leiden), July-Aug. 1963, relates that there was "a great deal of discussion" before the decision was taken to attack the prison. The author says that he had been one of those who argued that Portuguese reaction would be so "terrible" and instantaneous that it "might succeed in destroying our carefully created nationalist network." He does not identify the nationalist movement concerned.

[20] MPLA, *Angola, Exploitation esclavagiste, Résistance nationale* (Dakar: A. Diop, 1961), p. 41.

and the violence lasted on into the night.[21] Five days later a February 10 raid on another Luanda prison resulted in seven deaths and seventeen wounded.[22] Portuguese vengeance was awesome. The police helped civilian vigilantes organize nightly slaughters in the *muceques.* The whites hauled Africans from their flimsy one-room huts, shot them, and left their bodies in the streets. A Methodist missionary in Luanda at the time testified that he personally knew of the deaths of almost three hundred.[23] The full dimensions of the massacre will never be known. Local authorities promptly clamped down on foreign correspondents who, of course, undertook to investigate and report on the Luanda tragedy. The police confiscated their film and found space for them on outbound planes. There has been an almost complete blackout on free, unbiased reporting ever since.

Whereas the initial organization and direction of the February action remains in dispute, it is most generally attributed to the MPLA.[24] Former MLA partisans credit their group. Others probably joined in, including members of the FUJA, ELA, UPA, and JCA, and many who were not affiliated with any nationalist organization. The Portuguese government blamed the violence on unrepresentative groups of "hooligans and hirelings" and said that one of these groups was a "communist organization" known as the *Diretório Revolucionário de Libertação* (DRIL) which was acting on behalf of "international subversive forces." [25] There is some indication that the UPA may have been particularly vulnerable to Portuguese retaliation in the Luanda slums, as witness the fact that after the violence had subsided the "southerners" of the JCA were unable to reestablish contact with it. They did succeed in contacting the MPLA, however, and some began attending clandestine classes in techniques of sabotage organized by it. João Chisseva, who had earlier met Ilidio Machado and other MPLA leaders while in prison in Luanda, only to lose contact with their movement after being

21 World Assembly of Youth, "Report of the WAY Mission on Angola," Document 1984 (Brussels, June 1962, mimeo.), pp. 18–19.

22 United Nations, General Assembly, *Report of the Sub-Committee on the Situation in Angola,* 16th session, Suppl. No. 16 (A/4978), New York, 1962, p. 11 (cited hereafter as *Report of UN Sub-Committee*).

23 LeMaster, "Horror in Angola," p. 54. *Time* (Feb. 24, 1961) quoted a Luanda cab driver as having "told reporters that he saw five trucks loaded with corpses driven out to a mass burial in the bush."

24 Portuguese writers such as Hélio Felgas credit the MPLA. See Felgas, *Guerra em Angola* (Lisbon: Livraria Classica Editôra, 1961), p. 55.

25 *Report of UN Sub-Committee,* p. 12.

freed on May 29, 1960, joined an MPLA cell, *Bairro Operário* (Branch No. 7), on April 2, 1961.[26]

During February, in the wake of the rioting, a number of MPLA militants reportedly left Luanda for the interior, particularly the neighboring Dembos region, with the aim of organizing a resistance movement among the rural Mbundu. At the international level the MPLA benefited from the wide publicity given to the Luanda violence. In a front-page column, Paris's influential *Le Monde* described the MPLA as Angola's "most active" nationalist organization and quoted its acting president as saying that it had resorted to "direct action" only after exhausting all avenues for negotiation.[27]

The Fifteenth of March

It was the third upheaval of 1961 that thrust Angola into a protracted state of rebellion. The February violence in Luanda had attracted world attention,[28] and the Security Council scheduled a discussion of the matter for March 10. Five days later an insurrection broke out over a wide area of northern Angola.

The event has been described in widely differing terms.[29] A pro-Portuguese journalist, Pieter Lessing, has said that on March 15 "a terrible army . . . swept across the frontier from the Congo into Angola in a fifty-prong attack along a four hundred mile front, killing Africans and Portuguese men, women and children indiscriminately." Directed by Holden Roberto, whose past function in Léopoldville had been "to organize the distribution of Communist propaganda in the Portuguese territories," this army allegedly attacked under an "order of the day" which called for a three-way partition of West Africa: the northern part to be governed by Sékou Touré of Guinea, the center by Kwame Nkrumah of Ghana, and the southern segment by Holden Roberto. This same battle

[26] João Chisseva, "Ngau, Ngau, Ngau! O'Sino da Liberdade Tocou" (April 1966, unpublished typescript).

[27] *Le Monde,* Mar. 10, 1961.

[28] Taking advantage of this attention, Andrade had sent a telegram to Soviet Premier Khrushchev in which he said that his movement was counting on the Soviet government's support for the Angolan people's struggle. *Pravda,* Mar. 11, 1961.

[29] For a representative Portuguese account, see Hélio Felgas, "Responsabilidade dos grupos políticos angolanos do Congo ex-belga nos acontecimentos de Angola," *Revista Militar* (Lisbon), Supplement July 1962, as well as his *Guerra em Angola.*

order reportedly concluded with the slogans: "Long live Communism. Down with Concentric [*sic*] Tribalism." [30]

The order of the day cited by Lessing apparently refers to a "secret" document purportedly found on a rebel terrorist by his Portuguese captors. It was published in its improbable entirety under the heading "Orders from Moscow" by a conservative French weekly that described Holden Roberto as a Portuguese *métis* (mulatto).[31] This florid tract is illustrative of the sort of material offered by Lisbon (and sometimes taken) as serious evidence of a sinister conspiracy against a plucky, self-sacrificing Portugal engaged in defending the moral values of Western civilization. Allegedly an open letter to UPA militants, the "order" says more about the perception of its probable Portuguese author(s) than about Angolan nationalists.[32] (See Appendix D.)

In a pamphlet entitled *The Communists and Angola,* the Lisbon-

[30] A South African and one-time correspondent of the *Christian Science Monitor,* Pieter Lessing claimed to possess a photostat copy of the original of this order of the day. In a book published in the United States he also presented background information on Holden Roberto and the UPA, information which was as notable for its lack of supporting evidence as for its portrayal of a tidy drama of Communist conspiracy. According to Lessing, Roberto's "association with Belgian Communists is believed to have started soon after he left school. In subsequent years in France he became closely identified with the French Communist party. Roberto also spent a short time in Britain and in fact married an English girl, Susan Milton." (Milton was a family name of Roberto's Bakongo wife Suzanne). Then in 1954, still according to Lessing, Roberto "returned to Léopoldville and shortly afterward formed the UPA, at that time a small movement, which gained the support of members of the short-lived Angolan Communist Party after the latter had disbanded for tactical reasons." Lessing's book is noteworthy principally for its widely circulated misinformation. Pieter Lessing, *Africa's Red Harvest* (New York: The John Day Co., 1962), pp. 11, 15–18.

[31] Such references to Roberto as a mulatto in pro-Portuguese writing about the Angolan Revolution suggest a surprising degree of unfamiliarity with Angolan nationalist movements and their leadership. In *Guerra em Angola,* the historian Hélio Felgas describes Roberto as a "*mestiço* of Dutch and Angolan parentage born in the former Belgian Congo" (p. 53). An apparently authoritative British instructor with the Portuguese army, Col. Ronald Waring, dismissed Roberto as reputedly "a good friend of Mrs. Eleanor Roosevelt" but of "secondary importance" with no "significant following in Angola." See "The Case for Portugal," in *Angola: A Symposium, Views of a Revolt* (London: Oxford University Press, 1962), pp. 37-38.

[32] It appeared in an article by "Rémy" in *Carrefour* (Paris), Nov. 15, 1961, p. 20. It is described as a rather poor forgery by an American journalist who saw it. See Daniel M. Friedenberg, "Public Relations for Portugal. The Angola Story as Told by Selvage and Lee," *The New Republic,* Apr. 2, 1962, p. 12.

backed Portuguese-American Committee on Foreign Affairs[33] presented March 15 as part of a "Communist campaign" of "planned terrorism" and "skillful propaganda" designed "to separate Angola from Portugal" and weaken the NATO alliance. In its view the event combined an attack by terrorists trained in a "Communist camp" at Thysville in the Congo with a propaganda offensive against Portugal carried on by the American Committee on Africa (ACOA) in New York. Illustrated with hammers and sickles and Russian lettering, the Portuguese-American pamphlet cites predictions of Angolan violence made by members of the ACOA as evidence that "they were well aware of the plans" for the attack on Portugal, "foe of Communism and NATO ally of the United States." After charging that "the people who actually run the [ACOA]" had "records showing affiliation with, and sympathy for, Communist causes," and that some of the material they issued was "serving the Communist cause, possibly unintentionally," the pamphlet referred to "persistent reports that the Committee also [had] contributed directly to the terrorist cause."[34] March 15 was thereby portrayed as "part of the international Communist conspiracy" that benefited from the support of misguided American liberals. The picture was drawn by insinuation: "On February 16, 17, and 18 [1960] another member of the Committee, George Houser, now executive director, visited Léopoldville, where the pro-Communist leader, Holden Roberto, was planning the nationalist revolt."[35] As noted earlier, Roberto was absent from Léopoldville from September 1958 until July 1961.[36]

[33] A group of Americans of Portuguese descent organized to defend Portuguese colonial policy, headed by a Boston lawyer, Martin T. Camacho (chairman). See pp. 185–187.

[34] Portuguese-American Committee on Foreign Affairs, *The Communists and Angola* (Boston [1961]), pp. 1-2, 11, and 27.

[35] *Ibid.*, p. 10.

[36] ACOA board member William X. Scheinman initiated legal action against Selvage and Lee, Inc., for statements made in *The Communists and Angola*. The pamphlet's authors had gone beyond the innuendo of passages that noted that the Communist *Daily Worker* had "repeatedly reprinted" critical statements made by Scheinman and Frank Montero after their visit to Angola in February 1960. In general, the pamphlet's wording carefully skirted the edges of what might be libelous. For example: "The Portuguese government denied stories of racial strife and warfare, but the identical charges of Montero and Scheinman were repeated again and again in Communist propaganda" (p. 11). In a costly slip, however, after stating that Montero and Scheinman had driven into Angola "posing as tourists," it continued: "They flew out of Luanda on February 10. Scheinman had a second passport issued in the name of John Ball, and frequently used that name" (p. 10). Noting that to possess a second passport would be a

A member of Europe's unemployed royalty, the Archduke Otto von Habsburg, junketed through Spanish and Portuguese Africa in 1962 and then wrote a book in which he described the March 1961 uprising as "remarkably" well organized. Trained and equipped by professionals, small groups using identical slogans simultaneously cut communication lines and strategic roads. Their action was "clearly the result of precise plans and detailed studies" and not "spontaneous." Rebel leaders, according to the Archduke, hoped to jolt the Portuguese into abandoning Angola just as the Belgians had been precipitated into fleeing the Congo. After occupying northern Angola with the aid of a "massive entry" of Congolese "volunteers," he concluded, the rebels intended to rely on their international contacts with the Soviet bloc and with the United States via the American Committee on Africa to obtain sufficient political support to prevent Portuguese authorities from reacting.[37]

The writings of a few scholars, such as Lewis Gann (Rhodesian) and Peter Duignan (American) in their widely distributed paperback on *White Settlers in Tropical Africa,* have also presented the March uprising as "well planned and organized." Gann and Duignan divided Angolan revolutionaries into three elements: members of the Congolese *Force Publique* who had fled the Congo after the mutiny of July 1960, "Angolan nationalists," and "a small group of Angolan Communists who [had] been busy forming a revolutionary army since 1959." They concluded: "What is happening in

---

criminal offense punishable by a $2,000 fine or imprisonment up to five years, Montero filed suit for $2,000,000 in damages (New York Supreme Court, Appellate Division, First Department, William X. Scheinman v. Selvage and Lee, Inc., *Papers on Appeal from Order,* New York County Clerk's Index No. 19645-1962). In November 1964 Selvage and Lee settled out of court, paid Scheinman $7,827.96 in damages and issued the following statement signed by Morris M. Lee, president of Selvage and Lee:

To Whom It May Concern:

Selvage & Lee, Inc., expresses its regret to William X. Scheinman, a member of the Board of the American Committee on Africa, for including Mr. Scheinman in the pamphlet "The Communists and Angola," which it prepared as public relations counsel for the Overseas Companies of Portugal, and which was published by the Portuguese-American Committee on Foreign Affairs. Selvage & Lee retracts the statement made in that pamphlet that Mr. Scheinman had a second passport issued in another person's name and frequently used that name while in Angola and acknowledges the statement to be untrue" (Nov. 30, 1964, annex to Stipulation of Discontinuance, Index No. 19645/62).

[37] Otto de Habsbourg, *Européens et africains. L'entente nécessaire* (Paris: Librairie Hachette, 1963), pp. 221-222.

Angola may, in part, be a Communist-inspired war of national liberation." [38]

Still another presentation of March 15 as a carefully planned insurrection came from the UPA itself. As head of the party youth group, Johnny Edouard [39] wrote in 1962 that preparatory to the uprising the executive committee of the UPA met in private, top-level sessions "for several weeks during the course of which it elaborated a thoroughly studied battle strategy" which took into account all relevant factors including a careful study of topography.[40] Johnny Edouard's version constituted an apparent effort to counter charges by nationalist rivals that the northern uprising was a "spontaneous" or "unconsidered" act.

In reality, the UPA's official mythology about the outbreak of fighting in the north was not consistent with Edouard's version and may have been partly responsible for the very charges that he was attempting to refute. According to UPA president Holden Roberto, "The bloody events which took place in Angola" were unpremeditated and began at a farm called Primavera, situated near Madimba, some sixty-five miles from the Congo-Angola frontier. On the evening of March 14 the conscript laborers at Primavera gathered before the house of the coffee plantation manager, a Sr. Reis, and demanded six months' overdue back pay. He allegedly refused to listen, "and without further ado, took out his gun and fired at the workers, killing several of them." Armed with their *catanas* (machetes), the farm workers promptly fell upon Reis and killed him and his family. Hearing of the Primavera incident, other Portuguese settlers began shooting Africans on sight. The latter responded by burning crops, pillaging houses, and demolishing bridges. The news spread, incidents multiplied—the revolution had begun as a kind of spontaneous combustion.[41]

What, then, was March 15? A Communist invasion? A minutely

[38] Baltimore: Penguin Books, 1962, pp. 139–140. See also British (*Daily Telegraph*) journalist George Martelli, *The Future in Angola* (London: Congo-Africa, 1962), pp. 4–5.

[39] He sometimes uses the Portuguese spelling, Eduardo, as does his father, Eduardo Pinock.

[40] Johnny Edouard, "La Jeunesse angolaise accuse" (Léopoldville, 1962, mimeo.).

[41] Holden Roberto, "Angola and Portugal" (New York, 1961, unpublished typescript). The Primavera story appears in numerous UPA statements of that period, including a "Memorandum from the Union of the Populations of Angola to the Honorable Delegates of the Fifteenth Session of the General Assembly of the United Nations on the General Situation in Angola," New York, April 1961, p. 6 (hereafter cited as "UPA Memorandum to UN").

planned uprising? Or simply a chain reaction to a specific incident? A reconstruction of available facts suggests that the reports of Communist conspiracy were invented out of whole cloth, that there was some planning but some miscalculation as well, and that Primavera was more a symbol than an explanation of what happened that fateful day.

Moving toward Violence

The UPA turned to violent action out of disillusionment with years of peaceful protest. It was during his first sojourn in Ghana (1958–59) that Holden Roberto had begun thinking in terms of revolution, barring a change in Portuguese policy.[42] His friend Frantz Fanon spoke earnestly of the necessity of violent revolution for true liberation from the colonial condition and convinced him of the need for armed struggle in Angola.[43] In July 1960, shortly after his return to the Congo, Roberto sent UPA couriers to Luanda and Nova Lisboa with instructions to make contact with and distribute party tracts among African soldiers.[44] Among those who deserted the Portuguese army and escaped into the Congo during the second half of 1960 were a handful of noncommissioned officers, the highest rank to which Africans could aspire.[45]

One of these was a young Cuanhama born at Sá da Bandeira on February 3, 1933, Corporal João Batista (or Baptista) Traves Pereira. An *assimilado* who had completed a secondary school course for nurses' aides (rare for a Cuanhama, whose community has been especially deprived of educational opportunity), Batista reportedly had been associated with the ephemeral *União dos Naturais de Angola* (UNATA) of Sá da Bandeira before being conscripted into the army in 1959.[46] He was among the southerners who were moved to army posts along the Congolese border in the

[42] See pp. 68–69.

[43] According to Roberto, as interviewed by J. M'Ba in *Le Progrès* (Kinshasa), April 1–2, 1967. He saw much of Fanon in Accra in the spring of 1960 and then again that summer in Léopoldville, where Fanon attended an emergency meeting of African states, occasioned by the post-independence upheavals in the Congo. According to Roberto, Fanon urged him not to repeat Patrice Lumumba's mistake of overextending himself politically before he had built a solid political organization behind him.

[44] He later claimed that as a result of this campaign there were some 150 desertions before March 15, 1961. *Afrique nouvelle*, No. 740 (Oct. 11, 1961), p. 8.

[45] Interview with Holden Roberto, Léopoldville, Jan. 1, 1962.

[46] According to his friend from Sá da Bandeira, Marcos Kassanga.

months just before Congolese independence. Southerners were considered safe there because they did not speak local or neighboring languages, e.g., Kikongo, Lingala, or French. Nevertheless, possible contamination from broadcasts and tracts from the UPA in Léopoldville as well as some contact with the Congolese army finally rendered even these forces suspect in Portuguese eyes. At Noqui, where Batista was posted, Portuguese "paratroops" replaced Africans, and Batista himself fled to Matadi on the night of August 4–5, after learning that he was slated for arrest because of suspected nationalist sympathies.[47]

In Matadi Batista contacted the local UPA office and, after an interview with Eduardo Pinock, was given shelter at the home of another UPA official, Borralho Lulendo. Later in early autumn, during a visit to Matadi, Roberto met and took Batista with him back to Léopoldville. There Batista entered the UPA organization as assistant political director of the youth wing of the party (JUPA), formed in early November. In December, after returning from a second stint of lobbying at the General Assembly, and after consolidating his position at the head of the UPA (defeating the exponents of nonviolence), Roberto authorized Batista to assemble a group of ex-soldiers into a *Comissão da Revolução Nacional.* After two meetings the commission requested Roberto to obtain military training for them. This he did and in January eleven of them began night classes under a Tunisian officer at the Tunisian embassy. The military commissioners were scheduled to go on to Tunisia in March for more intensive training, but Captain Galvão's seizure of the "Santa Maria" on January 22 sparked a series of events that would upset this orderly time table.

In addition to laying the foundation for a future military force, Roberto worked from December through February on the dual task of building a broader political and diplomatic base from which to launch militant action. As part of his effort to give the UPA a more nationally representative ethnic leadership, he chose as the party's new vice-president Rosário Neto, the Mbundu exile who had opened the UPA's first office in Léopoldville at the time of Congolese independence. Born at Malange on April 3, 1927, Neto (no relation to the MPLA's Agostinho Neto) had been educated in the Catholic seminary at Luanda before deciding against the priesthood

[47] Much of the information in this and the following paragraph is based upon taped interviews with Batista inside nationalist controlled territory of Angola on Jan. 8 and 9, 1962.

and taking a post in the finance section of the colonial administration. He remained an active Church layman after leaving the seminary and wrote for the Catholic paper, *O Apostolado,* as well as for the *Diário de Luanda, Angola Norte* (Malange), and *Império* (Mozambique).

As a trusted assistant to one Captain Fernando Alves in the finance department, Neto gained access to confidential government documents such as circular letters to top administrators. Charged with making copies for intra-office use, he often made an extra one for himself. He also helped to prepare classified materials for shipment to Portugal pursuant to a regulation that all such materials be reposited in Lisbon within ten years of their date of issue. Some of these were politically revealing, and he took notes. It was apparently some of the fruit of his sleuthing that found its way from Catholic priests to whom he confided it to Frank Montero and William Scheinman during their visit in February 1960. Neto learned of the two Americans' subsequent press conference in New York from Radio Brazzaville and immediately realized that they had unveiled material that had passed through his hands.[48] Soon investigations were under way inside the government to discover the source of the leak. On the advice and with the help (e.g., falsified papers) of his clerical friends, Neto flew to Cabinda on June 3 and from there escaped into the Congo three days later. He had had some contact with the UPA's principal organizer in Luanda, but the party representative had been a bit reticent, in view of Neto's close associations with the local clergy, and it was only at Matadi, where he contacted Eduardo Pinock, that Neto joined the party and began his new career as a professional nationalist.[49]

Another Catholic and former student at the Luanda seminary, Alexandre Taty (born circa 1926 at Ndinji, or Dinge), joined UPA leadership ranks as a second vice-president and principal representative of another region of Angola, the enclave of Cabinda. The prominent Luandan mulatto Anibal de Melo became the party's *directeur politique.* And in Europe in early March Roberto made

[48] See p. 35 and Appendix B.

[49] Father Joaquim Pinto de Andrade, Chancellor of the Archdiocese of Luanda, who arranged for Neto's *laissez-passer,* was himself arrested June 25. Neto has said that, after his own departure, Luanda's ranking mulatto prelate, Msgr. Manuel Mendes das Neves, remained in contact with the UPA through a party courier, Correira Mekuiza. Mekuiza, he said, delivered UPA material to das Neves, which he in turn discreetly acknowledged by sending back newspaper clippings with dates written in by his own hand.

an initial contact with an Ochimbundu student, Jonas Savimbi, who had fled Portugal to escape harassment from PIDE and had enrolled at the University of Fribourg, Switzerland. An opinion leader among the Ovimbundu and other Angolan students in Europe, Savimbi had already been contacted by the MPLA. He was now presented with an alternative option but held back from an immediate commitment.[50]

On the diplomatic front, Roberto paid his third visit to Tunisia in January. There he solidified a deepening relationship with President Bourguiba and his *Néo-Destour* government.[51] En route to Tunis Roberto met in Rome with Gil Clemente and another member of the Portuguese opposition that was led by General Humberto Delgado. The meeting failed, however, to establish a basis for cooperation, which could only come, according to the UPA, when the Delgado group declared itself unequivocally on the question of self-determination.[52]

In February, after the outbreak of violence in Luanda, the UPA sent a memorandum to the Security Council urging that the United Nations go beyond the General Assembly resolution of December and press Portugal for an "immediate and unconditional withdrawal" of all its troops and the liberation of all political prisoners in Angola.[53] Then Liberia's move on February 20 to seize the Security Council with the Angolan issue provided the UPA with a clear and fateful opportunity to synchronize a limited act of violence with discussions at the United Nations, a technique that had been used earlier with considerable effectiveness by both its Tunisian mentors and the Moroccans in order to hasten their independence from France.

Within the UPA, opposition to plans for organized protest action sufficiently widespread and provocative to influence the course of diplomatic debate had been eliminated in the December showdown over party leadership. The "moderate" faction, consisting

[50] Savimbi later wrote that in February 1961 he sent a letter to both the MPLA and UPA in which he stated that he could not join either party, given their state of disunity. See Jonas Savimbi, "Où en est la Révolution Angolaise," *Remarques Africaines* (Brussels), No. 21 (Nov. 25, 1964), p. 7.

[51] The UPA party organ was still reporting such external ventures as undertakings of a Mr. J. Gilmore, who was in this instance received on January 28 at the Tunis headquarters of the *Néo-Destour*. *A Voz da Nação Angolana* (Léopoldville), Vol. 2, No. 2 (Feb. 2, 1961, mimeo.), p. 4.

[52] *Ibid.*

[53] UPA, "Memorandum presenté au Conseil de Securité des Nations Unies par l'Union des Populations de l'Angola" (Léopoldville [1961], mimeo.).

largely of Bazombo who had earlier belonged to Assomizo, then founded the *Mouvement de Défense des Intérêts de l'Angola* (MDIA) and declared themselves anti-Communist, anticolonialist, and in favor of negotiations with Portugal.[54] Leadership of the splinter party was assumed by Albert Matundu, president, François Ndombe, vice-president, and, most prominently, Jean Pierre M'Bala, secretary-general and prime mover of the organization. Having lived all his life in the Congo, M'Bala, born circa 1929, was a member of that generation of Angolan émigrés sometimes referred to as "Congolans," who spoke Kikongo and French, but little or no Portuguese. This was not to deter him, however, from becoming the main architect of an MDIA policy of collaboration with Portugal.

Publicly, the UPA's policy of nonviolence did not change. The party denounced the MDIA dissidents for their tendency toward Bakongo separatism but denied that it had refused to negotiate with the Portuguese. In an issue predated March 16, the official party organ restated that the UPA, as indicated by its platform, was "peaceful," but added a bit vaguely that in this regard it would be guided by "the attitude of the Portuguese government." [55] Certainly, by this time, "the attitude of the Portuguese government" had thoroughly convinced Roberto and other UPA leaders that

[54] Though their departure from the UPA dated back to December 1960, and the creation of their new party to January 22, 1961, it was only on March 1, 1961, that the MDIA group published a statement in the *Courrier d'Afrique* giving their version of what had happened. Under the caption, "Split within the UPA" they listed their grievances against their former associates as: (1) the "dictatorial attitude" of "so-called responsible founders" of the party; (2) their refusal to negotiate with Portugal; (3) the monopolization of international travel by one party member (aimed at Holden Roberto); and (4) the absence of a proper accounting system for party funds. The statement was signed by the following list of dissidents, with the position they claimed to have held within the UPA indicated in parentheses: Albert Matundu (general vice-president), Jean Pierre M'Bala (secretary-general), François Ndombe (responsible for scholarship matters), P. Kumbundu, Martin Nsumbu, Augustin Kaziluki (assistant director, political bureau), André Mwanza (secretary, political bureau), Francisco Mayembe, Michel Lusweki, and Léon Katende. The MDIA statement was followed immediately by a UPA rejoinder, which said that in fact the MDIA group had left some three months previously and that there was now complete unity within the ranks of the UPA. Indicative of the make-up of the UPA's new leadership, this rebuttal statement was signed by: Holden Roberto, [Anibal de?] Silva Melo, J. Pinock Eduardo, Borralho Lulendo, Octavio Belo, Pedro Rana, Rosário Neto, Alexandre Taty, Manuel Peterson, Frederico Deves, Barreiro Lulendo, Pedro Visão, António Luiz, and Luis Inglês. Absent from the list was the name of Barros Necaca. *Courrier d'Afrique,* Mar. 2, 1961.

[55] *A Voz da Nação Angolana,* Vol. 2, No. 4, Mar. 16, 1961.

Lisbon was not prepared to make meaningful concessions to Angolan nationalism. Commenting in retrospect, Roberto charged that to ceaseless requests that it "enter into negotiations for the decolonization of Angola" the Portuguese government had only repeated "the dogma of Portuguese Angola," and to each peaceful protest the Portuguese military had "replied with massive executions, deportations and intensified repression." [56] Angolans were thus constrained, he said, to use violence to obtain their independence.

In planning for action to coincide with the Security Council meeting, Roberto wished to avoid a repetition of the earlier ill-fated king palaver and demonstrations at São Salvador (1955–56). This time Africans were to be armed and primed for "defensive" action and not left to the mercy of the police.

Roberto personally confided his plans to his friend and revolutionary mentor, Frantz Fanon. The latter's widow, Josie Fanon, recalled later that, during a visit with them in Tunis shortly before the uprising, Roberto had commented in her presence: "Pay close attention to March 15th, the day of the debate in the U.N.; some very important things are going to happen in Angola." [57]

Widespread arrests in Luanda and elsewhere notwithstanding, had the Portuguese administration been alert, it would have taken preventive military action during this period and not allowed itself to be taken by surprise. This is the inevitable conclusion to be drawn from the observations of politically sensitive foreign missionaries then in Angola. One of those who sensed the impending explosion, Rev. Clifford Parsons, has written: "With some naïveté, [the UPA] made it known that something was going to happen on 15 March; but the authorities refused to take the warning seriously, so that the initial onslaught was a terrifying success." [58]

A Match to Dry Kindling

The uprising was organized in part by a number of young UPA militants who had been building an underground organization inside Angola for quite some time. Illustrative is the work done by

[56] Roberto, "Angola and Portugal."

[57] *World Outlook* (Paris), Vol. 2, No. 9 (Feb. 28, 1964), p. 19.

[58] Parsons, "The Torment of Angola," p. 73. Perry Anderson, director of the *New Left Review* (London), described the March 15 attacks as so overwhelming that "practically all" of Northern Angola was in nationalist hands a few days later. *Le Portugal et la fin de l'ultra-colonialisme* (Paris: François Maspero, 1963), p. 108.

a youthful (born 1939) party organizer from Nova Caipemba, Manuel Bernardo Pedro. At seven years of age he toiled alongside his mother as a contract laborer in a brick factory. After five years of this he was put to work on a European farm. Deprived of formal schooling, he was taught to read by his father. It was during a trip to São Salvador in November 1959 that he encountered the UPA. The local UPA chief organizer, Frederico Deves (born circa 1920), an African coffee farmer, tested him during a trial period of four months. Deves then instructed him and a group of his colleagues at Nova Caipemba in the art of building a clandestine political organization. In addition to mobilizing the Nova Caipemba area for the UPA, Pedro subsequently worked as a party messenger-propagandist as far south as Ucua, less than forty miles from Luanda. He and two of his fellow party workers were called to party headquarters in Léopoldville in late 1960. About February 28, 1961, they and others like them were sent back inside with instructions to prepare an uprising for March 15. Manuel Bernardo Pedro was given the job of readying the area of Nova Caipemba, Carmona (Uige), and Songo; Pedro Vide was assigned to an area closer to Luanda, i.e., Dange, Quicuzo, and Quitexe; and Pedro Santos was sent to the region of Nambuangongo, Quimbumbe, Quicabo, and Puri.[59]

On March 10, in the "bush" near Nova Caipemba, Pedro spoke to a revolutionary rally which he estimated at 3000 persons. His instructions to them were to burn bridges, crops, houses—to destroy property but not persons. The destruction of communications and transportation facilities, especially airfields, was given top priority. The fever of rebellion was mounting. Some workers on isolated coffee plantations, or *fazendas,* began attacking their *colon* bosses as early as March 12. By the morning of March 15, from the Primavera farm to the area around the coffee capital of Carmona, swarms of vengeful Africans armed with *catanas,* a few stolen rifles, and any blunt instrument they could lay their hands on had unleashed their bitterness in an indiscriminate deluge of violence.

In a subsequent analysis of these events based on a visit to Angola that April and on local missionary accounts, Rev. Parsons of the Baptist Missionary Society in London concluded that the guerrilla attacks of March 15 gave evidence of "little coordination" among different bands. The attacks pointed to loose over-all strategy based

[59] Based on interviews with Manuel Bernardo Pedro, Léopoldville, Aug. 1963.

on independent assaults against "isolated farms, commercial settlements and Government outposts, while at the same time disrupting communications by the destruction of bridges and ferries, the felling of trees and the digging of ditch-traps in the roads." [60]

On March 10 when final plans for synchronized incidents inside Angola had been completed, Roberto had left Léopoldville for the Security Council meeting in New York. By March 14 João Batista's military commissioners had moved inside in support of party organizers with orders to try to get African soldiers to defect and join the nationalists. Roberto gave a press conference in New York on March 15. He once again excoriated Portuguese colonialism and vaunted his movement's strength, claiming that the UPA now had 40,000 regular members and over half a million sympathizers.[61]

It was only gradually over the next ten days that reports from Angola revealed the extent of what was happening there. A general, not a limited, uprising was convulsing the northern part of the country. In an interview with *The New York Times* published on March 20, Roberto was quoted as deploring the "extreme violence" of African attacks on Portuguese settlers, attacks whose ferocity he described as an "expression of desperation against Portuguese terrorism over the past five hundred years." Allowing that UPA militants were involved in the assaults, he denied that they were acting on party orders (to destroy lives) and added, "We are deeply sorry that women and children have been killed." In this interview—which the MPLA subsequently cited as evidence of the "spontaneous character of [a] popular rebellion which, later on, the UPA claimed to have organized" [62]—Roberto expressed his fear of more violence by rebelling farm workers (*contratados*) unless the Portuguese made clear their intention to abolish forced labor. At the same time he identified himself as "a revolutionary" because "a Christian who remains silent before a crime becomes a partner in that crime." Bearing in mind American disenchantment with events in the Congo since its independence, he added: "We are trying to educate our people politically—to convey [the idea] that independence will not be won easily, and [that] freedom, once won, means

[60] Clifford Parsons, "The Making of a Revolt," in *Angola: A Symposium,* p. 66.

[61] "Statement of Mr. Holden Roberto, President of the Union of the Population of Angola" (New York, March 15, 1961, mimeo.).

[62] MPLA, "Dez Anos de Existência, Dez Anos de Luta em Prol do Povo Angolano" (Dar es Salaam, Feb. 4, 1967, mimeo.), p. 5.

discipline and responsibility. We are trying to insure against Angola's becoming another Congo."

Before hurrying back via Tunis [63] to Léopoldville, where Batista and others were clamoring for arms, Roberto addressed a memorandum to the United Nations in which he blamed Portuguese brutality for the outbreak of violence and made "a desperate and pressing appeal" for an "impartial Commission of Inquiry to visit Angola in order to ascertain the responsibility for the serious events which have recrudesced [*sic*] and in order to put an end to the useless bloodshed and to all the ills inflicted upon the weak and defenseless people by Portuguese ruffians under the facetious pretext of 'mopping-up operations among foreign elements.' " [64]

Once again the absence of free reporting renders an assessment of casualties approximate at best. The only third-party, on-the-spot accounts came from missionaries. Caught by surprise, perhaps 250 Portuguese civilians were killed during the first few days of the uprising, a figure which may have been closer to 750 by the end of three months.[65] Although UPA instructions from Léopoldville had reportedly been to attack property and not persons,[66] the leadership had underestimated the volatility of popular discontent and thus the sort of explosion that it would set off. Using what Roberto has termed their "garden tools," roving bands of Africans attacked any Portuguese within reach. As Rev. Parsons put it: "There were mutilations. It was a chilling demonstration of what the release

[63] "Conférence de presse donnée par Monsieur Gilmore, Président de l'Union des Populations de l'Angola à Tunis le 21.3.1961" (Tunis, 1961, mimeo.).

[64] "UPA Memorandum to UN," p. 10.

[65] Estimates by Rev. F. James Grenfell. Also see LeMaster, "Horror in Angola," p. 54. Hélio Felgas estimated 300 Europeans "assassinated" in the Nambuangongo area, as many more in the Dange-Quitexe region, and 200 in the north of the Congo district—the worst "massacre in memory in all Africa," *Guerra em Angola*, p. 33.

[66] Cyrille Adoula, at that time Congolese minister of interior, was told that these were the instructions given them when he talked with Angolan refugees during a visit to the frontier area shortly after the uprising began. Speech by Adoula, March 15, 1963, in FNLA's *Angola* (Léopoldville), Vol. 1, No. 3, Apr. 10, 1963. On April 1, 1961, according to the UPA, it issued new instructions to party militants in the light of the killing that followed the March 15 attacks. These read in part: "Your operations should be essentially military or paramilitary in nature and any violence which may occur as a result of your actions should be directed against military forces sent to repress your activities. Under no circumstances will violence against Portuguese women and children be condoned. Let our struggle for liberty not be stained with the blood of innocents" (Léopoldville, unpublished typescript).

of long pent-up feelings can do."[67] This aspect of the revolt was to be stressed later by Portuguese and pro-Portuguese publicists, describing what they viewed as the valiant defense of white Christian Portuguese against black heathen tribalists.[68] About this, James Duffy commented that ". . . if savagery and atrocities provide the index of tribalism, Portuguese soldiers and colonists are no less atavistic than their African opponents."[69] Indeed the Portuguese responded in like fury. Instead of *catanas,* however, they used machine guns and bombers; six months after the fighting had started African casualties were estimated at 20,000.[70]

Portuguese planes immediately brought in military reinforcements, with NATO trucks and other equipment that had been earmarked for defense of the North Atlantic area, and began striking back with indiscriminate wrath. They even bombed and strafed areas that had not been affected by the nationalist uprising. Rev. Malcolm McVeigh was near Ucua when the fighting started but observed that people in that area were in no way involved. Nonetheless, on March 18, the local *chefe de posto* asked him to leave immediately because the villages of the region were to be bombed —and they were. White militia roamed and killed at will. Protestant pastors and church members in the Mbundu areas of Golungo Alto, Ambaca, Dondo, Cacuso, and Libolo, "areas that never experienced any real rebel activity, were taken and many killed." A "reign of terror" had begun.[71]

To the northeast, at Quibocolo in the Bazombo country, Rev. David Grenfell reported much the same story. Though there had been no fighting in that area, on April 24 Portuguese aircraft dropped fire bombs and machine-gunned the nearby villages of Duimba, Condo, and others. By 6:00 P.M. a mass evacuation of heavily laden women with children running alongside had begun

[67] Parsons, "The Torment of Angola," p. 73.

[68] See Bernardo Teixeira, *The Fabric of Terror* (New York: Devin-Adair, 1965); Ronald Waring, *The War in Angola—1961* (Lisbon: Tipografia Silvas, 1962); Portuguese-American Committee on Foreign Affairs, *On the Morning of March 15* (Boston, 1961); Almeida Santos, ed., *Angola Mártir, Reportagens dos journais de Luanda de 20 de março a 19 de julho de 1961* (Lisbon: Agençia Geral da Ultramar, 1961); and Henrique Gago da Graça, *Angola Mártir, Angola Heróica* (Luanda: Tipografia Angolana, 1961).

[69] Duffy, *Portugal in Africa,* p. 216. For detailed reports on Portuguese counterterror and reprisals, see Len Addicott, *Cry Angola!* (London: SCM Press, 1962), pp. 64–65, 96–98, 107–111, 117–118.

[70] Parsons, "The Torment of Angola," p. 73.

[71] McVeigh, "The Bullets of Civilization," p. 7.

toward the north.[72] They joined a stream of refugees that was to pour 150,000 uprooted Angolans into the Congo before the end of the year.

By overreacting and flaying out with counterterrorism, the Portuguese helped to insure that this insurrection would not be localized and quashed like those of Kasanje and Luanda. Any hope for quickly containing the rebellion was lost when, in the words of a Baptist missionary, "the savagery of the Portuguese reaction kicked and scattered the fire until the whole of the north was ablaze." [73] On their side, nationalist forces found themselves in unexpected control of deserted towns, roads, airfields, and—until they ran out of fuel—vehicles. As surprised as the Portuguese by the extent of this initial success, they were not in a position to exploit fully the disarray of their adversary. They had few modern weapons, only what had been stolen by houseboys, brought over by (African) army deserters, or captured from the Portuguese. Otherwise they had just their *catanas* and *canhangulos*. Furthermore, in spite of the territorial extension of the conflict encouraged by Portuguese panic and bombs, the organized influence of the UPA had penetrated southward from its northern Bakongo base only as far as fringe regions of the Mbundu community, that is, the area around Nambuangongo, parts of the Dembos, and, of course, multiethnic Luanda, where the party had had a small following as early as 1958. This meant that the Portuguese could concentrate their forces in the north and, for purposes of both self-justification and international face-saving, could blame the violence on atavistic Bakongo tribalism. For his part, Roberto continued to express regret over the bloodshed, which, he said, could have been avoided had "the Portuguese government . . . not refused our offer of peaceful negotiations which is still open." "Painful" as it might be, however, he declared that the struggle would now have to "continue until the country is liberated." [74]

From what is known about these events, there is little to suggest that there was within the nationalist leadership either an expectation of or strategy for sustained military action, let alone for a

[72] Rev. David Grenfell, "The Quibocolo Story" (Chronology of events in Bazombo community of Quibocolo during Mar.–June 1961, mimeo. [1961]), p. 4.

[73] Addicott, *Cry Angola!*, p. 11.

[74] From Roberto's press conference at Léopoldville, Mar. 24, 1961, as reproduced in a UPA account of the 1961 uprising, "The Angola Revolution," *Présence Africaine* (English ed.), Vol. 17, No. 45 (1963), p. 159. See also *The New York Times*, Mar. 25, 1961.

direct overthrow of Portuguese rule by force. Attacks restricted to outlying settlements prompted the Europeans to retreat and reassemble in major settlements. There, "inflamed by the reports of outrage on their neighbors," they had time to build up their strength, receive reinforcements by air, brace for nationalist attacks, and then launch a general counteroffensive. Describing nationalist action as "patently hopeless in terms of military logistics," Rev. Parsons attributed faulty African strategy to a complex of motives. These included a compulsive despair over what had seemed to be a constant growth in Portuguese military power, an overoptimistic belief that a limited uprising could cause the Portuguese to break and run as the Belgians had done in the Congo, a conviction that the United Nations would take strong supportive action in recognition of "the essential justice of their cause," and a "naïveté in regard to the effectiveness of guerrilla tactics against the whole panoply of modern warfare." [75]

History will likely record that the Angolans underestimated the tenacity of the Portuguese and overestimated the responsiveness of the "Christian" West. The authoritarian Salazar government was immune to the sort of freely exercised domestic and international pressures of press and organized public opinion that had translated limited violence and United Nations debate into effective inducements for concessions in French policy toward Tunisia and Morocco. In other words, the tactics of "Bourguibism" worked well against the French but not against the Portuguese.

Two years earlier Roberto had predicted in a letter to a colleague that, in the event of an uprising in Angola or Mozambique, "Portugal will have no support, for its colonial system is known for being the most retrograde." [76] Within this idealistic misconception of what motivated the foreign policies of western countries—the homelands of sympathetic missionaries—however, may be found the grounds for later disillusionment with the West and its professed ideals.

In any case, when Roberto returned to Léopoldville in late March, he found that he was expected to equip, reorganize, and sustain an unplanned war. For João Batista, whose commissioners had returned from Angola to Léopoldville in quest of arms, he procured what he could locally—seven rifles, two machine guns,

[75] Parsons, in *Angola: A Symposium*, pp. 67–68.
[76] Letter from Accra dated April 19, 1959.

and some ammunition, according to Batista. On April 10 Batista went with his group back inside with the aim of converting an uncontrolled uprising into a centrally coordinated guerrilla war.

If it was needed, further evidence against the Portuguese conspiratorial theory that there had been a carefully organized Communist invasion of Angola was to come forth with the reporting of British journalist Gavin Young, who crossed into nationalist-held territory of Angola that August (1961). He discovered no signs of a well-trained and equipped Angolan force. On the contrary, he found the rebels "pathetic in [their] poverty and rags," lacking "the most basic supplies." They had a "few last-war Belgian rifles, smuggled out of the Congo" and a few "sporting guns" and submachine guns filched from the Portuguese. But they had no grenades, explosives, mortars, light machine guns, radio sets, or binoculars. Young reported that the rebels he saw "lacked even the most basic military training." They moved through open country "bunched up in a crocodile," failed to send out scouts, posted too few sentries, and made too much noise. "There is," he concluded, "little discipline. . . . The rebels have no knowledge of elementary tactics; an Algerian or a Naga would shudder to see them. Clearly the Angolans desperately need instructors as well as arms." [77]

Retaliation against Protestants

The Portuguese could not entertain the suggestion that they were reaping a bitter harvest of their own planting. They seized upon two outside forces as the principal scapegoats, i.e., Communists and Protestants. Congolese independence and Lumumba's anticolonialism, Afro-Asian hostility toward Portugal at the United Nations, and the activities of Bakongo émigrés (disdained as *"deslocados"*), prophet sects, and political parties were all viewed by the Portuguese as part of the conspiracy.[78] But the Communists and Protestants

[77] *The Observer* (London), August 20, 1961. These observations contrasted sharply with those of a British officer visiting the Angolan front on the Portuguese side who reported: "There is no doubt that amongst the leaders there are specialists in jungle warfare, and for some months past specialist instructors have been training terrorist gangs both in Angola and in the Congo." Waring, "The Case for Portugal," in *Angola: A Symposium*, p. 38.

[78] Felgas, *Guerra em Angola*, pp. 40–59. For the official Portuguese Information Ministry's view of all this, see "The Attack on Portugal in Angola and in the United Nations Organization," *Portugal: An Informative Review* (Lisbon), No. 2 (Mar.–Apr. 1961), pp. 63–82.

were the principal villains, and, though the myth of Communist conspiracy was presented to Atlantic allies as *the* explanation for the revolt, an internationally less plausible myth of Protestant conspiracy was equally, if not more, convincing to the Portuguese themselves. After Chief Buta's revolt of 1914, colonial authorities had blamed his action on a British Baptist, Rev. J. S. Bowskill, and had seriously circumscribed the activities of the Baptist Missionary Society (BMS). This time the Baptists were simply sent packing, and those of their churches and schools that were not destroyed by Portuguese action were closed down. Rev. David Grenfell, who reluctantly left his church at Quibocolo only to resume work among the Angolan refugees at Kibentele, near the Congo-Angola frontier, ended a chronicle of the final days of the Quibocolo station where he had spent twenty-one years with the words: "The place is now a shambles, with doors off and windows broken." [79] In Britain the BMS charged the Portuguese with "utmost barbarism," including the lynching and massacring of tens of thousands of men, women and children.[80]

In Portuguese eyes, Protestants only compounded their sins when they charged that their African pastors and teachers had been singled out for elimination and imprisonment, that forced labor and educational neglect were at the root of the revolt, and that there was "no evidence of Communist agitation." Yet such were the conclusions of the report of an inquiry conducted along the Congo-Angolan border in August 1961 by two British observers, George Thomas, M.P, a former vice-president of the Methodist Conference, and Rev. Eric L. Blakebrough, a Baptist. So convinced were they that the revolt had been an expression of genuine indigenous grievances that the two observers urged against any British economic aid or "gestures which might be interpreted as support for Dr. Salazar's regime." They went on to volunteer that "a review of Portugal's membership [in] the NATO alliance is long overdue in view of her denial of the Christian and democratic principles which are supposed to form the basis of the NATO alliance." [81]

[79] Grenfell, "The Quibocolo Story," p. 10.

[80] *The Guardian* (Manchester), June 19, 1961, and letter from Rev. Clifford Parsons expounding Baptist charges, *ibid.,* July 18, 1961. See also Addicott, *Cry Angola!, passim.*

[81] George Thomas, M.P., and Rev. Eric L. Blakebrough, *Congo-Angola Border Enquiry* (Southend-on-Sea, England: Angola Action Group, 1961), pp. 12, 16, and 20. The former British missionary Len Addicott concludes his sympathetic account of the Angolan uprising, *Cry Angola!,* with a resolution passed unanimously

Given the fact that most Methodist posts lay south or east of the original insurgency, Portuguese action against them was especially gratuitous. Yet it was also a glaring fact that Protestant missions and missionaries, unlike their Catholic counterparts, were not harmed by Africans in the areas of violence. The Catholic church, in the minds of rebelling Africans, was closely associated with the Portuguese administration. As a British Catholic journalist sympathetic to Lisbon has put it, whereas in "most mission countries" the church had sought "to build on indigenous culture, baptising and purifying them, and marrying them to Christian civilization, Portugal still [worked] on the basis that the best way to Christianize is to Europeanize." [82] The church was thus used as an instrument of Portuguese nationalism—the number of non-Portuguese priests was kept to a minimum. And though a few voices were raised by clerics such as the Bishop of Malange, who spoke out in 1959 against the "get rich quick" psychology of Europeans in Angola, Catholic missions were physically attacked in 1961 as symbols of colonial authority.[83] These attacks encouraged distraught settlers to conclude that there was Protestant collusion in the revolt, even where there had not yet been any revolt.

After seventy-six years of work among the Mbundu, the Methodists had built up a total of 292 churches, with 42 resident missionaries, 124 African pastors and 140 African teachers, 10,000 students in 125 schools, a hospital a Quessua, and a clinic in Luanda. "Then," in Rev. LeMaster's words, "the Portuguese went to work." A year later, only eight missionaries were still at their posts, 130 of 165 African pastors and teachers in the Luanda-Dembos area were dead, in prison, or missing.[84] The Luanda clinic was destroyed by a white mob under police escort. White terrorists, inspired by plantation owners who resented Protestant schools, which they held responsible for reducing the availability of farm labor, demolished

---

by the Baptist Union Assembly at Westminster Chapel, May 2, 1961. The Assembly petitioned the British Parliament to "manifest its disapproval" of Portugal's policy of "continuing harsh and oppressive" acts against "many of its subjects" in Angola and went on to "humbly pray" that no military supplies be sent from Britain to Portugal or its overseas territories "while such repressive policy is continued" (p. 144).

[82] Hugh Kay, "A Catholic View," in *Angola: A Symposium,* p. 101. At the time of the revolt there were some 452 priests in Angola, of whom 70 were African. *Ibid.,* p. 102.

[83] *Ibid.,* p. 87.

[84] LeMaster, "Horror in Angola," p. 54.

churches and schools in the countryside. Writing in *The Christian Century* in November 1961, Methodist Bishop Ralph E. Dodge charged that the Portuguese had climaxed a standing policy of harassment and discrimination against Protestants with a reign of terror that had brought the total loss of lives since the outbreak of the revolt to 45,000 Africans as against 1,000 Europeans.[85] Such figures, however, were estimates at best. Moreover Rev. Clifford Parsons, who actually visited the north after the outbreak of fighting, concluded that Portuguese publicity and statistics sought to exaggerate the extent of African atrocities. Specifically he stressed that the Annual Report of the Diamang (diamond) Company, dated June 30, 1961, estimated that only two hundred Europeans had been killed, some two and a half months after the outbreak of fighting.[86] Supporting evidence for such a low estimate of Portuguese civilian losses could also be found in the reporting of on-the-spot missionaries. For example, Rev. F. James Grenfell, who was working at São Salvador at the time of the March uprising, made the following comment on publicity claims that forty Portuguese were killed at Luvo: "I happen to know there were no more than twelve civilians living in the place at that time. It was not attacked until May 1961, and when it was, no one on either side was killed or wounded." [87] In this light the scope and ferocity of Portuguese countermeasures seem to have been even more disproportionate than might immediately have been apparent.

Of the thousands of Africans slain most, according to Rev. Malcolm McVeigh, came "from the better educated, more stable sectors of the African community." [88] Not only Protestants, but Catholic priests, nurses, chiefs, and other educated Africans were singled out in what appeared to religious observers to be a calculated effort "to wipe out" all present and potential African leadership.[89]

Rev. Guilherme Pereira Inglês, an African Methodist minister in

[85] Ralph E. Dodge, "Angola and Protestant Conscience," *The Christian Century*, Nov. 22, 1961, p. 1396. Bishop Dodge charged that Portuguese "deviousness" had been "an offense against the Protestant conscience, which believes in dealing with all religious groups openly and on a basis of equality."

[86] Parsons, in *Angola: A Symposium*, p. 67.

[87] Statement made at Kinshasa, April 26, 1967, with reference to a pamphlet, *On the Morning of March 15* [1961], issued by the Portuguese-American Committee on Foreign Affairs (Boston, 1961).

[88] Quoted in George Daniels, "Agony in Angola," *The Christian Century*, Nov. 15, 1961, p. 1366.

[89] Addicott, *Cry Angola!* p. 111.

his fifth year as district superintendent in the Dembos, remained in his village after most others had fled from Portuguese air raids. There Portuguese soldiers sought him out. He was "beaten, then shot and, along with his local pastor, Christovão da Silva, dumped into the Danges River." [90] Some two hundred miles from the nearest revolt area, at the southernmost edge of Methodist activity, a local pastor, Mateus de Almeida, was arrested and was presumed to have been killed. Four American missionaries were also arrested and imprisoned for three months on charges of running a school for terrorists, teaching courses with hidden meanings, and importing refrigerators filled with guns.[91]

One Methodist pastor and teacher, Rev. Domingos da Silva,[92] has even suggested that it was Portuguese action against him personally that really sparked off the March 15 revolt. He has said that, after having been denounced as a conspirator by a Catholic catechist, he was interrogated on March 14 and asked to sign a collective telegram to the United Nations which professed loyalty to Portugal and opposition to independence. This he refused to do. Warned of danger by the washwoman of a local administrator, he and his family managed to escape their home just fifteen minutes ahead of a lynch mob of white farmers and traders.[93] In his view, shots fired in the mob assault on his home, followed by a rumor that he was dead, "inflamed" the populace and prompted them to launch an attack on the Portuguese in the early morning hours of March 15.

Also central to Rev. da Silva's interpretation of events is his assertion that "all the forces" that attacked in the Dembos and Nambuangongo areas were Mbundu and belonged to the MPLA, and that it

[90] LeMaster, "Horror in Angola," p. 54.

[91] The four were Rev. LeMaster, Fred Brancel, Rev. Wendell Lee Golden, and Marion Way. *Ibid.*, p. 56.

[92] Rev. Domingos Francisco da Silva, born circa 1913, in the Ambaca region of the Quanza Norte district, studied for five years at the Luanda *Liceu Salvador Correia* before beginning a long career as a teacher in Methodist schools. From his first visit to Angola in 1936, Bishop Ralph E. Dodge recalls da Silva as a "rural pastor deeply interested in social questions."

[93] According to da Silva's account, in early 1961 the MPLA sent him into the interior from Luanda, where he had been teaching, so that he could mobilize support and exhort nationalist elements in the Dembos "to back up the revolution immediately when it broke out on the fourth [of February]." For reasons that he has said may remain a "mystery" until after the revolution, African units of the Portuguese army which had promised to join in the February attack failed to do so. Because of this misfire, it follows from his account, no supporting action was then mounted in the Dembos area. Davezies, *Les angolais*, pp. 223–227.

was their attacks that really marked the beginning of the revolution. As for the UPA, he acknowledged that "in a narrow belt to the north of Nova Caipemba there were also some attacks," but asserted that they did not compare in either destructiveness or ferocity with those led by the MPLA.[94]

On the other hand, Rev. da Silva's thesis that the MPLA should be given credit for the March 15 uprising is at variance with the accounts of two other young MPLA partisans who were in the same general area as he at the time, and whose stories appear alongside his in a volume of interviews edited by a French priest, Robert Davezies. According to these two, military instructions to forces in the Dembos came initially from the UPA in Léopoldville and, contrary to MPLA policy, included orders to attack *assimilados* and mulattoes, but not to molest airplanes because the chief of the revolution, a certain "Mbuta Muntu," would be flying in to take command.[95] Instead of claiming MPLA credit for the destructiveness of the March attacks, these two observers criticized the peasant-oriented UPA for allegedly killing educated persons and for causing people to expose themselves to Portuguese bombers.[96] In their description of events they specifically referred to the ambush of a Portuguese military convoy near Ucua in the Dembos as having been executed according to orders received from Léopoldville (from Mbuta Muntu) and to the accompaniment of the rebel commander's cry "UPA!" [97]

Another Methodist minister, Rev. Julião Webba, Mbundu *assimilado,* an active member of the UPA, and pastor in the Dembos village of Mucondo of the Nambuangongo region, has related the following sequence. In late 1960 the local *chefe de posto* sent for

[94] *Ibid., p. 228.* In *Guerra em Angola* (p. 108) Hélio Felgas expressed doubt about MPLA claims [see Andrade, *Liberté pour l'Angola* (Paris: François Maspero, 1962), pp. 44–45] that its members were responsible for assaults taking place "from Ucua to Tombôco" [northeast of Ambrizete]. Instead, he largely blamed UPA "terrorists."

[95] Home from school (Luanda) visiting his father at a village near Quiteche, a young nationalist, referred to here as "Ciel," replied as follows to Davezies' question about how orders were received from Léopoldville: "How? They had men who made the trek from Léopoldville, sent down by Holden. In this way they began to fill peoples' heads with the name UPA, and now everyone had begun to talk of UPA, UPA, UPA, UPA, UPA." *Les angolais,* pp. 31–32; see also pp. 63, 67.

[96] *Ibid.,* pp. 33, 39.

[97] As related by "Gabriel," a young Mbundu from Piri in the Dembos. *Ibid.,* p. 67.

him and advised him to close down the school he had just opened because it was considered to be a menace by Portuguese farmers who wanted workers, not educated Africans that might clamor for independence. The government, according to Rev. Webba, had already decided to arrest all such Protestant and Catholic clergy and teachers as might be spreading subversive ideas. After the attacks to the north on March 15, fears and tensions mounted rapidly and exploded into violence five days later in Nambuangongo. Portuguese planes bombed Mucondo, killing among others Rev. Webba's wife and a son. *Catanas* in hand, the local population, joined by Ovimbundu farm workers, attacked the nearby Portuguese settlement. Then the Portuguese army moved in, and all Protestants became fair targets.[98] Rev. Webba joined another Methodist pastor, a mulatto who had been for several years a UPA activist in Luanda and Nova Caipemba, Rev. Fernando Pio Amaral Gourjel, and together they made their way to Léopoldville where they offered their services to Holden Roberto and the UPA.

To all of this it should be added that the African in general, and the Protestant African in particular, was not the only victim of the government's decision to repress the Angolan insurrection mercilessly. Psychologically, the Portuguese soldier or vigilante also suffered. Just how has been described in a striking eyewitness account of the first months of fighting written by a Portuguese doctor whose conscience forced him to defect and seek asylum in Brazil. Dr. Mário Moutinho de Padua saw the war brutalize Portuguese soldiers and turn them into hardened men who competed for kills like game hunters, and who collected the ears of dead Africans as souvenirs.[99] Most significant of all, the grievances of the poor, often illiterate Portuguese foot soldiers and the muted idealism of their relatively well-paid young officers could all be turned with cathartic relief away from the Salazar regime, the real source of oppression for their own people. The rebellion offered the government an opportunity to deflect and redirect latent popular dis-

[98] In an interview taped by George Houser at Léopoldville, Jan. 1, 1962, Rev. Webba described the fate of some of his colleagues: "The fascist soldiers cut off the arms of Rev. [Guilherme Pereira] Inglês after shooting him with seven bullets. Before dying, he asked to be allowed to pray. Rev. Cristovão was crucified. The Portuguese assassins violently pulled out the eyes of Rev. Manuel André, but he said, 'I can teach the Word of God without eyes or mouth. I teach with my heart.' "

[99] Mário Moutinho de Padua, *Guerra em Angola, Diário de um Médico em campanha* (Sao Paulo: Editôra Brasiliense, 1963).

content into a furious campaign to smash the rebelling African. In the process Angola's adversaries were all losers.

PIDE and Prison: Zones of Silence

As part of their argument that all the violence in Angola had been the work of foreigners, whether Communists, Protestants, or Bakongo tribalists, the Portuguese generally insisted that only those northern portions of the territory exposed to external infiltration offered any opposition to continued European rule. In order to protect the credibility of this thesis they had to suppress all news about such events as the cotton strike and Maria's War in Kasanje.[100] They also encouraged the notion that the Africans of central and southern Angola were especially pro-Portuguese. Reacting to this official view, Rev. McVeigh has commented that by their "constant reiteration that the Bailundos [and other South Angola people] are loyal, [the Portuguese] hope to divide the Africans into two camps. They recognize that the most valuable African weapon is unity." [101]

There is good reason to believe that the myth of a happy, docile Ovimbundu community has also owed much of its credibility to the silencing impact of PIDE and the absence of a free press or free speech. As mentioned earlier, at least one rebellious group of young Africans centered in the Lobito-Nova Lisboa region had determined to launch an insurrection—on April 2, 1961.[102] Their principal organizer, fund raiser, and propagandist, Julio Cacunda, traveled all over the country from Sá da Bandeira to Luanda, spreading tracts and holding palavers. The uprising in the north spurred him to redouble his efforts to contact soldiers and collect arms for his own campaign.[103] He journeyed from his home base at Bocoio (or Vila Sousa Lara), a small town a few miles inland from Lobito, up the railroad to Vila Luso and south to Sá da Bandeira, distributing typewritten flyers in Umbundu, some of which read: "Freedom is coming. Now the time has come. Show yourselves so that we can

[100] In his April 1961 "Memorandum" to the United Nations, Holden Roberto charged that, already during December 1960, 216 Africans had been killed and their bodies buried by fearful Portuguese authorities in the villages of Cacuaco, Golungo Alto, and Funda. See "UPA Memorandum to UN," p. 5.

[101] McVeigh, "The Bullets of Civilization," p. 7. For such a description of the loyal Bailundu as "hero," see Felgas, *Guerra em Angola,* pp. 37 and 97.

[102] See p. 111.

[103] Luciano Kassoma, "The Outbreak of the Angolan Revolution in the South" (Lincoln University, 1965, unpublished typescript).

save our country from the whites. Freedom! On the 2nd of April wherever you see a white man, kill him." [104]

Portuguese authorities, nervous since the outbreak of fighting in the north, discovered some of Cacunda's tracts while searching African dwellings in Balombo. They arrested him and colleagues such as Arão Cunga, hauled them off to the Mombaka prison in Lobito, and there reportedly executed them. Leaving aside the question, whether the rather disorganized, idealistic activities of these hapless young men really constituted a serious threat, the reports of missionaries in the area confirm that the government carried out mass arrests during this period in Bocoio-Balombo, Andulo, Bailundu, and neighboring regions.[105] According to Africans present at the time, the police shipped a boatload of persons presumed to be infected with nationalist sentiments to sea, and that was the last that was heard of them. European vigilantes, *dragões de Angola,* backed by the army, hunted down educated Africans, raided villages, and killed untold hundreds suspected of nationalist sympathies. Europeans such as Dr. António Ferronha, a Portuguese teacher at Nova Lisboa, who interceded on behalf of the Africans, were arrested. Surveillance over and restrictive measures against American and Canadian missionaries intensified. The government radio station at Silva Porto employed Africans to broadcast in Umbundu and other vernacular languages an official version of events in the north. Their broadcasts combined anti-Americanism and exhortation to reject the rebels of the north because they were killing loyal "Bailundu" soldiers (recruited to fight them).[106] Yet the fires of nationalism were not stamped out.

By May African nationalists had formed a new underground

[104] "Eyovo lu Viali. Kaliyi otembo ya pitila. Limalehi oco tu popele ofeka yetu ko vindele. Eyovo! Eteke lia vali ko sai ya kupupu apa posi wa muili ocindele pondi."

[105] Dr. Ian Gilchrist of Canada, among others. In his book, *Angola in Ferment* (Boston: Beacon Press, 1962), Rev. Thomas Okuma cited the Portuguese campaign against Protestants in the Bocoio area during Easter week [1961]: "The Protestant pastor and church elders were arrested and beaten by the police. They were accused by the *chefe de posto* of being leaders of a terrorist plot" (p. 89). Dondi Mission sources have reported that the casualness with which he submitted to arrest and the confidence he expressed about an early release suggested that Arão Cunga's behavior was not that of some one whose actions might justify arrest. On the other hand, the mere fact that Cunga, who was completing his last year of *liceu,* had indicated a desire to study law was sufficiently daring in itself to get him into trouble with suspicious authorities.

[106] See *The Atlantic,* Vol. 209, No. 3 (Mar. 1962), p. 28.

organization in Lobito, the *Comitê Secreto Revolucionário do Sul de Angola.* It regrouped a number of those who had been involved in Julio Cacunda's movement and who were determined to profit from the lesson of his recent fatal experience. They organized quietly as a small, clandestine committee and avoided any flamboyant action such as the distribution of party cards and political tracts. The Secret Revolutionary Committee cautiously built and maintained a new nationalist underground under the leadership of three Lobito residents: Osseia Oliveira Chinyama, president, Adão José Domingos Kapilango, vice-president, and Luciano Kassoma, secretary.[107] The severity of police repression dictated a policy of caution and total secrecy during the remainder of 1961. (According to Portuguese sources, the police uncovered three alleged "terrorist" plots centered in other Angolan coastal communities during June: at Porto Alexandre, Baía dos Elefantes, and Novo Redondo.)[108]

In May 1961 nearly five hundred miles to the east along the railroad from Lobito in the district of Moxico, a very different kind of effort was made to organize Africans. The president of *Ukwashi Wa Chokwe,* Smart Chata, sent a representative, Paulo Ndala, from Northern Rhodesia to make contact with Chokwe chiefs and commoners at Leua, Luso, and Lumége with the idea of forming a branch of the Chokwe self-help association inside Angola. Ndala learned that Ambroise Muhunga of ATCAR had already written from Elizabethville seeking support for his movement, but that Muhunga and his organization had been judged too political for what the situation in Angola would then allow. Ndala presented the *Ukwashi Wa Chokwe* as a nonpolitical mutual-aid association, however, and won local acceptance for it. (The Chokwe of the Lunda district to the north, on the other hand, appear to have had considerable and protracted contact with ATCAR.)

Ndala persuaded a teacher by the name of Lwiji Cemp to take on the task of organizing a local branch of the association in cooperation with the chiefs. Cemp gained the approval of the district governor at Luso for the association's constitution, which emphasized its educational purposes, and the matter was then sent on to the governor-general in Luanda for final action. After a delay of some weeks, however, the order came back to arrest Cemp, impose travel restrictions on the chiefs of the area, and proscribe the new organi-

[107] Other members included Jeremias Cussia Arão Chinhundo, Noé Adolfo Capinala, Abreu Moises Kayaya, and Castro Tadeu. Kassoma, "Outbreak."
[108] Felgas, *Guerra em Angola,* p. 115.

zation. Viewed by the governor-general and PIDE as a potential incubator of trouble, the *Ukwashi Wa Chokwe* was denied a legal existence inside Angola. As for Cemp, he reportedly spent two months in prison before being released on the condition that he report weekly to the local administration.[109]

It was just such negative reactions to the slightest signs of independent collective action by Africans that persuaded an increasing number of politically sensitized and geographically well-situated young men from the southern half of Angola that they should join the rebellion in the north. Already an untold number of Ovimbundu working as *contratados* on coffee farms of the north had leagued up with Bakongo and Mbundu peasants fighting the Portuguese. And as the insurrection demonstrated its staying power, more southern soldiers deserted from the Portuguese army, in which they figured rather prominently and, when it was possible and they were not caught, they escaped to the Congo. There they joined the UPA's fledgling military organization which by midyear had been given a formal structure with southern leadership. In addition to the Cuanhama officer, João Batista, the nationalist forces were headed by a Ganguela, Marcos Xavier Kassanga, born on March 20, 1937, at Vila Artur de Paiva. Kassanga studied for four years at the Seminário de Caála near Nova Lisboa and then at a private school in Sá da Bandeira, where he has said he was associated with the *União dos Naturais de Angola* (UNATA). Drafted into the army in 1957, he attended an infantry school for noncommissioned officers at Nova Lisboa before being stationed at army headquarters in Luanda. In February 1961 he joined a small group of nationalists at Luanda in a dash to the Congo, where he promptly sought out the UPA. Professional military skill was sorely needed after the northern rebellion broke out, and in June Roberto converted João Batista's military commission into an Angolan National Liberation Army (*Exército de Libertação Nacional de Angola* [ELNA]), appointed Kassanga chief of staff in Léopoldville, and made Batista field commander inside Angola. Roberto himself, however, assumed the over-all position of commander-in-chief.[110]

Commander Batista established his military headquarters in the forest near Bembe, south of the M'Bridge River, and set about

[109] Information for the two previous paragraphs from Smart Chata, interview, Lusaka, May 12, 1967.
[110] *Le Monde,* June 9, 1961.

trying to structure a chaotic, free-wheeling rebellion into a coordinated guerrilla war. For a longer-term answer to military needs Roberto turned to North Africa. On May 4, *Le Monde* carried an item from Tunis, little noted at the time, saying that Roberto had acknowledged that he was now receiving political and military counsel from the Algerian FLN. In fact, while giving Kassanga and Batista the job of holding down the fort, he had sent some two dozen others, mostly ex-army men, to be trained by the Algerian Liberation Army as the nucleus of an ELNA officer corps.

CHAPTER FIVE

FOUR ANGOLAN RESPONSES TO THE NORTHERN REBELLION

Referring to the failure of past uprisings to overthrow Portuguese colonial rule, Holden Roberto wrote in late 1961: "Perhaps the most important thing that has been lacking these years has been a suitable jumping-off place for an armed force. Independence for the Congo resolved this problem." [1] What he did not say was that for the UPA, which was well ensconced in Léopoldville and possessed the necessary political contacts, operational experience, and knowledge of local affairs to work effectively from there, Congolese independence represented a great advantage over political rivals, in particular, the MPLA. This advantage became even more pronounced as a result of the sequential explosion of January to March 1961.

The MPLA: For Revolution by Coalition

Under the circumstances, it was predictable that the People's Liberation Movement would respond with a certain sense of urgency to the northern uprising by resuming its campaign for a common front of all Angolan movements. From its headquarters in Conakry the MPLA launched a twofold, diplomatic-political offensive designed first to gain increased international support and then, with this added bargaining power, to persuade the UPA to agree to a common-action front that would give it access to that strategic "jumping-off place," the Congo.[2]

On the international side, the MPLA chalked up some notable

[1] Holden Roberto, "The Angolan Revolution" (New York, 1961, unpublished typescript).

[2] Mário de Andrade stressed the case for such a common front in a letter published in *Le Monde,* Apr. 1, 1961.

gains. In March while the UPA was preoccupied with trying to give some direction to affairs on the home front, an MPLA delegation attended the Third All-African Peoples' Conference in Cairo, where, in the absence of UPA representation, Mário de Andrade was elected to the Conference Steering Committee, replacing Holden Roberto. Though the Conference resolution on Angola did not expressly recommend a common front of Angolan nationalist movements, it did warn against "imperialist or neocolonialist" maneuvers tending to provoke "divisions among the people." [3] The MPLA also participated in the third session of the Council of the Organization of the Afro-Asian Peoples' Solidarity Conference, held in April at Bandung.

Also in April 1961 the MPLA and its allies in FRAIN, who before that were allied in MAC,[4] convoked a new gathering of nationalist movements from Portuguese colonies in Casablanca. During their meeting (April 18 to 20), which opened with an address by Andrade, they dissolved FRAIN and formed a new coalition, the *Conferência das Organizações Nacionalistas das Colónias Portuguêsas* (CONCP).[5] The core of the grouping remained, as it was in the two earlier versions, the tandem of the MPLA and the *Partido Africano da Independência da Guiné e Cabo Verde* (PAIGC).[6] The UPA declined an invitation to attend. Had it been present, it would have been under great pressure to join the new interterritorial group CONCP, and that in itself would have represented a step in the direction of agreeing to a common front with the MPLA. The UPA later publicly claimed that its absence was unavoidable. As of April 1961, Morocco was one of those countries (Casablanca powers) where persons resident in the Congo-Léopoldville were not permitted to visit under penalty of being barred from re-entry into the Congo, a fact that the UPA said it had explained privately at the time to the Conference organizers.[7]

[3] MPLA, *Angola, Exploitation esclavagiste, Résistance nationale* (Dakar: A. Diop, 1961), p. 60.

[4] *Frente Revolucionária Africana para a Independência Nacional* and *Movimento Anti-Colonialista.*

[5] For the text of Andrade's opening address, see his *Liberté pour l'Angola* (Paris: François Maspero, 1962), pp. 29–34.

[6] Also present at CONCP's founding conference at Casablanca were representatives of the *União Nacional dos Trabalhadores de Angola* (UNTA), *União Democrática Nacional de Moçambique* (UDENAMO), *Comitê de Libertação de São Tomé e Principe* (CLSTP), *Movimento de Libertação da Guiné e Cabo Verde* (MLGC), and four groups from Portuguese Goa.

[7] GRAE, Ministère des Affaires Étrangères, "Le GRAE et la CONCP" (Léopoldville, Apr. 17, 1965, mimeo.).

The Conference established a joint Consultative Council, elected Andrade president, and set up a permanent secretariat in Rabat, Morocco, headed by Marcelino dos Santos of Mozambique.[8] King Hassan II received the Conference delegates in an audience at Fez,[9] and from that time on Morocco became an important source of support for the MPLA, counterbalancing Tunisia's assistance to the UPA.

As the political part of its April offensive the MPLA sent a two-man delegation to Léopoldville to discuss a draft proposal for a common front with the responsible leaders of the UPA, Aliazo, and the *Mouvement de Libération de l'Enclave de Cabinda* (MLEC). The MPLA project called for the creation of a *Front de Libération de l'Angola* (FLA), which would unite but not merge all Angolan nationalist groups and which during the course of the liberation struggle could evolve toward the status of an Angolan government.[10] According to MPLA sources, their mission met with the executive committees of the three aforementioned parties headquartered in Léopoldville. There was agreement concerning the necessity for creating a front and it was decided that a conference to discuss the structure and program of this front should be held at Monrovia in May.[11]

Aliazo subsequently presented a different version of these April discussions. Its leadership was still rankled by the decision of the MPLA's Conakry executive to disavow its own Léopoldville committee and break up the Aliazo-MPLA alliance of November 1960 to February 1961. Aliazo leadership had also been irritated by a proposal made by Luis de Azevedo, Jr., an MPLA official from Conakry, that together the two parties mount a military effort to rival that of the UPA. According to Emmanuel Kunzika, the Azevedo formula called for Aliazo to provide the men and for the MPLA to furnish the arms. When Azevedo rejected a counter-suggestion that each party muster a contingent of one hundred men,

[8] Assistant secretaries: João Cabral of Goa and Alfredo Bangura of Portuguese Guinea.

[9] *Le petit marocain* (Casablanca), Apr. 23, 1961.

[10] MPLA, "Memorandum aux gouvernements africains sur la formation d'un prétendu gouvernement provisoire de la république de l'Angola" (Léopoldville, Apr. 15, 1962, mimeo.).

[11] MPLA, "Déclaration," at "Conférence de presse de M. Dr. Eduardo dos Santos, membre du comité directeur du MPLA" (Léopoldville, Apr. 5, 1962, mimeo.).

Aliazo officials rejected the Azevedo proposal as iniquitous. Yet they did agree to new discussions. Then at this delicate time, Azevedo made a visit to Pointe Noire in Congo-Brazzaville in order to arrange for the departure of a contingent of MPLA students for Eastern Europe. There he was reported to have made a somewhat premature statement before Aliazo's local Pointe Noire branch. The word received back in Léopoldville was that Azevedo had boasted that "the MPLA had succeeded in uniting around itself such parties as Aliazo and MLEC." Whatever he meant to convey, his remarks were taken by Aliazo leaders to represent a deliberate attempt to give the impression that their party and MLEC "were satellite organizations of the MPLA." [12]

MPLA negotiations with the UPA were stymied by the absence from Léopoldville of the key man to be convinced, Holden Roberto. Talks therefore did not progress beyond the stage of a general agreement that everyone favored unity. Learning that Roberto would be attending the Conference of Heads of African and Malagasy States to be held in Monrovia (May 8–12), however, the MPLA promptly dispatched a delegation headed by Andrade to talk with the UPA leader and to present him with proposed statutes and a "common minimum program" for a united front (FLA).[13]

Support for an entente between the two parties was also being exerted within the top leadership of the UPA. This was evident in the following letter of early May by UPA *directeur politique* Anibal de Melo to a fellow Luandan:

Dear Compatriot Mário de Andrade,

I received your telegram and immediately acted on it. We have all agreed that because it is impossible for any of us here to travel by the date set, inasmuch as we have failed to obtain the passports for which we long ago made requests, there is only one solution: for us to delegate Holden Roberto, who is at Monrovia to attend the Conference of Heads of States, to represent us.

Therefore we have cabled him as follows:

MPLA HAS SET MEETING WITH UPA 20 MAY AT MONROVIA. STOP. HAVE INDICATED ONLY YOUR NAME TO REPRESENT OUR PARTY GIVEN LACK OF PASSPORT[S] UNDERSCORE URGENT NECESSITY THIS MEETING. STOP.

[12] *Partido Democrático de Angola* (PDA), "Conférence de presse" by Emmanuel Kunzika (Léopoldville, Apr. 12, 1962, mimeo.).

[13] See Andrade, *Liberté pour l'Angola*, p. 41. The respective positions that Andrade and Roberto took publicly at the Monrovia meeting concerning both the issue of a common front and other matters are reported in interviews each accorded to Sylvain Camara in *Afrique Nouvelle*, No. 740 (Oct. 11, 1961), pp. 8–9.

and you as follows:

BY VIRTUE NOT YET HAVING PASSPORTS WE ASK YOU CONTACT HOLDEN PRESENT AT CONFERENCE TO WHOM WE HAVE ALREADY COMMUNICATED. STOP.

We so acted in order not to delay the date for the meeting, since we are of the view, as seen even in the text of the cable sent to Holden, that the joining of our efforts constitutes an urgent necessity.

Thus I have lost an opportunity to know you (to be included in the delegation) as well as other compatriots of the MPLA, but for all that I am satisfied because I know that the interests of the *Patrie* have been put above personal interests which can be delayed.

Therefore, I express my hope that our meeting may satisfy all the Angolan family.

Please give our greetings to Viriato da Cruz, Eduardo Santos, Hugo Menezes and Américo Boavida and let them know that I wish them, as well as all the others, good luck in our common labor.

With an embrace, I wish you good luck also.[14]

ANIBAL MELO

Yet in spite of supportive pressure for an accord by some African presidents, notably Fulbert Youlou of Congo-Brazzaville, the MPLA delegation was unable to move Roberto. An MPLA official later recounted somewhat bitterly that "Holden, pretending to be unaware of the substance of the discussions in Léopoldville, refused to discuss problems concerning the creation of the Front." [15] Roberto, at the very least not sharing the MPLA's sense of urgency about the matter, continued to frustrate his rivals. He maintained that he could not undertake negotiations without prior consultation with his own party.

Nevertheless in July Andrade expressed the hope that the leadership of the UPA would yet agree to meet with that of the MPLA and "any other Angolan nationalist movement" so that all Angolan patriots might fight under a "unified command." To this end he invited independent African states "to intervene" in favor of Angolan unity. As our "elders," he said, they could at least determine who sought unity and who opposed it.[16]

Meanwhile the keystone of the MPLA's "foreign policy" consisted in mobilizing Afro-Asian and other anticolonialist forces to bring pressure on Portugal's allies, principally the United States, Great Britain, and West Germany, and in pushing for an economic

[14] Open letter dated May 9, 1961 (Léopoldville, mimeo.).

[15] dos Santos (see ftn. 11 above).

[16] An interview first published by *Afrique Action* (Tunis), July 24, 1961; and then in Andrade, *Liberté pour l'Angola,* p. 41.

and diplomatic boycott to be directed against Portugal. To begin with, Andrade advised, African states that traded with Portugal "could get along without Porto and Madeira wines." [17]

Bakongo Moderates: Continuing the Search for Nonviolent Alternatives

After the outbreak of hostilities, Angolan Bakongo movements opposed to the UPA adopted one of two courses: either they joined in more-or-less open collaboration with the Portuguese or else they held to the increasingly difficult policy of nonviolent resistance to Portuguese rule. The Ngwizako, Nto-Bako, and MDIA were within the first category, Aliazo was in the second.

The Portuguese refusal to allow an Ngwizako delegation to enter Angola on February 17, 1961, did not discourage its organizers from continuing their efforts to elect a new king. They rebounded quickly by sending their president, José Kasakanga, a grandson of Dom Pedro VII and long-time resident of Boma in the Lower Congo, to establish a permanent party office at São Salvador.[18] There on March 3 Kasakanga made a formal inquiry whether a date had been fixed for the election and received a negative reply the next day from the local administrator, Eduardo Pio.[19] On March 11 the Ngwizako leader and two associates, identifying themselves as members of the royal family (Kivuzi clan), sent a letter to Pio, putting on record a statement of their aims, much as they had already set them forth in an interview with the administrator and one Dr. Lopes of PIDE a few days earlier. They explained that they had come to establish residence in their "native land" and to await a government announcement setting the king's election day in conformity with the understanding given them on February 17.[20] They went on to allege that district officers and others had been secretly pressuring the administration to ignore royalist demands and said that if such "provocation" should result in "prolonged silence" concerning the election, Ngwizako would appeal over local heads directly to Portugal. "In any case," they wrote, "we repeat our desire to continue

[17] *Ibid.*, p. 40.

[18] *Courrier d'Afrique,* Mar. 6, 1961.

[19] Information contained in registered letter to the governor of the Zaire district, São Salvador, dated Aug. 19, 1961, São Salvador, and signed by José dos Santos Kasakanga, president-general, and Garcia Monteiro H. Diasuka, counselor and secretary.

[20] See p. 92, ftn. 105.

peaceful and dignified negotiations with Portugal concerning the matter of our king." [21]

The uprising of March 15 interrupted Ngwizako's effort to turn a royal monologue into a new king palaver. In a move to gain some advantage out of the new situation, however, Kasakanga sent the following telegram on April 4 to the governor-general at Luanda:

NGWIZAKO REPROVES TERRORIST ACTS COMMITTED BY OUR RACIAL BROTHERS. STOP. SUCH ACTS ARE CONTRARY TO RESPECT FOR HUMAN PERSONALITY. STOP. NGWIZAKO AFFIRMS ITS DESIRE TO CONTRIBUTE IN RESTORATION OF ORDER NORTHERN ANGOLA IN PERSON OF CONGO KING. STOP. THEREFORE ESTIMATE NECESSARY THAT WE ARE ACCORDED PROMISED AUTHORIZATION FOR ELECTION NEW KING. STOP. OUR VIEW CLOSE COLLABORATION CONGO KING WITH PORTUGUESE GOVERNMENT IS INDISPENSABLE IN THESE TIMES TO RE-ESTABLISH LASTING TRANQUILITY CONGO SO AS TO EFFECTIVELY DEFEND POSITION PORTUGAL BEFORE WORLD. STOP. SIGNAL THAT AT MOMENT CURRENT CLANDESTINE EMIGRATION CONGO POPULATION TO CONGO REPUBLIC CONSTITUTES IN OUR VIEW NEW DANGER FOR CONGO DISTRICT AND GRAVELY COMPROMISES PORTUGAL'S PRESTIGE IN AFRICA. STOP. CURRENT EVOLUTION OF AFRICA CONSIDERED WE REPEAT REQUEST AUTHORIZATION ELECTION CONGO KING TO COMBAT COMMUNIST INFILTRATION OUR TERRITORY. FULLSTOP.

On April 7 Sr. Pio informed Ngwizako that it would not be possible to conduct elections until after the storm had passed. On April 24 he told them, even more negatively, that, in view of the flight of the local population, the election of a king had been rendered quite impossible. What he neglected to say or perceive was that the administration itself was largely responsible for this demographic hemorrhage. São Salvador itself had been free of violence on March 15, although there had been many incidents in surrounding villages. It was Portuguese reprisals against these outlying villages, some of which were burned down, and a new wave of arrests in the town itself by PIDE that had caused some 90 per cent of São Salvador's population to flee. Everyone knew that arrested persons had a habit of "disappearing" from prison and there was thus an incentive for flight before arrest. An eyewitness, Rev. F. James Grenfell, has said that prisoners were simply not present when their relatives took them food. In the absence of any explanation, it was "difficult to avoid the conclusion that they were liquidated," a conclusion "confirmed" by later information. One of the last British Baptists to leave northern Angola, James Grenfell

[21] Letter PG/SS/1/3/61, São Salvador, dated Mar. 11, 1961, and signed by Kasakanga, Diasuka, and André Pecado, counselor.

has affirmed that he could personally supply the names of "over a dozen folk whom I saw arrested and who have never been heard of or seen since." [22]

Kasakanga argued that, at the very least, those people who had not fled should be permitted to elect a regent. This proposal met the same fate as all his others. Then on May 27 he sent another telegram, this time to the overseas minister, Dr. Adriano Moreira, in Lisbon. Revealing his growing frustration, the Ngwizako president complained of government "disregard" for the "legitimate aspirations of the natives of the Congo." "This attitude," he cabled, "is considered by Ngwizako as tacit government support for the Communist action which is taking hold in our Congo." Urging the Portuguese minister to add São Salvador to the itinerary of his scheduled forthcoming visit to Angola in order that he might study the election issue on the spot, Kasakanga warned that Portuguese forces alone could hope to restore only a "superficial peace," but that the situation would remain far from normal so long as the government remained hostile to local aspirations. He also pointed out that African states were reacting to Portuguese policy by taking concerted action that weakened Portugal's international position. An "important part" of the population of the Congo, he said, was still "impatiently awaiting" His Excellency's decision on the kingship.

On July 15 Ngwizako royalists in Léopoldville announced wishfully that the sojourn of their president and other party officials at São Salvador had "given assurance of the beginning of frank negotiations with responsible authorities." Party spokesmen explained that they had initiated a "dialogue" with Portugal in order to persuade the latter to respect the Kongo's international identity, abandon the policy of assimilation, and agree to a program of political reforms leading to self-determination for the (Portuguese) Kongo. Re-affirming their dedication to nonviolence, they also volunteered their good offices for the negotiation of a cease-fire between Portuguese and African nationalist forces.[23] During this protracted "dialogue" Kasakanga made three trips to Luanda [24] but also sent a rather anti-Portuguese "confidential" letter to the BMS

[22] James Grenfell (a nephew of David Grenfell), handwritten notes, Kinshasa, Apr. 26, 1967.

[23] Ngwizako press conference of July 15, 1961, reported in *Mondo* (Léopoldville), No. 3, Sept. 25, 1961.

[24] *L'Homme nouveau* (Brazzaville), No. 122, May 13, 1962.

mission at São Salvador asking for help.[25] In early August he tried to influence Portuguese officialdom with a party tract which juxtaposed his claims to royal descent with charges that Haldane Roberto [*sic*] and the UPA "terrorist" organization had embraced Communist doctrine.[26]

Sadly for him, however, none of Kasakanga's various initiatives bore results. In mid-August he and his secretary, Garcia Monteiro Diasuka, lamented in a letter to the governor of the Zaire district (which included São Salvador) that they had been waiting for three months for an audience with him while the situation in the Portuguese Kongo continued to go "from bad to worse." They repeated their arguments in favor of the immediate election of a king, or at least a regent, and disclaimed any intention of wishing to reunite the separate parts of the old Kongo kingdom, avowing instead that they preferred to leave their Kongo free to maintain its traditional ties with Portugal. Nonetheless, the will to preserve these ties would depend, they warned, "on the generosity of Portugal vis-à-vis the present position of Ngwizako." And only a new king might win back those of their brothers who had been "led into error and transformed into terrorists." Then, slipping into the language of black nationalism, they explained: "In these times only a Negro can penetrate the interior of a brother Negro. This may seem paradoxical but it is thus in the world today." [27]

Grasping at yet another straw, on August 31 Kasakanga cabled the overseas minister in Lisbon again, this time welcoming his recent (August 28) declaration which affirmed government respect for traditional rights in Portugal's overseas provinces. For his part, Kasakanga committed Ngwizako to maintain the Kongo's respect for the Berlin Convention of 1885 and reaffirmed his desire to see "traditional and secular" relations between the Kongo and Portugal continue through the person of the Kongo's king. Specifically, he argued that it was totally contrary to tradition for a queen to assume the regency of the throne and complained that Portuguese authorities had elevated Queen Dona Isabela to this position without consulting the people.

Following up his cable to Lisbon, on September 4 Kasakanga and his associates, displaying more courage than prudence, sent a new

[25] See Appendix C.

[26] Ngwizako, "A Cerca dos acontecimentos na Norte de Angola" (São Salvador?, Aug. 4, 1961, typescript).

[27] Letter of Aug. 19, 1961 (see ftn. 19).

letter to the governor of Zaire in which they chose to interpret the overseas minister's declaration of respect for local traditions as an "implicit authorization for us to exercise our traditional and sacred right without any impediment." Therefore, they wrote, "we respectfully take the liberty of informing Your Excellency that as of September 9, 1961, joined by the king's counselors and the rest of the people, we will begin to deal with the question of selecting a new king." [28] Such boldness was also doomed to failure. On September 8, just one day before the scheduled deliberations were to begin, the Ngwizako representatives at São Salvador sent a rather contrite follow-up letter to the governor, noting that, in spite of the fact that their missive of four days before had cost them forty-eight hours in detention, they wished to assure him that their desire to enthrone a successor to Dom António III was motivated by the "primordial aim of maintaining the friendship that has existed for centuries between Portugal and the Congo."

While Kasakanga persevered in his fruitless pleading at São Salvador, the Ngwizako organization in Léopoldville, optimistically produced a new draft constitution for the Kongo kingdom. Released by the party's "political secretariat," the constitution proposed to concentrate power in the hands of a king elected for life from any of the kingdom's "twelve free and sovereign clans." The monarch was to be chosen by a bicameral legislature composed of a National Council of Resistance, elected by provincial councils, and a Council of State "chosen from among the Kongolese elite," in both of which houses the minimum age would be forty. The king was to take the following oath: "I swear in the name of my illustrious predecessors and my grandparents to observe the constitution and laws of the Kongolese people and to maintain the national independence and territorial integrity [of the kingdom], all in affirming my faith in God." And just to make certain that he did not again sign away his kingdom, no act of the king was to be valid unless countersigned by a responsible minister.

In keeping with Ngwizako's intention that Bakongo compatriots residing in the Congo Republic should return to play a role in the resurrected kingdom, French as well as Portuguese was to be made an administrative language (Kikongo being the "national" lan-

[28] Letter dated Sept. 4, 1961, return address P.O. Box 46, São Salvador, signed by Kasakanga, Diasuka, and Pecado, with copies sent to the governor-general at Luanda and the overseas minister in Lisbon.

guage). For purposes of "technical assistance," the draft constitution provided that "Portuguese, notably those who speak French so that they can have direct contact with the Kongolese elite born and schooled in the former Belgian Congo, will occupy certain top posts in the administration, army, and gendarmerie." [29] Though there was no mention made of a political party in the draft constitution, Ngwizako leaders reportedly had in mind the idea of creating a new governing party, or *União das Populações de Kongo Angola* (UPKA), from which the prime minister and his cabinet would presumably be chosen by the king.[30]

As for the Nto-Bako during this period, in addition to serving the Portuguese as informants, its members cooperated with anti-UPA elements inside Abako in inciting police and army harassment of UPA partisans moving in and out of Angola. More dramatic, however, was a "peace offensive" launched by the third group of Bakongo moderates, the ex- and now very anti-UPA leaders of the MDIA. In July their secretary-general, Jean Pierre M'Bala, traveled to Lisbon where he reportedly presented a petition signed by chiefs and several thousand Angolan commoners to Portuguese Foreign Minister Alberto Franco Nogueira. He put his case for "independence in collaboration with Portugal" and returned with a reward of some forty scholarships for study in Portugal. Then in September a five-man MDIA delegation went to Luanda for discussions with Governor-General Deslandes, and again in October M'Bala made a return trip to Lisbon where, it is claimed, he once again met Nogueira. Finally, at the end of the year (December 26–January 16) a group of MDIA members went on a tour of northern Angola, visiting Maquela, Quibocolo, Damba, and São Salvador.[31]

Yet outside of some pleasant educational travel, a consistently good press in Abbé Youlou's Brazzaville, and possibly some financial aid, it is difficult to see what tangible results the MDIA leaders gained from all these trips. On August 13, nonetheless, the secretary-general presented an optimistic report—before a crowd which he generously estimated at between 7000 and 8000 persons, though Léopoldville's Maison des Combattants could hold at most 1000

[29] Ngwizani a Kongo, "Constitution du Royaume du Kongo" (Léopoldville, Nov. 26, 1961, mimeo.).

[30] D. Grenfell, *Notes* (Kibentele), No. 46, Oct. 19, 1962.

[31] *L'Homme nouveau,* No. 126, June 10, 1962; and MDIA, "Le problème angolais. Textes et documents vus par le comité directeur du Mouvement de Défense des Intérêts de l'Angola" (Léopoldville, July 29, 1962, mimeo.).

persons—in which he praised Lisbon's decision to abolish formally the legal distinction between *assimilados* and *indígenas* and repeated his plea for "peace and liberty through negotiations." [32] In September M'Bala and party president Albert Matundu sent a letter to the United States government, seeking scholarships and restating their faith in the cause of "independence in collaboration with the former colonial power, Portugal, as has been the case with most French-speaking African states." [33]

In Léopoldville the MDIA was widely assumed to be collaborating with the Portuguese Embassy, even to the extent of maintaining an office on the Embassy's premises.[34] Apparently MDIA ranks furnished some of the impecunious African informers who were to help keep the Portuguese government apprised of the activities of Angolan nationalists in the Congo.

The only Bakongo party that held to a nonviolent but uncompromisingly nationalist position was the Bazombo movement, Aliazo. In February, following the collapse of its alliance with the MPLA, the leaders of Aliazo turned their attention toward the possibility of cementing ties with the local line-up of other northern parties, MDIA, Ngwizako, and Nto-Bako, as well as Cabinda's MLEC. The Nto-Bako was negative from the outset, wishing to preserve its freedom of action. The others, however, proceeded with negotiations almost to the point of signing a convention. Then, in the words of Aliazo's Emmanuel Kunzika, "we were surprised by a radio announcement telling of the departure of an MDIA delegation alone to Lisbon," where it seemed to be confident of receiving the grant of "we know not what sort of independence." [35] This MDIA break from the ranks was especially irritating to Aliazo. The MDIA leadership constituted, after all, the same group of Bazombo that had left Aliazo (then Assomizo) to join the UPA in July 1960, attracted, in Kunzika's words, by "the revolutionary propaganda of [the UPA] President, who had just returned from a

[32] *L'Homme nouveau,* No. 86, Sept. 10, 1961.

[33] Letter to Bureau of Educational and Cultural Affairs, Department of State, Washington, D.C., Nov. 16, 1961.

[34] Antoine Matumona wrote that a Portuguese vice-consul at Léopoldville, Raoul da Souza, admitted paying traveling expenses for MDIA trips to Lisbon. See "Angolan Disunity," in *Angola: A Symposium, Views of a Revolt* (London: Oxford University Press, 1962), p. 123. Hélio Felgas described the MDIA as representing "Angolans of good will." *Guerra em Angola* (Lisbon: Livraria Classica Editôra, 1961), p. 149.

[35] PDA, "Conférence de presse" (Léopoldville, Apr. 12, 1962, mimeo.).

long stay in Ghana and Guinea." While in the UPA, this group, he said, had embittered the party's relations with other nationalist organizations. Now, instead of returning to its original associations, i.e., to Aliazo, it appeared to be embarked upon a "counterrevolution" which "consisted of preaching a nonviolence that already had been rendered illogical by the fire [March 15] which it [as part of the UPA] had just ignited."[36] At this point Aliazo dropped its effort to create a Bakongo front, an effort which predated aforementioned and similarly ill-fated April 1961 unity discussions with the MPLA.

After the outbreak of violence in March Aliazo sent a letter to Premier Salazar appealing for negotiations to restore political rights, including the right of self-determination, to the Angolan people. Since "freedom of expression" had been banished in "all forms" within Angola, the letter pointed out that the only way it had of making its voice heard was to sound its "cry of alarm" from outside the country.[37] The Portuguese response to such appeals was simply more repression, as evidenced in what happened to Kunzika's father-in-law, Pedro Sadi, the Baptist pastor at Quibocolo. Sadi, a witness to Portuguese counterterror, who was himself arrested "by mistake" and beaten into unconsciousness, concluded along with thousands of others that there was only more of this treatment, not reform, ahead and trudged north to asylum in the Congo.[38]

At a June press conference Aliazo called for an "entente" among Angolan nationalist leaders in order to eliminate destructive political intrigues.[39] No entente was forthcoming, though one more fruitless discussion of unity reportedly took place with the representatives of the MPLA and MLEC at Aliazo's offices on July 12.[40] During July Aliazo began publishing a "monthly" newspaper, *Mondo,* which under the editorship of Kunzika adopted a generous but politically unorthodox policy of granting space to rival movements, e.g., Ngwizako. Its generosity went unreciprocated.

[36] Quoted from an open letter by Emmanuel Kunzika to António Josias, PDA. Dir. 1503/66 (Léopoldville, July 25, 1966, mimeo.).

[37] An open letter dated Mar. 26, 1961 and signed by André Massaki, Emmanuel Kunzika, Antoine Matumona, Ferdinand Dombele, Emmanuel Ziki, David Livromentos, André M'Vila, and Samuel Silva.

[38] Len Addicott, *Cry Angola!* (London: SCM Press, 1962), pp. 95–96.

[39] Aliazo, "Conférence de presse donnée par l'Alliance des Ressortissants de Zombo 'Aliazo' sur la situation générale en Angola" (Léopoldville, June 10, 1961, mimeo.).

[40] Matumona, "Angolan Disunity," p. 128.

Aliazo, both repelled by the inhumanity and unconvinced of the efficacy of violence, was unwilling to be bought with escudos or manipulated by Portuguese guile. It found itself in an increasingly isolated and beleaguered position as 1961 progressed.

The Cabindans: A Marginal Reaction

Physically separated from the rest of Angola by Congo-Kinshasa's corridor to the sea, the Portuguese enclave of Cabinda was nonetheless caught up in the Angolan revolution. Though perhaps only a tangential issue, it deserves some special consideration. Furthermore, Cabinda's modest proportions, 2895 square miles and 60,000 people, do not give an adequate measure of its importance. Its valuable hardwood forests and plantations (cocoa and coffee) provided economic rewards for some two thousand Portuguese settlers, and this abundance gave rise, in turn, to a lively, competitive interest on the part of both Brazzaville and Léopoldville in this potential African Danzig. As of early 1961 the enclave was administered by a forty-four-year-old, reform-minded district governor, José Barrados. His regime was widely viewed as constituting a progressive and honest contrast to its predecessors, which dated back to the securing of Portuguese sovereignty in 1866.[41]

Inhabited mainly by Bakongo peoples, the enclave is linked demographically to the two Congo republics and historically to the Loango (Vili-speaking) kingdom, which was located in the area astride its borders to the north before it collapsed like the Kongo kingdom under the impact of the slave trade. Not only does the Bavili community of the Pointe Noire region of Congo-Brazzaville extend southward across the border into Cabinda, but over the years some ten to fifteen thousand Bavili and other coastal Cabindans have crossed over to find jobs and settle in and around Pointe Noire. Portuguese traders, who have long controlled much of the commerce in Congo-Brazzaville, habitually hired Portuguese-speaking Cabindans in preference to French-speaking Congolese, thus helping to spread a Cabindan émigré population from Pointe Noire along the railroad to Brazzaville. The relatively well-educated Cabindan mulattoes did particularly well in obtaining posts as teachers, telecommunication operators, and even army officers within the former *Moyen Congo.*

[41] *The New York Times,* Feb. 21, 1961.

In due course this Cabindan émigré population became a source of embarrassment and anxiety for the Portuguese in much the same manner as the Angolans living in Congo-Léopoldville. The continued inflow and outflow of persons and ideas between the enclave and its émigrés provided a conduit for the introduction of modern African nationalism. There are reports that PIDE became sufficiently exercised in 1959 to send its operatives into Congo-Brazzaville in order to kidnap some of those Cabindans who appeared most dangerous.[42]

It was indeed in 1959 that the first signs of an organized and separate Cabindan nationalism became visible in the activities of an émigré group in Congo-Brazzaville known as the *Association des Ressortissants de l'Enclave de Cabinda* (AREC). During 1960 this mutual-aid association underwent a familiar transformation into an overtly political movement, the *Mouvement de Libération de l'Enclave de Cabinda* (MLEC). In August 1960 MLEC sent letters to the Portuguese president, prime minister, and other authorities presenting a long list of grievances, asking for the recovery of Cabinda's independence, and suggesting a monetary union and other links between the enclave and the two Congo republics.[43] Then in September the party issued a communiqué in which it charged that Portuguese police had opened fire and killed ten persons in a crowd of 5000 demonstrating in Cabinda city for the independence of the enclave. MLEC requested a United Nations mission of inquiry.[44] Portugal denied the charges, and there was no international investigation.[45]

The membership of MLEC consisted mainly of coastal Cabindans, i.e., Bavili, Baoio, Cacongo, and mulattoes living in and around the economic and administrative center of Cabinda city. The Mayumbe (or Maiombe) peasantry of the northeast interior constituted a separate, often hostile, minority community, relatively untouched by mission schools or Portuguese settlement. Thus even in tiny Cabinda the familiar coastal-urban versus interior-peasant dichotomy influenced nationalist politics. Resentful of the favored position of the coastal population within the enclave, the Mayumbe remained aloof from MLEC. On the other hand, the rural, peasant-

[42] The author is indebted to Dieudonné Mahoungou and Francisco Xavier Lubota, among others, for background information on Cabinda.

[43] Letter dated Aug. 12, 1960, see *Courrier d'Afrique,* Sept. 27, 1960.

[44] *Courrier d'Afrique,* Sept. 24–25, 1960.

[45] *Ibid.,* Sept. 28, 1960.

oriented UPA was more in tune with Mayumbe political attitudes, and Roberto's party therefore garnered a number of adherents from the Mayumbe community, both within Cabinda and in the border area around Tshela in Congo-Léopoldville.

As part of its program for a sustained and expanded military challenge to Portuguese rule, the UPA relied upon the Mayumbe in extending its military campaign to the Cabinda enclave after the outbreak of fighting in March 1961. Roberto chose a Cabindan, Alexandre Taty, to take charge of the Cabindan sector. Taty, who it will be recalled had left seminary studies in Luanda for Léopoldville where he joined the UPA in 1960, was aided in his assignment by a number of defectors from Portuguese army units stationed in the enclave. Deserters such as António Calvino Manuel Major, an Umbundu-speaking corporal from Novo Redondo on the coast north of Lobito, brought their arms, training, and knowledge of the local Portuguese establishment in Cabinda to the rebels. By the end of 1961 the UPA guerrilla force within Cabinda numbered about three hundred as against a Portuguese garrison force ten times its size.

Guerrilla war and police repression again led to an outpouring of refugees, mostly into Congo-Brazzaville. Reporting on an inspection by President Fulbert Youlou of the reception area around N'zassi and Tchintanzi, the Brazzaville press put the refugee total as high as 7000 by early May 1961.[46] In the face of these events MLEC renewed its appeals for the intercession of the United Nations. In a memorandum signed by its president, Louis Ranke Franque, and secretary-general, José Candide Ramos, the Cabinda Liberation Movement claimed that, by the Treaty of Simulambuco of 1885, Cabinda had become a Portuguese protectorate but not a part of Portugal and, for that matter, not a part of Angola. (Concerning its relations with the nationalist movements of Angola proper, MLEC had participated in common-front negotiations in November 1960 [UPA, Aliazo, MPLA], and again in February [Aliazo, MDIA, Ngwizako] and April [Aliazo, MPLA] 1961, but had entered into no agreements.) The MLEC memorandum to the United Nations went on, rather expansively, to charge that Portuguese atrocities had by this time resulted in 5000 deaths, 1500 deportations, and an out-flow of 44,000 refugees—all this from a total population of 60,000.[47]

[46] *L'Homme nouveau,* No. 68, May 7, 1961; and No. 69, May 14, 1961.
[47] *Ibid.,* No. 87, Sept. 17, 1961.

With due allowance for exaggeration in MLEC's statistics, Cabindans had clearly been sorely affected by the outbreak of fighting in Angola. Whether a free ballot would find them choosing independence as part of Angola, as a separate state, or as an incorporated area of one of the Congolese republics, they and their enclave would be a factor within the over-all nationalist effort to overthrow Portuguese rule.

The UPA: Adding New Structure—and Surviving

The rebellion placed on the UPA apparatus a wide range of new demands for disciplined leadership and both military and financial resources. One of Roberto's answers, as noted earlier, was to send a group of more than twenty men to be trained by the Algerian FLN at their Tunisian bases at Ghardimaou and Melègue. In December a *New York Times* correspondent reported that six Algerian advisors would soon accompany a returning contingent of twenty-five Angolan officer trainees. He quoted an Algerian source at the United Nations as saying that the North African advisors "would particularly stress the importance of political indoctrination along the lines of the Algerian rebels' slogan: 'The leaflet precedes the bullet.' "[48] Anxious not to lose political control over its fledgling National Liberation Army (ELNA) to the army's Arab mentors, however, the UPA ultimately welcomed back its returned trainees without Algerian advisors.

In addition to building a more solid military apparatus Roberto created another subsidiary to complement the work of his party, i.e., a labor union. There were several ways in which such an organization could be helpful. By organizing Angolan émigré workers in collaboration with the Congolese trade unions, it could dramatize the absence of workers' rights inside Angola; it could train leadership cadres for a future professional trade union movement in independent Angola; and it could serve as a funnel through which financial aid from the international trade union movement could be channeled to the Angolan nationalist fight for independence.

An Angolan labor organization in exile had, in fact, already been established in Léopoldville as early as February 1960. Known as the *União Nacional dos Trabalhadores de Angola* (UNTA), it had been founded by French-speaking Bakongo émigrés and had devel-

[48] Lloyd Garrison in *The New York Times,* Dec. 18, 1961.

oped early international ties with the World Federation of Trade Unions (Prague) and political ties with the MPLA. During May 1961, after participating in the founding congress of the All-African Trade Union Federation (AATUF) at Casablanca in April, UNTA secretary-general Pascal Luvuala led a four-man UNTA delegation on a trip to China at the invitation of the All-China Federation of Trade Unions.[49] In the Soviet Union *Pravda* published an article by Luvuala,[50] and a Moscow publisher issued a Russian language edition of an MPLA booklet (*Svobodu Angola*) which asserted that all "progressive" Angolan workers belonged either to a clandestine *União dos Trabalhadores e Operários Negros de Angola* (UTONA), allegedly organized inside Angola, or to the *União Nacional dos Trabalhadores de Angola* headquartered in Léopoldville.[51] UNTA's leadership sent members to Eastern Europe and Israel[52] for training in trade unionism, and in December (4–15) 1961 its deputy secretary-general, Bernard Dombele, attended and addressed the Fifth Congress of the World Federation of Trade Unions (WFTU) at Moscow. At the same time, though not officially affiliated with the MPLA, UNTA consistently supported the latter's common-front policy[53] and acknowledged it as the "vanguard party" of the Angolan revolution.[54]

The idea for creating a labor union linked with the UPA grew out of Holden Roberto's discussions with Tunisian trade unionists in January and again in May 1961. A draft proposal for an Angolan union was submitted in February by a representative of the *Union Générale Tunisienne du Travail* (UGTT) for consideration by Roberto and his party. In May the UGTT secretary-general, Ahmed Tlili, agreed to Roberto's request that the author of the project be sent to Léopoldville as a technical advisor to help put the plan into operation. It was with this assignment that Carlos Kassel,[55] a Cuban trade unionist working for the UGTT, arrived

[49] *The Mizan Newsletter,* Vol. 6, No. 5 (May 1964), p. 6.

[50] *Pravda,* April 30, 1961.

[51] *The Mizan Newsletter* Vol. 5, No. 5 (May 1963), p. 5. MPLA publications which refer to UTONA provide no information about the nature or locale of its activities in Angola.

[52] For example, UNTA sent the secretary of its affiliated *Syndicat National des Enseignants Angolais,* Emile Mbidi, to study trade unionism at the Afro-Asian University of Tel Aviv. *Courrier d'Afrique,* Aug. 31, 1962.

[53] UNTA, *Bulletin-Mensuel,* No. 1 (Léopoldville, Oct. 1961, mimeo.).

[54] UNTA, *Le Travailleur de l'Angola,* No. 4–5 (Léopoldville, Apr.–May 1965, mimeo.).

[55] Also known as Carlos Gacel Castro.

in Léopoldville on May 24, 1961. With the approval of Prime Minister Cyrille Adoula (himself a former trade unionist) and Holden Roberto, Kassel contacted Angolan exiles with prospective leadership ability, and on June 13, 1961, an agreement was drawn up launching the *Liga Geral dos Trabalhadores de Angola* (LGTA).[56]

The new movement was given professional counsel and eventually office and meeting hall space by the Congo's *Fédération Générale du Travail du Kongo* (FGTK). The LGTA's organizing manifesto acknowledged that without FGTK help "the setting up of our League would not have been possible," and the Congolese union exerted considerable influence over its protégé right from the beginning. In spite of close functional ties with the UPA, which were justified as a temporary concession to the exigencies of revolution, the LGTA officially endorsed the "nonpolitical" orientation of western trade unionism as advocated by the Congo's FGTK, Tunisia's UGTT, and the International Confederation of Free Trade Unions (ICFTU), to which both the FGTK and UGTT belonged. Accordingly the LGTA proclaimed that it was "strictly" a labor organization and had grouped together "Angolan workers of all political tendencies, without regard to religion or philosophical doctrine"—which in itself, of course, reflected a clear western, pluralist orientation.[57]

The top LGTA leadership post of secretary-general went to a recent arrival from Luanda, André Martins Kassinda. Born at Nova Lisboa on October 10, 1936, of Sele parents from Gabela, Kassinda was educated in the Catholic schools and seminary of Luanda. His lieutenants included Pedro Rana, Félix Lubota, and Pedro Saldanha Hagalhãos. Within two months of its founding the LGTA claimed 800 members, and branches—more simulated than real—were set up within UPA-controlled villages inside An-

[56] *Le Progrès* (June 12, 1964) published an interview with the LGTA secretary-general, Pedro Barreiro Lulendo, which traced the activities of the organization since its creation in June 1961.

[57] LGTA, Executive Committee, "Manifesto" (Léopoldville, no date, mimeo.), p. 2. A companion document, entitled "Structure et Plan de l'Action," which outlined the LGTA's organizational structure and program, described the union in its Préambule as "politically independent at both the national and international level" and declared that its members were free to belong to any political party they wished. In its statutes the LGTA further undertook to support "all organizations fighting for the independence" of Angola. LGTA, *Estatutos,* Sept. 15, 1961, Art. I, § e 2. But in practice the LGTA supported only the UPA, maintaining that it was the sole organization engaged in real combat.

gola, in order to give popular instruction in the purposes and techniques of trade unionism. With the patronage of the UGTT, the LGTA applied for and obtained membership in and some financial assistance from the ICFTU in Brussels.

In addition to the army and trade union, a third new component was added to the UPA's new complex of revolutionary organizations. With the massive influx of refugees following the explosion of March 1961, there was an urgent need for medical and social relief work. Rather than rely solely on international agencies and local Catholic and Protestant relief programs, the UPA determined to organize a relief effort of its own. Humanitarian considerations aside, such an effort was indispensable if the UPA was to command the loyalty of the tens of thousands of refugees streaming into the Lower Congo.

The UPA's initial relief work was organized by João César Correira Mekuiza, a male nurse trained in Benguela and an early UPA organizer, who had escaped to the Congo from Luanda in 1960. He was joined later in the year by José Liahuca, an Ochimbundu medical student (born May 4, 1929, at Elende-Cuma) who had fled Portugal in mid-1961 shortly before completing his medical degree; Manuel Barros Necaca, the former head of the UPNA and a Dondi trained medical technician; and Dr. Rui Teixeira, an Angolan pharmacist. The son of an African pastor, Liahuca had been educated at Protestant mission schools (Elende and Dondi) before being sent by the United Church of Christ to the University of Lisbon, where he studied to become the first fully qualified physician in the Ovimbundu community of a million and a half persons. Obliged to complete his M.D. at Lovanium University, Dr. Liahuca assumed the directorship of the UPA relief program, which was now organized in a nominally independent, apolitical *Serviço de Assistência aos Refugiados de Angola* (SARA). With its independent format, the refugee service could qualify for international assistance as a nonpolitical agency, even though it remained closely associated with the UPA.

All these UPA activities, of course, depended upon the good will of the central Congolese government. As the war continued refugees poured into the Lower Congo and fears grew that Portuguese forces might invade or bomb Congolese soil in "hot pursuit" of retreating Angolan "invaders." Congolese good will was less and less assured. In particular, the long-standing rivalry and bad blood between the

UPA and Abako was exacerbated by the war. In June 1961 Abako authorities were reported to have labeled Holden Roberto a Communist and to have prohibited his entry into the Lower Congo region.[58] Portuguese sources attributed anti-UPA sentiments to the powerful Abako leader in the strategic Lower Congo, Faustin Vital Moanda, and quoted him as saying: "We know that among the Angolan parties some are communist, and we do not want such a regime established in Angola."[59] For its part, the UPA accused Abako leaders of the Congo Central Province, such as Moanda and Senator Isaie Kuyena, of maintaining undercover ties with the Portuguese government.[60]

Much more serious were signs that the central government might clamp down on Angolan rebel activity. In an interview with a correspondent of *Le Monde* in early July, President Joseph Kasavubu indicated that, though the Angolans had always supported the Congolese in their struggle for independence, the responsibilities of independence dictated a Congolese policy of "strict neutrality" in the Angolan conflict. He agreed to humanitarian aid for refugees but added: "Above all, it is essential to prevent our soldiers from selling their arms to the Angolans." He even implied that the Léopoldville government might ask the Angolan nationalists to cease all activity on Congolese soil.[61] According to *Le Monde*'s reporter, conversations with Joseph Kasavubu, Justin Bomboko, and General Joseph Mobutu had revealed that they were giving consideration to the idea of expelling Roberto from the Congo in order to avoid the risk of Portuguese retaliation.[62] Another conceivable rationale for such a Congolese move could be found in the fear that the UPA would create a state within a state and act in disregard of Congolese interests. Such apprehensions could only be nourished by journalists' reports that the UPA exercised an "iron discipline" over its members and that its militants made those of the well-organized Abako look like "boy scouts" in comparison.[63]

If there really was a danger that the central government would adopt the Abako position and crack down on the Angolan rebels, it was short-lived. Things took a marked turn for the better in

[58] *Le Monde,* June 28, 1961.
[59] Felgas, *Guerra em Angola,* p. 149.
[60] *Le Monde,* June 28, 1961.
[61] Interviewed by Pierre de Vos, *Le Monde,* July 6, 1961.
[62] Pierre de Vos, "Angola: avec les rebelles," *L'Express,* July 6, 1961, pp. 15–16.
[63] *Le Monde,* July 6, 1961.

mid-July, when Roberto's old friend Cyrille Adoula became premier. Though local conflicts with Abako were to continue, the UPA's over-all situation was secured. And in September Roberto finally put aside his preoccupation with the day-by-day demands of the revolution long enough to fly with Adoula to Belgrade, Yugoslavia, where he attended the first Conference of Non-Aligned States.[64]

[64] For the text of the UPA memorandum presented at Belgrade by Roberto, see *A Voz da Nação Angolana* (Léopoldville), Vol. 2, No. 7, Sept. 22, 1961.

CHAPTER SIX

RESPONSES AND REPERCUSSIONS: THE WORLD AND PORTUGAL

On April 20, 1961, the United Nations General Assembly, by a vote of seventy-three to two (Spain and South Africa), with nine abstentions, called upon the Portuguese government "to consider urgently the introduction of measures and reforms in Angola for the purpose of the implementation of General Assembly resolution 1514 (XV)" dealing with preparation for independence.[1] To the consternation of the Portuguese and the delight of the Africans, the American delegation representing the new administration of President John F. Kennedy voted with the majority.

The American Response

Already on March 15 the United States had voted in the Security Council in support of a Liberian resolution calling for a United Nations inquiry into the Angolan situation. Britain, France, Turkey, Nationalist China, Chile, and Ecuador had abstained, thus killing the motion.[2] Before that time the outgoing government of President Dwight Eisenhower had been among the abstainers. In December 1960 it abstained in votes on General Assembly resolutions dealing with colonial independence and Portugal's obligation to submit information concerning its overseas territories. Earlier, in May 1960, President Eisenhower had visited Lisbon where he praised the "real progress" achieved by Dr. Salazar's government. Moreover the President reportedly had "listened sympathetically and respectfully to the Portuguese premier's request that the United

[1] United Nations, General Assembly Resolution 1603 (XV), Apr. 20, 1961.

[2] For the statement (Mar. 15) by Adlai Stevenson in support of the Afro-Asian resolution on Angola, see *Department of State Bulletin,* Vol. 44, Apr. 3, 1961, p. 497.

States not 'allow' official or semi-official" American agencies to foment anti-Portuguese sentiments in Portugal's African territories.[3]

The Angolan rebellion seemed to coincide with a new attitude in Washington, and the American vote in the Security Council on March 15, 1961, was viewed by some as "a reversal of fundamental past policy." [4] Holden Roberto had met the new President while he was still a senator and, like many African nationalists, had admired him for his public support for the cause of Algerian independence. The Angolan leader was prompt to react to the new stand against Portuguese colonialism by the leading power of the North Atlantic Alliance. "We wish to take this occasion," he told the press, "to pay a ringing tribute to the new American administration and its young and dynamic chief, John Kennedy. Our country will be proud to have helped solidify the sharp change in American policy concerning Africa and decolonization." [5]

Walter Lippmann also approved of the change in American policy. To have abstained in the Security Council vote, he said, would have left the Soviet Union as "the only great power in the white man's world which took the other side." If the United States had, by abstention, supported Portuguese colonialism "timidly and apologetically," he added, "what an 'image' that would have been of the leadership of the 'free world.' " [6]

Two Republican leaders, Senator Everett Dirksen and Representative Charles Halleck, struck a different note. They issued a joint statement which alleged that American support for Security Council resolutions critical of Portugal had cast the United States in the role of siding with the Soviet Union on a losing issue and was "hardly a proud moment for Uncle Sam." [7] On April 4 Roberto wrote to Senator Dirksen, describing the colonial abuses that had caused the Angolans to take to arms. He cited Portugal's refusal to meet its obligations concerning non-self-governing territories under Article 73e and declared that, when the American delegation's vote

[3] *The New York Times,* May 21, 1960.

[4] Arthur Krock, *ibid.,* Mar. 21, 1961.

[5] *Courrier d'Afrique,* Mar. 25–26, 1961. In contrast to this praise of the Kennedy administration, Roberto used the occasion of a press conference in Tunisia to criticize the French and British governments for their abstention in the Security Council vote. "Conférence de presse donnée par Monsieur Gilmore, Président de l'Union des Populations de l'Angola à Tunis le 21.3.1961" (Tunis, 1961, mimeo.).

[6] *New York Herald Tribune,* Mar. 22, 1961.

[7] *New York World Telegram,* Mar. 23, 1961.

had "proved that ideals were more important than the support of an erring friend, your nation once again lived through a moment of magnificence, a moment which should thrill you for having done right, a moment which reaffirmed the pledges of the founders of your country." He continued: "Obviously a country cannot frame its foreign policy on the basis of being opposed to the foreign policy of another. It would not be useful to catalog the many issues which have had the joint accord of the United States and the Soviet Union. The very fact of the United Nations' existence is proof that they must occasionally be on the same side. Why, then, cannot the issue be isolated from the Cold War and judged on its merits?" On April 11 Senator Dirksen wrote back explaining that his statement had been prompted by the fact that the UN action seemed like "an intrusion . . . into the internal affairs of a country in direct violation of Article 7, which prohibits such interference." He "quite agreed," however, "that every case must be resolved on its merits."

Lisbon's reaction to Washington's position was one of deep shock and resentment. On March 22 a group of white settlers organized an anti-American demonstration in front of the United States Consulate at Luanda and pushed the American Consul's car into the harbor.[8] Six days later on March 28 a crowd estimated at 20,000 protested in a two-hour demonstration outside the American Embassy in Lisbon.[9] The Portuguese government seized the opportunity offered by a ministerial meeting of NATO powers on May 8, 1961, at Oslo, Norway, to vent its anger, and privately it threatened to leave the alliance. It claimed the right to use NATO-equipped troops in Angola, and Foreign Minister Alberto Franco Nogueira pointed to France's use of NATO units in Algeria as a precedent. The Norwegian foreign minister, Halvard Lange, declared that Norway felt obliged to take into account the reality of African nationalism when voting at the United Nations—a promise that was to distinguish Norway's position from that of other NATO members in the future.[10] In spite of Lisbon's displeasure, the United States joined with the Soviet Union and Afro-Asian members of the Security Council in June in passing a resolution that

[8] *The New York Times,* Mar. 23, 1961.

[9] *Le Monde,* Mar. 29, 1961.

[10] *The New York Times,* May 10, 1961. On June 21, 1961, the Norwegian government announced that it had refused to license the sale of arms to Portugal because of the latter's colonial policy. Norwegian Information Service, *News of Norway,* Vol. 18, No. 25, June 29, 1961.

called upon Portugal to desist forthwith from repressive measures in Angola.[11]

In July, after a group of African students had fled Portugal, the White House directed the State Department's Bureau of Educational and Cultural Affairs to organize a scholarship program for refugee students from the Portuguese colonies. In addition, a review of the military assistance program, under which the United States had already provided Portugal with approximately $300 million for NATO defense purposes, resulted in a cutback from a planned delivery of $25 million to only $3 million in assistance during 1961.[12] Washington also imposed a ban on commercial sales of arms to Portugal, which was enforced as of mid-1961 by the State Department's Office of Munitions Control.

American commitments to Portugal under the NATO treaty together with a new Berlin crisis, which dramatized the strategic value of American refueling facilities in the Azores, soon started eroding the new American policy that Holden Roberto had hailed. Washington's troubles, which eventually produced a "credibility gap" concerning American behavior, could be traced back to the days just after March 15 when a panicky Portuguese government flew military reinforcements into Angola armed with NATO weapons. In Paris *Le Figaro* carried a prominent story on April 19, 1961, reporting that Lisbon was sending to Angola a division of troops that had been earmarked and armed for NATO. Caught between its desire to please African opinion and yet not wholly to alienate Portugal, the United States at first publicly denied that NATO equipment had been involved. Challenged by the Liberian representative on the Fourth Committee of the General Assembly to express regret over the use of NATO arms "to massacre the people of Angola," the American representative, Jonathan Bingham, replied that he had no apologies to make since NATO arms furnished by the United States were not being used in Angola.[13] That was at the Sixteenth General Assembly in November 1961. A year later at the Seventeenth General Assembly, the same American representative admitted that the United States had really known

[11] Britain and France abstained. United Nations, Security Council Resolution S/4835, June 9, 1961.

[12] U.S. Department of Commerce, *Statistical Abstract of the United States, 1961*, 82nd ed. (Washington, D.C.: U.S. Government Printing Office, 1961), p. 879; and *ibid.*, 83rd ed., 1962, p. 251.

[13] United Nations, General Assembly (XVI), Fourth Committee, 1201 meeting, Nov. 8, 1961.

all along that the Portuguese had sent NATO arms to Angola.[14] In fact, Washington had made immediate representations to the Portuguese government in the spring of 1961, protesting this misuse of NATO arms but Lisbon had ignored the protest and continued using them.[15]

American support—or at least benevolent neutrality—in the war against African nationalism was crucial for Lisbon. Accordingly, Portugal hired a New York public relations firm, Selvage and Lee, to build up American support for its cause.[16] With the aid of a Portuguese-American Committee on Foreign Affairs, organized, on Selvage and Lee's initiative, among Portuguese-Americans in New England, its campaign concentrated on two arguments expected to impress Americans. First, the Angola revolt was inspired and organized by external Communist forces. Second, it was racist and barbaric.[17] These contentions were spread far and wide. Two pro-Portuguese articles appeared in the November 1961 issue of the *Reader's Digest,* one by a Negro writer, Max Yergan, and another by a retired army officer and vice-president of New York University, Brigadier General Frank L. Howley. Thousands of reprints of these articles were distributed, along with a special supplement on "Portuguese Africa" in the July 1, 1961, issue of the Pittsburgh *Courier.* The lead article in the supplement, aimed at the *Courier's* Negro readership, was entitled "Racial Integration and Intermarriage Promoted for 500 Years."

The organizer of the Portuguese-American Committee on Foreign Affairs was a Portuguese-born (San Martin, Madeira, 1913) Boston lawyer with a Harvard doctorate in political science, Martin Thomas Camacho. He received four hundred dollars a month from Selvage

[14] United Nations, General Assembly (XVII), Fourth Committee, 1402 meeting, Nov. 20, 1962.

[15] See U.S. House of Representatives, Committee on Foreign Affairs, *Foreign Assistance Act, 1962.* Pt. I (Washington, D.C.: U.S. Government Printing Office, 1962), pp. 145–146. See also *The New York Times,* Apr. 11, 1962.

[16] The Selvage and Lee contract was arranged by a group known as the Overseas Companies of Portugal at the instance of the Portuguese government. For details of the Selvage and Lee combined public relations and lobbying campaign and the cooperative role of Portuguese officials and diplomats, see U.S. Senate, *Hearings before the Committee on Foreign Relations,* 88 Congress, 1st session, pt. 8, Apr. 12, May 6, 1963 (Washington, D.C.: U.S. Government Printing Office, 1963), *passim* (cited hereafter as *Hearings before the Committee on Foreign Relations*).

[17] See Portuguese-American Committee on Foreign Affairs, *The Communists and Angola* (Boston, 1961). See also illustrated pamphlet by Portuguese-American Committee on Foreign Affairs, *On the Morning of March 15* (Boston, 1961).

and Lee. In July 1961, even before creating his committee of approximately seventy New Englanders of Portuguese descent, Camacho succeeded in having President Kennedy presented with a "memorial" on behalf of the "Luso-American community of the eastern seaboard states." This petition defended Portugal's "enlightened multi-racial policy" in Africa, charged Communist complicity in the Angolan uprising, and stressed the value for the United States of continued friendship with Portugal, "a Christian country with a long, consistent record of resistance to Communist wiles and pressures." In addition to citing American military bases in the Azores, it reminded the President that "Radio Free Europe's principal transmitting service [was] situated in Lisbon" and that all these facilities were being provided "rent-free." Above all, the petition argued that the American government should reverse the ill-advised policy that had resulted in its siding "with the Soviet Union and against Portugal in votes at the United Nations on matters involving the Portuguese Province of Angola."[18] Camacho and his associates also petitioned and talked with congressmen and State Department officials.

The Angolans lacked the funds that the Portuguese government and the Overseas Companies of Portugal could lavish on such a press and lobbying campaign. The *Reader's Digest* refused to publish a reply to the Howley and Yergan pieces by someone sympathetic to the African cause, and a letter from Roberto to the editor went unanswered and unpublished.[19] Concerned lest United States public opinion be mobilized against the Angolan nationalist cause by default, Roberto wrote a series of letters to American publications responding to their articles on Angola.[20]

[18] Dated July 20, 1961. See *Hearings before the Committee on Foreign Relations,* pp. 1185–1186.

[19] See Appendix D.

[20] A partial listing of these letters with dates written includes: *New York World Telegram,* Mar. 19, 1961; *New York Post,* Apr. 3; *New York Herald Tribune,* Apr. 4, Apr. 11 (published Apr. 20); *The Wall Street Journal,* Apr. 11, (another published Apr. 12); *The New York Times,* Apr. 11; *The New Republic,* Apr. 18; *New York News,* Apr. 20; *Time,* Apr. 25; *Providence Journal* (R.I.), Apr. 27; *Milwaukee Journal,* June 14; *U.S. News and World Report,* Nov. 17; *Minneapolis Star,* Nov. 20; *The Telegram* (Worcester, Mass.), Nov. 20; *Richmond Times Dispatch* (Va.), Nov. 21; *Houston Chronicle,* Nov. 26. At the same time, Roberto wrote to political figures all over the world seeking aid and sympathy for his movement, e.g., a letter to Prime Minister Jawaharlal Nehru, Apr. 21: "Your Excellency, an African population is fighting for survival against tremendous odds, naked and unarmed against a depraved and vicious foe. We must have immediate help if we are to avoid being exterminated."

In an effort to discredit critics Camacho and his Luso-American group launched a campaign against the American Committee on Africa (ACOA). Camacho's "memorial" to President Kennedy charged that the ACOA was echoing "Communist propaganda" and "condoning terrorism." [21] The anti-ACOA offensive reached a peak in November when Camacho issued a statement demanding a Congressional investigation of the ACOA, which, he said, was "ardently supporting communist goals." He urged that such persons as presidential aide Arthur M. Schlesinger, Jr., and Mrs. Eleanor Roosevelt, along with other prominent members of the ACOA, "immediately resign" from it.[22] ACOA executive director George Houser responded by inviting "any responsible investigation" of his organization's "activities and policies" and reaffirmed the Committee's dedication to "the American tradition of equality, freedom, and independence for all people"—including Angolans.[23] Another ACOA member, Professor Reinhold Niebuhr, responded by refuting Camacho's "implausible attacks" on American liberals, attacks that accused "anyone devoted to justice in any dimension [of being] tainted with Communism." [24]

In addition to the ACOA's monthly *Africa Today,* however, the American press during 1961 did in fact publish some sympathetic and probing accounts of the Angolan uprising and its background. These included articles in *Harper's, Christian Century, Foreign Affairs,* and *Look,* as well as *The New York Times.*[25] In June a group of eighty leading American and Canadian Christians sent an open letter to Portuguese President Américo Thomaz calling for major political reforms in Angola. Sponsored by the Africa Committees of the National Council of Churches and the Catholic Association for International Peace, the letter argued that only bold moves in Angola to "eliminate social injustices" and rapidly increase African "participation in the processes of government" might avoid an interracial "war of extermination." [26]

[21] *Hearings before the Committee on Foreign Relations,* p. 1186.

[22] Associated Press dispatch, Boston, Nov. 16, 1961.

[23] Statement by George M. Houser (New York, Nov. 17, 1961, mimeo.).

[24] Open letter from Niebuhr to Camacho, dated Jan. 26, 1962.

[25] See "The Kingdom of Silence," *Harper's,* Vol. 222, No. 1332 (May 1961), pp. 29–37; Ralph E. Dodge, "Angola and Protestant Conscience," *Christian Century,* Nov. 22, 1961, pp. 1395–1397; James Duffy, "Portugal in Africa," *Foreign Affairs,* Vol. 39 (Apr. 1961), pp. 481–493; Ernest Dunbar, "Angola," *Look,* Mar. 28, 1961, pp. 42 ff.

[26] Letter of June 4, 1961, distributed for signatures by Rev. Dr. Theodore L.

Other NATO Allies and Brazil

Although Portugal's other NATO allies expressed a general belief in the principle of self-determination, they were not so troublesome as the United States. In particular, Lisbon's traditional ally, Great Britain, was not moved by the outrage of the Baptist Missionary Society, criticism from the Labour Party opposition, or appeals from Commonwealth leaders to desist from a policy of diplomatic and military cooperation with Lisbon.[27] Not only did British representatives abstain in United Nations' votes against Portugal, but on June 17 London revealed the sale of two frigates to the Portuguese navy.[28] At the same time, on June 27 London announced that it had suspended licenses for the export of military equipment for use in Portugal's overseas territories.[29]

Britain's Conservative government held that the Angolan uprising constituted a problem within the domestic jurisdiction of Portugal, which should not be allowed to weaken Portugal's role within the NATO alliance.[30] France, still embroiled in its Algerian war, maintained a similar hands-off policy, consistent with President Charles de Gaulle's disdain for United Nation's anticolonialist resolutions. French military writers, however, argued the strategic importance of preserving Portuguese rule in Africa.[31] Belgian economic and political interests, implicated in the secession of the Congolese province of Katanga, relied upon Angola and the Benguela railroad for access to and evacuation of its mineral wealth;

Tucker, secretary of the National Council's African Committee and Dr. Thomas Patrick Melady, chairman of the Catholic group, was signed by such persons as Robert F. Goheen, president of Princeton University, Edward Skillen, editor of *Commonweal*, Rev. W. J. Gallagher, general secretary of the Canadian Council of Churches, and A. Philip Randolph, president of the Brotherhood of Sleeping Car Porters. *The New York Times*, June 5, 1961.

[27] See Len Addicott, *Cry Angola!* (London: SCM Press, 1962), for Baptist action; and "Some Facts about the Situation in Angola" a supplement to *This Week* (Transport House, London), Vol. 3, June 22, 1961, for the Labour party's views.

[28] See Basil Davidson, "The Oldest Alliance Faces a Crisis," in *Angola: A Symposium, Views of a Revolt* (London: Oxford University Press, 1962), p. 154.

[29] *Parliamentary Debates, House of Commons* (Hansard), June 27, 1961, "Written Answers to Questions," col. 18.

[30] See Prime Minister Harold Macmillan in *Parliamentary Debates, House of Commons* (Hansard), July 4, 1961, cols. 1256 ff. Also see Patrick Wall, "Britain and Angola: The Attitude of the British Government," in *Angola: A Symposium*, pp. 130–137.

[31] Louis Axel, "La Congolisation de l'Angola: une grave menace pour l'Occident et pour l'Otan," *Revue militaire générale* (Paris), Oct. 1961, pp. 392–409; George Gayet, "L'Angola, porte du Katanga," *Revue de Défense Nationale* (Paris), Vol. 17 (June 1961), pp. 1029–1040.

and like London and Paris, Brussels refrained from joining the censorious majorities that condemned Portugal at the United Nations. There were reports that some of Portugal's closest friends, i.e., Britain, France, and Spain, "exerted pressure on the Kennedy Administration not to jeopardize America's defense ties with Portugal." [32]

Apart from Scandinavia, Portugal's European allies were as predictably indulgent as the Soviet Union, China, and other Communist states were denunciatory. It was the Western Hemisphere that provided a second unpleasant surprise for Lisbon. At the same time that the New Frontier of President John F. Kennedy had brought a new look to the African policies of the United States of North America, the election of Jânio Quadros as president of the United States of Brazil on October 17, 1960, had resulted in strikingly new thinking in that Portuguese-speaking republic of nearly eighty million people. Quadros set forth a new, independent foreign policy for Brazil, with increased importance attached to relations with Africa. To aid the foreign minister, Afonso Arinos, in the design of such a program, Prof. Cândido António Mendes de Almeida was named to head a new Brazilian Institute of Afro-Asian Studies, attached to the Foreign Ministry in Rio de Janeiro.[33] While the Quadros government sought ties with states like Senegal and supported Algerian independence, it was careful not to alienate Portugal completely, and it abstained in United Nations votes on the Portuguese territories, preparing itself for a future role as intermediary between African nationalists and the Portuguese.[34] Foreign Minister Arinos reportedly urged political liberalization in the overseas territories during his visit to Lisbon in April 1961.[35] The most important consequence was that Portugal could no longer count on automatic support from Brazil, where the MPLA in particular was winning a considerable private audience within intellectual circles and among politicians.[36]

[32] *The New York Times*, Apr. 16, 1961.

[33] See Cândido António Mendes de Almeida, *Nacionalismo e Desenvolvimento* (Rio de Janeiro: Instituto Brasileiro de Estudos Afro-Asiáticos, 1963).

[34] See José Honório Rodrigues, *Brazil and Africa* (Berkeley: University of California Press, 1965), pp. 322–337.

[35] *The New York Times*, April 15, 1961.

[36] Rodrigues, *Brazil and Africa*, pp. 285–286. Brazilian observers such as Prof. Mendes of the Brazilian Institute of Afro-Asian Studies viewed Holden Roberto as too committed to the United States and consequently a potential "Trojan Horse" for extending America's influence from the Congo into Angola. Sympathy

The Portuguese Response: Administrative Reforms

All empirical evidence notwithstanding, Lisbon refused to recognize the Angolan rebellion as an indigenous uprising against foreign rule. Yet there was widespread expectation that military, economic, and diplomatic pressures unleashed by the conflict would finally induce the Salazar government to start down the "slippery path" of major, though piecemeal, reform that would eventually lead to local self-government and independence.

It soon became clear, however, that fierce national pride would at least delay such a response. In April *The New York Times* correspondent at Lisbon, Benjamin Welles, wrote that precisely because steps to liberalize Portuguese rule "might be widely interpreted as yielding to . . . foreign pressures," and because of criticism "by high United States officials," the government had decided to postpone the enactment of an urgently needed reform program. In the words of one Portuguese official, his was a nation of "sensitive people" who tended to react to outside criticism by rallying around Salazar and "refusing to be pushed." [37]

Although major reforms were delayed, a limited program of administrative change, which the government had already begun before the uprising, was continued and expanded. It called for improving labor conditions, prohibiting forced cultivation, creating elective councils in communities of five hundred or more inhabitants, and broadening social and health services.[38] By the end of June, while Premier Salazar still attacked the United States for serving the cause of Communist subversion by supporting terrorism in Angola,[39] he admitted that his government might have "erred on the side of excessive caution" in the past and promised a speed-up in the process of modernization and assimilation.[40] He also pledged that his government would restore order, continue "that reformative effort in which the nation [had] engaged for many years in all her component parts," and "work toward the formation

---

for the MPLA was also manifest in a Brazilian anthology on the Angolan crisis, *Angola, Através dos Textos* (São Paulo, Brazil: Editôra Felman-Rêgo, 1962).

[37] *The New York Times,* Apr. 16, 1961.

[38] *Ibid.,* July 27, 1961.

[39] *Ibid.,* July 1, 1961. For the text of Dr. Salazar's address to the Portuguese National Assembly, June 30, 1961, see Portugal, Secretariado Nacional da Informação, *The Portuguese Overseas Territories and the United Nations Organization* (Lisbon, 1961).

[40] *The New York Times,* May 31, 1961.

of nations which may eventually become the substructure of potential future states." [41]

There were some cautious internal pressures for substantive reform. In April, for instance, the Roman Catholic hierarchy in Angola issued a pastoral letter which condemned the "criminal acts" of "terrorists" but also said that the "legitimate and just aspirations" of the African people had to be considered. "The Church," it commented, "is entirely within the limits of its mission in advising citizens to unite themselves for the moralization of laws and institutions and for the formation of a more perfect social situation, more supported by justice and charity." [42]

On August 28 in a speech at Oporto, Portugal, Prof. Adriano Moreira, who had been elevated to the post of overseas minister in April of that year, announced what was to be Lisbon's maximum reform program. It called for speeding up European settlement so as to defend Portuguese sovereignty, abolishing the *indigenato* and reclassifying all Africans as Portuguese citizens, and reorganizing rural districts (*regedorias*) to provide for elections to choose their administrators and for legal safeguards to protect their African inhabitants from expropriation of their land.[43] On September 6 sixteen settlement boards "were set up to facilitate European immigration, and the *Estatuto dos Indígenas* of 1954 was officially repealed.[44] Though the invidious distinction between "civilized" and "noncivilized" was now abolished, the general upgrading meant a doubling of taxes from five to ten dollars per head for former *indígenas.*

The reforms also included a sharply expanded program of education with the state assuming responsibilities previously left to the Catholic Church. A crash program was established to train rural elementary teachers (*monitores*).

Though they applauded the expansion of educational opportunities, many informed observers viewed the reforms in general with considerable skepticism. American Methodist E. Edwin LeMaster charged, some eight months after their promulgation, that "for external consumption the Portuguese announced they were aban-

[41] *Ibid.*

[42] *Diário de Notícias* (Lisbon), Apr. 16, 1961; *The Times* (London), Apr. 17, 1961.

[43] For text of the Oporto speech, see Adriano Moreira, *Portugal's Stand in Africa* (New York: University Publishers, 1962), pp. 181–201.

[44] Decrees Nos. 43,895 and 43,893, *ibid.*, pp. 225–256.

doning the legal distinction between the *assimilado* and the *indigena,* but our missionaries in Angola report it is merely a paper reform, without any apparent implementation, and more likely to reduce the status of the few *assimilados* than to improve the condition of the mass of *indigenas.*"[45]

Most disappointingly, Portuguese reforms failed to introduce freedom of press, speech, or ballot, and made no concessions to rising sentiments of African nationalism. A June announcement that Angolan municipal councils were to become elective rather than appointive bodies, and a September provision for three additional Angolan representatives in Portugal's nearly powerless one-party National Assembly left the basic issues of political freedom unresolved. These moves simply recalled to mind efforts by the Fourth Republic of France to stave off the disintegration of the French Union by belatedly increasing African representation in the French parliament.

Lisbon's determination not to budge from its basic contention that Angola formed an integral and inalienable part of Portugal remained unshaken by rebellion or criticism, American or otherwise. The fact that Spain and South Africa might be the only two countries supporting it in votes at the General Assembly only revealed the enormity and pervasiveness of human ignorance and perfidy. Portugal was right and the world was wrong. Accordingly, Lisbon refused to cooperate with a five nation Sub-Committee on the Situation in Angola established by the General Assembly, or to allow the committee to enter Angola.[46]

Portugal not only claimed it was right but soon asserted that it was winning its fight to hold Angola. In an interview published at the end of October 1961, the Portuguese ambassador to the United States announced: "The military phase of the operation against the terrorists in northern Angola is now almost complete." Ambassador Pedro Theotónio Pereira said that the main villages, farms, and means of communication had been recaptured and that law and order had been restored to the "relatively small area, which the terrorists sought to devastate and control." Angola, he assured

[45] E. Edwin LeMaster, "I saw the Horror in Angola," *Saturday Evening Post,* May 12, 1962, p. 50. See also A. R. Kasdan, "An Examination of Portugal's Announced Reforms for African Territories" (American Committee on Africa, New York, mimeo.).

[46] Members: Bolivia, Dahomey, Malaya, Finland, and Sudan; Chairman, Dr. Carlos Salamanca (Bolivia).

Americans, was now entering upon a period of national reconstruction aimed at "rebuilding racial harmony" and restoring confidence and security in areas affected by the rebellion.[47]

The Impact of Rebellion on Portuguese Guinea

While Portuguese officials claimed to be restoring confidence and harmony within Angola, the uprising there had already encouraged an ominous growth in nationalist sentiment and new security moves to counter it in Portugal's other African territories. It helped to speed both Portuguese Guinea and Mozambique along their own collision courses with Portugal.

In small (14,000 square miles), forested, and swampy (rice-growing) Guinea-Bissau, efforts of local nationalists to organize had begun in the early 1950's. By July 1959 they had already led to a costly dockers' strike, which the administration broke with the "massacre of Pigiguiti quay," in which some fifty Africans were killed. The strike had been organized by the *Partido Africano da Independência da Guiné e Cabo Verde* (PAIGC), founded in September 1956 by local *assimilado* townsmen and educated mulattoes from the Cape Verde Islands. The quick and pitiless repression of the 1959 strike convinced the PAIGC of the futility and high cost of peaceful urban protest. Accordingly, it shifted its action to rural areas and thereafter concentrated on organizing clandestinely within the ethnically diverse rural population of some 600,000 Portuguese Guineans. The party secretary-general, Amilcar Lopes Cabral, who was an agronomist and had served earlier in the Portuguese administration in Angola, was keenly aware of the importance of bridging the inevitable gulf between intellectual and peasant, between urban modernist and rural traditionalist. The PAIGC therefore instituted a program to educate the countryside politically in order to develop common loyalties and ideological cohesion and thereby transcend the rivalries of communal fragmentation.[48]

As a student in Portugal and then as an exile in France, Cabral worked closely with MPLA leaders, notably Mário de Andrade, whom he joined in forming the *Movimento Anti-Colonialista*

[47] Pedro Theotónio Pereira, "Wars of 'Liberation' in Africa. What They Mean," *U.S. News and World Report,* Oct. 30, 1961, pp. 74–76.

[48] See William Zartman, "Africa's Quiet War," *African Report,* Vol. 9, No. 2 (Feb. 1964), pp. 8–12; also Gérard Chaliand, *Guinée "portugaise" et Cap Vert en lutte pour leur indépendance* (Paris: François Maspero, 1964).

(MAC) (Paris, 1957), and the successor, *Frente Revolucionária Africana para a Independência Nacional* (FRAIN) (Tunis, January 1960). He wrote on Portuguese colonialism under the name Abel Djassi,[49] traveled and lobbied for support abroad, and in early 1960 joined the MPLA in establishing exile headquarters in Conakry. Meanwhile, under the presidency of a public works employee, Raphael Barboza, the party built a clandestine apparatus at home.

Following the outbreak of fighting in Angola in 1961, Lisbon dispatched army reinforcements to Guinea, bringing their total there to some 6000, more than twice the size of the normal resident population of Portuguese traders and administrators. In July of that year the PAIGC joined with other Portuguese Guinean nationalist movements operating in exile in Senegal to create an abortive common *Front Uni de Libération de Guinée et du Cap Vert* (FUL). Days later the most important of the Dakar-based organizations, the *Mouvement de Libération de la Guinée dite Portugaise* (MLG), which enjoyed a considerable following among the Manjak people living in areas along the Senegalese frontier, launched an armed assault from Senegal on three Guinean border towns. Under the ambitious leadership of Senegalese-educated François Mendy, the MLG and other Dakar-based movements then refused to implement their projected union with the stronger PAIGC, whose Cape Verdian leaders they resented. At the same time they created a public clamor that helped to deepen Portuguese apprehensions and that encouraged PIDE to undertake a series of arrests which began in August 1961 and continued intermittently from then on.

The Impact of Rebellion on Mozambique

Security in the vast (302,000 square miles) East African territory of Mozambique made even more serious demands than Guinea-Bissau on a Portuguese economy that was losing some 117 million dollars in foreign currency reserves during 1961 because of the Angolan fighting. Like Angola, Mozambique had been the scene of determined traditionalist resistance to Portuguese rule until the First World War: its large northern districts of Cabo Delgado and Niassa were progressively occupied for the first time between 1906 and 1912, and the Barué region of the south was not brought

[49] Abel Djassi, "The Facts about Portugal's African Colonies" (London: Union of Democratic Control, 1960, pamphlet).

under Portuguese control until 1902, and then revolted again in 1917. The distance and hazards of the trip around the Cape reduced the impact of the slave trade and kept down the number of white settlers relative to Angola. Yet a similar pattern to that in Angola characterized the development of Mozambican nationalism —forced labor (*shibalo*), marginal or token assimilation (4300 *assimilados* representing 0.08 per cent of 5,700,000 Africans by 1950), and growth of modern protest through journalism, voluntary associations, and finally scattered and ephemeral political movements.[50]

In 1931 the American consulate at Lourenço Marques sent a dispatch to Washington that suggests something of the nature and fate of protest action of that period: "On May 25, political deportees, some twenty in Lourenço Marques and four in Inhambane, attempted to join forces near the latter place and to incite the native soldiery to revolt. All conspirators were captured and deported to Cape Verde, but the ringleader escaped to Angola where he may foment trouble if not promptly captured." [51] Every effort was made to stamp out the contagious spirit of nationalism in its most formative stages. In the 1950's an *Associação dos Naturais de Moçambique* developed as a social organization that accepted African membership, favored racial integration, organized scholarship aid for young Africans seeking secondary, technical, and commercial education, and became a focal point of autonomist, even prenationalist, sentiment. The government therefore arrested its top leaders and replaced them with safe, pro-Salazar men, just as it had with the *Liga Nacional Africana* in Angola. Dr. Eduardo Mondlane, later to emerge as Mozambique's most prominent nationalist leader, has written of this episode: "One might venture the prediction that the Portuguese people, a European white group, will regret the emasculation of this organization, for with its demise as a multiracial nucleus may have gone all the hopes for a racially tolerant Mozambique." [52]

Mozambicans, some half a million at any given time, working in neighboring countries (65,000 to 80,000 a year in South African mines alone) were exposed to the then politically more permissive

[50] See Ronald H. Chilcote, "Les Mouvements de libération au Mozambique," *Le mois en Afrique,* No. 7 (July 1966), pp. 30–42.

[51] Dispatch from Mr. Cameron, Lourenço Marques, No. 42, 853N.00/9, July 9, 1931, U.S. Archives.

[52] Eduardo Mondlane, "The Struggle for Independence in Mozambique," *Présence Africaine* (English ed.), Vol. 20, No. 48 (1963), p. 35.

environment of South Africa and Southern Rhodesia. In Rhodesia young men from Mozambique sought asylum, work, and education and began to organize their own social and self-help organizations in the period 1958–1960. According to one of them it was "in these small gatherings [that] discussions in a serious sense regarding national politics began." Thus, according to David J. M. Mabunda, Mozambicans went to Rhodesia "with the express desire to engage in some activity" that might enable them to change things in their own country. There they sought experience in and support from African nationalist movements.[53] Ultimately, in October 1960, a group of them working in and around the city of Bulawayo founded a nationalist party, the original *União Democrática Nacional de Moçambique* (UDENAMO).

Led by a young man in his early twenties, who claimed to have already helped organize a nationalist movement inside Mozambique,[54] UDENAMO moved its headquarters to Dar es Salaam in February 1961.[55] Because of the close cooperation between the European governments of Southern Rhodesia and Mozambique, the party had found it impossible to function in Rhodesia. In Dar es Salaam its president, Hlomulo Chitofo (Adelino) Gwambe, originally from the Gaza district of southern Mozambique, contacted the leadership of another exile movement which had organized among Mozambicans working in British East Africa, principally in Tanganyika. This was the Mozambique African National Union (MANU), which derived from the reorganization of an ethnic cultural and self-help organization, the Tanganyika Mozambique Makonde Union founded in 1954 among Maconde émigrés from Northern Mozambique.[56] Reflecting the KANU/TANU nomenclature of the area, MANU had been organized in February 1961 in consultation with the East African Goan League.[57] Much of MANU's leadership, including its president Matthew Mmole and

[53] David J. M. Mabunda, "The Liberation Movement of Mozambique" (unpublished typescript, Oct. 1965).

[54] The *Partido da Unidade Nacional,* some 200 miles north of Lourenço Marques (Inhambane?). *African Mail* (Lusaka), Jan. 31, 1961. Eduardo Mondlane has charged that this young man, Adelino Gwambe, was sent to Rhodesia by the PIDE as an informer but then threw in his lot with the nationalists. Mondlane, "Struggle for Independence," p. 36.

[55] See *The Economist* (London), Aug. 26, 1961, p. 809.

[56] The Makonde Union had represented Mozambique at the Conference of Nationalist Leaders from Portuguese Colonies held in London on December 6, 1960. See p. 45.

[57] *East African Standard* (Nairobi), Feb. 20, 1961.

its secretary-general Lawrence M. Millinga (Kenya trade unionist), was English-speaking. Whereas UDENAMO established branch offices in Accra and Cairo and drew international attention, MANU limited itself to Tanganyika, Zanzibar, and (Mombasa) Kenya, where it organized among Mozambican plantation and dock workers.

When in July 1961 in an oratorical response to the rebellion in Angola, Adelino Gwambe announced to the press that UDENAMO was preparing to liberate Mozambique with the aid of several African states and some 70,000 soldiers, he was expelled from Tanganyika.[58] Marcelino dos Santos, the Mozambican secretary-general of the CONCP alliance, which had been founded that April and which linked UDENAMO with the MPLA, PAIGC, and the several Goan movements, promptly flew from his headquarters in Rabat to Dar es Salaam. There he undertook to investigate the events surrounding Gwambe's expulsion and to salvage what he could. Avoiding any repetition of the "invasion" threat made by Gwambe, dos Santos then issued a locally more acceptable warning that a popular uprising was imminent inside Mozambique.[59]

In November 1961 Paulo José Gumane, a former schoolteacher from Inhambane, joined the ranks of Mozambican nationalists in Dar es Salaam. He had had his political apprenticeship in South Africa where he served as branch secretary of the Laundry and Dry Cleaner Workers' Union at Cape Town. Reportedly named national organizing secretary of UDENAMO while still in South Africa, he had earlier belonged to the African National Congress (ANC) 1946–1958 and to the Pan-Africanist Congress (PAC) 1959–1960.[60] Gumane was one of a considerable number of Mozambicans who, while working in South Africa, became involved in its nationalist politics. Some tried to organize Mozambican mine workers.[61] Then

[58] See *Daily Nation* (Nairobi), July 18, 1961; *Contact* (Cape Town), July 27, 1961. Some TANU leaders reportedly suspected that Portuguese circles had engineered Gwambe's announcement so as to implicate them and cause Britain to delay Tanganyika's accession to independence. See Richard Cox, *Pan Africanism in Practice* (London: Institute of Race Relations, Oxford University Press, 1964), p. 46.

[59] *Remarques Congolaise* (Brussels), Vol. 3, No. 44–45 (Nov. 24, 1961), p. 447.

[60] Paulo José Gumane, "Biography" (Lusaka, June 1966, unpublished typescript).

[61] According to Mozambique nationalist sources, such an effort was made by Diniz Mengame and Tomas Betulane Nhantumbo, who founded a *Partido de Libertação de Moçambique* in Johannesburg during 1956–57. The South African police blunted their action and reportedly delivered them to Portuguese authorities in 1962.

as the South African situation tightened up after the Sharpeville emergency of March 1960, a number of Mozambicans moved northward to participate in the development of an organized political movement in exile. Thus it was that, after spending three months in jail and while awaiting deportation to Mozambique because of his political activities, Gumane jumped bail and escaped through Bechuanaland to Southern Rhodesia and Tanganyika.[62]

Another new and noteworthy arrival in Dar es Salaam was the leader of a regional party, the *União Nacional Africana de Moçambique Independente* (UNAMI), José Baltazar da Costa Chagong'a from Zumbo, Mozambique. For many years a medical orderly, he had been jailed briefly in 1960 for his criticism of the government's repression of students and workers, after which he had taken asylum in Nyasaland. Avowedly the organizer of a social group at Moatize (Tete district) known as the *Associação Nacional Africana de Moçambique,* an antecedent of UNAMI, Baltazar Chagong'a, on his arrival in Dar es Salaam in 1961, surveyed the status of Mozambique exile politics and then wrote to Professor Eduardo Mondlane at Syracuse University in the United States, urging him to come to Africa to help create a united nationalist movement.[63]

While Mozambique nationalist organizations were only in the formative stage of their development, violence had already broken out in June 1960 at Mueda in the Maconde country of the far north. Initiatives by a local leader, Kibiriti Diwani, to create an African association ended in tragedy when Portuguese troops moved in from Porto Amélia and reportedly shot several hundred people in what will probably be known in the future history of Mozambique as the Massacre of Mueda.[64] Six months later, following the hijacking of the "Santa Maria" in January 1961, reports reaching Salisbury indicated that the troubled administration was arming white Mozambicans. According to the *Rhodesia Herald,* "The [Portuguese] army [had] stopped training its African soldiers in arms drill and [was] absorbing them into engineering and labor units." [65]

After the February-March 1961 sequence of explosions in Angola,

[62] Gumane, "Biography."

[63] Mondlane, "Struggle for Independence," p. 37.

[64] See J. M. A. Khamba, "Historical Background to the National Liberation Struggle in Mozambique," *The Voice of Africa* (Accra), No. 5–6 (May–June 1964), p. 32; Chilcote, "Les Mouvements," p. 31.

[65] *Rhodesia Herald* (Salisbury), Jan. 31, 1961.

tension mounted sharply in Mozambique. In April seven European businessmen, members of a small white *Movimento Democrático de Moçambique* (MDM) were arrested in Beira for circulating an antigovernment petition.[66] In May the police suddenly executed a defiant chief, Zimtambira Chicusse from Vila Coutinho (near the Malawi border) who had been detained since 1955.[67] By July the South African press was printing such headlines as "Jittery Mozambique Alerted for Trouble." [68] An outflow of money was matched by an inflow of army reinforcements. In September the MDM circulated another tract calling on Portuguese soldiers to revolt against the "reactionary" colonial administration and to establish Mozambique's independence under majority (African) rule.[69] Such appeals, however, proved ineffectual, as police raids and the military buildup underscored Portugal's resolve to concede nothing more in Mozambique than in Angola.

As the year drew to a close the administration nevertheless felt constrained to cancel provincial elections scheduled for November. And though there was no uprising to match that of Angola, police action and military reinforcements could not prevent Mozambican nationalists from congregating and organizing in exile in an effort to mount a serious challenge to Portuguese rule from outside.

[66] *The New York Times*, June 22, 1961; and *Sunday Times* (Johannesburg), July 2, 1961.

[67] Chilcote, "Les Mouvements"; and UDENAMO memorandum, "United Nations Committee on Territories under Portuguese Administration" (Dar es Salaam, May 12, 1962, mimeo.).

[68] *Sunday Times*, July 2, 1961.

[69] See MDM tract, "Proclamação do Movimento Democrático de Moçabique [*sic*] (MDM) aos Soldados de Portigal [*sic*] em Missão de guerra em Moçambique" (Sept. 1961, mimeo.). Also see *Spearhead* (Dar es Salaam), Vol. 1, No. 2 (Dec. 1961), p. 6.

CHAPTER SEVEN

THE EMERGING STRUGGLE FOR REVOLUTIONARY LEADERSHIP

As 1961 progressed and fighting in northern Angola continued, a struggle for revolutionary leadership developed as an increasingly central motif of Angolan nationalist politics. In considerable measure it became a two-way competition between a movement associated with the Luanda-Mbundu area and another associated with the northern Bakongo region.

The MPLA's Autumn Offensive

In October, as part of a major effort to assure itself a place in the revolutionary picture and to break up what had become the UPA's near-monopoly of access to, and thus control over, the northern zone of rebellion, the MPLA moved its headquarters from Conakry to Léopoldville. This move followed upon the considerable success of Mário de Andrade in mustering external support for his movement during the spring and summer of 1961. For example, Soviet Premier Nikita Khrushchev had responded to a message from Andrade and expressed his sympathy and confidence in the ultimate victory of the Angolan people,[1] and Soviet representatives consistently supported the nationalist cause at the United Nations. In France, Andrade was able to launch an appeal for support from intellectuals and liberals through the medium of Paris's most influential paper, *Le Monde*.[2] A private *Comité de Soutien à l'Angola et aux Peuples des Colonies Portugaises* was already functioning in Paris in cooperation with the MPLA, and similar groups were formed in Belgium, the Netherlands, Italy, the Scandinavian coun-

[1] *Pravda,* June 16, 1961.

[2] An appeal transmitted via interview with Ernest Milcent, *Le Monde,* July 2, 1961.

tries, and West as well as East Germany, in both of which the MPLA was able to place a number of students.[3]

The failure of the MPLA to make a similar effort to influence North American opinion left Holden Roberto and the UPA as the unchallenged spokesmen of Angolan nationalism in the United States—thus counterbalancing the MPLA's distinct advantage in Europe. Deriving in part from the happenstance of early contacts and associations at home and later in exile, this division of activity abroad added a complicating international dimension to UPA-MPLA rivalry.

Deeper reasons for relative MPLA disinterest in the United States, however, were suggested in late 1961 by one of the party's veteran leaders in Europe, Lucio Lara. Even America's much-praised votes against Portugal at the United Nations, he said, were a sham designed "to make believe that American policies towards colonial countries had changed." Washington voted "reluctantly" under pressure from Afro-Asian countries, continued to express its "good will and friendship" for Portugal, and criticized the action of Angolan "patriots" defending themselves against Portuguese "atrocities."

Manifesting a systematic hostility and distrust that suggested that the MPLA could anticipate nothing positive from America, Lara charged that, when Washington voted to please, it did so without sincerity. Accordingly it revealed its true attitude and undermined Security Council action by failing to deliver the support of those (in this case Chile, Ecuador, and Nationalist China) "who always vote with the United States." The reasoning was clear: for the United States, even a good vote stemmed from bad motives. "The most shocking thing," Lara said, "is that while they strain to be on the side of the African peoples, the United States government continues to favour Portugal through NATO. In June last, it was announced that the Portuguese Air Force was about to purchase from the United States $6,440,000 worth of military equipment."[4]

In Brazil, as has been mentioned earlier, the new government of

[3] Such groups helped the MPLA to put its case before the European public through existing publications, e.g., "Statuten der Volksbewegung für die Befreiung Angolas (M.P.L.A.)," *Deutsche Aussenpolitik* (East Berlin), Vol. 6, No. 4 (1961), pp. 482–487; or through mimeographed material such as the communiqués of the Paris *Comité de Soutien* concerning the arrest of Father Joaquim Pinto de Andrade in 1960.

[4] Lucio Lara, "The Struggle for Freedom in Angola," *Voice of Africa* (Accra), Vol. 1, No. 11 (Nov. 1961), p. 27.

Jânio Quadros, like that of John Kennedy, displayed a new interest in the Afro-Asian world, and MPLA intellectuals and students formed contacts with their Brazilian counterparts, trade unionists, and parliamentarians. At São Paulo, university professors formed a Solidarity Committee,[5] and students created an Afro-Brazilian Movement for the Liberation of Angola (MABLA) to popularize the Angolan cause as represented by the MPLA.[6]

In the United Kingdom a group of liberals and intellectuals headed by Sir Leslie Plummer, M.P., and Anthony Wedgewood Benn, in cooperation with representatives of the Portuguese opposition and the MPLA, established a Council for Freedom in Portugal and Colonies.[7] During August the Council participated in a campaign to obtain offers of a position abroad for Dr. Agostinho Neto, the MPLA's "honorary president," who was still being held under house arrest in the Cape Verde Islands. The CONCP organization had mounted an international campaign charging that Portuguese officials on the island of Santa Antão, where he was held, planned to murder Neto. In an undated press release distributed in London, CONCP quoted the Angolan leader as having written in a worried letter, dated March 21, 1961: "The authorities have put out rumours that I am trying to escape by Russian submarines. At any time the police can kill me and announce that I have escaped." He went on to say that people in contact with him had been advised to avoid seeing him or face imprisonment and concluded that the police might "incite people against me so that a gang may be gathered to provoke and kill me." [8]

A series of letters by Thomas Fox Pitt of the Anti-Slavery Society, which requested action concerning the plight of Dr. Neto, mobilized among others Bishop Ralph E. Dodge of the Methodists and George Houser of the ACOA, both of whom attempted to obtain a medical internship for Dr. Neto in the United States. It was, however, the London-based Council for Freedom in Portugal and Colonies that produced the publicity and concrete offer to place Dr. Neto that

[5] Members included Florestan Fernandes, Josue de Castro, Caio Prado, Jr., Edison Carneiro, Buarque de Holando, and other political and cultural personalities.

[6] MPLA, *Angola, Exploitation esclavagiste, Résistance nationale* (Dakar: A. Diop, 1961), p. 45.

[7] The Council's sponsoring committee included such names as Fenner Brockway, Basil Davidson, and Sir Julian Huxley.

[8] A later appeal appears in CONCP, *Bulletin d'Information* (Rabat), No. 1 (Dec. 30, 1961), p. 6.

did the most to embarrass and possibly to deter Lisbon from allowing the Angolan doctor's fears to materialize. On October 17 he was transferred to Aljube prison in Lisbon and was subsequently permitted to live outside under house arrest.

In Africa, in addition to consolidating support among the "radical" Casablanca states—Ghana, Guinea, Mali, Morocco, and the United Arab Republic—Andrade solicited support from the leaders of newly independent French-speaking states, notably from a fellow poet and *Présence Africaine* intellectual, President Léopold Sédar Senghor of Senegal.[9] While in Dakar, Andrade published a party booklet setting forth the MPLA's "minimum and maximum" programs.[10] Its minimal goals focused on the need for a common front in the fight for independence. And in the interests of the masses of peasants and workers, they called for an alliance with the "progressive forces" of the world. The much more detailed maximum objectives included pledges to install democratic government and economic justice, to nationalize "land belonging to the enemy of the nationalist movement," to carry out educational reforms including the prohibition of "colonial and imperialistic culture and education," and to bar the establishment of foreign military bases on Angolan soil—but also to protect private enterprise and "foreign economic activities which were useful" to the society.[11]

In September the MPLA took a leading role in the organization of a conference of thirty-one students from Portuguese colonies at Rabat, Morocco. Twenty-two of the participants were Angolan; three were from Portuguese Guinea and three from São Tomé-Principe; two were from Cape Verde and one from Mozambique. At the student level, the meeting represented the same political coalition that had already formed the CONCP, headquartered in the Moroccan capital. From September 22 to 26 the students met as the constituent congress of a *União Geral dos Estudantes da Africa Negra sob Dominação Colónial Portuguêsa* (UGEAN). They denounced colonialism, neocolonialism, and imperialism, called upon

[9] Andrade was received by Senghor and other government officials in Dakar, June 15–24, 1961. The official organ of the ruling party, the *Union Progressiste Sénégalaise,* carried an interview with Andrade which stressed the need for a common front, *L'Unité Africaine* (Dakar), No. 93, June 20, 1961.

[10] MPLA, *Angola, Exploitation esclavagiste,* pp. 63–67.

[11] For English translation of both programs see Thomas Okuma, *Angola in Ferment* (Boston: Beacon Press, 1962), pp. 112–118. For a general review of MPLA goals, see Mário de Andrade, "Évolution du mouvement de libération angolaise," *Études méditerranéennes,* Vol. 10 (Autumn 1961), pp. 86–97.

"the nationalist parties and organizations of Angola to form one united front to destroy the Portuguese colonial system." They blamed the "imperialist bloc" of NATO for enabling the small and poor state of Portugal "to continue the colonial war of extermination," and elected an Angolan, Desidério da Graça (MPLA), as their first president.[12]

The fact remained that international support, pamphleteering, conference resolutions, and military communiqués implying that the MPLA (alone) had given leadership to the uprising in the north[13] could not make up for its being at least partly shut out of the action on the home front. Therefore, when the MPLA, with the approval of the Adoula government, set up its headquarters in well-furnished offices at 51 Avenue Tombeur de Tabora, Léopoldville, it immediately made a series of moves designed to put it back into the revolutionary equation.

First, it relaunched its campaign for the common *Front de Libération de l'Angola* (FLA) broached in the abortive negotiations of April. The FLA proposal was resurrected in a memorandum presented by MPLA observers to the Conference of Non-Aligned States at Belgrade in September and re-endorsed in a press conference by Mário de Andrade on October 30 at Léopoldville.[14] In his October statement Andrade affirmed that the MPLA Steering Committee was prepared to make "all necessary concessions" required to open the way for the creation of such a front.[15] Once again, however, the MPLA got off to a bad start with its most willing prospective partner, Aliazo. According to Aliazo, shortly before its move to Léopoldville the MPLA announced that José Bernardo Domingos, who Aliazo said enjoyed the respect of "Angolan patriots," had been named to the vice-presidency of the party. Yet when the MPLA headquarters team arrived from Guinea, Domingos was "automatically evicted"

[12] The strongest member of the executive committee was reputed to be its secretary-general and treasurer, José Fret, a mulatto from São Tomé-Principe. Other officers were Alberto Passos (Angola), vice-president for external affairs, Carlos Correia (Portuguese Guinea), vice-president for social and cultural affairs, and Daniel Neves (Cape Verde Islands), vice-president for press and information. UGEAN, "Resolutions," Constituent Congress, Rabat, Morocco, Sept. 22–26, 1961.

[13] See, for example, an MPLA communiqué of June 22, 1961, and elaborations on it in Lucio Lara, "Struggle for Freedom."

[14] See "Porquê uma frente de libertação de Angola," in *Unidade angolana,* No. 1, Dec. 1961.

[15] For the text of this statement, see *ibid.*; and Mário de Andrade, *Liberté pour l'Angola* (Paris: François Maspero, 1962), pp. 43–47.

from the party steering committee, which was "recomposed entirely of learned members tried and tested in Lisbon and Conakry." Such "political instability within the MPLA" and disregard on the part of MPLA leaders for local party workers was enough to raise Aliazo's doubt of the "good faith" of persons once again preaching unity. Furthermore, according to Aliazo sources, talks with Andrade convinced them that the MPLA leaders might be approaching them only because efforts to negotiate a front with the UPA, without Aliazo, had failed. In any case, the mutual confidence necessary for an alliance did not yet exist. Basically, the leaders of Aliazo feared that the MPLA would use them and their movement as a "springboard" to success for what they considered "ill-defined" aims. Following this they suspected that the MPLA would drop them as they said it had dropped others.[16] In general, it appears that the MPLA leaders had not yet effectively reckoned with local sensitivities and therefore remained "outsiders" in the Léopoldville context.

The *União Nacional dos Trabalhadores de Angola* (UNTA) was the only group to respond affirmatively to Andrade's call for unity negotiations. Contrarily, in a November press statement Holden Roberto simply invited members of other political parties to join the UPA, which he said was the only political movement conducting a military campaign inside Angola.[17] He clearly intended to bar the door to an alliance with a party whose array of poets, doctors, and theorists seemed to him and some of his associates to be only too anxious to take over the leadership of the revolution from the less polished directorate of the UPA.

The MPLA then tried another approach. Having formed a party youth group (*Jeunesse,* or JMPLA) upon arriving in Léopoldville in October, it set about trying to promote a common front of youth organizations as a step toward the ultimate objective of an Angolan Liberation Front (FLA). On October 29 leaders of the J-Aliazo, JMPLA, and JUPA met at the office of the MPLA's refugee service and agreed in principle to form a joint *União Democrática da Juventude Angolana,* which was to be organized by a provisional committee of twenty-one, seven representatives from each member youth group. But the JUPA representative at the meeting, Johnny Edouard, was immediately thereafter called to task by his seniors. The next day, October 30, he dispatched a letter of withdrawal

16 PDA, "Conférence de presse" (Léopoldville, Apr. 12, 1962, mimeo.).
17 *Courrier d'Afrique,* Nov. 23, 1961.

from the projected youth front, a turnabout which he attributed rather laconically to the "lack of seriousness or sincerity on the part of some of our brothers in other organizations." [18]

In spite of that withdrawal, an announcement was circulated in Léopoldville on December 5 stating that the youth affiliates of all three parties had joined to found a *Rassemblement Démocratique de la Jeunesse Angolaise* (RDJA). In fact, the representatives of the J-Aliazo and JMPLA only had met on November 1 and formed a two- not three-member front, with a fourteen-man executive committee headed by Pedro Ngadimpovi (J-Aliazo), president, Georges Manteya Freitas (JMPLA), vice-president, and Dr. João Vieira Lopes (JMPLA), secretary.[19] The withdrawal of the JUPA had crippled the RDJA from its beginning, and the apparent misrepresentation of the December 5 announcement only increased distrust of its promoters' intentions and hastened its early demise.[20]

If it did not succeed in creating a common front, the MPLA did nonetheless succeed in making its new presence felt in Léopoldville. It established a refugee medical service which was staffed by eight doctors and interns, headed by Dr. Américo Boavida,[21] and was well supplied with medicines, powdered milk, rice, and other staples for refugees. The services of the MPLA's *Corpo Voluntário Angolano de Assistência dos Refugiados* (CVAAR) quickly eclipsed those of the UPA's SARA and its overworked, undersupplied staff. Despite superior means,[22] however, CVAAR met strong, sometimes violent, resistance when it tried to establish branch dispensaries in areas of

[18] JUPA, Communiqué, P/CIRC/3/62/JE/BS (Léopoldville, Feb. 6, 1962, mimeo.). Johnny Edouard stated that JUPA had really supported the idea of forming a "comité unique d'assistance aux combattants angolais," which would have meant a joint committee to assist UPA fighting forces if one accepted the UPA thesis that it was the only organization on the battlefield.

[19] "Porquê uma frente de libertação." Other officers included Sebastien Bongo, assistant secretary; Simon Makonda, treasurer; André Kukia, assistant treasurer.

[20] In an interview at Léopoldville on January 21, 1962, João Lopes (secretary) maintained that the RDJA was very much alive and wished to develop connections with such organizations as the World Assembly of Youth and the U.S. National Student Association. The J-Aliazo had, however, withdrawn from any active participation in the RDJA by the time its parent party joined with the UPA in a political front in March 1962.

[21] Trained in gynecology and obstetrics, Faculty of Medicine, Barcelona, Spain; author of *Angola: Cinco séculos de exploração portuguêsa* (Rio de Janeiro: Editôra Civilização Brasileira, 1967), which lays stress on economic factors and determinants in the conflict over Angola.

[22] CVAAR announced that it had received medicines from the Swedish Red Cross, 3000 pounds sterling from War on Want (London) and help from numerous other sources. CONCP, *Bulletin d'Information,* No. 1 (Dec. 30, 1961), p. 10.

UPA influence in the Lower Congo. UPA partisans viewed CVAAR as a vehicle for MPLA political penetration. On the other hand, elements of the locally powerful Abako party, led by Vital Moanda and long at odds with the UPA, were ready to welcome both CVAAR and the MPLA.

One of the MPLA's major breakthroughs came in late 1961, during the absence of Holden Roberto and the UPA's vice-president and regular voice on Radio Léopoldville, Rosário Neto. During their absence, the MPLA took advantage of political rivalries within the Congolese government to persuade Interior Minister Christophe Gbenye to turn the Angolan broadcasts over to it.

At about the same time, a senior member of the party executive committee, Matias Miguéis, was chosen to launch and edit a new tabloid-size party organ, *Unidade Angolana,* which published its first issue in December. Miguéis, born August 15, 1917, at Novo Redondo, had studied at Luanda's Catholic seminary before completing a course at its commercial school. In 1945 he took a job with the Benguela Railroad and worked later as an accountant with the Mampenza Company. He was among the founding members of the *Ngola Ritmo* dance and folklore group and a one-time leader of Luanda's *Liga Nacional Africana* (LNA). In 1957 he left Angola and settled at Pointe Noire, where he reportedly served as a political liaison man between exiles Mário de Andrade and Viriato da Cruz in Europe and the MPLA organization inside Angola. In 1960 he became a member of the steering committee of the MPLA in exile, and as editor of its Léopoldville paper he emerged in 1961 as one of the MPLA's principal leaders.[23]

The occasion of its autumnal entry upon the Léopoldville scene prompted the MPLA to launch a publicity offensive and to explain in some detail those of its policies which had heretofore provoked criticism or which distinguished it from other movements headquartered in the Congolese capital. Answering questions at the end of a press conference on October 30, Andrade said that since its creation the MPLA had been proud to attract intellectuals. After all, throughout history intellectuals had put themselves in the *avant garde* of national liberation movements. Thus the MPLA had been proud to appeal to writers, doctors, and Catholic and Prot-

[23] *Angola 66* (published by Jorge Valentim, Oegstgeest, Netherlands, 1966, mimeo.), p. 7; and MPLA/Viriato, Comitê Director Provisório, "Commemoration de la deuxième anniversaire de la mort de deux patriotes assassinés à Brazzaville en Novembre 1965" (Kinshasa, Nov. 12, 1967, mimeo.).

estant clergymen with its political program. Furthermore, referring obliquely to charges that the MPLA was dominated by a mulatto leadership, Andrade pointed out that the existence of some tens of thousands of mulattoes in Angola was the result of Portuguese appropriation of African women since the fifteenth century and asked: "But are they not fully Angolan?" He argued that only a few mulattoes lived as privileged members of the colonial order, and that most first-generation mulattoes were abandoned by their European fathers. He made it clear, moreover, that the MPLA regarded any reservations about a political role for Angolan mulattoes as constituting a form of African racism.[24]

Andrade also declared that the MPLA was nonaligned internationally and prepared to cooperate with Portuguese democrats. During the subsequent legislative election campaign of November 1961, the party directorate declared its support for anti-Salazar candidates. In spite of the disunity of the Portuguese opposition, the MPLA professed to find in the opposition's ranks a "common denominator" that consisted of "a realistic and democratic spirit that would have permitted a solution to colonial conflict without requiring the use of armed violence," had this been the spirit of those in power. Stressing that its own opposition was to the Salazar regime, not to Portugal, the MPLA expressed the hope that the Portuguese people would use the elections, which were, it should be noted, anything but free, as a means of replacing the "fascist" Salazar regime with a democratic one.[25] This stand was consistent with MPLA efforts to coordinate all African and European opposition to Salazar in the belief that what would happen in Angola would be tied inevitably and closely to the political situation in Portugal.[26] The UPA, by way of contrast, took little heed of the Portuguese elections, considered the results a foregone conclusion, tended to write off the Portuguese opposition as merely liberal colonialists, and continued to work alone.

Another feature of the MPLA's autumn offensive which deserves special attention was something called the Khatib Plan. As of late 1961 the Casablanca powers, united in their support for Lumumbist nationalism in the Congo, were championing the cause of militant

[24] See *Le Monde*, Nov. 8, 1961; and MPLA, Mimeographed questions and replies (Léopoldville, Nov. 1961).

[25] MPLA, "Déclaration" by the Comité Directeur (Léopoldville, Nov. 3, 1961, mimeo.).

[26] See *The Atlantic*, Vol. 209, No. 3 (Mar. 1962), p. 26.

pan-Africanism. Thus it was logical that the MPLA and its Moroccan supporters should produce a well-publicized scheme known as the Khatib Plan designed to implement the militant, Casablanca-style resolutions of the All-African Peoples' Conferences and Afro-Asian Solidarity Conferences that now annually called for the liberation of southern Africa.

The plan was named for its author, Dr. Abdelkrim Khatib, then minister of African affairs in the Moroccan government. He first set it forth as a series of proposals put to a Seminar on the Problems of Portuguese Colonies held at New Delhi in October 1961 under the aegis of the Indian Council for Africa. His proposals called for the following: (1) an Afro-Asian conference of foreign ministers or "experts" for the sole purpose of discussing alternative courses of action regarding the Portuguese colonies, and particularly Angola; (2) a timetable for political decolonization in the form of an ultimatum to Portugal; and (3) in the probable event of Portuguese defiance, an African expeditionary force formed under the Joint African High Command of the Casablanca Charter to be sent to help national liberation movements overthrow Portuguese rule.[27] The Khatib Plan was officially endorsed by the MPLA and the Conference of Nationalist Organizations of the Portuguese Colonies (CONCP).

In January 1962, in a meeting that the Washington *Evening Star* described as "a semi-official council of war," the CONCP reportedly decided to push ahead with the Khatib Plan.[28] The paper reported that "the prospect of a concerted military move by several African states" was "being taken seriously" by western diplomatic circles in Washington, in the wake of India's seizure of Goa. Going on to say that a successful attack on Portuguese Guinea, Angola, or Mozambique would "have the most serious implications for NATO," the *Evening Star* proceeded to draw attention to a widely held assumption that the American government feared actions that might topple the Salazar regime, in view of the apparent absence of an acceptable noncommunist alternative in Portugal. Commenting on Washington's presumed "Batista or Castro" thinking, the widely

[27] *Jeune Afrique,* No. 68 (Jan. 17, 1962), p. 22. Mário de Andrade outlined the plan in a press conference at Rabat on Dec. 11, 1961. CONCP, *Bulletin d'Information,* Dec. 30, 1961, p. 7.

[28] Reportedly, if the Khatib Plan were to fail, it had been decided to concentrate on initiating military action in Portuguese Guinea. *Evening Star,* Feb. 12, 1962.

read Franco-Tunisian weekly *Jeune Afrique* predicted that in the event of an upheaval, the *Junta Patriótica Nacional Revolucionária* of the extreme left would probably come to power in Portugal. This would not be the same thing, it noted, as replacing a pro-NATO Adnan Menderes with a pro-NATO Ismet Inonü. Portugal was not Turkey, and Britain and America knew it.[29] To this alleged Anglo-Saxon-NATO perception of things Portuguese, *Jeune Afrique* attributed "the violence of American and English reactions" against the Indian seizure of Goa. From this analysis it followed logically to *Jeune Afrique* that Washington and London were obliged to oppose the liberation of the Portuguese colonies in order to sustain Salazar—a widely held Afro-Asian interpretation of western motives and actions.

Chetniks and Partisans: The Ferreira Affair

During the autumn of 1961 the MPLA made strenuous efforts to achieve a political and military breakthrough. On October 30 Mário de Andrade claimed that MPLA units had occupied regions from Tombôco southward through Nambuangongo to Ucua for five months (March to July) and were continuing to fight against heavily armed Portuguese reinforcements that had reoccupied parts of these areas.[30] Andrade expressed concern over the "curious notion" found in "certain circles of the international press" that "the conduct of and responsibility for the military operations in Angola" depended "upon one political movement only." His concern and a corrective "survey of [MPLA] activities" in the military domain was aired in a New York monthly alongside a UPA communiqué signed by Roberto and Batista which claimed that the UPA's army of "25,000 men" occupied a "vast area" in the northwest of Angola and constituted "the only nationalist military force engaged in military operations against Portuguese colonialism in the interior of our country." Appearing in *Liberator,* the organ of an Afro-American "Liberation Committee for Africa," these juxtaposed contradictory statements symbolized the dilemma that would long confront foreign analysts and persons sympathetic to the Angolan nationalists' cause. In due course some observers would get ensnarled in or become critical of the crossfire of conflicting claims

[29] *Jeune Afrique,* No. 68 (Jan. 17, 1962).
[30] Andrade, *Liberté pour l'Angola,* pp. 44–45.

to revolutionary legitimacy. The conflict was highlighted in the UPA communiqué's rejection of the "recent statement by Mr. Mário de Andrade . . . who claims for his party a military anti-colonialist activity which, unfortunately, does not correspond to reality." [31] What were the bases for MPLA claims to revolutionary leadership in northern Angola or for UPA counterclaims to exclusive credit?

A Swedish journalist, Anders Ehnmark, visited Léopoldville during late summer 1961 and wrote about it in a book translated into English and published in New York.[32] He reported that refugees arriving in the Songololo area of the Congo credited "UPA (pronounced 'oopa')" with "being behind the whole business." Two of the UPA's leaders, he said, were well known: "Holden Roberto and Pinoquio." Whereas Roberto lived in Léopoldville, "Pinoquio [presumably Eduardo Pinock] often traveled about in Angola. At any moment, anywhere, he might come through the savannas to supervise the rebellion." [33]

A few pages later Ehnmark described a meeting in Léopoldville with a handsome young MPLA militant by the name of Tomas Francisco Ferreira. While he found it "hard to say exactly" what Ferreira's role might be, he described him as "at once a sort of military commander, recruiting agent, and courier." When Ehnmark asked such questions as where the MPLA got arms for the forces it claimed to have inside Angola, Ferreira replied vaguely that "Angola is full of weapons," and his admirers in the courtyard applauded.[34] Some pages further on, however, the Swedish observer struck a somber note. "Ferreira, the dandy of Léopoldville's African quarter" had been killed. On a mission to carry ammunition and bring relief to nationalist forces in the Nambuangongo area of Angola, he and his patrol had been surprised, captured, and killed by troops of the UPA.[35]

The Ferreira affair was to be one of the most discussed, most deplored, and most difficult to explain in the long chain of human tragedies that have plagued the Angolan revolution. Without judging the arguments of the contending parties, it is now possible to

[31] *Liberator* (New York), Vol. II, No. 2 (Feb., 1962), p. 2.

[32] Anders Ehnmark and Per Wästberg, *Angola and Mozambique* (New York: Roy Publishers, 1963).

[33] *Ibid.*, pp. 72–73.

[34] *Ibid.*, p. 77.

[35] *Ibid.*, pp. 81–82.

piece together some of what probably happened and to fit this into the over-all picture of the nationalist struggle.

After the February uprising in Luanda was smashed, a number of MPLA partisans escaped into the Mbundu countryside, principally the Dembos. One of them was a young man known as Ferraz Bomboco. According to the accounts of men who served under him, Bomboco established himself at the village of Colua, not far from Quiteche, where he found the populace already organized by the UPA.[36] Accepting military orders from UPA headquarters in Léopoldville, he organized a military band which assaulted Quiteche on March 15 and which subsequently operated as a guerrilla force out of Colua and later Kaluanda. Such was local support for the UPA and its chief, "Mbuta Muntu," that the commander was reportedly "afraid to reveal the name of [his] Organization," for if he did so "he would risk his life." As months passed the Portuguese brought in sizable reinforcements and intensified their air attacks, and the rebel band, like many others, ran out of both ammunition and hope for an early victory. On August 9, 1961, Portuguese troops reoccupied the nationalist town of Nambuangongo. Some of the rebels were by then disillusioned by delinquent promises, whether real, rumored, or just imagined—promises of material, reinforcements from a trained guerrilla force of 25,000 in the Congo, and even aid from America.[37] So in August Commander Bomboco sent a five-man mission, headed by Rev. Domingos da Silva, to Léopoldville to assess the political situation and seek help.

After traveling a month through rebel-held (UPA) territory, the da Silva mission from Colua arrived in Léopoldville and went straight "to the home of an MPLA official" (José Bernardo Domingos). It spent the next few days in discussions with MPLA

[36] Robert Davezies, *Les angolais* (Paris: Les Éditions de Minuit, 1965), pp. 30–33.

[37] *Ibid.*, p. 35. For Portuguese assessments of the Nambuangongo campaign as a "rude blow" and political and psychological defeat for the UPA, see Artur Maciel, *Angola Heróica* (Lisbon: Livraria Bertrand, 1963), pp. 167–180; and Hélio Felgas, *Guerra em Angola* (Livraria Classica Editôra, 1961), p. 160. A Britisher, Col. Ronald Waring, for some years an instructor at the Portuguese Staff College, who visited the war zones, has written that the only "direct evidence in Angola of direct Communist indoctrination or interference" that he could find was the creation of a "People's Socialist Republic of Nambuangongo, which clearly was intended to have a Communist-type administration." "The Case for Portugal," in *Angola: A Symposium, Views of a Revolt* (London: Oxford University Press, 1962), p. 39.

leaders, to whom it turned over funds that it had brought from Colua with instructions not to deliver them until it knew "the truth." [38] Seizing the opportunity that was thus presented, the MPLA organized an armed patrol and sent it off to Bomboco's rescue.

To lead this mission the MPLA chose Tomas Ferreira. According to Marcos Kassanga, Ferreira, a dark African-oriented mulatto from Benguela, had been his classmate at the *Escola de Aplicação Militar de Angola* at Nova Lisboa. Ferreira fled to the Congo in 1960 ahead of Kassanga and was one of the original members of João Batista's military commission in Léopoldville. Dissatisfied with Roberto's political leadership, however, he reportedly quit the UPA in early 1961. Again according to Kassanga, after the outbreak of fighting in March, Ferreira entered Angola at the head of a group of some seven men to organize an independent military campaign in the Tombôco region southwest of São Salvador. Then a few months later he returned to the Congo and joined the MPLA.[39]

On November 10 MPLA officials dispatched a letter to the Steering Committee of the UPA, charging that an MPLA military patrol, headed for Nambuangongo to relieve Angolans surrounded by Portuguese troops, had been "encircled and taken prisoner" by armed forces of the UPA operating in the corridor through which all "Angolan patriots" must enter and leave their country. The letter charged that this "anti-patriotic act" would reduce the effectiveness of the Angolan resistance movements by introducing a "fratricidal" conflict onto the Angolan battlefield, and it demanded the immediate release of the patrol and all its confiscated equipment.[40] This letter was followed on November 23 by an MPLA communiqué which announced and denounced the slaying on October 9 of Commander Tomas Ferreira and his squad of twenty men by the UPA's militia.[41] The MPLA patrol had been stopped when trying to cross the M'Bridge River at the UPA village of Caluca. From there it had been taken to the UPA regional headquarters post known as Fuesse, a forest hideaway that had been

[38] Davezies, *Les angolais,* p. 37.
[39] Interview with author, Sept. 3, 1968.
[40] MPLA, "Note" No. A/M/F, Nov. 10, 1961, circulated in Léopoldville as an open, mimeographed letter, signed by Messrs. Andrade, da Cruz, Miguéis, Santos, and de Menezes.
[41] MPLA, Communiqué (Léopoldville, Nov. 23, 1961, mimeo.).

established near São Salvador by Roberto's aide and trouble shooter, José Manuel Peterson. There the "intruders" were put to death.[42]

After an initial expression of surprise at the MPLA charges and a promise to investigate the affair, the UPA issued a *pro forma* communiqué signed by vice-president Rosário Neto and the military chief of staff Marcos Kassanga, which denied the MPLA's accusations and suggested that if there really had been a massacre the Portuguese were responsible.[43] Subsequently, however, Holden Roberto confirmed that he had in fact given orders to intercept and annihilate MPLA columns that were trying to infiltrate into Angola.[44]

The Ferreira mission had been designed to wrest control of the village militia centered at Colua from the UPA and thereby to establish a military front linked to the MPLA headquarters in Léopoldville. Apparently this goal was at least partially achieved, in spite of the elimination of Ferreira's patrol, when two of the guides sent with Rev. da Silva from Angola to Léopoldville managed to return safely to Colua and report back to Commander Bomboco. They reportedly told Bomboco that "Holden had lied when he pretended to have 25,000 men and airplanes in Léopoldville"; and after some palaver, the Kimbundu-speaking villages of the area led by Bomboco switched allegiance to the MPLA.[45] On the other hand, Kikongo-speaking villages in this ethnic transition zone remained loyal to the UPA.[46]

[42] Davezies, *Les angolais,* pp. 38, 78, and 232.

[43] The UPA responded first with an open letter (Reference 621/3/VP/961) of November 14, signed by Rosário Neto, which professed no knowledge of the affair, and second with a communiqué (Léopoldville, no date, mimeo.), denying the charges and adding that for the MPLA to send a patrol into the zone of military action without having alerted the UPA in advance was a "grave error."

Marcos Kassanga later told the author in an interview (Sept. 3, 1968) that he and Rosário Neto were the last to be told the truth about the UPA's responsibility for the fate of the Ferreira patrol, but the first to be pressured by the UPA's Bakongo leadership into denying such responsibility. According to Kassanga, Jonas Savimbi, in whom he and André Kassinda had confided, had already alerted Holden Roberto to their growing dissatisfaction with his leadership. Therefore, to have refused to sign the communiqué, Kassanga reasoned, might have cost him his post and ended his chances of working for a new party leadership from within the UPA structure.

[44] See interviews with Roberto in *Révolution africaine* (Algiers), No. 83, Aug. 29, 1964; and in Davezies, *Les angolais,* p. 189. There was some suspicion within UPA circles at Léopoldville that the Ferreira mission had instructions to build an airfield in the Nambuangongo area so that arms could be flown in from Stanleyville, the center of Antoine Gizenga's dissident, Eastern-backed Congolese regime.

[45] Davezies, *Les angolais,* p. 40.

[46] *Ibid.,* pp. 40–41 and 242.

During the last months of 1961 several other complicated cases of concealed, confused, or switched loyalties—all characterized by the same ethnic undertones—further envenomed UPA-MPLA relations. For example, as the Portuguese counteroffensive progressed in August and September, Mbundu forces which had earlier attacked Ucua under the leadership of a UPA commander, Domingos Miguel, now joined by villagers from different parts of the Dembos, withdrew northward across the Dange River into the rebel-held forest area around Nambuangongo, only to find that the Portuguese were beginning to move their forces back into that area as well. In desperation they dispatched a mission of six Dembo people to Léopoldville to seek help. The mission met Roberto but also sought out MPLA leaders. It accepted gunpowder and medicine from Roberto, received party cards, rubber stamps, pistols, and other medicine from the MPLA, and after six months returned to report that to remain with the UPA would mean never to get out of the forest.[47] (These same six delegates reportedly made a return trip to Léopoldville in August 1962, accepted arms and military orders from the UPA, and once again accepted medicine, letters, and party insignia from the MPLA. They then returned to Nambuangongo, where, discouraged by the course of the revolution, they crossed the Dange River and gave themselves up to the Portuguese.)[48]

What Roberto denounced as MPLA efforts to "infiltrate" the UPA's military zone in Angola, Matias Miguéis praised in *Unidade Angolana* as a series of successful tactical moves by the MPLA designed to obtain the adhesion of important groups of people inside the country. These political-military exploits of mid- and late 1961 were, according to Miguéis, the work of several MPLA commanders, i.e., Ferraz Bomboco, António Fernandes, Pedro Mussadi, and João Gonçalves Benedito.[49] The UPA was of course hurt by such group defections. They were organized by persons whose loyalties it had taken for granted, and UPA bitterness showed in a new communiqué that was issued over the names of Rosário Neto and Marcos Kassanga and dealt with a statement to *Agence France Presse* that had been made by Commander Benedito,

[47] *Ibid.*, p. 77.

[48] *Ibid.*, pp. 78–79. Illustrative of how loyalties were disguised, an MPLA partisan at Nambuangongo said that the delegates to Léopoldville, after receiving MPLA medical supplies, "had a receipt made out at a pharmacy and then claimed: 'These are not MPLA medicines, we bought them ourselves.' In their clothes they hid secret letters, insignia, and rubber stamps."

[49] *Unidade Angolana*, Feb. 4, 1962.

one of the MPLA organizers cited by Miguéis. Benedito had told the official French news service that he led a group of 1000 MPLA partisans inside Angola. The UPA charged that, on the contrary, Benedito had until recently served under the orders of the National Liberation Army (ELNA) and had come to Léopoldville at the end of July 1961 under a "safe conduct" pass delivered by a UPA party secretary, António Simão da Silva. There he had presented a report on activities in the Nambuangongo region to the political director of the UPA, Luandan Anibal de Melo—who defected to the MPLA a few months later—a report stating that military operations had begun in his area on March 19, 1961, under UPA direction.[50]

Kassanga has since recounted that Benedito arrived in the Congo with 500,000 escudos taken from Portuguese posts in the Nambuangongo area. In Léopoldville, according to Kassanga, Benedito found disgruntled groups that had preceded him to UPA headquarters where they had given over their escudos and then waited in vain for the military equipment they had expected in return. Benedito, Kassanga has said, therefore concluded what he, Kassanga, was also beginning to conclude, that Roberto was more concerned with collecting escudos than with procuring arms, and Benedito went straightaway to the MPLA.[51]

Benedito later gave his own version of these events, which were shrouded by a haze of confused and disputed loyalties, in an autobiographical article entitled "Five Months of Independence in Angola." Born in 1927, the son of a Luanda railway worker, he spent two years in a Catholic seminary before taking a job with the administration. He served as a "liaison officer" and grew coffee in the Nambuangongo region before coming into contact with the MPLA while visiting with his family in Luanda. His introduction to nationalist politics came in the form of an MPLA tract left under the front door, which read: "Long live Angola! Long live Queen Jinga! Rise up Angolans!" Benedito showed the leaflet to a friend with "progressive opinions" and the friend then "started [Benedito's] political education."

Returned to Nambuangongo, Benedito organized political meetings and in January 1961, upon learning of the imminence of politi-

[50] UPA, "Communiqué conjoint UPA-ALNA" (Léopoldville, Jan. 15, 1962, mimeo.).

[51] Interview with author, Sept. 3, 1968.

cal action in Luanda, he helped local forces prepare to fight with such weapons as incendiary bombs in the form of bottles of palm oil and gasoline with short cotton wicks. In mid-March, following the February riots in Luanda, Benedito's rural forces occupied trading posts and *fazendas* in the Nambuangongo area, and together with those whom he would later describe as "MPLA officers from the neighboring regions" they liberated "a vast area containing more than 60,000 people."

In one startling passage which suggests an absence of planning, strategy, or real links with political movements within either Angola or the Congo, Benedito recounted that some $300,000 in escudos collected at captured Portuguese posts was burned at a public assemblage in order "to prevent people squabbling over the money and because we had no need of it." Obviously, if such funds were indeed useless, then the local nationalist council "governing" the area had no access to sources of supply through either an internal Angolan underground or an exile movement.

Benedito wrote that in the aftermath of the deaths of a fellow commander Maneco-Paca and others, during fighting around Ucua, nationalist forces withdrew into the bush and mountains. They were confronted by an impending Portuguese assault on the nationalist stronghold of Nambuangongo. At this point Benedito set out for Léopoldville on a mission "to contact the external organization of the MPLA so that they would send us arms and ammunition." Accompanied by "seventy young soldiers" on a twelve-day trek to the border, Benedito perforce traversed areas under UPA control, and it may be presumed that he and his large—and thus visible—contingent had at least to feign some sort of loyalty to the UPA at the time. Nothing of this is suggested in his account, however, which states only that once in the Congo he met with "the MPLA delegate and gave him a report on the situation." [52]

From such accounts by MPLA partisans active in areas contested by the two rival parties, it would appear that military leaders like Bomboco, Benedito, and others, mostly Luandans, had in fact maintained a latent sympathy for the MPLA even when obliged to take orders from the UPA. They had been familiar with the names and reputations of Dr. Agostinho Neto and Mário de Andrade, but not of Holden Roberto.[53] In due course, war weariness, the absence of

[52] Commander João Gonçalves Benedito, "Five Months of Independence in Angola," *African Revolution* (Algiers), Vol. 1, No. 1 (May 1963), pp. 26–29.
[53] Davezies, *Les angolais,* p. 38.

outside help, and the inclination to blame Léopoldville for mounting reverses[54] rendered them increasingly receptive to charges that the UPA had ordered the killing of *assimilados*,[55] was antimulatto,[56] or was motivated by Bakongo tribalism.[57] (On the other hand, assertions that the MPLA, unlike the UPA, was not ethnocentric had to be matched against reports that all defections from the UPA to the MPLA were among the Mbundu.)[58] The extent to which ethnic sentiments underlay the deepening animosity between the MPLA and UPA stood out clearly in Rev. da Silva's accusations against the UPA. Contradicting the accounts of several of his younger MPLA associates, the Methodist pastor claimed that from the beginning all fighting in the Dembos and Nambuangongo areas had been led by the MPLA and added that with "some rare exceptions" the people of the north (Bakongo) "lack the fighting spirit of those who come from the regions south of Nova Caipemba." In fact, the military exploits of the Mbundu, he said, had been the cause of the "jealousy" which had prompted Holden Roberto, backed by the Adoula government of the Congo, to bar the transit of men and arms across Bakongo country to the real center of the Angolan revolution.[59]

Most international reaction to the Ferreira affair and UPA-MPLA conflict was to deplore it, often in condescending terms, as a manifestation of African tribalism. Western analysts seldom made mention of what were innumerable historical precedents of revolutionary rivalry between Chetniks and Partisans. A journal of the Trotskyite Fourth International, however, viewed the event somewhat differently. It attributed the affair to the hatred of the African peasant for the more privileged mulatto (there were mulattoes in Ferreira's

[54] Resentment against Léopoldville centered about (1) alleged unfulfilled promises of help which may have been occasioned, in part, by the excessive enthusiasm of UPA couriers, and (2) alleged orders not to shoot down Portuguese aircraft bombing and strafing African villages, because "Mbuta Muntu" (a term which Eduardo Pinock has suggested was a reference to himself) might be aboard. It is somewhat difficult to understand what motive UPA headquarters would have had for giving such an order or why any rational local leadership would have taken it seriously.

[55] Davezies, *Les angolais*, pp. 31–34, 39.

[56] *Ibid.*, pp. 33–34, 39, 78.

[57] *Ibid.*, p. 110.

[58] *Ibid.*, pp. 40 and 242. The UPA was alternately accused of being anti-Mbundu because the Mbundu all joined the MPLA or anti-MPLA because the MPLA was not a Kikongo party.

[59] *Ibid.*, pp. 244–245.

squad) and commented that only those suffering from "political angelicism" and knowing nothing of the "brutal conditions of colonial wars for independence" would be surprised by it. The journal went on to suggest that violent competition between Angolan nationalists was also linked to the division of all African anti-colonial movements into two types: (1) Bourguibists, who were bourgeois and pro-western; and (2) Castroists, who were socialist in orientation. The UPA "nationalists," it said, fell within the first category, the MPLA "revolutionary leftists" within the second.[60]

However analyzed and categorized, the UPA and MPLA were to clash in military combat again in the future. Significantly, their sporadic armed encounters always occurred in either the Lower Congo-Angolan frontier region, which was vital for access to the fighting zones in northern Angola, or in ethnic transition zones such as Nambuangongo, where political and ethnic rivalry were most likely to reinforce one another.

The End of the Year: Off to New York

As 1961 closed, attention turned to New York and the Sixteenth General Assembly of the United Nations where the Angolan question was once again on the agenda. This time Holden Roberto was not the only Angolan to attend. In November Aliazo sent its vice-president, Emmanuel Kunzika, along with Sanda Martin, a prominent Bazombo business man and member of the party executive, to the United Nations—with stops in Belgium and Britain. Aliazo thus made its entry into the international arena as the "third party" in the Angolan nationalist equation. At the General Assembly Kunzika sounded an "SOS" urging the world body to "disarm Portugal" and send two commissions to the revolt-torn country, one on a fact-finding mission and another to establish the machinery for general elections.[61] He also lobbied, with some diplomatic assistance from Ambassador Emmanuel Dadet of the Congo-Brazzaville, among African and other delegations.

Aliazo's political options remained those of nonviolent nationalism. Yet it was becoming increasingly difficult to remain aloof from the war. Already in September the party president, André Massaki, had given an indication of this in a statement which was carried in

[60] *L'Internationale* (Paris), Oct. 1962.

[61] Aliazo, "Petition pour l'Angola presentée à la 16ème Assemblée Générale des Nations Unies à New York" (Léopoldville, no date).

the British press. Speaking of Portugal's response to the rebellion in the north, he said that in the Bazombo region "the Portuguese came and took all the educated people, especially chiefs. Later they came back to some of our villages with trucks, and dumped out the clothing of the men who had been taken. Our people assumed they were killed—we have never heard from them again, and it was then that some Aliazo supporters began taking rifles and machetes and resisting the Portuguese military power." [62]

Mário de Andrade also crossed the Atlantic. Just before leaving he told the press in Rabat that the MPLA had consistently worked "to remove any obstacles" that could stand in the way of the creation of an Angolan Liberation Front and warned that only political-military coordination, including "a single command over the maquis," could save Angola from a "fratricidal" war. He also called for an all-African conference to implement the Khatib Plan.[63] He was quoted as saying that he would use the occasion of his trip to New York to begin preparations for such a conference. Lisbon thereupon protested in vain against Washington's decision to grant him an entry visa.[64] With his program he went to the United States where, like Kunzika, he lobbied for support within diplomatic and university circles. On January 11, 1962, at the invitation of Professor Immanuel Wallerstein, he gave a lecture at Columbia University on the relationship between "Literature and Nationalism in Angola." [65]

Andrade's visit gave him an opportunity to refute the charge made against the MPLA that had most damaged its chances for influencing American opinion. In an interview published by the *Christian Science Monitor* he met head-on the issue of his and the MPLA's reputed Communist sympathies. So long as the MPLA had maintained its offices in Conakry, Guinea, he said, it had found itself "being lumped with Guinea as a target for propaganda." Since moving to Léopoldville, however, the situation had changed so that "we are no longer called Communists. And to reply directly—no, we are not pro-Communists." [66]

In another interview during his American visit, the MPLA

[62] *The Guardian,* Sept. 20, 1961, p. 2.

[63] "Conférence de presse," Dec. 11, 1961, in CONCP, *Bulletin d'Information,* No. 1 (Dec. 30, 1961), p. 7. Also in Andrade, *Liberté pour l'Angola,* pp. 48–51.

[64] *The New York Times,* Dec. 14, 1962.

[65] Extracts of which are published in *Présence Africaine,* No. 41 (1962), pp. 91–99.

[66] *Christian Science Monitor,* Jan. 8, 1962.

leader asserted that it was personal ambition and not ideology that prevented the UPA from joining in a front with his party. In his estimation, Holden Roberto constituted the real obstacle to unity and, just as Lisbon charged, Roberto was not really Angolan, because he had lived for so long in the Congo. Nevertheless, Andrade indicated that he was prepared to meet with his rival at any time in order to negotiate a common front. Andrade acknowledged too that the area of northern Angola under UPA control was of great importance as a zone of access to the north-central areas of Angola, which constituted the MPLA's stronghold. He said that a special MPLA commission was working on the problem of arms transit through the zone. If the UPA continued to block access from the north, he added, "We will infiltrate through other border areas." [67]

The third new visitor to the United Nations and New York speaking in the name of Angola was the president of Nto-Bako, Angelino Alberto. His trip was sponsored by the Portuguese-American Committee on Foreign Affairs, registered as a foreign agent with the Department of Justice. To the press, Alberto denounced nationalist violence in Angola and released pictures showing himself addressing peaceful Angolan villagers, who were in turn surrounded by Portuguese military personnel.[68]

For Holden Roberto, it was his fourth trip to New York and his third appearance at the General Assembly. This time, he was accompanied by Jonas Savimbi, whom he had persuaded to leave his studies in Lausanne long enough to join him at the Belgrade Conference of Non-Aligned States and to visit Léopoldville, where Savimbi took the plunge, made his political commitment, and became secretary-general of the UPA. The appointment of an Ochimbundu to this key post in the party did much to blunt charges that it was tribalist. Together, Roberto and Savimbi submitted a joint memorandum to the United Nations Sub-Committee on Angola, arguing that recognition of the right to self-determination should constitute the *sine qua non* of any Angolan settlement.[69]

At a New York press conference on November 22, Roberto announced that he intended to ask the American government to

[67] Interview with author, New York, Feb. 1, 1962.

[68] *Christian Science Monitor,* Feb. 10, 1962.

[69] Memorandum submitted to "His Excellency Sr. Carlos Salamanca, chairman, Sub-Commission on Angola, United Nations Secretariat, New York" (typescript, Nov. 22, 1961).

place an embargo on all arms shipments to Portugal.[70] Hopeful that the Kennedy administration and American public opinion could be persuaded to take such a firm stand against Portuguese colonialism, he then made a number of public appearances during December, speaking, among other places, at the University of Pennsylvania and at Georgetown University.[71] In these addresses he presented a balance sheet for 1961, the year of rebellion.[72] He said that although Angola's "harsh war" might "go on for a long time," the "tactical objectives" of the war's first phase had been substantially achieved. These were (1) to obtain modern weapons to replace the "garden tools" with which the first attacks had been launched, and (2) to destroy the war potential of the enemy. The cost had been high: 50,000 civilian dead and untold thousands of wounded, "who, lacking medicine or refuge, would eventually die or face the future crippled for life."

According to the UPA president, the rebellion had now entered its second or guerrilla phase. Portuguese troops had reoccupied all major centers during the summer dry season, but nationalist forces occupied the forests and mountains, from which they mounted raids and ambushes, destroyed plantations, disrupted transportation, and captured arms. The war of attrition would continue, he added, until Portugal, a nation of limited resources, would be prepared to negotiate an Évian-type agreement granting self-determination to Angolans.

In terms that recalled and possibly reflected the thinking of Frantz Fanon, whom he had visited at the latter's Bethesda Hospital deathbed that autumn,[73] Roberto professed to find some compensatory

[70] *Le Monde,* Nov. 24, 1961.

[71] Dec. 2 and Dec. 12, 1961, respectively.

[72] These speeches form the major ingredients in Roberto's unpublished manuscript, "The Angolan Revolution" (New York, 1961), from which the quotations in this paragraph are taken.

[73] Because of his deep hostility toward American racial and colonial policies, Fanon had earlier resisted advice that he go to the United States for specialized medical treatment. He died at the age of thirty-six, convinced by his Bethesda doctors, according to Roberto, that his political convictions had fatally delayed treatment that might have saved his life.

Writing shortly before his death in December 1961, Fanon, like Roberto, described the Angolan rebellion as having entered a new, guerrilla phase. Following upon the spontaneous and impetuous nature of the initial explosion, he wrote, the "hard lesson of facts, the bodies mowed down by machine-guns: these [called] forth a complete re-interpretation of events." The instinct to survive devalues in the continuation of the war. If it had made Angolans suffer, he said, it had also unified them. Some countries that had won their independence without a struggle had weakly allowed selfish tribal and regional interests to prevail over "the needs of the masses." Angolans had been forced to suppress such parochial interests "in order to save [their] skins. Perhaps, if it had not been for the catharsis of the war, sectional and ethnic divisions might have played a disturbing role for a long time to come." Traditional rivals, however, had been obliged to fight side by side and to sacrifice their lives for one another. "This," he continued, "is what produces nationhood, and our future tasks will be easier with our people so aware of the necessity of sticking together." To encourage this process of national unification, he added, the UPA was "discouraging regional and tribal competition at the top echelons of the Party," which, moreover, had been "organized in such a way as to discourage any attempts at political domination by any one group."

Discussing the UPA's program for an independent Angola, Roberto emphasized four things: education, land reform, economic development, and diplomatic nonalignment. Couched in terms of a pragmatic, agrarian radicalism which reflected the UPA's peasant roots, his political prescription for an independent Angola called for: (1) a massive educational effort at all levels to create the popular and technical basis for effective, stable government, an effort to which the government would devote "the greatest part of [its] budget"; (2) land reform to redistribute, limit the size, and increase the productivity of freehold land, much of which was "in the hands of Portuguese settlers"; (3) development of mineral, petroleum, fish, and other resources for the profit of "all the people of Angola";

---

manded a switch away from the optimistic or Utopian tactics of mass popular assault:

". . . We may remember that on the 15th of March 1961 a group of two or three thousand Angolan peasants threw themselves against the Portuguese position. Men, women and children, armed and unarmed, afire with courage and enthusiasm, then flung themselves in successive waves of compact masses upon the districts where the settler, the soldier and the Portuguese flag held sway. Villages and aerodromes were encircled and subjected to frequent attacks, but it must be added that thousands of Angolans were mown down by colonialist machine guns. It did not take long for the leaders of the Angolan rising to realize that they must find some other methods if they really wanted to free their country. So during the last few months the Angolan leader Holden Roberto has reorganized the National Angolan Army, using the experience gained in various other wars of liberation, and employing guerrilla techniques." Fanon, *The Wretched of the Earth* (New York: Grove Press, 1963), p. 107.

and (4) real independence achieved by means of a "nationalist policy" which avoided "dependence upon the ideologies of any outside groups" and barred a cold-war "alliance with one or another great power." At the same time that he declared for a policy of nonalignment, however, Roberto warned that all Angolans "know that the napalm which has burnt out our villages and the bullets which have murdered and wounded our fighting men—as well as a helpless civilian population—have been supplied to Portugal through NATO in order to let her participate in the defense of the so-called Free World." He appealed to the United States to halt further military shipments to Portugal and concluded: "We can only say to Americans: our ideals are your ideals, our hopes are the same that you had once for yourselves. If you help destroy us, you are only destroying a part of yourselves." [74]

The Portuguese were also present in New York in December 1961, but the principal focus of their concern was not Angola. Instead, they were involved in a vain effort to obtain United Nations action against India, which had just occupied Goa and other Portuguese enclaves on the Indian subcontinent. Following the New Delhi seminar on Portuguese colonies of October, in which Mário de Andrade had participated, the CONCP *Bulletin* had characterized the liberation of Goa as of "exceptional importance for the liberation of other Portuguese colonies." Yet as the year ended this assessment was already proving illusory. The traumatic loss of Goa simply steeled Portuguese nationalists to an even more intransigent determination to hold on in Africa. Portuguese troops and supplies formerly held down in Goa could now be diverted to Angola, whereas India promptly lost much of its interest in the anticolonial struggle against Portugal in far-off Africa. Indeed Portugal, martyred and righteous, benefited from a new wave of sympathy in the United States and other western countries, a sympathy that would hurt the fledgling forces of African nationalism more than it would an unrepentant but giant India. A coordinated program of military and diplomatic pressure mounted by India and African nationalists together might have produced different results. As it was, considerations of Afro-Asian solidarity as against Indian national interests seemed to count for little or nothing. Such was the final lesson of Angola's year of rebellion.

[74] Roberto, "The Angolan Revolution."

PART III

A REVOLUTION IN TRANSITION

CHAPTER EIGHT

FROM REBELLION TO GUERRILLA WAR AND A GOVERNMENT IN EXILE

In July 1961 an American television team traveled into the rebel area of Angola. It met streams of refugees heading north toward the Congo, eluded Portuguese bombers, and captured the chaos, suffering, and exhilaration of the newly exploded war.[1] That autumn, at about the same time that the hour-long documentary, "A Journey to a War," was televised by the National Broadcasting Company, the *Reporter* magazine published an article recounting another journalist's summer journey inside rebel territory, where he had visited the UPA's forest base of grass and mud huts at Fuesse and then witnessed the base's destruction during a Portuguese air attack.[2] Following these accounts, however, months passed without any further first-hand reports on the war. In *Guerra em Angola* published in late 1961, Hélio Felgas asserted that Portuguese counterinsurgency operations, begun in the north at Lucunga on June 13, 1961, had been a brilliant success and had resulted in "the reoccupation of all North Angola in less than four months." [3] In spite of the uninterrupted exodus of war refugees that totaled 150,000 by the end of December, there was a growing tendency to give credence to assertions, such as those made by Angola's Governor-General Augusto Venâncio Deslandes in October, that African forces had been dispersed, all administrative posts, villages, and hamlets reoccupied, and the rebellion "terminated." [4]

[1] NBC reporter Robert Young and photographer Charles Dorkins. See Robert Young, "Values in Revolt," *Africa Today,* Vol. 8 (Nov. 1961), p. 4.
[2] Richard Mathews, "A Visit to the Rebels of Angola," *The Reporter,* Sept. 28, 1961, pp. 41–44.
[3] Hélio Felgas, *Guerra em Angola* (Lisbon: Livraria Classica Editôra, 1961), p. 201.
[4] *Le Monde,* Oct. 12, 1961.

Nevertheless Portuguese claims were soon revealed as overstated. In late 1961 George Houser of the ACOA undertook to organize an emergency refugee relief program designed to extend help to the thousands of Angolans shown by the NBC documentary to be hiding in the forests of northern Angola as well as those pouring into the Congo. On January 5, 1962, after studying the refugee situation in the Lower Congo, Houser, accompanied by the author, entered the Angolan fighting zone. During a period of nearly two weeks in nationalist-held territory, they hiked more than two hundred miles over an interwoven network of trails leading through forests and elephant grass, across vine and single-log bridges, and around open-pit animal traps to the hidden, semiportable villages that constituted Nationalist Angola. The journey made possible some empirical observations within a specific, if limited, area of the revolt and permitted some inferences to be drawn about conditions prevailing in neighboring regions. As was pointed out in the published accounts of it, however, this inquiry did not and could not purport to present a picture of "the entire revolt." [5]

Inside Rebel Angola

Far from being "terminated," the conflict was found to be shifting from the fluid chaos of the initial uprising into an organized guerrilla insurgency. Orders and arms were carried in from the Congo and disseminated from forest hideaways over an intricate, constantly altered system of footpaths which would quickly lead an unguided interloper to disaster. In the grass shelters of a relocated and rebuilt headquarters known as Fuesse—which had two predecessors and untold numbers of successors—military information was assembled under the supervision of a veteran of Eduardo Pinock's group at Matadi, Eduardo Frederico Deves, and sent on by messenger to central headquarters in Léopoldville. Military field headquarters under Commander João Batista, lay some fifty miles

[5] Its findings were made public at a press conference in New York and in subsequent articles. See "Joint Press Statement by George M. Houser and John A. Marcum," Overseas Press Club (Feb. 1, 1962, mimeo.); Houser, "Report on a Journey through Rebel Angola" (American Committee on Africa, New York, 1962, mimeo.), appearing as "Journey to Rebel Angola," in *Africa Today,* Vol. 9 (March 1962), pp. 4–7; Houser, "The Rebellion in Angola," *Concern* (Pittsburgh, Pa.), July 1, 1962, pp. 3–6; Marcum, "Progress toward Independence in Angola," *Lincoln University Bulletin,* Vol. 65, No. 2 (Winter 1962), pp. 4–8; and Marcum, "The Revolt in Angola," *The New Leader,* Apr. 30, 1962, pp. 17–18.

south of the Fuesse-São Salvador region, across the sometimes impassable M'Bridge River. There in the vicinity of Bembe, Commander Batista had established the nucleus of an over-all military command and was laboring to bring some coordination into rebel activity while awaiting the return of his colleagues, the future officer corps training in Tunisia.

Nationalist forces, made up of young men from the area and of army deserters and contract laborers from all over Angola, organized themselves into small (10 to 12 men) mobile groups suited to hit-and-run guerrilla action. During January they received their first sizable shipment of arms from outside. The presence in the Congo of military units from a variety of countries participating in United Nations operations provided channels through which modest supplies of arms could be obtained. These desperately needed weapons and munitions were rationed out under the supervision of Batista to the representatives of forty-odd military sectors gathered together in an abandoned village. After receiving their allotment of rifles, shells, grenades, plastic bombs, and, for the more fortunate, a few land mines and machine guns, nationalist patrols hoisted their loads onto woven palm leaves and trekked for as long as two to three weeks to their respective posts in the interior—as far south as Ucua.

Outside of beleaguered towns and patrolled roads, rebel forces controlled an area estimated to be roughly 150 miles wide and 200 miles deep within northern Angola. Typical was the situation at a nationalist village in the hills of the N'Gunda forest near Buela. This newly constructed and concealed complex of grass huts and bamboo tables, sheltering a community of about one hundred militants with an inadequately armed military patrol commanded by an army deserter from Nova Lisboa, looked down upon an empty town (Buela), abandoned farm houses, and a besieged garrison of Portuguese troops which used searchlights for protection from night raids.

By this time, however, the Portuguese were making increasingly effective use of what was their most potent physical and psychological weapon, the airplane. By January 1962 outside observers could watch Portuguese planes bomb and strafe African villages, visit the charred remains of towns like Mbanza M'Pangu and M'Pangala, and copy the data from 750-pound napalm bomb casings from which the Portuguese had not removed the labels marked "Property U.S.

Air Force."[6] One rebel response to these raids was to build a few "Potemkin villages" designed to lure Portuguese bombers into unloading their destruction on false targets. The nationalists also created "air raid shelters" (deep trenches that resembled open graves) and warning systems (plane spotters with police whistles), but the air raids were devastating.

Portuguese planes bombarded nationalist held areas with political leaflets as well as napalm. In Kikongo, Kimbundu, and Portuguese, these tracts called upon the insurgents to leave the cold and hunger of their forest hideouts and to forsake the war into which they had been misled by a UPA that only fleeced their pockets. In return, the Angolans were promised that "the whites" would protect them and give them jobs on the coffee plantations, all of which would enable them once again to purchase "cloth, shoes, jackets, shirts, food, and wine" (see Appendix D). One leaflet pictured a black hand clasped by a white hand over the advice: "The people of Camabatela, Carmona, Negage, Buango, and Pedra do Feitici and others have *returned.* Do like them. Troops are waiting for you to come in groups of ten bearing a white flag."

The nationalists had established a rudimentary system of self-government in areas under their control. Many villages had an elective council, a youth group (JUPA), a dispensary (SARA), a simulated labor union (LGTA), and a Protestant or, less frequently, a Catholic school teacher with a few tattered books. In the Fuesse region, this organization was watched over by José Manuel Peterson, who acted as a roving UPA "administrative secretary" inside Angola.[7] The relationship of this "civil" organization to the military command was not always clear, however, and sometimes led to confusion or disputes, for example, a disagreement over whether the youth group (JUPA) should be considered part of the army. Clear lines of authority had yet to be worked out.

Everyone traveled with *guias* (passports) delivered by Léopoldville and checked at guard posts scattered along the paths and at village entrances. Slits dug across paths demarcated the borders of new "administrative districts." The nationalists claimed to have organized over fifty such districts, most of which had headquarter

[6] For example, M116A1 fire bomb with manufacture No. E14–5–1500, government order No. ? NY 51–1?–8. (? = illegible digit).

[7] In charge of compiling and reporting military information back to Léopoldville from the rebel base at Fuesse was Frederico Deves, veteran UPA organizer in the São Salvador region. See p. 141.

villages like Fuesse. These districts, however, were not yet tied together, and "independently, each one [went] about the business of menacing roads, ambushing Portuguese soldiers and attacking plantations." [8] In the villages, which resembled rustic boys' camps in the mountains, days began and ended with mass prayers and patriotic ceremonies, during which little paper UPA flags were hoisted up and down tree poles. The villagers sang new versions of old hymns and work songs from the coffee and cotton plantations, adding nationalist words which recounted how Roberto had gone to Lisbon and how he had told "old Salazar" this . . . and that. . . .

Interviews revealed a generally high morale based in part, at least, on two assumptions: (1) that only Portuguese air power stood in the way of an early military victory over a dispirited Portuguese army; and (2) that once the facts were presented to the United Nations, mobilized international pressure—and especially American power—would force Portugal to come to terms with the forces of Angolan nationalism.

As he traveled among these nationalist centers, Batista inspected local militia in their scraps and shreds of uniform and delivered a standard talk in Portuguese. In his talk, which was translated by a village official into the local vernacular, he urged the villagers (1) to rise above all tribal divisions and face the future united as Angolans and (2) to view independence not as the end of their labors but as the beginning of an era of hard work through which a new society would be created with educational and economic opportunities for everyone. Those who heard him were already savoring a real if Spartan *independência* in the wet forests, and it would be difficult for them to return to the old order—to the unquestioned acceptance of Portuguese authority—whatever the outcome of the war. With the rebellion African nationalism had sunk its roots more deeply into Angolan soil. The essence of what was happening was captured in three words scrawled on the side of a gutted Catholic church amidst the empty ruins of what had been the town of M'Pangala: "Angola, Kimpwanza, Amen." [9]

Such was the changing picture of insurgency at the beginning of 1962. Contrary to some accounts, northern Angola was the scene of an active revolution that was neither communist nor

[8] Arthur Herzog, "An Unknown War for Freedom," *True,* Vol. 43, No. 302 (July 1962), p. 88.

[9] Kimpwanza means independence in Kikongo.

antiwhite.[10] Angolan refugees continued to flee into the Congo, and the Red Cross and other relief agencies there discerned no appreciable response to Portuguese efforts to get these displaced people to return to Angola and settle under military protection at official relocation centers. In successfully demonstrating the possibility of delivering medical supplies inside the country, the Houser mission confirmed the presence in rebel territory of untallied thousands of other displaced people suffering from new ailments such as rheumatism and bronchitis brought on by the dampness of the forest.[11]

[10] London's *West Africa,* No. 2343 (Apr. 28, 1962), p. 462, published a letter from one Charles Stephens who denounced what he termed the impropriety of the Houser mission, in view of existing "friendly diplomatic" relations between the United States and Portugal. He commented: "As for acceptance of terrorists' assertions that the revolt is not Communist inspired I can only refer to the early speeches of Fidel Castro: no revolutionary ever admits to Communist support until it has secured power."

[11] Approximately 250 pounds of medical supplies were donated for this test run by private agencies in New York. Under the supervision of Dr. José Liahuca (SARA), these supplies were divided into forty-three packets and distributed to approximately that many villages in Angola. The supplies were transported to distant sectors by the same nationalists that had assembled to receive arms. The medicines were given over to local "dispensaries" which were supervised by Angolans who had either had nurses' training or some experience in hospital work. Houser and Marcum themselves delivered the packets, which included antibiotics, antimalarials, antidiarrheals and other medicines, to seven village centers. See "Joint Press Statement," ftn. 5. As a result of this pilot project, the ACOA organized a special on-going program known as Emergency Relief for Angola (ERA). Under ERA, medicines, clothes, and other supplies were sent to the SARA organization for distribution to refugees in both Angola and the Congo.

The Houser mission also spoke out on the issue of private and public American policy toward Angola. It recommended stepped-up medical and educational assistance for African refugees and called for a "vigorous U.S. policy" that would bar Portugal from using NATO equipment in Angola and would prevail upon Lisbon "to end the conflict" by agreeing to negotiations for independence and to an orderly transfer of political power to be achieved in collaboration with the services of the United Nations. *Ibid.*

In Europe this journey was attacked from right and left as evidence of both American complicity in the revolution and American designs on the economic wealth of the colony. In Lisbon the *Diário da Manha* (Apr. 5, 1962) reproduced a story that had already appeared in the Johannesburg *Star* and Luanda's *A Provincia de Angola,* which described the two travelers as contemptible spies (*"salafrários"*), who had walked only 30 kilometers inside Angola but who had nonetheless written a 6400-word secret report for President Kennedy. In a similar vein, the left-wing Brussels periodical *Remarques Africaines* (Vol. 6, No. 12 [June 13, 1964], p. 270) later referred to a "confidential report" written for President Kennedy by Messrs. Marcus (*sic*) and Houser and charged that, by delivering medicines and foodstuffs to Angolan rebels and by establishing relations with leaders such as Holden Roberto, these two "secret commissars" acted

Then finally, a year after the rebellion had begun, eyewitness accounts, the continuing exodus of refugees, and mounting casualty lists forced the Portuguese government to abandon its position that the conflict had been "terminated." On March 9, 1962, Radio Lisbon announced that "small groups" of terrorists continued to be active and were able to "lay ambush for a vehicle, or carry out small surprise attacks on isolated plantations and farms." The broadcast went on to acknowledge that, because Portuguese forces were unable "to completely close the frontier," supplies from the Congo were reaching the "terrorists." [12]

Bakongo Moderates and the Revolution

In addition to contending with the Portuguese, the UPA had to face African movements that sought to reduce or destroy its political-military supremacy within rebel areas of northern Angola and to block its access to those areas through the Lower Congo. In the Fuesse-São Salvador region, Ngwizako royalists provided the most trouble. Collaborating with the colonial authorities, they led Portuguese patrols to the sites of UPA villages. The butt of UPA marching songs because of their support for the discredited relic of Kongo kingship, some Ngwizako members were captured by UPA forces and put to work as "prisoners of war" building grass huts. Others were used by the Portuguese in the effort to appeal to Bakongo loyalty through the traditional institution of the monarchy. As part of this effort, government authorities persuaded the aging queen regent Dona Isabel M. da Gama to issue an appeal urging those thousands of her subjects who had taken refuge in the forests

---

in support of an over-all American scheme for control of Angola. This scheme, it said, called for replacing Portuguese authority with an indigenous government "formed by rightist elements who would not significantly alter the system of forced labor established by Salazar, which permits companies like 'Angola Diamond,' the Comgéral Purigina, the Sociedade Aquecolo, and others to continue to pocket profits reaching as high as a net 50 per cent on capital invested." The MPLA later expressed the view that the press report of the "two Americans who claimed to have visited the UPA maquis" was designed to prepare the public for "the launching of [a] so-called Angolan Government in Exile." *African Association Review* (Cairo), Vol. III, No. 44–45 (Nov.-Dec. 1965), p. 29. In fact, Houser and Marcum traveled as private citizens without governmental approval, made no report to President Kennedy (who sought none), and rendered their findings public. Their trip was followed by those of a number of European and American journalists. See Arthur Herzog, "An Unkown War"; and "The Roots of Revolution," *The Observer* (London), Apr. 29, 1962.

[12] Lisbon Overseas Service in English, 0200 GMT, Mar. 9, 1962.

or across the border in the Congo to return home—with white flag in hand and nothing to fear. Her invitation to submit to the forgiving "Authority" of the state was mimeographed and scattered by planes across the green countryside.[13]

Nto-Bako supporters also helped to guide Portuguese troops and otherwise cooperated with Portuguese efforts to "pacify" the country.[14] According to Rev. David Grenfell, Angelino Alberto sent his men to refugee hiding places "saying that all was now settled and that he was negotiating with Salazar for independence in a peaceful way." Therefore, all should return to their homes, for if they did not his efforts "would come to naught and the Portuguese would send troops and planes and kill them all." Alberto convinced some people who then came with him in groups of about a hundred to be delivered to the administration.[15]

To the nationalists, even more disconcerting than the actions of these Angolan collaborators was the attitude of local Congolese officials and the Abako party. They controlled the border posts and road junctions commanding access to the Angolan frontier. Following his September visit to UPA territory during which he spent two days in a Congo jail, journalist Richard Mathews wrote: "If the local Congolese authorities along the frontier are not in the pay of the Portuguese (and many share my opinion that they are), they behave as if they were."[16] Whether subsidized or not, it is understandable that there would have been some antagonism on the part of the local Congolese toward those who had triggered a revolution that had brought upon them a flood of refugees. Now those revolutionaries wished to mobilize the refugees to help sustain a war that was dangerously close at hand. The Congolese press carried reports both of incursions by Portuguese troops into the Congo following border clashes[17] and of the detention of Angolan "com-

[13] An open letter addressed "Aos Meus Queridos Filhos, Homens e Mulheres, Rapazes e Raparigas," São Salvador, Sept. 1961. See Appendix C.

[14] *Christian Science Monitor*, Feb. 10, 1962 and United Nations, General Assembly, *Report of the Sub-Committee on the Situation in Angola*, A/5286, Nov. 14, 1962, pp. 23–24.

[15] Grenfell, *Notes* (Kibentele), No. 12, 1966.

[16] Mathews, "A Visit to the Rebels," p. 44. Arthur Herzog reported similarly after his trip in March 1962. He and the UPA's José M. Peterson were arrested by a Congolese policeman at the border when they crossed back into the Congo. "Most Congolese officials," Herzog wrote, "favor the Angolans; the local administrator . . . unfortunately did not. 'Viva l'Angola,' Peterson said, and we went off to jail." Peterson spent eighteen days in prison before being allowed to rejoin the revolution. Herzog, "An Unknown War," p. 92.

[17] *Courrier d'Afrique*, Mar. 7, 1962.

mandos" detected by Congolese police while transporting arms and munitions through the Lower Congo.[18]

Angelino Alberto both fostered and exploited such Angolan-Congolese antagonism in the region of the frontier. There, according to reports in late 1961, Alberto, financed by the Portuguese embassy in Léopoldville, employed an Nto-Bako militia backed up from Angola by Portuguese "para-commandos" in a campaign to terrorize Angolan refugees into returning to Portuguese Angola.[19] In March, reacting to just that sort of engineered mayhem, a local Congolese Bakongo group known as the *Union Congolaise pour la Libération de l'Angola* (UCLA) asserted Congolese over Angolan interests and sent a letter to the premier of the Léopoldville province requesting (1) increased security measures along the border to provide protection from Portuguese troops chasing Angolan refugees into the Congo and (2) less government tolerance toward Angolan political and youth movements that were engaged in "perpetual slaughter in the frontier villages occupied by Angolan refugees."[20]

The war also brought new friction to relations between the UPA and Aliazo. Military action spread into the Bazombo area, brought by both Portuguese bombs and roving UPA patrols. There were local incidents in which overzealous UPA soldiers shot Aliazo partisans as "collaborators" because the latter could not produce "proper," meaning UPA, *guias*. Emmanuel Kunzika protested to UPA leaders. He also organized a basic review of Aliazo's political position. A party conference was held in Léopoldville from January 12 to 15. Following the earlier example of the UPNA (UPA), Aliazo dropped its parochial label, became the *Partido Democrático de Angola* (PDA) and launched an unrewarding drive to recruit new members from outside the Bazombo community, e.g., local MPLA leadership that had been shunted aside by the incoming committee from Conakry.[21]

A few days after the party conference, PDA leaders suggested that they still hoped to play the role of balancer and conciliator between

[18] *Ibid.*, May 7, 1962.

[19] *Ibid.*, Feb. 3, 4 and 5, and July 13, 1962.

[20] *Ibid.*, Mar. 14, 1962.

[21] Discussions were held with a disgruntled MPLA member, José Bernardo Domingos, but in the final count he and his supporters did not join the PDA. The former president of the MPLA's Léopoldville committee, António Josias, did resign from the MPLA in 1962 but took a two-year hiatus from politics before joining the PDA in 1964.

the UPA and MPLA. They believed that the danger of being dominated by MPLA mulattoes would not be great under a "one man, one vote" system, in which the latter would constitute only a small minority. At the same time, however, they expected that Lisbon, should it ever agree to the principle of self-determination, would use the period of political transition to build up the position of both the MPLA and "southerners," because it would consider these two groups to be Portuguese in cultural orientation. (Such Portuguese action would, of course, be to the disadvantage of the PDA, most of whose leaders had been educated in French in the Léopoldville and Brazzaville republics.) Viewing themselves and the UPA as "populists," the PDA leaders were not eager to risk a two-party front with an MPLA that they considered elitist. They became even more skeptical of MPLA objectives when, according to Kunzika, they learned from Andrade that he had made unilateral though futile efforts to engage the UPA in bilateral talks without the PDA. Still they continued to favor a three-party coalition in which they might hold the balance of power. Keeping all options open, they also increasingly envisioned some sort of entente with the UPA, all the while hoping, if possible, to avoid any aggravation of the north-south cleavage in Angolan nationalism. PDA leaders sought to strengthen their bargaining position by giving their movement a broader ethnic base. Also, crediting international support with having had much to do with the relative success of their two competitors, they sought to develop their own international contacts.[22] They also brought some new talent into their top leadership ranks which were now headed by André Massaki, president, Emmanuel Kunzika, first vice-president, Antoine Raphael Matumona, second vice-president, Ferdinand Dombele, secretary-general, and David Livromentos, political director.[23]

The Kassanga-Kassinda Affair

In late January 1962 Commander João Batista, twenty-nine years old, who, wherever he might be, read from his Bible at the beginning and end of each day, arrived back at his headquarters near

[22] Interviews with Emmanuel Kunzika, André Massaki, Ferdinand Dombele, and other PDA officials, Jan. 18 and 20, 1962, at Léopoldville.

[23] Matumona and Livromentos were both journalists working in Léopoldville, the first with the Catholic daily *Courrier d'Afrique,* the second with the Protestant monthly *Envol.*

Bembe. A few weeks later, while Roberto was still at the United Nations in New York, news reached Léopoldville that Batista was dead. On February 23, the UPA announced that its young field commander had fallen on the battlefield. The following day the chief of staff of the National Liberation Army (ELNA), Marcos Kassanga, who was headquartered in Léopoldville, dissociated himself from the UPA announcement. In a one-sentence communiqué he stated that concrete information concerning the circumstances surrounding Batista's death had not yet been obtained. Meanwhile another version of what had happened circulated in Léopoldville, in the form of a mimeographed "communiqué" dated February 6 and purportedly issued at Batista's Bembe military headquarters. According to that account, put out in the name of a dissident and ephemeral UPA *Comitê da Revolução Nacional de Angola,*[24] Commander Batista, a southerner, had been killed on that day by undisciplined Bakongo tribalists.

Kassanga issued a second ELNA communiqué on February 26, in which he announced that after an *"in loco"* investigation he would make "an important declaration" concerning Batista and the armed conflict inside Angola. For the occasion he invited "Angolan nationalist leaders, interested observers, and the press."

Indicative of the political maneuvering that underlay his pending declaration, an MPLA official, Luis de Azevedo, Jr., paid a visit to PDA headquarters. There, according to top PDA sources, Azevedo briefed Kunzika and his associates on what was about to happen and urged them to attend Kassanga's press conference scheduled for March 3.[25] Kassanga made his much-anticipated declaration to a crowd gathered that day in the open-air pavilion of Léopoldville's Zoo Restaurant, a favorite site for Congolese political rallies. He startled many of his listeners by charging that Commander Batista, as well as 8000 other innocent Angolans, had been murdered by northern (Bakongo) tribalists. He accused Roberto of interfering in military matters and of arrogating to himself the title of com-

[24] UPA, Comitê da Revolução Nacional de Angola, Quartel no Bembe, "Communicado" (Feb. 6, 1962, mimeo.), signed by one Pedro Zala (of Silva Porto), whose name has never appeared before or since the event in any other connection.

[25] According to Emmanuel Kunzika, his party distrusted the motives behind both the invitation and the conference but did send its general treasurer, Domingos Vetokele, to attend the meeting and report back on what took place.

mander-in-chief without the consent of the army.[26] Moreover, reversing his earlier position, he now endorsed MPLA charges that Roberto had sparked a "fratricidal" war, accused the UPA president of ordering the deaths of the Tomas Ferreira patrol as well as that of his own field commander João Batista,[27] and called upon all Angolan nationalist movements to unite within a new *Front de Libération Nationale de l'Angola.* The same day, March 3, UPA vice-president Rosário Neto denied and denounced these accusations as treasonous, and announced Kassanga's dismissal as chief of staff.[28]

A less partisan account of Batista's death which subsequently came to light contended that the young officer fell during an attack on the Portuguese fort at Bembe. In June 1964 the secretary of the BMS church at Bembe, António Gabriel, recounted to Rev. David Grenfell that he was summoned to Batista's headquarters on January 29, 1962, to attend a conference called for the purpose of discussing plans for an attack on the Bembe fort. As was customary on such occasions, Gabriel opened and closed the meeting "with a Bible reading and a prayer, on Batista's orders." According to the church secretary's report:

An attack on the fort was planned for the 6th of February, and this duly took place. At this time the people were hiding not very far from Bembe, and the soldiers (most of them with little training) were billeted out in the various surrounding hiding places. There were twelve men at the place where Gabriel was, and they went, and all returned. One of the twelve was Adolfo, and he was the first to return with the news of Batista's death. The attack was at night, and the soldiers succeeded in entering the fort and surprising the Portuguese soldiers. However, there were more Portuguese soldiers there than expected, and the fighting was very hot. Batista was badly wounded, so the attackers withdrew under heavy fire, carrying Batista along. However, soon after they passed the gates of the fort Batista died, so because of the heavy fire, they abandoned the body. With this

[26] In one of his frequent news columns on Angolan affairs, Antoine Matumona of the PDA suggested that Kassanga's action represented a desire of the army (ELNA) to conduct its own affairs "without pressure or influence from the political leaders of the UPA." *Courrier d'Afrique,* Mar. 3–4, 1962.

[27] ELNA, Marcos Kassanga, "Conférence de presse" (Léopoldville, March 3, 1962, mimeo.). See also *Courrier d'Afrique,* Mar. 7, 1962; *Remarques Congolaises* (Brussels), Vol. 4, No. 11–12 (Mar. 22, 1962), p. 115; and *Le Monde,* Mar. 15, 1962.

[28] UPA, "Communiqué" (Léopoldville, Mar. 3, 1962, mimeo.). Kassanga in turn charged that irresponsible leaders of the UPA, who lacked "any notion of military affairs," were the real "traitors." ELNA, "Communiqué" (Léopoldville, Mar. 4, 1962, mimeo.).

group was a man called Madalia, who assured everyone that Batista was actually dead.[29]

Asked by Grenfell whether Batista had been critical of Roberto in the days leading up to his death the secretary replied "never." Indeed just a month before his death, in interviews taped in northern Angola during which he related details of how he had been given successive military assignments by Roberto, Batista had manifested what appeared to be unqualified loyalty to the UPA president.[30]

The fact remains that Batista's death became a bitterly divisive issue and was followed by a determined effort to topple Roberto from his position of rebel leadership. Kassanga was joined in this undertaking by the secretary-general of the *Liga Geral dos Trabalhadores de Angola* (LGTA), André Kassinda, in whose company he had escaped from Angola to the Congo in February 1961. Recently returned from the founding conference of the African Trade Union Confederation (ATUC) at Dakar (January 9–14, 1962), where in the name of the UPA he had negotiated an alliance with a group of Portuguese Guinean nationalists,[31] Kassinda announced that the executive bureau of the union had been "dissolved" on March 2 because it had acted as a tool of the UPA and "against the legitimate interests of Angolan workers." He said that the UPA had prevented thousands of Angolan workers from joining the LGTA simply because they were not of "the UPA-São Salvador." As secretary-general, he continued, he had wished to place the LGTA "above the narrow quarrels" of the party, but his union had been obliged to give to the UPA two thirds of the aid it received from the ICFTU —that is, sixty out of ninety thousand Congolese francs. Considering these grievances, Kassinda said, he had decided to form his own LGTA executive committee and therefore declared the old one, which had already fired him, to be in dissidence.[32]

Kassanga sent a memorandum to the American Committee on Africa detailing charges against Roberto and asking George Houser

[29] Grenfell, *Notes*, No. 13, 1964.

[30] Interviews with author, January 7 and 8, 1962, at Angolan villages of Ina and Kindualu.

[31] See pp. 309–310.

[32] LGTA. "Conférence de presse faite par André Martins Kassinda, secretaire général de la Ligue Générale des Travailleurs de l'Angola" (Léopoldville, Mar. 16, 1962, mimeo.).

to "order an inquiry into the facts,"[33] The MPLA soon joined in by giving wide circulation to the accusations of assassination and tribalism,[34] and by once again inviting the PDA to join with it in a common front, this time with the Angolan National Liberation Army (ELNA) led by Marcos Kassanga as the third unit. The PDA, however, was not interested. Its leaders reasoned that, as chief of staff, Kassanga shared responsibility for any of the alleged misdeeds for which he was now denouncing his former colleagues in the UPA; and in any case they judged that Kassanga had no following.[35]

Just as he had been obliged to do the previous year, Roberto rushed back from the United Nations in New York to face a political-military crisis that had exploded in his absence. He quickly reasserted his political authority. In a press conference on March 12 he refuted all charges leveled by Kassanga, whose actions, he implied, were linked to the machinations of the local Portuguese embassy. Roberto acknowledged that Kassanga had taken "some ELNA military documents" with him when he left the UPA, but no men. Questioned about reports of Polish promises of support (including military officers) for Kassanga, Roberto predicted that if

[33] "Memorandum à l'intention du American Commite of [*sic*] Africa," dated Mar. 11, 1962, sent in the name of the Angolan National Liberation Army (ELNA), Léopoldville. Kassanga later wrote that he and Batista had come from families of Ganguela and Cuanhama chiefs, respectively, who were traditional allies in the history of resistance to Portuguese rule. While attending military school (*Escola do Aplicação Militar*) at Nova Lisboa in 1959, he added, both he and Batista belonged to a clandestine group of African soldiers known as the *Grande Vanguardo-Commando*. Marcos Kassanga, "Aspecto real do problema angolano" (Léopoldville, Mar. 15, 1965, unpublished typescript).

[34] MPLA, Comité Directeur, "Communiqué" (Léopoldville, Mar. 26, 1962, mimeo.). Reports circulated in LGTA circles that in January, during talks with Dr. Hugo de Menezes of the MPLA, Kassanga and Kassinda decided to organize a campaign to discredit and overthrow the UPA's top leaders. Consequently, it was said, Batista's death then provided them with an appropriate incident around which to build such a campaign. Whatever the truth of these reports, the MPLA and Kassanga and Kassinda were united in their desire to get rid of Roberto. In an interview at MPLA headquarters on January 19, 1962, Dr. Eduardo dos Santos of the *comité directeur* said that it was important to distinguish between Roberto, who willfully blocked unity, and his party, which did contain nationalists of good will. For Kassanga and Kassinda, Roberto was the one who imposed UPA party supremacy over their respective spheres of influence, the army and labor union.

[35] The PDA considered that an MPLA-PDA-ELNA front would be "prejudicial" to PDA interests because in reality it would be just a bilateral MPLA-PDA front in which the PDA would be junior partner. See PDA (Kunzika), "Conférence de presse" (Léopoldville, Apr. 12, 1962, mimeo.).

the Poles did in fact intend to give such support they would find that Kassanga was alone and did not lead a force that could really be assisted. Roberto further announced that Commander Batista had been elevated *post mortem* to the rank of colonel by the UPA executive bureau and revealed that he, Roberto, had personally stopped in Tunisia, en route from New York, in order to visit [and ensure the loyalty of] Angolan officers training there with the Algerian FLN. He reported that the Angolan officers were progressing well in their training and that more men would be sent for such training as they returned, in order to build rapidly a skilled and experienced leadership cadre for the Angolan Liberation Army (ELNA).[36]

Roberto issued a military order on March 15 commending ELNA soldiers for their valor in a "year of battle" for independence,[37] and the army, in the main Bakongo, remained loyal. So did the bulk of the LGTA, also predominantly Bakongo. Undaunted, Kassanga and Kassinda, traveling as Messrs. Kalada and Kilouba, stumped the African continent denouncing Roberto.[38] They concentrated in particular on Tunisia, a major source of support for the UPA leader. There they endeavored to persuade the Tunisian government and the Algerian National Liberation Front to halt their assistance to the UPA and related organizations, and at the same time they tried to influence Angolans training with the Algerians to defect.[39] They also tried to get the Tunisian labor movement to use its influence to convince the ICFTU to switch its support from the loyalist LGTA to Kassinda's breakaway union, a largely paper organization which was renamed the *Union Générale des Travailleurs Angolais* (UGTA). On all counts, the two travelers were essentially unsuccessful.

The Kassanga-Kassinda affair did, on the other hand, constitute a *cause célèbre*, which was effectively exploited by the Portuguese

[36] UPA, "Conferência de Imprensa" and "Relatório da Conferência de Imprensa" (Léopoldville, Mar. 12, 1962, mimeo.). Also *Courrier d'Afrique,* Mar. 13, 1962.

[37] "A 15 de Março Começoua Revolução Angolana" (Léopoldville, no date, mimeo.).

[38] *Le Monde,* Apr. 22, 1962.

[39] According to one unconfirmed report, four of forty-one Angolan officers being trained in Tunisia did defect to a new rebel organization known as the *Frente Angolana de Libertação Nacional* (FALA) [*sic*], led by Marcos Cassanga [*sic*]. *Hispanic American Report* (Stanford), Vol. XV, No. 3 (Mar. 1962), p. 202.

press and radio,[40] and long remained a bitterly disputed issue among Angolan nationalists. It severely shook the UPA, whose multiethnic leadership and primarily Bakongo following had yet to transcend regional loyalties fully or to transform personal ambitions into collective teamwork. There was still a certain lack of mutual confidence within the organization, especially as concerned the definition and allocation of responsibilities. Under these circumstances, Batista's death and the political defections that followed put the UPA on the defensive and suggested to some that, having been chastened, it might now be more receptive to the idea of a common front—without Kassanga and Kassinda, to be sure. Thus in mid-March, the leaders of the *União Nacional dos Trabalhadores de Angola* (UNTA) took their turn at initiating proposals for such a front.

First, in order to establish his movement's credentials as a bridge builder despite its close relations with the MPLA, the UNTA's secretary-general Bernard Dombele stated publicly and emphatically that the union was not dependent on any political party. On the contrary, he said, the UNTA wished "to serve as a force linking all Angolan parties in spite of the different political ideologies that separated them," and supported the creation of a multiparty Angolan Patriotic Front.[41] On March 10, the labor union sent a letter to the UPA requesting a meeting between the two organizations' respective executive committees. When the UNTA committee arrived for talks at UPA headquarters on March 23, however, it found itself meeting with Holden Roberto alone—thereby deprived of an opportunity to canvass for common-front support within the whole UPA executive. Not unpredictably, Roberto responded to the UNTA proposals by saying that national unity would be built on

[40] For example, on March 6, 1962 (1830 GMT, English), Radio Lisbon commented on an article in *O Comércio* (Luanda), which repeated the Pedro Zala story on Batista's death, and concluded: "Tribal instincts proved stronger than political necessities. A mere diplomatic maneuver, a journalistic artifice, or a unilateral decision on the part of some U.N. committee cannot really transform bandits into politicians, guerrillas into regular soldiers, or tribal instincts into patriotism."

[41] Statement by Dombele, Léopoldville, March 12, 1962, published in *Remarques Congolaises,* Vol. 4, No. 13–14 (Apr. 5, 1962), p. 131, and interpreted by the journal as a victory for Andrade's common-front policy. In May during roundtable discussions on Angolan unity called by Congolese minister of interior Cléophas Kamitatu, UNTA representatives maintained that they were "apolitical" and attending only in order to urge the political parties to unite. See "Réunion du 10 mai, 1962 avec le ministre Kamitatu" (Léopoldville, 1962, mimeo.). Hereafter cited as "Réunion du 10 mai."

the battlefield and not in Léopoldville.[42] Yet as it turned out, the idea of a common front—of his own choosing—was very much on Roberto's mind.

The Angolan Revolutionary Government in Exile—GRAE

In late December 1961 the UPA had released a statement that Roberto made first in New York, predicting that a rebel government would soon be set up inside Angola.[43] Roberto's statement was followed a few days later by an army (ELNA) communiqué that called for the creation of a provisional government "under the banner of the UPA, the *avant garde* of our masses and proper guide of our military organization." Endorsing Roberto's call for such a government, ELNA commanders Kassanga and Batista, among others, exhorted their "25,000 comrades in arms" to intensify their military action and to focus on "the occupation of a major portion of northwestern Angola where the Provisional Government of our Republic should be established" as the "immediate objective" of the revolution.[44] Together, Roberto and Batista declared that "thanks to the gracious and unlimited support of certain brother countries," the ELNA now possessed a staff trained in guerrilla warfare, as well as quantities of modern weapons, and was "certain to occupy all of the far north of Angola in the near future." For this reason, they said, the UPA was "directing the preparatory work for the setting up of a National Liberation Front composed of organizations which have deep roots in the heart of our masses." Moreover, "the formation of such a Front under the direction of UPA" was "unreservedly" supported by the army as a "step toward the establishment of a Provisional Government inside Angola."[45] Within three months a government was established, but as the product of a limited two-party coalition and with its headquarters in Léopoldville, not inside Angola. The failure of Angolan nationalist forces to secure large, fixed areas as had been hoped, and the ina-

[42] *Remarques Congolaises,* Vol. 4, No. 21–22 (June 7, 1962), p. 196.

[43] UPA, "Communiqué" signed by Rosário Neto (Léopoldville, Dec. 20, 1961, mimeo.). See also *The New York Times,* Dec. 19, 1961.

[44] UPA-ELNA, "Communiqué" (Léopoldville, Dec. 27, 1961, mimeo.), signed by Commanders Marcos Kassanga, chief of staff, F. Salavu, chief of military information, João Baptista Traves, chief of operations, Alexandre Taty, chief of Cabindan operations, and Gunda C. Kalei, political commissioner.

[45] UPA, "Joint Declaration of Messrs. Holden Roberto and João Batista" (Léopoldville [Dec. 1961?], mimeo.).

bility or unwillingness of UPA leaders to repair to the remote, dangerous, and constantly shifting interior areas under nationalist control meant that the original plans to establish a provisional government within Angola were to be deferred and then abandoned for years to come.

Much political groundwork lay behind the creation of the new front and government in exile. Whereas the Luanda-Mbundu region had been represented in the UPA's leadership ranks for many months, most notably by party vice-president Rosário Neto and Fernando Gourjel, it was only with the appointment of Jonas Malheiro Savimbi as secretary-general in late 1961 that the party had hoisted a spokesman for the populous Ovimbundu into a position of major responsibility. With the appointment, Roberto succeeded in associating the Ovimbundu stream of Angolan nationalism more closely with the UPA and in giving the party a more inclusive national image.

Savimbi belonged to a prominent Ovimbundu family from Chilesso (near the town of Andulo in Bié district). He was born on August 3, 1934, at Munhango in the Moxico district where his father, Lot Malheiro Savimbi, was employed by the Benguela railroad.[46] Lot Savimbi not only had been converted to Christianity by Protestant missionaries but had himself started a church and school at the small rail center where he served as stationmaster. Protests by Catholic clergy resulted in his being transferred to another station; but the local population continued to support and thus keep alive the church and school that he had founded. At his next post, Lot Savimbi did the same thing and was again transferred to another place. The end result was that all up and down the railroad there developed a string of strong churches and elementary schools. When he later returned to his home village of Chilesso on a small pension (reportedly about $15.00 a month), the elder Savimbi continued his educational work in that area by organizing a chain of modest mud-walled, thatch-roofed primary schools run by local African Protestants.

Jonas Savimbi inherited his father's educational drive. His early training, which began in the local Protestant school at Chilesso, continued successively at the Dondi Mission school and Silva Porto secondary school, and concluded at the *liceu* of Sá da Bandeira where he completed his sixth year at the top of his class.

[46] Interview with author, Nov. 1961. Father's name also spelled Loth.

In September 1958 Jonas Savimbi was one of the pioneer group of students sent to Portugal by the United Church of Christ. He and his fellow students were housed by the church and had little or no contact with Portuguese government scholars (and future MPLA-CONCP leaders) living at the *Casa dos Estudantes do Império* in Lisbon. Badgered by the political police, who were unable to persuade him to serve as a paid informer, Savimbi left Portugal during a school recess in 1960 and did not return. Instead, he persuaded his sponsors to allow him to transfer to the University of Fribourg, Switzerland, and then subsequently to the University of Lausanne, where he switched from premedical studies to political science.

Savimbi has said that he was influenced in his ultimate decision to accept the secretary-generalship of the UPA by the advice of Tom Mboya of Kenya during the course of a student conference at Kampala, Uganda, in the summer of 1961.[47] His decision in turn influenced other Angolan students in Europe to join the party and thus helped to counterbalance what some people considered to be the UPA's anti-intellectual or exclusively rural orientation. Savimbi's decision also helped reduce PDA fears that by joining in an alliance with the UPA they would be promoting a north-south breach between Angolan nationalists. Thus, the Kassanga-Kassinda affair notwithstanding, Jonas Savimbi's sudden rise to political prominence within the UPA did much to pave the way for Roberto's creation of an exile government in April 1962.

Roberto and Savimbi approached the PDA and engaged that organization in formal negotiations. On March 27 the two parties announced that they had joined together in a *Frente Nacional de Libertação de Angola* (FNLA), which was to function under the direction of a National Council composed of ten (later fifteen) representatives from each movement.[48] David Livromentos (PDA), the

[47] According to unpublished typescript, "UNITA," by British journalist John de St. Jorre (Lusaka, July 26, 1966).

[48] The convention establishing the FNLA was signed by ten UPA representatives: Holden Roberto, Rosário Neto, Alexandre Taty, Jonas Savimbi, José Liahuca, Johnny Eduardo, Eduardo Pinock, Vasco José António, Fernando Pio Amaral Gourjel, Francisco Paka; and ten PDA representatives: Emmanuel Kunzika, David Livromentos, Ferdinand Dombele, Sebastien Lubaki, Domingos Vetokele, Sanda Martin, Lulukilavo Antoine Dontoni, Norbert Kiatalua, André M'Vila, Simon Kumpesa. FNLA, "Convention" (Léopoldville, Mar. 27, 1962, mimeo.).

The ceremonies announcing the new Front to a gathering at the Léopoldville

twenty-eight-year-old director of the Protestant review *Envol,* and product of the Salvation Army school at Léopoldville, was named president of the National Council, and Holden Roberto assumed the chairmanship of the executive committee. The new front declared its aims for Angola to be independence under a democratic system based on the Universal Declaration of Human Rights, agrarian reform, a planned economy, industrialization, and diplomatic nonalignment.[49]

Commenting later on the negotiations that led to the creation of the front, Emmanuel Kunzika said that, because the UPA had been "the only organization reputed to be hostile to a Front," the PDA had sought and "obtained without objection" a provision that left the front door open for other Angolan movements to enter later.[50] For his part, Roberto emphasized that the front was based on a common dedication to the principle of revolution and, accordingly, excluded the participation of pacifist elements so as to prevent the enemies of the revolution from entering that which they would destroy.[51]

On April 5, one week after it was founded, the FNLA announced that it in turn had formed a Government of the Angolan Republic in Exile (later altered to read Revolutionary Government of Angola in Exile [*Govêrno Revolucionário de Angola no Exílio*], the GRAE. In the view of some observers, the decision not to wait until it was possible to locate such a government on Angolan soil was made because of the need for a dramatic move to counter MPLA activity.

Andrade's party was making strenuous efforts to build "a mass following among the very people upon whose support the UPA was built," that is, among the Angolan émigrés and refugees of the

---

Zoo on March 27 were reportedly marred by a group of MPLA youth who distributed "subversive" leaflets among the audience. See UPA, "A Intenção do Povo Angolano (Léopoldville [1962], mimeo.).

[49] FNLA, "Convention."

[50] PDA, "Conférence de presse," Apr. 12, 1962. The FNLA convention specified that the candidacy of any organization applying for membership in the front would be "the object of a study in depth" by an internal commission of the FNLA. In July 1966 Kunzika recapitulated the founding of the FNLA as follows: The PDA tried to revive the tripartite alliance with the UPA and MPLA. "Disdained by the MPLA in the final analysis, however, the PDA decided to find a common meeting ground with the UPA for the formation of a Front, which represented only a partial solution, but which was at least that much achieved in the face of the virulent antagonism and unyielding positions of the other parties." Quoted from an open letter from Kunzika to António Josias. PDA, Dir. 1503/66 (Léopoldville, July 25, 1966, mimeo.).

[51] "Réunion du 10 mai."

Léopoldville-Lower Congo region. The MPLA's well-organized "camps, clinics, schools, and indoctrination program" threatened to undercut the UPA in the UPA's own political territory. In this light, the creation of the GRAE could be viewed as designed to secure the UPA's Bakongo base by preempting all claims to revolutionary legitimacy. It could be asserted that the GRAE constituted the "single proper focus for Angolan loyalty as well as for international support." [52]

Less than a month earlier Roberto had stated publicly that the timing for the establishment of a provisional government would depend on military considerations, since it would be located "in part if not entirely in the interior of the country." He had also said that it was essential first to be in a position to "protect it from possible attacks by the Portuguese army." [53] The formation of a government in exile therefore appeared to be a recognition of military weakness as well a response to political dictates. The example of Algeria may also have been a factor in the decision. In April 1962 Radio Ghana speculated that the recent cease-fire agreement heralding the successful conclusion of the Algerian war for independence had inspired emulation of Algerian political and military strategy among Angolans. Analogous action, it could be reasoned, might be expected to produce analogous results. The creation of an Angolan equivalent of the Algerian Provisional Government (GPRA) looked to Radio Ghana "very much like history repeating itself." [54] Such an interpretation was rendered even more plausible by Roberto's penchant for identifying the FNLA-GRAE and its leaders with Algeria's FLN-GPRA, and for equating his principal opposition, the MPLA and Mário de Andrade, with the ill-fated *Mouvement National Algérien* (MNA) of Messali Hadj.[55] On April 24 it was announced that Mohamed Ben Bella had met with the twenty-three Angolans training in Tunisia, who would soon return to assume command posts inside Angola.[56]

[52] Andrew Westwood, "The Politics of Revolt in Angola," *Africa Report*, Vol. 7 (Nov. 1962), p. 10.

[53] UPA, "Relatório da Conferência de Imprensa, dada pelo Senhor Holden Roberto, Presidente-geral da UPA" (Léopoldville, Mar. 12, 1962, mimeo.).

[54] Radio Ghana, Accra (1450 GMT-English), Apr. 9, 1962.

[55] This GRAE-GPRA versus MPLA-MNA analogy was suggested in an article in *L' Étudiant Congolais* (Brussels), No. 2, May 1962; reproduced and distributed in GRAE, *Revue de Presse* (Léopoldville), No. 9, June 18, 1962.

[56] GRAE, "Communiqué de presse" (Léopoldville, Apr. 24, 1962, mimeo.).

In a Declaration of Principles, the new "government" declared that those who had created it, the UPA and PDA, constituted "the two authentic representatives of the legitimate aspirations of the people of Angola." Because of "new problems made more delicate each day by the extension of the struggle to the interior of Angola," it continued, these parties established a "Provisional Government" that was "legally mandated by the people in armed struggle to assure careful conduct of the Revolution and the official representation of Angola, whether to International Organizations or to sympathetic and friendly countries." To reinforce this claim to exclusive legitimacy, the GRAE said that it would "solicit the early recognition of all [African] Governments." [57]

Roberto assumed the presidency of the GRAE, and Kunzika became first vice-president. An aging (seventy-one years) and respected mulatto prelate, Msgr. Manuel Mendes das Neves, former vicar-general of Luanda, who had once been expected to become Africa's first cardinal but who instead had been jailed in March 1961 for his nationalist sympathies, was named "honorary" vice-president, presumably without having been consulted in prison.[58] Jonas Savimbi became foreign minister, seconded by Antoine Matumona (PDA) as secretary of state for foreign affairs (Africa) and Johnny Eduardo (Europe). An Ochimbundu, Dr. José Liahuca of SARA, was named minister of interior [59] but declined the post, preferring the less partisan work of the relief organization. Instead the interior ministry went to a veteran UPA leader with a strong following in the strategic Lower Congo, Eduardo Pinock, seconded by Sanda Martin (PDA). [Other important posts were filled as follows: minister of armaments, Alexandre Taty, seconded by Fernando Gourjel and Norbert Kiatalua (PDA); minister of information, Rosário Neto; minister of social and refugee affairs, Ferdinand Dombele; minister of education, André Massaki; and minister of finance, Emmanuel Ziki (PDA).]

[57] GRAE, "Declaration of Principles" (Léopoldville, Apr. 17, 1962, mimeo.).

[58] The GRAE was promptly confronted by an MPLA contention (Andrade at Rabat, Apr. 5) that Msgr. das Neves had been a member of their movement before his incarceration, a claim which the GRAE denied with promptness. "Communicado," No. 001 (Léopoldville, Apr. 6, 1962); see also *Washington Post,* Apr. 6, 1962.

[59] *Washington Post,* Apr. 6, 1962.

The MPLA: Response and Crisis

The reaction of the MPLA was swift. For over two years the party had been promoting various projects for a common front only to find itself excluded from the one that was finally created. The day before the UPA and PDA announced their bipartite front, and seemingly unaware of the negotiations in course, the MPLA executive committee had issued a strongly worded statement endorsing charges leveled against the persons of Roberto and Rosário Neto by Kassanga and Kassinda. "By virtue of their crimes," the committee said, the two top UPA leaders had been "unmasked" as "chiefs of a band of traitors." It described Roberto as an ambitious opportunist who had never lived in and knew nothing about Angola, a tribalist who recruited his principal aides from São Salvador and a religious sectarian who sought support from the world Protestant movement, divided Angolans along religious lines, and ordered measures designed "to impose the Protestant faith in the regions of Angola inhabited by Africans he had misled." The MPLA statement also accused Roberto of falsely branding other nationalist organizations as Communist in order to attract Western sympathy, receiving money from Portuguese planters in northern Angola, displaying vanity by refusing to make public mention of "the great patriot and fighter Dr. Agostinho Neto," and carrying out a program of racial genocide against mulattoes.[60]

As for Roberto's first lieutenant, UPA vice-president Rosária Neto, a Catholic and an Mbundu, the MPLA described him as a former thief who had served a prison sentence in Angola, who now collaborated in Roberto's use of UPA funds for political blackmail, and who translated "the lies, calumnies, and criminal orders of his chief" into Portuguese. The MPLA statement then concluded with an appeal for unity and the creation of an Angolan Liberation Front that would include "all Angolan patriotic organizations." [61] This appeal did not prompt Roberto to change his mind and invite the MPLA to join the FNLA then in the process of formation.

Soon after the Angolan National Liberation Front was founded, Dr. Eduardo dos Santos of the MPLA steering committee denounced

[60] MPLA, Comité Directeur, "Communiqué" (Léopoldville, Mar. 26, 1962, mimeo.); also published in *Remarques Congolaises*, Vol. 4, No. 15–16 (Apr. 19, 1962), p. 145.

[61] *Ibid.*

it as an unrepresentative improvisation created to divert attention from the "revelations" made by Kassanga and Kassinda, revelations which he repeated at some length while denying that they were "inspired" by the MPLA.[62] By praising Kassanga and Kassinda as representing the "true patriots" of a UPA torn by a "profound schism," Dr. dos Santos pursued the MPLA effort to isolate Roberto, by now the *bête noire* of Angolan common-front enthusiasts.

Knowing that relations between the UPA and PDA had been strained in the past and that some PDA leaders had been critical of Roberto's opposition to a three-party front, the MPLA moved quickly to exploit this potential weakness in the new two-party front. Just a few weeks earlier the PDA's Antoine Matumona had written an article in the *Courrier d'Afrique* in which he charged that the UPA was receiving nearly all its material and financial support from the American Committee on Africa. "If one believes the numerous bits of gossip in circulation," wrote Matumona, this aid has been given on the condition that the UPA will not ally itself with the MPLA, "which American circles accuse of being pro-communist." Such an undertaking, he concluded, "would explain the radical intransigence always manifested by Holden Roberto against merger with the MPLA or participation in any front to which the MPLA should belong." [63] Alexandre Taty had answered these charges against the UPA by contending that the UPA's opposition to a common front reflected neither external influence nor a desire "to monopolize the liberation of Angola." Instead, he said, such opposition was based on "reasons" which Matumona might learn about if he would just consult the UPA instead of publicly criticizing it in his news reports. The *Courrier d'Afrique,* for its part, refused to publish letters by Taty denouncing Matumona as a more Congolese than Angolan journalist who wrote in "bad faith." [64] Yet when the MPLA now asserted that Matumona and

[62] MPLA, "Conférence de presse de M. Dr. Eduardo dos Santos" (Léopoldville, Apr. 5, 1962, mimeo.).

[63] *Courrier d'Afrique,* Feb. 5, 1962.

[64] Taty's unpublished letters of Feb. 5 and 13, 1962, were released by the UPA in a *Communiqué de presse* (Léopoldville, no date, mimeo.). Rosário Neto had signed an earlier "Communiqué" (Dec. 1961?) in the name of the UPA Executive Bureau which had questioned the value of any "purely political common Front." In terms clearly meant to exclude the possibility of an understanding with the MPLA, the communiqué argued that national unity could "result only when there is a fruitful collaboration between fighting brothers who have common aspirations and who cooperate fraternally and frankly to the exclusion of any attempt at mutual denigration and destruction."

Massaki had not been among the "several individuals" of the PDA who had illegally committed the PDA to an alliance with the UPA, Matumona promptly issued a rejoinder claiming that, to the contrary, he had been a "promoter" of the new front. And as for Massaki, Emmanuel Kunzika announced that before leaving on a previously scheduled trip to Rhodesia, he had given the PDA executive committee a mandate to act in his name during negotiations with the UPA.[65]

The MPLA's principal effort to discredit the FNLA and block the GRAE from gaining diplomatic recognition took the form of an eighteen-page memorandum sent to all independent African states. Issued in the name of the MPLA steering committee, this memorandum traced the history of the party's efforts to persuade the UPA to join with it in a liberation front, reproduced excerpts from some of the Kassanga-Kassinda blasts against Roberto,[66] laid out the statutes of Aliazo in order to show that the latter (and thus the PDA) was a strictly ethnic party and quoted Matumona as saying that a UPA-Aliazo alliance would open the way for the UPA to impose northern rule over the south of Angola.[67] It denied that the UPA-PDA possessed any "administrative, judicial, or military apparatus that would permit the effective exercise of control over any part of Angolan national territory," implied that close links between Roberto and "interests foreign to Africa" foreclosed any independence of action on his part, and denounced the Government in Exile as constituting an assault upon the unity of the Angolan people.[68] Whether or not this "confidential" memorandum along with the personal intercessions of MPLA leaders and the traveling team of Kassanga and Kassinda should be credited for it, the fact was that, for the duration of 1962 and contrary to Roberto's stated expectations, no government recognized the GRAE.

As for the MPLA itself, though it maintained a public appearance of monolithic unity and, unlike its rivals, revealed little about its

[65] See PDA, "Conférence de presse" [Kunzika] and "Mise au point" signed by Matumona (Léopoldville, Apr. 12, 1962, mimeo.). Neither Matumona's nor Massaki's name had appeared among the ten PDA signatures on the FNLA convention. See ftn. 48.

[66] As published in the daily organ of Mali's ruling *Union soudanaise* party, *Essor* (Bamako), Mar. 12 and 19, 1962.

[67] *Courrier d'Afrique,* Feb. 5, 1962.

[68] MPLA, Comité Directeur, "Memorandum aux gouvernements africains sur la formation d'un prétendu Gouvernement Provisoire de la République de l'Angola" (Léopoldville, April 15, 1962, mimeo.).

own internal organization or external support, it betrayed signs of traversing a major crisis during April and May 1962. This crisis was related to the frustration of both its common-front policy and of its efforts to break the monopoly of access to Angola enjoyed by the forces of the FNLA (UPA) supported by the Congolese central government.

One reason for the inability of the MPLA elite to rally other nationalists to their common-front projects was a suspicion by some that Andrade, da Cruz, and others were concealing extra-African ideological and political commitments. The president of the party's local Léopoldville committee, António Josias, resigned and quit politics after reportedly quarreling with Andrade over the latter's refusal to disclose the source of party funds. Both friends and critics of the MPLA to some extent defined the party in terms of the early left-wing training and associations of its leaders while in Europe. António de Figueiredo, a well-known Portuguese economist and supporter of General Humberto Delgado, who lived for twelve years in Portuguese Africa, wrote in 1962: "The MPLA can be said to be an essentially Portuguese socialist-minded movement." At the same time, he warned, one should not assume that that orientation, coupled with persistent efforts to achieve a common front with other movements, is an indication of "communist affiliations." To so interpret, he said, would be to ignore "the fact that [the] Portuguese democratic opposition is faced with a task of fighting the last bastions of Fascism in the world and that it therefore accepts an alliance with Communists in the same spirit that during the last war Great Britain and the United States accepted an alliance with Russia against the common enemy." [69] Nevertheless, back-handed compliments from Radio Lisbon encouraged a continuing wariness on the part of African skeptics. For example, a Radio Lisbon broadcast on March 9, 1962, described the MPLA as an "openly Communist" organization and Andrade personally as a "suitably trained, indoctrinated Communist who had carried out the necessary trips to Moscow, Peking, and Prague." Alleging that the MPLA enjoyed the "backing" and "financial resources of international Communism," along with Communist "instructors, arms, and technicians of sabotage, propaganda, and subversive war," the broadcast concluded on a theme that was bound to hurt the MPLA

[69] António de Figueiredo, "The Case Against Portugal," in *Angola: A Symposium, Views of a Revolt* (London: Oxford University Press, 1962), p. 55.

in the eyes of African rivals. Stating that the MPLA had eclipsed Roberto's UPA as a force to be reckoned with in Angola, Radio Lisbon explained: "The most important thing is that the MPLA is controlled by European brains and is not a purely African organization." [70]

Ten days after this broadcast, *Pravda* carried an article that praised the MPLA's "militant program" and charged that Roberto's refusal to cooperate with the MPLA was weakening the forces of the Angolan liberation movement and "playing into the hands of Portuguese and other colonialists." *Pravda* went on to say, however, that "progressive forces within the UPA" were striving to unite the efforts of both parties and concluded: "They rightly regard the unity of the nationalist forces as the inevitable prerequisite for the victory of the Angolan people over the Portuguese colonialists." [71]

Twice during May, the Congolese minister of interior, Cléophas Kamitatu, convoked meetings of representatives from all Angolan parties headquartered in Léopoldville in order to discuss possibilities with them for Angolan unity. An official communiqué issued after the first meeting on May 3 stated that Kamitatu had won general support—with the notable exception of the FNLA—for the creation of a single front to represent all Angolan nationalists in dealings with the Congolese Central Government.[72] At the second meeting on May 10, Andrade repeated MPLA support for the creation of a broad Angolan Liberation Front but also suggested that, as a modest beginning, Angolan nationalists might agree to (1) a propaganda truce that would halt the flow of mutually defamatory communiqués and (2) the creation of a liaison council to represent all Angolan nationalists in their dealings with the Congolese government. His suggestions went unheeded. Representatives of the FNLA maintained that they had already established a bona fide front, that it was open to others who supported the revolution, and that it should not be dismantled for the sake of creating a different front.[73]

Reflecting a continued desire within PDA circles for the creation of an enlarged common action front that would include all

[70] Lisbon Overseas Service in English (0200 GMT), Mar. 9, 1962.

[71] Article by V. Midtsev and P. Yevsyukov in *Pravda,* Mar. 19, 1962.

[72] *Courrier d'Afrique,* May 5–6, 1962.

[73] "Réunion du 10 mai." Participating in these meetings were representatives of the FNLA, FNA (*Frente Nacional Angolana*—later MNA), MPLA, MDIA, MLEC, Ngwizako, RCCKP (*Rassemblement des Chefs Coutumiers du Kongo Portugais*), and UNTA.

revolutionary parties while excluding the partisans of nonviolence, Antoine Matumona used his newspaper column to comment on these meetings and to reaffirm that the door was open for the MPLA to join as the third member of the FNLA—an affirmation that the MPLA chose not to test.[74] If the Congolese minister's offer of "good offices" brought about no change in basic positions, these meetings did give him an opportunity to serve formal notice on all Angolan groups that they should keep their quarreling within bounds and respect the peace and security of their host country.[75]

It was on May 13, 21, and 22, following these latest abortive unity discussions, that the MPLA steering committee met in special, stormy sessions and ousted Viriato da Cruz from the post of secretary-general that he had held since the founding of the party in 1956 at Luanda. The secretary-generalship was abolished and replaced by a three-man secretariat, or *troika,* composed of Desidério da Graça, João Vieira Lopes, and Graça da Silva Tavares. Mário de Andrade continued as acting president, Matias Miguéis moved up to the vice-presidency, and a new thirteen-man executive committee, from which da Cruz was excluded, took office.[76]

da Cruz had a reputation for being one of the ablest tacticians and most disciplined Marxists in the top ranks of MPLA leadership. His removal was followed by a perceptible effort on the part of the reorganized party executive to give their movement a more neutral tone. On May 24 Andrade submitted a report to the United Nations Special Committee on Territories under Portuguese Administration which stressed his party's determination to avoid entanglement in the East-West "cold war." He acknowledged that in the past the MPLA, for which he claimed 50,000 card-carrying members, had been attracted by "the dynamism of the Casablanca group of states." The party, he said, had nevertheless "always tried to keep the Angolan question outside of any considerations of choice among our African brothers." If in the past the MPLA's presence had been insufficiently felt outside the more radical Casablanca group, he added, this would now be remedied. Dealing with the suspicion that

[74] *Courrier d'Afrique,* May 10, 1962.

[75] "Réunion du 10 mai."

[76] The new MPLA steering committee was composed of: (1) Mário de Andrade, (2) Matias Miguéis, (3) Hugo de Menezes, (4) Luis de Azevedo, Jr., (5) Graça da Silva Tavares, (6) Déolinda de Almeida, (7) José Bernardo Domingos, (8) Georges Manteya Freitas, (9) Rev. Domingos Francisco da Silva, (10) Desidério da Graça, (11) João Vieira Lopes, (12) João Gonçalves Benedito, (13) José Miguel. MPLA, "Communiqué" (Léopoldville, May 25, 1962, mimeo.).

the MPLA had committed itself in the international cold war, Andrade assured the United Nations committee that "the positive neutralism that we practice in our foreign policy conceals no deliberate ideological choice, and there is no question of its being considered as a blackmail [bargaining] tactic." [77] Though his flight to Moscow and well-publicized address to the World Congress for General Disarmament and Peace on June 12 did not reinforce this desired new image, in a July interview with the French Communist weekly *France-Nouvelle,* Andrade rejected exclusive ties with either East or West "during [the current] phase of the struggle" and said that his party would "sincerely work to counteract" any moves to bring the "cold war" into Angolan politics in order to avoid "the complications of international intrigues" in the Angola of tomorrow.[78]

The GRAE in Quest of African Recognition and Support

Compared with the Casablanca group of Ghana, Guinea, Mali, the UAR, Morocco, and the Algerian Provisional Government (GPRA), the less ideological but more numerous Monrovia states were generally less enterprising and less daring in response to requests for aid from southern African liberation movements. Yet it was principally from within this Monrovian bloc that Holden Roberto and the GRAE had to seek African recognition and support. By early 1961 the MPLA had sewed up the backing of the Casablancans, although Roberto continued to receive some help from Algeria. Competition for the favor of Algeria, which gained independence in July 1962 after seven years of revolution, was in fact intense. The MPLA's advantage became apparent, however, by early November when Andrade announced from Algiers both the opening of a local party office and plans to recruit Algerian volunteers to fight in Angola.[79] By December the press was publishing MPLA claims that it had a thousand men undergoing mili-

[77] MPLA, "Rapport présenté devant le comité spécial des Nations Unies sur les territoires sous administration portugaise," by Mário de Andrade (Léopoldville, May 24, 1962, mimeo.). See also *Remarques Congolaises,* Vol. 4, No. 25–26 (July 12, 1962), pp. 226–228.

[78] See "Address to World Congress for General Disarmament and Peace" (Moscow, July 9–14, 1962, mimeo., 2 pp.); *France-Nouvelle* interview in Mário de Andrade, *Liberté pour l'Angola* (Paris: François Maspero, 1962), pp. 56–57.

[79] *Courrier d'Afrique,* Nov. 9, 1962.

tary training in Algeria.[80] GRAE-MPLA competition for Algerian support nevertheless continued and flared up dramatically in January 1963 at Algiers when Roberto, seeking to gain some points, clashed publicly with the local MPLA representative, Eduardo dos Santos, during a congress of the General Union of Algerian Workers (UGTA).[81]

One of Roberto's other major hopes was Nigeria. But Nigeria pursued what one of its diplomats once described as an "introspective foreign policy." In spite of the bravado and flamboyance of its foreign minister Jaja Wachuku, the giant Nigerian federation from its inception was preoccupied with domestic problems of national unity and economic development. Nigerian independence, like that of most African states, had come as an orderly peaceful transfer of power hastened by the legal pressure brought to bear by tolerated African nationalist movements. Thus when Roberto went to Lagos in April 1962, shortly after the formation of his Exile Government, he was welcomed with nonrevolutionary sympathy. The prime minister, Sir Abubakar Tafawa Balewa, offered to train medical and administrative staff for the GRAE. But he refused to offer military or police training and expressed the wish that some means might be found to "work out ways of winning freedom without bloodshed." In an apparent reference to the fact that the GRAE's forces were fighting in the northern part of Angola, the Nigerian prime minister told Roberto that he was obliged to withold military aid because it would "mean training you to fight your African brothers in thc South." [82]

The fourteen French-speaking states of the *Union Africaine et Malgache* (UAM) were even less openhanded. The UAM secretariat, under an enterprising young Dahomean, Albert Tevoedjre, submitted a report to the organization's summit conference at Bangui in March 1962, urging collective material support for African independence movements. The report suggested: (1) diplomatic initiatives, including "the expulsion of colonialist and racist powers from international organizations" and measures to prevent South African

[80] *The New York Times,* Dec. 7, 1962.

[81] See *Africa 1963* (London), No. 3, Feb. 1, 1963.

[82] Nigeria, Federal Ministry of Information, *News from Nigeria* (Lagos), No. 34, Apr. 28, 1962. Implying that some Casablanca states (viz. Ghana) were aiding nationalist movements in such a way as to extend their own political influence, Balewa said that Nigeria wished in its disinterested fashion to help Angolans win an independence which they could retain. *Ibid.*

and Portuguese planes and ships from landing on UAM territory; (2) organized public collections, performances, and lotteries for financial assistance; and (3) creation of an Institute for Training of Leaders so as to avoid a repetition of events in the Congo caused by "the grave insufficiency of trained political leaders." The report argued that it was the "inescapable duty" of the UAM to establish such an Institute and thus "save our struggling brothers the trek to Peking and Moscow" and also "give an African direction to their liberation movements." As for military training, however, the report simply asked: ". . . is this measure truly practical or feasible given the present conditions of our armies?" [83]

The secretariat's report produced little support and no consensus. Furthermore, subsequent appeals by Angolan nationalists made little impact.[84] The UAM heads of state could agree only to inexpensive generalities, i.e., a pledge "to pursue vigorous and concerted diplomatic action in behalf of the African nationalists." They and their governments then dropped the whole matter, escaping into continued inaction, concerning which Albert Tevoedjre later wrote: "In reality nothing was done until Addis Ababa [the All-African Summit of May 1963], when the UAM left to Algeria, Ghana, and Guinea the role of defender of the interests of African countries still under foreign domination." [85] Put in financial terms, $900,000 was spent in organizing three UAM conferences during 1962–63, and $329,000 was put into a functionless UAM defense organization, but nothing was contributed to the cause of Angolan independence.[86] Most UAM states, including contiguous Congo-Brazzaville, limited their support to pronationalist statements at the United Nations and elsewhere.[87]

Roberto did receive some modest assistance from other Monrovia countries such as Ethiopia and Liberia. Next to the Congo, among

[83] "Report of the UAM Secretary-General on Concrete Measures to Assist African Countries not yet Independent," in Albert Tevoedjre, *Pan-Africanism in Action, An Account of the UAM,* Harvard University Center for International Affairs, Occasional Papers in International Affairs, No. 11 (1965), pp. 82–84.

[84] For text of FNLA memorandum presented to the next UAM conference of heads of state held at Libreville, Gabon, September 12–14, see *Courrier d'Afrique,* Sept. 13, 1962.

[85] "Report of the UAM Secretary-General," p. 19.

[86] *Ibid.,* pp. 17–18 and 65.

[87] For example, République du Congo-Brazzaville, "Déclaration de son Excellence M. Emmanuel Dadet à la Dix-Septième Session de l'Assemblée Générale de l'ONU sur la question de l'octroi de l'indépendance aux pays et aux peuples coloniaux" (New York, Nov. 26, 1962, mimeo.).

the Monrovians Tunisia, though limited in resources, was Roberto's most reliable source of arms, financial aid, and counsel.[88] In January the head of Tunisia's trade union movement, Ahmed Tlili, helped the LGTA win admission as a founding member to the continental African Trade Union Confederation (ATUC) at the latter's inaugural conference at Dakar.[89] Of still greater importance, President Bourguiba continued to patronize the arrangements under which Angolan guerrilla soldiers were training with Algerian FLN units at bases in Tunisia. Some twenty-four of them completed eight months of training there before returning to Léopoldville on June 1, 1962.[90]

In July the GRAE foreign minister Jonas Savimbi—using the pseudonym Matos Sayaya—issued a statement from Khartoum, Sudan, which shed further light on the importance of Tunisia's role. Savimbi said that the GRAE intended to (1) move its ministries of interior and defense into nationalist-held areas of Angola; (2) leave its presidency and ministry of information at Léopoldville where they would keep close contact with insurgent forces; and (3) transfer its ministry of foreign affairs to Tunis, where it would have at its disposal "all the means necessary for conducting relations with Africa and the rest of the world." [91] This plan was never implemented.

Throughout this period the Congo's central government remained Roberto's one really indispensable ally, as is illustrated by the following sequence. In March Roberto announced that he had offers of volunteers for his army, including Algerians, Germans, Spaniards, and Americans. Noncommittally, he said that he would study these offers.[92] What he needed most, however, was not men but funds and matériel and, with the return of his newly trained officer cadre in June, a secure base where he could build a disciplined guerrilla army. In spite of rumors of important American financing [93] and Abako charges that the GRAE had recruited French

[88] Journalist Arthur Herzog reported in April 1962, after returning from UPA-held territory: "A sizable new arms shipment, 100 machine guns were in it, for instance, was arriving in the north. It is an open secret that these arms came from Tunis." *The Observer,* Apr. 29, 1962.

[89] ATUC was the Monrovian response to the Casablancan All-African Trade Union Federation (AATUF) founded in May 1961 at Casablanca.

[90] *The New York Times,* June 3, 1962.

[91] *Courrier d'Afrique,* July 15–16, 1962. Savimbi also announced that the Sudanese government had offered financial aid to the GRAE.

[92] *Ibid.,* Mar. 13, 1962.

[93] Such as those cited by Matumona, see p. 250.

Algerian OAS mercenaries[94] the GRAE was facing a danger of financial collapse just as military needs promised to soar. In order to secure the loyalty of his new officer corps, whose Algerian political exposure had inevitably sowed doubt as to the wisdom of his past American associations, Roberto had to produce results—or face the likelihood of losing control over his army. He was bailed out by the Congolese, by the personal generosity of his old friend Cyrille Adoula, who dug into his own pocket, and by the political generosity of Adoula's government, which granted his army the use of an abandoned military campsite.[95] On August 14 GRAE ministers Taty (of armaments) and Pinock (of interior) left Léopoldville in the company of the Algerian trained officers to install the new base, an event described by the GRAE as "one of the most decisive steps in the history of the Angolan Revolution." [96] In the empty, isolated hills of a place called Kinkuzu, some four and a half hours by sturdy Land Rover north of Thysville, the returned trainees began to train a new Angolan Liberation Army (ELNA). José Kalundungo, a twenty-eight-year-old Bailundu, educated at a Protestant mission, was named base commander and chief of staff. Like his predecessors, Commanders Batista and Kassanga, he was not only a southerner but a veteran of the Portuguese army from which he had deserted in March 1961.[97]

The Portuguese chargé d'affaires at Léopoldville protested the action of the Congolese government. Responding over the Congolese radio, Foreign Minister Justin Bomboko defended his government's right to aid Angolan nationalists in the same manner as Morocco and Tunisia had helped Algerian nationalists to win their protracted independence struggle. Moreover Bomboko said his government intended to continue such aid to the "fullest extent of its possibilities" until Portugal "understood the futility" of a war it was bound to lose.[98] On September 3 Premier Adoula also took to the radio to criticize Portugal for allowing Katanga secessionists

[94] Coming as they did from an Abako senator and founder in 1961 of a dissident *Union Démocratique de l'Ancien Royaume du Kongo* (UDAKO), Gabriel Toto Kinkela, such allegations followed the pattern of continuing harassment of the UPA-GRAE by partisans of Kongo separatism. In a communiqué of May 7, 1962, the GRAE ridiculed charges of collusion with the OAS and reaffirmed its support for the Algerian Provisional Government (GPRA).

[95] *The New York Times*, Aug. 21, 1962.

[96] GRAE, "Communiqué" (Léopoldville, Aug. 17, 1962, mimeo.).

[97] Other officers trained in Algeria included assistant chief of staff Norbert Sengele, political commissioner Alberto Pires, and Jacinto Isaias Kiela.

[98] *Le Progrès*, Aug. 29, 1962.

to move in and out of Angola, and to reaffirm what he had said about self-determination at the Belgrade Conference of Non-Aligned States a year previous, i.e., "that the Congo will not hesitate to give its moral and material support to all people struggling for their freedom." Continuing his statement, which did much to explain his policies toward Angola, he asserted that the Congo had a special mission to fulfill: "Our geographic situation in the center of Africa means for us that the liberation of other African peoples still under foreign domination depends in large measure upon our support, and to aid these peoples is for us a duty of solidarity that we must not shirk." [99] Adoula's words drew praise from Gilbert Pongault, vice-president of the African Trade Union Confederation (ATUC), across the river in Brazzaville (though not from Premier Youlou),[100] and on September 7 provoked a formal note of protest from Lisbon.[101]

In Portugal, Overseas Minister Adriano Moreira denounced the Congo for granting a "privileged sanctuary" to Angolan terrorists. He said that the Portuguese Army had refrained from pursuing Angolan raiders and from destroying their Congolese bases only because of a hope that world opinion would come to understand the merits of Portugal's case.[102] In this regard, Dr. Moreira could take some encouragement from western press reactions to the Kinkuzu affair. *The New York Times* concluded that if there was anything that the Congolese government "should not be doing at this moment it is to play host to the preparation of military adventures against other countries." Though the "Angolan uprising commands some sympathy" as a "natural response to the urge for independence," continued the *Times,* "the Léopoldville government has, and will have, troubles enough of its own without asking for more." [103]

The GRAE received only a modicum of extra-African assistance.

[99] *Courrier d'Afrique,* Sept. 6, 1962.

[100] At Pongault's initiative ATUC had adopted a set of resolutions on Angola at its founding conference at Dakar in January. Anticipating later pan-African projects on the same subject the resolutions proposed, among other things, that African governments contribute 0.1 per cent of their national budget to a fund to be used to provide arms, training, and refugee relief support to Angolan nationalists. Pongault argued that, unless African states took such drastic action, rivalry between Angolan nationalists would be aggravated by the cold-war competition of East-West powers and would lead to fratricidal conflict. *Ibid.,* Sept. 9–10, 1962.

[101] *Ibid.,* Sept. 12, 1962.

[102] *The New York Times,* Sept. 29, 1962.

[103] *Ibid.,* Aug. 22, 1962.

Interested in African friends and indifferent to Portuguese displeasure, Israel joined the sparse ranks of those helping it. Among other things, Israel trained a group of young SARA volunteers as medical corpsmen. The forthcoming Israeli attitude was calculated to strengthen its image among anticolonial Afro-Asian states. It contrasted sharply with the hands-off, hand-wringing posture of most western countries, including the United States and Great Britain.[104] By accepting Israeli assistance, however, the GRAE, like some other southern African liberation movements, risked incurring the wrath of the Arabs and cutting itself off from the kind of help that Egypt could provide, i.e., military training and arms.

As for American assistance, there was a good deal of smoke but less fire. In May 1962 William J. van den Heuval of the New York-based International Rescue Committee (IRC) announced an ambitious Angolan refugee aid program which promised to provide SARA with massive assistance, including fifteen Cuban doctors.[105] The IRC eventually produced one Haitian surgeon, along with some medical equipment, to supplement relief and medical supplies being provided through the ACOA's Emergency Relief to Angola (ERA) and the Catholic-linked African Service Institute of New York. Overly expansive promises and publicity like those of the IRC soon led to disillusionment as GRAE leaders calculated the political costs of a poorly compensated identification with the United States.[106] American support was not only nongovernmental, modest, and slow, but it was also limited to the "humanitarian" sector, whereas the nationalists' greatest needs were for cash and arms.

Roberto might have had both cash and arms from Ghana, but only at President Kwame Nkrumah's price. According to Roberto, this would have meant moving the GRAE's political headquarters to Accra and, of course, agreeing to a united front with the MPLA. Ghana and the other Casablanca states were actively pressuring

104 See Israeli press *Ma'ariv* (Tel Aviv), Aug. 14, 1962, and *Davar* (Tel Aviv), Aug. 15, 1962.

105 GRAE, Ministère d'Information, "Revue de Presse," No. 4 (Léopoldville, May 17, 1962, mimeo.); also *World News Service* (Chicago), Vol. 19, No. 3, May 11, 1962.

106 In the view of the Fourth International and many others who suspected American intrigue, the magnitude of the Congolese central government's aid to Holden Roberto could only be explained in terms of American "consent." As the United States supported Adoula against Gizenga, the reasoning went, so Adoula supported Roberto against Andrade. *L'Internationale* (Paris), Oct. 1962.

African nationalist movements of all remaining colonial areas to coalesce into single "united fronts." Even as early as September 1961 at Conakry, the Casablanca-oriented Steering Committee of the All-African Peoples' Conference had deplored "continued disunity within African Nationalist movements in certain dependent countries where a united stand and united fronts are urgently needed to ensure victory against colonialists," and had called upon all such movements "to take urgent steps to constitute United Fronts."[107]

In June 1962 President Nkrumah carried the campaign a step further. He organized a special Conference of African Freedom Fighters at the Kwame Nkrumah Institute for Ideological Training at Winneba, Ghana. After appealing to independent African states to create a joint military command, rather than remain divided and ineffective in the face of South African and allied military power, he told the assembled African Freedom Fighters that they should close their own ranks, overcome both "the sectionalism of separate organizations" and the divisiveness of competing leadership, and unite in the struggle against imperialism.[108]

Some ephemeral united fronts were announced as a result of Ghanaian prodding. One of these was an accord signed by representatives of the FNLA and MPLA. The FNLA delegation led by David Livromentos and Rosário Neto was cajoled into accepting Nkrumah's minimal formula for cooperation with the MPLA.[109] Accordingly, Rosário Neto joined Mário de Andrade and President Nkrumah himself in signing an agreement by which the two movements undertook to place their respective armed forces under a single unified military command.[110] The agreement was described as a "nonpolitical" military arrangement.

In the absence of a political understanding, however, it was unrealistic to attempt to implement such a military alliance. As soon as the two delegations were back in Léopoldville, the agreement broke down. FNLA council president Livromentos demanded

[107] "Resolution on Unity," *Bulletin of the Permanent Secretariat of the All-African Peoples' Conference* (Accra), No. 2, Oct. 31, 1961.

[108] For President Nkrumah's address, see Ghana Information Service, New York, "Press Release," No. 183, June 12, 1962.

[109] The other members of the FNLA/GRAE delegation were Antoine Matumona, Pedro Gadimpovi, André M'Vila, Nicolas Vieira, and Antoine Mouzinho.

[110] This agreement was embodied in a document entitled "Problème angolais. Formation d'une alliance militaire et création d'une commande militaire nouvelle des combattants angolais pour la libération" (Accra [July 1, 1962], mimeo.).

that the MPLA recognize and negotiate with the FNLA as distinct from the latter's constituent parties,[111] while the MPLA held fast to its policy of nonrecognition. And that was the end of the Accra agreement.[112]

Regional, ethnic, ideological, and personal differences did not dissolve into desired consensus because of strategic or moral imperatives. In some measure, the failure of Ghanaian pressure to produce any lasting unity among Angolan, South West African, and other liberation groups could be traced to fears on the part of a peasant-based movement, led by either little-educated or self-educated men, often restrictively ethnic in origin, that merger with an organization led by an elite, better educated and ideologically more sophisticated or disciplined, would prove suicidal. They suspected that the common front would only prove to be a vehicle by which university-educated mulattoes and African Marxists might pluck power from their less experienced hands. Therefore, the leaders of movements like the FNLA-GRAE spoke enthusiastically of the need for unity and avoided it like the plague—foregoing in the process material support from common-front advocates such as Ghana.

Agostinho Neto: Last Hope for a Common Front?

In July 1962 Dr. Agostinho Neto's escape from forced residence in Portugal across the straits to Morocco thrust a martyred symbol of Angolan nationalism into the rough and tumble of Angolan exile politics. Years of jail and rustication had transformed the life of the MPLA's "honorary president" into a political legend well before he had the opportunity to exercise public political leadership. The previous December a Methodist scholarship student from Luanda, Elisio Figueiredo, had told a Chicago conference of African students studying in the United States that the campaign for Neto's release bore the same significance for Angola as campaigns for the

[111] In an open letter to the MPLA dated July 25, 1962 (Léopoldville, mimeo.).

[112] A similar fate befell an agreement between the South West Africa National Union (SWANU) and Peoples' Organization (SWAPO), who undertook to establish "a working relationship" by creating "consultative committees" made up of executive members of their two organizations. Arranged by the Ghanaians, this accord was apparently implemented for a time inside South West Africa but never outside. See "Recommendation to the National Executive Committees of the South West Africa Peoples' Organization and South West Africa National Union" (Accra, June 1962, mimeo.). See also *Contact* (Cape Town), Vol. 5, No. 14, July 26, 1962.

release of Jomo Kenyatta and Ben Bella had borne for Kenya and Algeria. "Dr. Neto," he said, "is the only leader able to save us from eventual divisions among the Angolan nationalist parties." [113] Considered a hero by his constituents in Catete, he was widely admired by Angolan students and intellectuals, many of whom hoped and anticipated that his escape would now provide new leadership around which all Angolan nationalists might rally and transcend their partisan differences.[114] Dr. Neto was expected to be the arbiter, the unifier.

Stopping along the way at MPLA-oriented capitals like Rabat and Conakry, Neto made his way to Léopoldville where, in early August, he initiated unity talks among Angolan nationalists. He did so, however, not by seeking private exploratory talks with Holden Roberto and others as a means to pave the way for an understanding, but by calling straightaway for a formal meeting between FNLA and MPLA delegations empowered to negotiate a unifying agreement. Putting aside any ambition that he might have had of rising like a Charles de Gaulle "above the quarreling parties" —his honorary presidency of the MPLA, after all, had not represented a public partisan commitment on his part—he decided to attend unity talks, to which the FNLA agreed, as a member of the MPLA delegation.

At 10:45 A.M., August 5, 1962, in the Hall de Buvetta, Léopoldville, the two delegations confronted each other in a tense but polite exchange. Antoine Matumona, known for his past advocacy of a common front, headed an FNLA team, which included Jonas Savimbi, Fernando Gourjel, Emmanuel Ziki, and Johnny Edouard. In addition to Neto, the MPLA delegation was composed of Rev. Domingos da Silva, José Bernardo Domingos, and Luis de Azevedo, Jr.[115] After some initial sparring about whether the MPLA would consent to negotiate with (and thus recognize) the FNLA, as a united front, Dr. Neto conceded the point, urged that past recriminations be put aside, proposed three possible formulas for unity, and de-

[113] Speech delivered to the Conference of the All-African Student Association, Chicago, Dec. 1961; excerpt published in *Liberator* (New York), Vol. II, No. 4 (Apr. 1962), p. 4.

[114] Andrade also expressed such sentiments in December 1961; see his *Liberté pour l'Angola,* p. 49. The *World Marxist Review* (Prague), Vol. 5, No. 9 (Sept. 1962), hailed Neto's escape as of undoubted "significance for the unity of all the nationalist forces of Angola fighting against the colonialists" (p. 93).

[115] For an account of the meeting, see press release, "Entretien FNLA-MPLA, 5 août 1962" (Léopoldville, Aug. 5, 1962, mimeo.).

clared his own preference for the first, i.e., a rapid, "fusion" by stages into a single movement. His second alternative called for "close collaboration" in political-military action under a common organic body; and his third, in line with the Accra accord of July, proposed simply a joint military command over all Angolan forces under the umbrella authority of a national council.[116] The FNLA agreed to study the three proposals.

Once again, however, hopes for unity crashed in mid-takeoff. On August 8, before a second meeting could take place, FNLA headquarters issued a statement denying press reports that an agreement had already been reached.[117] Such was the atmosphere of mistrust that some UPA partisans suggested, whether skeptically or expediently, that these reports had been planted in order to bring pressure on Roberto. The same day Dr. Neto dispatched a letter to Roberto in which he referred to and implicitly accepted earlier accusations of racism, sectarianism, tribalism, and treason leveled against Roberto and his government.[118] Stung by this resurrection of charges that had formed an obstacle to a political détente in the past, Roberto, followed by Kunzika and Dombele of the PDA, seized upon the letter as new evidence that MPLA leadership lacked the

[116] MPLA, "Conférence de presse de M. Dr. Agostinho Neto, président d'honneur du MPLA" (Léopoldville, Aug. 10, 1962, mimeo.).

[117] GRAE, Ministère de l'Information, "Communiqué" (Léopoldville, Aug. 8, 1962, mimeo.).

[118] For text see GRAE, Ministère de l'Information, "Le FNLA et l'unité angolaise" (Léopoldville, Aug. 5, 1962, mimeo.); also published in Pierre Moser, *La révolution angolaise* (Tunis: Société l'Action d'Édition et de Presse, 1966), pp. 201–203. In his letter, Dr. Neto alleged that anyone who tended to perpetuate division within Angolan ranks was supporting Portuguese colonialism and adding to the political disarray into which the Angolan masses had fallen. In the passages to which the FNLA took particular exception, he went on to say:

> "When Angolans fleeing from the cruelty of Portuguese settlers arrive in the Congo only to be imprisoned, maltreated, and even exterminated by other Angolans, whatever the pretext, this is a crime, a betrayal of the aims of the Angolan revolution, collaboration with the occupying power.
>
> "When medical-social teams working among the abandoned are subjected to persecution or aggression by Angolans inspired by racism, sectarianism, and tribalism, thus preventing needy Angolans from receiving the assistance they require, this constitutes an inhuman crime, a collaboration with Portuguese colonial repression."

The letter concluded with an invitation to Roberto to meet in a tête-à-tête with or without other political leaders present. Roberto, however, rejected the whole letter as gratuitously "insinuating, vexatious, and provocative," and the two leaders never met to discuss their differences.

requisite qualities of trust and good faith essential for serious unity negotiations.[119]

Probably not yet aware of the storm his letter was creating, Neto followed it with a press conference on August 10, at which he outlined the three proposals that he had made at the meeting five days previous (which had already been publicly circulated by both groups in a common *compte rendu* of the August 5 meeting) and announced that the MPLA was awaiting "with anxiety" for an affirmative response from the FNLA. By this time all possibilities for private negotiations uncompromised by publicity and the competitiveness of partisan communiqués had evaporated. Neto also chose the occasion of his press conference to identify himself even more exclusively with the MPLA, which he said had organized his escape "with the aid of Portuguese and other European anti-colonialists."[120] He implied that his ties with the MPLA were of long standing—"we organized the Anti-Colonialist Movement [MAC]"—and praised the work of Mário de Andrade, Lucio Lara and Amilcar Cabral, who since 1950, he said, had been "pillars of the anti-colonialist struggle abroad." (He made no mention of Viriato da Cruz.) After denouncing Portuguese colonial rule by "iron and fire," he praised the MPLA, which, he said, was "in the midst of expansion." It was the MPLA, he continued, that had "best known how to interpret the meaning of Angolan nationalism" and had struggled for "national unity and against all sorts of discrimination," whether "racial, regional, ideological, or otherwise." These last comments probably further undercut precisely what was Neto's "principal" stated objective, i.e., the ever-elusive common front.[121]

That same month, Neto also gave a press interview to a corre-

[119] Letters dated Aug. 9 and 13, 1962, *ibid.*

[120] In an interview published in Robert Davezies' *Les angolais* (Paris: Les Éditions de Minuit, 1965), Roberto later spoke openly of his suspicion that Neto's escape might not have been without some Portuguese collusion. This feeling, shared by other adversaries of the MPLA, had lingered in the background of the unity talks of August 5, 1962. Roberto told Davezies that he considered it "strange" that Neto should have been able to escape with his wife and children. (Though it was not mentioned, the fact that his wife was Portuguese was very much in mind.) "We know PIDE. Less important people than he have disappeared. In any case, the circumstances surrounding his escape have never been clarified" (p. 187). On the other hand, in order to protect those who had helped to organize his escape and perhaps to leave open the possibility for others to follow suit, it might well have been difficult, if not impossible, for Neto to reveal such details of his flight as could have disarmed skeptics.

[121] "Conférence de presse de M. Dr. Agostinho Neto" (see ftn. 116).

spondent of the Cuban government paper *Revolución*. He was reported as saying that some "imperialist and neocolonialist forces" had given up their support of Portugal's colonial war as a lost cause. They had now chosen instead, he warned, to disrupt the unity of Angolan nationalists by concluding "agreements with false leaders who would safeguard the interests of the imperialists" while continuing to give lip service to nationalism and independence. The MPLA leader dwelt at length upon what he alleged to be the UPA's dependency upon American assistance and its willing cooperation with American "imperialist maneuvers." He scarcely mentioned Portugal.[122]

[122] Interview with Ithiel Leon, *Revolución* (Havana), Aug. 17, 1962.

CHAPTER NINE

AMERICAN, PORTUGUESE, AND COLONIAL RESPONSE TO CONTINUING REVOLUTION

The year 1962 witnessed a gradual but unmistakable shift in the international power equation concerning Angola and Portugal. At the beginning of the year, in January, the United States voted with a Sixteenth General Assembly majority of ninety-nine against two (Spain and South Africa) and a solitary abstention (France) in approving a resolution which reaffirmed Angola's right to self-determination. The General Assembly resolution both "deprecated" and asked Portugal "to desist from" repressive measures and urged member states to use their influence to persuade Portugal to institute an extensive program of political, economic, and social reforms in its African territory.[1] In contrast, less than a year later, in December, the American delegation to the Seventeenth General Assembly voted with a minority of seven (five NATO countries, Spain, and South Africa) against a majority of eighty-one and thirteen abstentions (of which eight were NATO countries) in opposing a resolution which severely condemned Portugal's rule in all its overseas territories. The new resolution added to earlier ones a request that all states refrain from offering assistance that could enable the Portuguese government to continue its repression of the peoples of these territories. Specifically it urged that they take whatever measures necessary to prevent the sale and supply of arms and military equipment to the Portuguese government.[2]

[1] United Nations, General Assembly Resolution 1742 (XVI), Jan. 30, 1962.

[2] United Nations, General Assembly Resolution 1807 (XVII), Dec. 14, 1962. The United States also voted against a similar resolution concerning only Angola, which requested that the Security Council take appropriate measures, including sanctions, so as to secure Portugal's compliance with Assembly demands for an orderly transfer of power to a freely elected Angolan government. General Assembly Resolution 1819 (XVII), Dec. 18, 1962 (approved by 57 to 14, with 18 abstentions).

The American Retreat

Caught between its public commitment to the principle of self-determination on the one hand and its incompatible obligations to support a NATO ally on the other, the United States equivocated during 1962. Portugal insisted that America's contractual responsibilities as a NATO ally included an inescapable duty to support Portuguese colonial policy. At the same time, African, Asian, Latin American, and Communist states were responding to Lisbon's defiance of the United Nations with increasingly severe censure. Thus the United States found itself more and more isolated—a fence straddler pleading for pale, inoffensive resolutions.

In November the American General Assembly delegation circulated and lobbied for a proposal designed to establish a temporary United Nations "presence" in Angola and Mozambique in the person of a one-man visiting mission, or *rapporteur,* to be appointed by the President of the Seventeenth Assembly.[3] Clearly a "gradualist" measure, it was designed to extend United Nations influence and establish a useful precedent. The United Nations-sponsored Carpio Mission to South West Africa the year previous, however, had resulted in a tragicomedy of conflicting statements and diversionary controversy that Africans were loathe to see repeated. And the fear that a single *rapporteur* might succumb to Portuguese wine and wile became a real obstacle when it became known that the Portuguese were prepared to receive the visit of such an observer—assuming the selection of an acceptable person. Moreover, Holden Roberto rejected the American proposal as a delaying action, arguing that the circumstances demanded immediate remedy and could not wait for a report that would be presented a year hence to the

[3] The text of the American draft resolution (undated [Nov. 1962], mimeo.) read:

"The General Assembly
Recalling its previous consideration of Angola and of Mozambique;
Having concluded that there is a need for further accurate and detailed information from within Angola and Mozambique on conditions there;
(1) *Requests* the President of the Seventeenth General Assembly to appoint a United Nations Rapporteur for the purpose of gathering information on Angola and on Mozambique, visiting those two territories and such other places as the Rapporteur may deem necessary;
(2) *Requests* the Government of Portugal to extend to the United Nations Rapporteur such assistance as he may require pursuant to his mandate;
(3) *Requests* the United Nations Rapporteur to draw up a report for the consideration of the Eighteenth General Assembly."

Eighteenth General Assembly.[4] Faced with resolute African opposition and a general lack of enthusiasm among other delegations, the United States quietly withdrew its proposal without formally presenting it for approval.[5]

American efforts to bring pressure upon Portugal through Brazil,[6] by virtue of the latter's special historical and cultural ties, were similarly ineffectual. The government of President João Goulart, which had in September 1961 succeeded the brief administration of Jânio Quadros, was internally weaker and internationally rather less enterprising. Brazil did employ the forum of the General Assembly to urge Portugal to "take the lead in the movement for the emancipation of Angola and its transformation into an independent state which would be as friendly toward Portugal as is Brazil." [7] Yet visits to Lisbon by the American, Brazilian, and British foreign secretaries, intent upon reasoning with Portugal, were rendered more difficult by the very fact that these visitors or their governments had made critical statements or voted against Portugal in the United Nations and had thereby incurred "Portugal's wrath." [8] Lisbon meanwhile made considerable use of its "traditional tactics" in dealing with "more powerful foreign governments" with whom its relations were strained. That is to say, it responded with "injured silence." [9]

As an illustration of this withdrawal into silence, Benjamin Welles of *The New York Times* reported in April 1962: "Requests by American or British attachés to visit Portuguese Government installations are neither approved nor disapproved; they are pigeonholed." Portuguese rancor, he continued, stemmed from a "widely held belief that President Kennedy personally has ordered his administration to side with the African and Asian bloc at the United Nations whenever they are in conflict with Portugal." Recognizing the limits of their own power, the Portuguese believed that American policy would "inevitably wrest away the nation's overseas territories and leave Portugal bankrupt." [10]

Premier Salazar broke this silence in May, when he publicly blamed both the United States and the Soviet Union for Portugal's

[4] JUPA, *Juventude revolucionária*, No. 10 (Jan. 11, 1962), p. 6.
[5] See *Le Monde*, Dec. 20, 1962.
[6] *The New York Times*, Apr. 13, 1962.
[7] United Nations, Document A/PV, 1091 (Jan. 18, 1962), p. 37.
[8] *International Conciliation*, No. 539 (Sept. 1962), p. 57.
[9] *The New York Times*, Apr. 1, 1962.
[10] *Ibid.*

colonial difficulties. While the two great powers were busily "banning wars that do not exist," he said, they were "stimulating those that do." Alluding to western pleas for democratic reform and the failure of western powers to stand up to India when it occupied Goa in late 1961, the Portuguese leader charged the United States, as well as the Soviet Union, with "ideological interference" and with giving financial, military, and political support to Portugal's enemies. Portugal, he said, was confronted with a costly and difficult war in Africa, which it was fighting "not without alliances but without allies." [11] Nor was Salazar content with verbal protest. In July the American director of Methodist missionary work in Africa, Rev. Dr. C. Melvin Blake, announced in New York that the Portuguese Government was refusing visas and barring Methodist missionaries from entering Angola and Mozambique.[12]

Unwilling to endorse collective measures that might have offered some hope for persuading Portugal to alter its policies, the United States was left to argue with decreasing effect that it had "publicly and privately and continuously urged Portugal to accept" the principle of self-determination.[13] In reality, however, by blocking efforts to organize an arms embargo against Portugal, Washington had made a choice.

The reasons for the increasingly apparent shift in American policy toward a position of uneasy but unequivocal support for Lisbon were not difficult to find. Within the State Department itself, Assistant Secretary G. Mennen Williams' Bureau of African Affairs had its hands full trying to ward off attacks on the administration's Katanga policy. The Katanga lobby, led by Senator Thomas J. Dodd of Connecticut, and the British, Belgian, and French governments sought to persuade Washington to withdraw its support for the Congolese central government in that government's struggle to undo Katangese secession. As a result, Williams' capable deputy and director of the African Bureau, J. Wayne Fredericks, found it impossible to fight on two fronts. It was also true that in the main the older European Bureau (EU) still attracted abler career personnel and carried more weight than its African counterpart (AF), and so it was only normal that the Portuguese desk (EU) should eclipse the Angola-Mozambique desk (AF) in departmental infighting. Furthermore, the enthusiasm with which the Kennedy admin-

[11] *Ibid.*, May 29, 1962.
[12] *Ibid.*, July 22, 1962.
[13] United Nations, Document S/PV, 1045 (July 26, 1963), p. 22.

istration had first approached Africa waned by mid-1962, partly as a result of disenchanting entanglement in the complicated, seemingly ungovernable Congo, whose civil conflict had only been stalemated but not resolved by a protracted and costly United Nations occupation. Under these circumstances, the public relations program conducted for the Portuguese by Selvage and Lee, which gave maximum publicity to the myth of a "Communist invasion" of Angola, may have had some effect on American thinking, especially in the absence of any comparable publicity for the African case.[14] Over $200,000 was spent during 1962 alone on that public relations campaign, which succeeded in organizing an Angolan tour for fifty-six newsmen traveling under the auspices of the National Editorial Association.[15] For its part, the Portuguese-American Committee on Foreign Affairs worked on Massachusetts congressmen who were desirous of pleasing voters within the state's Portuguese-American community. On October 4 and 5 twelve Massachusetts congressmen, including House Speaker John W. McCormack and former Speaker Joseph W. Martin, made speeches in the House of Representatives praising Portugal as a faithful and indispensable NATO ally and condemning Angolan nationalist insurgency as communist-inspired terrorism.[16] Yet all these factors were secondary. The principal reason the United States buckled under Portuguese pressure was embarrassingly simple—the Azores bases.

The agreement under which the United States used the air and sea bases in the Azores was due to expire on December 31, 1962. The influence of this deadline on American attitudes was decisive. An influential exponent of NATO-first policy, former Secretary of State Dean Acheson, writing after the outbreak of the Angolan war, had described these refueling, communications, and antisubmarine bases as "perhaps the single most important [set of bases]

[14] For a description of the Portuguese-American Selvage and Lee campaign, which included use of the forged "order of the day" that purported to prove Holden Roberto to be a Communist, see Daniel M. Friedenberg, "Public Relations for Portugal: The Angola Story as Told by Selvage and Lee," *The New Republic*, Apr. 2, 1962, pp. 9–12.

[15] *Evening Star* (Washington), Feb. 16, 1963. Selvage and Lee also produced a 23-page brochure of favorable press items entitled *Eyewitness Reports from Portuguese Africa.*

[16] Speeches printed and distributed as pamphlet: *Friendly Relations Between Portugal and the United States—A Victory for Freedom.* Speech of Hon. Thomas P. O'Neill, Jr., Oct. 5, 1962 [et al.] (Washington, D.C.: U.S. Government Printing Office, 1962).

we have anywhere." [17] The Defense Department agreed. The Lajes air base on Terceira Island and its back-up field on Santa Maria Island reportedly handled 14,000 aircraft departures in the fiscal year 1961—more than forty long-range planes per day. They were crucial in the November 1961 redeployment of American troops in Europe and represented an investment of approximately a hundred million dollars.[18] And though the American installations provided jobs for 3000 Portuguese nationals and annually poured between ten and fifteen million dollars in wages, rents, and purchases into the Portuguese economy, Lisbon threatened to let the base agreement expire in retaliation for American failure to give unqualified support to its African policies. In July Prime Minister Salazar granted a carefully timed interview to the conservative weekly *U.S. News and World Report.* Asked whether Portugal was likely to extend the Azores agreement, he replied ominously: "I would like to be excused from replying to the question." [19] A few weeks earlier the same periodical had offered its millions of readers an article on the Azores entitled "A Key Base U.S. Could Lose." [20]

In January Secretary of State Dean Rusk traveled to Lisbon to smooth ruffled feelings,[21] and the United States went ahead with deliveries of approximately four and a half million dollars in military aid to Portugal, in spite of African resentment of such aid.[22] The Portuguese government encountered no difficulty in floating a twenty million dollar long-term loan with a group of American banks, the United States purchased thirty seven million dollars' worth of Angolan coffee during the year,[23] and the Defense Department pulled out all stops in its effort to obtain a renewal of the Azores base agreement. On July 19 American Air Force Chief of Staff Curtis E. LeMay placed the ribbon of the Legion of Merit about the collar of Portugal's Air Force Chief of Staff General Bernardo Tiago Mira Delgado. Secretary of Defense Robert McNamara,

17 Dean Acheson, "Fifty Years After," *Yale Law Review,* Vol. 51 (Autumn 1961), p. 9.

18 For a report on the operations and importance of the bases, see Harold K. Milks, "Azores—Vital to U.S. Air Defense," *The Sun* (Baltimore), Mar. 25, 1962.

19 *U.S. News and World Report,* July 9, 1962, p. 78.

20 *Ibid.,* May 21, 1962, p. 86.

21 *The New York Times,* Jan. 29, 1962.

22 *Statistical Abstract of the United States, 1963,* 84th ed. (Washington, D.C.: U.S. Government Printing Office, 1963), p. 259.

23 U.S. Department of Agriculture, Economic Research Service, "United States Agricultural Imports from Angola, 1962, 1963, and 1964" (Washington, D.C., Sept. 1965, mimeo.).

speaking at the decoration ceremonies held in Washington, cited the Portuguese general for his contribution to Portuguese-American friendship at a time when the principal function of General Delgado's air force consisted in spreading bullets, rockets, and American-made napalm over a wide area of northern Angola.[24]

Lisbon bargained shrewdly. It demanded evidence of "friendly" behavior as a prerequisite to any base-renewal agreement and so intimidated the State Department that the Department reportedly sent orders to New York that members of the American mission to the United Nations were not to speak to Angolan nationalist petitioners under any circumstances.[25] Lisbon also sought to halt American scholarship aid for African refugee students from Angola and Mozambique, letting it be known that the students were only being deprived of their Portuguese cultural heritage and rendered irrelevant to the future of their countries by virtue of their studies under government and private scholarships in the United States. By December the United States was back voting with Portugal's NATO friends, Spain, and South Africa.[26] Yet having exacted its price, Lisbon still chose not to sign a long-term contract for American use of the Azores. It understandably preferred to hold on to its leverage in case the United States should again stray into misguided anticolonial behavior. Thus Lisbon agreed only to permit American use of the Azores facilities on an *ad hoc* basis after the base agreement expired on December 31.[27] Washington quietly accepted Lisbon's terms and thus became dependent upon the latter's continued and uninterrupted good humor.

[24] *Washington Post,* July 20, 1962.

[25] According to Angolan petitioners, these orders were carried to such an extreme that American officials whom the Angolans knew looked the other way and pretended not to see them in the event of a chance encounter in a United Nations elevator. The ACOA was unable to arrange, as in the past, for nationalist leaders from Portuguese Africa to meet appropriate State Department officials. See George Houser, "The Danger of United States Vacillating Policy toward Portuguese Africa" (Dec. 1962, unpublished typescript).

[26] At the end of the year Selvage and Lee published a congratulatory foldout entitled "U.S. Votes *With* Portugal *Against* Communist Bloc and Afro-Asian Extremists at U.N.," in which it claimed that, in U.N. committee votes, "The U.S. had begun quietly to shift its position as early as August and September." Hailing the American General Assembly vote "with Portugal" on December 14, the publicity sheet reproduced favorable articles from the *Evening Star* (Washington), Dec 21, *Washington Post,* Dec. 26, *The Catholic News* (New York), Dec. 22, and the *Post Tribune* (Jefferson City, Mo.), Dec. 21.

[27] *Christian Science Monitor,* Jan. 8, 1963; and *Philadelphia Inquirer,* Jan. 16, 1963.

To many people, the picture of giant America being outmaneuvered by little Portugal was bewildering. Having first denied and then admitted that American-supplied NATO arms were used in Angola, American delegate Jonathan B. Bingham assured the Fourth Committee of the General Assembly in late 1962 that promises had been sought and received (in the summer of 1961) that the Portuguese would not again use NATO arms in Angola.[28] In fact, it was impossible for the small American consular staff in Luanda to check thoroughly enough to know whether small arms provided to Portugal under NATO accords were being sent to Angola. And in any case almost no one took very seriously Washington's assertions that it was not helping Lisbon materially in its military campaign to wipe out African nationalism.[29] In August 1962, for example, the United Nations Special Committee on Territories under Portuguese Administration issued a report which concluded that NATO arms had been "extensively used and continue to be used by Portuguese military and other Portuguese forces of repression to suppress the people of Angola." By way of contrast with American eagerness to accept Portuguese denials of this, the Committee found that "so long as these [NATO] arms are in the hands of Portugal they will be used against African nationalist movements regardless of any assurances to the contrary that Portugal might have given. It is obvious that any such assistance so rendered represents an implication in the suppression of the movements for freedom in the territories under Portuguese administration." [30]

Meeting at Harriman, New York, in November, the first American Negro Leadership Conference on Africa raised a new voice in support of a stronger American policy that would include "immediate steps to insure that no arms, weapons or war material supplied to Portugal by the United States are used against the peoples of Portuguese Territories in Africa in its efforts to keep these peoples in subjugation." Sponsored by all the principal civil rights organizations of the country, the Conference also deplored "Portugal's ex-

[28] United Nations, General Assembly, Fourth Committee, 1402 meeting, Nov. 29, 1962; and U.S. Delegation to the General Assembly, Press Release No. 4107, Nov. 29, 1962.

[29] Afro-Asian states at the United Nations assailed the United States and other "NATO powers" for extending economic and military assistance to Portugal and for thus helping it to suppress the Angolan independence movement. *The New York Times,* Dec. 7, 1962.

[30] United Nations, General Assembly, *Report of the Special Committee on Territories under Portuguese Administration,* A/5160, Aug. 15, 1962, p. 142.

penditure of large sums of money on public relations designed to misinform and mislead the American public," and called upon the United States government "to use its influence to persuade other Western powers to urge Portugal to grant Angola, Mozambique and Portuguese Guinea their independence."[31] Emmanuel Kunzika attended the Conference as an "observer" on the behalf of the FNLA.[32]

Dr. Martin Camacho of the Portuguese-American Committee on Foreign Affairs responded to the Conference by charging that Negro leaders "apparently have embarked on an organized campaign to use the political power of the Negroes in this country to force the Federal Government to align itself with racists and other extremist elements in Africa." Should a Communist or Castro type of government take over a Portugal weakened by the loss of its African possessions, he warned, the West would see "key areas" astride Atlantic sea routes fall into "enemy hands" and the United States "would lose its vital air base on the Azores."[33]

In an address on Independence Day 1962, President John F. Kennedy proclaimed that the United States had "no intention of abdicating its leadership in [the] world-wide movement for independence to any nation or society committed to systematic human oppression."[34] Yet by subsequently voting against the tough General Assembly resolutions of December 1962, the United States seemingly abdicated just such leadership. This left the way open for the Soviet Union to argue with enhanced credibility and justification that only NATO assistance to Portugal and exploitative Western economic interests in its colonies could account for the Salazar government's ability to pursue its colonial war.[35] Already in his May 1962 report to the United Nations, Mário de Andrade had

[31] Sponsors included the Congress of Racial Equality, National Association for the Advancement of Colored People, National Urban League, Southern Christian Leadership Conference, Brotherhood of Sleeping Car Porters, and Student Non-Violent Coordinating Committee. See American Negro Leadership Conference on Africa, *Resolutions*, No. V (Harriman, New York, Nov. 23–25, 1962). For Conference background paper on Angola, see John Marcum, "The Angolan War and American Ambivalence" (Nov. 1962, mimeo.).

[32] Mozambique nationalist, Dr. Eduardo Mondlane, who was then completing his final semester as a professor at Syracuse University, also attended the conference.

[33] *The Sun* (Baltimore), Dec. 11, 1962.

[34] *The New York Times*, July 5, 1962.

[35] For an analysis of General Assembly debate, see Patricia Wohlgemuth, "The Portuguese Territories and the United Nations," *International Conciliation*, No. 545 (Nov. 1963), pp. 21–37.

expressed a view concerning the real locus of responsibility for the protracted war in Angola that was to gain ever wider acceptance as the years progressed. Portugal, he said, had practically no war industry, and "it is evident that it would not have the slightest inclination to continue its armed action against the Angolan people if it were not for the military aid furnished to it by a number of western countries." [36]

One of the consequences of the American decision to choose NATO over Africa, or the Azores over Angola, was to drag the cold war deeper into Angolan nationalist politics. The epithet "pro-American" became about the most damaging charge that could be hurled against an African nationalist. Private American citizens in refugee relief and educational fields found that their assistance was increasingly viewed as suspect or as a political liability not worth the marginal help rendered. Disillusionment among earlier admirers of the United States and intensified hostility on the part of those who had been critical to begin with would, in fact, turn anti-American sentiment into a powerful common denominator and unifying factor among Angolan nationalists from 1962 onward. Among some Africans, anti-Americanism came to outweigh antipathy toward Portugal.

Portuguese Tenacity and Treason

From Dr. Salazar's vantage point, 1962 was a better year than 1961. After an abortive army coup staged at Beja, south of Lisbon, in January—a coup which may have been connected with army discontent over the conduct of the war in Angola—Salazar's power and policies were not seriously challenged. His ability to contain the rebellion, on the other hand, was improved by the construction of a large new air base in northern Angola at Negage, the institution of special counterinsurgency training, and the intensification of air attacks in rebel zones.[37] Under a new (June 1961) governor-general, Augusto Venâncio Deslandes, Portuguese tactics had been revised, and stringent measures were now taken to prevent Angolan rebels from capturing arms and ammunition. Portuguese soldiers were

[36] Andrade charged that Portuguese paratroops were using NATO automatic weapons. MPLA, "Rapport présenté devant le comité spécial des Nations Unies sur les territoires sous administration portugaise" (Léopoldville, May 24, 1962, mimeo.).

[37] *The New York Times,* June 3, 1962.

strapped to their jeeps, their weapons tied to their bodies, and they began to move in large, air-protected convoys. It thus became more difficult for Angolan snipers and patrols to fell individual soldiers or to ambush small Portuguese units, the means by which they had heretofore been able to recuperate desperately needed small arms.[38]

The Portuguese government inaugurated or accelerated local economic development schemes during the year and related them to defense priorities. In September, for example, it hired South African contractors to begin work on a $160,000,000, three-thousand-mile road complex in southern Angola that was closely tied in with "military strategy." [39] Lisbon also accelerated its assimilation or de-Africanization program. It encouraged the return of European families who had fled during the first frightening months of the uprising and promoted settlement by Portuguese soldiers, to whom it offered land and financial inducements to stay in Angola after their period of military service expired—with easily procured African wives if they wished. As part of this same effort, four hundred families from the Cape Verde Islands arrived at Luanda in late summer en route to new settlements in the north.[40]

Lisbon even considered the idea of recruiting Chinese settlers. A Portuguese official, the director of Information and Tourism in Angola, visited Taipeh, Formosa, in June 1962 on what he described as "a mission to invite Chinese immigrants, to solicit Chinese investment, and to seek Chinese technical cooperation." He sought an initial contingent of at least five hundred families for Angola, who he said would be free to set up Chinese schools and live together in Chinese communities. The Chinese Nationalist radio quoted him as saying that, if the Chinese government would provide transportation, the Angolan (Portuguese) government would assist with resettlement costs. He even proposed to accept Chinese refugees from Hong Kong provided the Nationalist Chinese would first investigate and screen them.[41] Though these settlers might not make

[38] See Robert Davezies, *Les angolais* (Paris: Les Éditions de Minuit, 1965), p. 243.

[39] *The Star* (Johannesburg), Sept. 29, 1962. South African forces patrolling the nine-hundred-mile South West African border with Angola prevented SWAPO organizers from infiltrating into the Ambo regions of southern Angola.

[40] *Hispanic American Report,* Vol. XV, No. 10 (Oct. 1962), p. 882.

[41] Chinese Central News broadcast to the United States, June 23, 1962, as quoted in David Nelson Rowe, *Free Afro-Asia, Cooperation between the Republic of China and African Countries* (New York: American Afro-Asian Educational Exchange, Feb. 1, 1963), p. 7.

Angola more Portuguese, they would, presumably, make it less African. The scheme was not implemented, however.

The colonial administration intensified its drive to get African refugees to return from the Congo and from their forest hideouts within Angola to specially constructed resettlement centers. To put more steam behind this effort, it released the venerable religious prophet Simão Toco. After a long rustication that had effectively isolated him from the developing forces of contemporary African nationalism, Toco was now prepared to tour northern Angola and areas along the Congo frontier in a campaign to encourage his remaining followers to return to the Portuguese fold.[42] The PDA angrily charged the Portuguese embassy in Léopoldville with "actively corrupting" Angolans and expressed its concern over the fate of Simão Toco, whom it said the Portuguese were using as a "tool."[43]

Though their situation had improved, the Portuguese were nonetheless not out of trouble. In late November a correspondent of the London *Times* estimated that between three and eight thousand armed rebels were still "subverting" an area of approximately 35,000 square miles which hung "like a sack from the northern frontier to within thirty miles of the Luanda-Malange railway, about one-twentieth of the whole of Angola." Their losses of two hundred and fifty to four hundred men per month could be made up by reinforcements from the training base at Kinkuzu, he concluded, and the guerrillas appeared capable of fighting on "indefinitely."[44]

Taking a page from the French counterinsurgency campaign in Algeria, the Portuguese army launched a psychosocial campaign designed to win over the population. Accordingly the army itself became a source of teachers and social workers—nation builders, though, of course, still Portuguese nation builders. Yet Portugal's much-publicized colonial reforms, of which this campaign was a part, offered little immediate hope for a peaceful solution. The reforms gained neither African nationalist nor international acceptance as a substitute for self-determination. In his July interview with *U.S. News and World Report,* Salazar solemnly restated the legal fiction that "Angola is already an independent territory

[42] *Courrier d'Afrique,* July 13, 1962.
[43] *Ibid.,* July 27, 1962.
[44] *The Times* (London), Nov. 26, 1962.

within the Portuguese nation." [45] Yet both the MPLA and GRAE reacted to "the hypocrisy of Portuguese colonial reformism" by repeating demands for the right to self-determination.[46] It was precisely this refusal to recognize "the legitimate aspirations of the indigenous population," including the right to separate independence, that the United Nations Special Committee on Portuguese Territories found to have been the principal cause of the revolt of 1961 and to be the major obstacle to peace in 1962.[47]

A few members of Angola's Portuguese community agreed with the United Nations assessment. Some were organized within a separatist movement centered in the central Lobito-Nova Lisboa area that surfaced in mid-1962. Speaking out from the safety of exile in France, leaders of a *Frente de Unidade Angolana* (FUA) revealed that their independence movement had been founded at Benguela in January 1961 and that it had subsequently gained support among European Angolans living in Luanda, Léopoldville, and Lisbon, especially among students and "progressives." [48] FUA's membership, they said, included some who had earlier collaborated with Viriato da Cruz's *Mensagem* (1950) and its successor publication *Cultura* (1957). FUA's political antecedents, they said, could be traced back to 1940, when a group of young whites and mulattoes in Nova Lisboa had attempted to form an opposition movement and had organized protests against the dispatch of forced laborers to São Tomé—an initiative that had led to numerous arrests, including that of a noted poet, Alexandre Dáskalos.[49] The organization founded at Benguela in 1961 was said to comprise "elements linked to the 1940 movement," members of "secret organizations" that had been making some progress toward unity before they were suddenly "wiped out" by PIDE in March 1959, and "some members of the Portuguese democratic opposition in Angola." All of these groups "succeeded in settling their differences and decided to unite within

[45] July 9, 1962, p. 79.

[46] Quote from MPLA, Comitê Director, "Communicado" (Léopoldville, Nov. 3, 1962). See also GRAE, Ministère de l'Information, "Memorandum du FNLA aux Membres du sous-comité chargé d'examiner la situation en Angola" (Léopoldville, Aug. 19, 1962).

[47] United Nations, General Assembly, *Report of the Special Committee on the Situation in Angola,* Document A/5160 (Aug. 15, 1962), p. 142.

[48] *Le Monde,* May 16, 1962.

[49] Marie-Thérèse Maugis, "Entretien avec des 'pieds noirs' angolais," *Partisans* (Paris), No. 7 (Nov.-Dec. 1962), p. 96.

a single political movement"—the Angolan United Front (FUA).[50]

In May 1961 PIDE cracked down on liberal whites suspected of nationalist-separatist sentiments. Many of FUA's leaders in Angola, including a well-known Lobito engineer named Fernando Falçao, were then arrested and deported to Portugal.[51] Some subsequently escaped to France where in September 1962 they founded a committee of exiled FUA leaders. Headed by one of FUA's original founders, Sócrates Mendonça de Oliveira Dáskalos (president), this new Paris committee declared itself committed to the principles of multiracialism and economic justice and unreservedly in favor of Angolan independence.[52] It thus moved beyond the position reportedly held by the party while functioning within Angola, where FUA had called for political and social reforms but had argued that Angola was not yet prepared for "immediate independence."[53] FUA's Parisian exiles sent a petition to the United Nations Sub-Committee on the Situation in Angola in which they denounced Portuguese colonialism.[54] At the same time they undertook to establish contacts and to cooperate with both exiled Portuguese democrats and exiled African nationalists, in particular, with the MPLA.[55] They sent circulars to both the MPLA and the UPA, as well as to other movements, proposing a meeting "with the least possible

50 "Facts about the Angolan United Front," *Présence Africaine* (English ed.), Vol. 17, No. 45 (1963), p. 169.

51 Prominent FUA deportees to Portugal included Socrates Dáskalos, Carlos Morais, Alberto Morais, Luis Porto Carrero, João Mendes, and Anibal Vasconcelos. *Ibid.*, p. 97.

52 Other members of the Paris executive committee included Adolfo Rodrigues Maria, secretary-general, Carlos Morais, João Mendes, and Ernesto Larafilho, a former Luanda correspondent for the Spanish journal *ABC*, who assumed responsibility for what were ambitiously termed FUA's "press relations." *Le Monde*, Sept. 14, 1962. Also see "Angola: la troisième force," *Jeune Afrique*, No. 107 (Nov. 5–11, 1962), p. 20.

53 As reported by Elizabeth White of *The Scotsman*. See *Hispanic American Report*, Vol. XV, No. 3 (Mar. 1962), p. 203.

54 Frente de Unidade Angolana, O'Comitê Director, "Ao Chairman da Sub-Commissão para a Situação de Angola da Organização das Nações Unidas" (Paris, Sept. 4, 1962, mimeo.).

55 See *France Observateur*, March 9, 1961. Prior to this time, the MPLA's insistence on immediate independence had formed an obstacle to cooperation between the two movements. *Hispanic American Report*, ftn. 53. The UPA publicly dismissed FUA as inimical to African interests and desirous only of gradualist moves toward Angolan autonomy. UPA, "Atenção Angolanos" (Léopoldville [1962], mimeo.). The PDA wrote off FUA as an impotent group of Paris exiles (Kunzika interview).

delay" of all Angolan political and trade union organizations to prepare for the creation of an all-party National Liberation Front.[56]

Moving toward Revolution in Guinea and Mozambique

The example and lessons of the Angolan revolution strongly influenced the policies of the nationalist movements of Guinea-Bissau and Mozambique as these movements expanded their activities during 1962. Nationalist leaders of Guinea and Mozambique generally concluded from Portugal's response to the Angolan uprising that they could expect no concessions to demands for self-determination but on the contrary should expect vigorous police and military repression of any nationalist protest action, be it violent or nonviolent. The nationalist strategy of using limited violence to produce diplomatic and political gains that had often worked earlier against France and Britain had proved ineffective with Portugal. Portuguese preparedness to bomb, burn, and machine gun any communities suspected of being linked to rebellion or subversion had been devastatingly demonstrated, and the lesson was clear. Only a carefully organized insurgency might crack Portuguese resolve and keep African losses within acceptable bounds during the ensuing struggle.

In Guinea the PAIGC intensified its program of *sub rosa* political education and organization within the peasant population. Concurrently PIDE strove to break up all organized opposition. On March 13, 1962, the police arrested Raphael Barboza (or Zian Lopes), president of the PAIGC's Central Committee.[57] Though Portuguese troops were increased to 6000, the PAIGC launched and gradually stepped up a systematic program of sabotage of roads and farms. By the turn of the year 1962–63, its North African and Eastern-trained military commanders were leading guerrilla forces that set about, with increasing effectiveness, to ambush, raid, mine, and otherwise harass Portuguese forces.[58]

If the Angolan rebellion had revealed the need for careful planning and organization prior to the launching of military action, it was also widely viewed as having shown the need for at least a

[56] "Facts about the Angolan United Front," p. 172.

[57] See William Zartman, "Africa's Quiet War," *Africa Report,* Vol. 9, No. 2 (Feb. 1964), pp. 8–12.

[58] For an admiring presentation of the PAIGC approach to revolution, see Gérard Chaliand, *Lutte armée en Afrique* (Paris: François Maspero, 1967).

minimal unity among nationalist forces. During 1962 the PAIGC emerged as so much more effective than its rivals, who fell to quarreling among themselves along ethnic lines, that it managed to attract and unite most serious Portuguese Guinean nationalists. On the other hand, as of mid-1962 disunity was still a major affliction handicapping the nationalists of Mozambique.

The consultative council of the CONCP, meeting in Rabat from June 13 to 15, publicly "deplored the state of weakness of the liberation struggle in [Mozambique] and noted the difficulties [that] the two principal organizations, MANU and UDENAMO, [had] in leading the liberatory struggle." After studying the situation and pointing out that the CONCP's permanent secretariat had "received no news whatever on the struggle in Mozambique from the leadership of UDENAMO," the CONCP council cited criticism of UDENAMO president Adelino Gwambe, paved the way for MANU's admission to the CONCP, and appealed to the two organizations "to come together." [59] In late May the two movements had already indicated their intention to create a united front, though the issue of leadership remained a contentious obstacle.[60] Some progress was subsequently made during unity discussions held under the guidance and pressure of President Kwame Nkrumah at the Conference of Freedom Fighters at Winneba, Ghana, in mid-June 1962.[61]

A decisive confrontation finally took place later that month in Dar es Salaam, where Adelino Gwambe (UDENAMO), Matthew Mmole (MANU), and José Chagong'a (UNAMI) were joined by Dr. Eduardo Mondlane, who had flown out to East Africa for the avowed purpose of helping to mold together a united nationalist movement.[62] Discussions got under way on June 20 under the aegis of the local governing party, the Tanganyika Africa National Union

[59] CONCP, *Information Bulletin* (Rabat), No. 4 (Sept. 5, 1962, mimeo.), pp. 5–7, 27.

[60] New China News Agency (NCNA, Peking), May 28, 1962.

[61] According to Adelino Gwambe, the UDENAMO and MANU delegations while in Ghana "met and gave the name of the proposed common front as FRENTE LIBERTADORA MOÇAMBICANA (FRELIMO) or MOZAMBIQUE LIBERATORY FRONT and the agreement was reached that [as] soon [as] we got back to Dar es Salaam the two unions were going to work in the same office and prepare a conference jointly for both memberships to approve the formation of the front and the constitution and programme." Hlumulu Jani Chitofu Gwambi [*sic*], "My Concise Autobiography" (Lusaka, June 1966, unpublished typescript).

[62] Eduardo Mondlane, "The Struggle for Independence in Mozambique," *Présence Africaine* (English ed.), Vol. 20, No. 48 (1963), pp. 41–42.

(TANU). They ended successfully five days later with the creation of a single *Frente de Libertação de Moçambique* (FRELIMO), which elected Dr. Mondlane as its first president.[63]

FRELIMO was given a proper launching by an inaugural national conference, September 23–28, at Dar es Salaam. The new movement declared its determination to promote "unity among Mozambicans," to develop literacy, women's education, and cadre training programs, and to seek broad international support for the forthcoming struggle to liberate Mozambique.[64] In anticipation of that struggle, FRELIMO was soon sending young volunteers to newly independent Algeria for military training. Months later Mondlane was still quoted as saying that FRELIMO sought its goals through political-diplomatic pressure and would turn to "direct action" only if it should become "desperately necessary." [65] Yet as 1962 drew to a close there were no signs that the Portuguese government would respond to anything short of force.

At the same time Portuguese authorities were determined not to be caught off guard again as they had been in Angola. Within a year of the uprising in northern Angola, an American correspondent reported that Lisbon had "vastly increased its military forces" in Mozambique from 3000 to 13,000 men and had organized a special civil voluntary force, new riot police units, and an improved intelligence network.[66] By late September the Johannesburg *Star* estimated Portuguese troops in Mozambique at between 30,000 and 50,000, some of whom were patrolling the Tanganyika and Nyasaland borders reconnoitering for nationalists moving in and out of the country.[67] Both sides were preparing for a protracted struggle with a full awareness of their adversary's intentions. Nationalist strategy in Mozambique, as well as in Guinea-Bissau, promised to develop more openly than it had in Angola. It promised just as certainly to add to Portugal's burdens.

[63] Announced by a press relase entitled "Mozambique Political Parties Fuse" (Dar es Salaam, June 26, 1962, mimeo.). Other officers elected include Uria T. Simango, vice-president, and David M. Mabunda, secretary-general.

[64] Resolutions and reports of the conference published in FRELIMO organ *Patriota* (Cairo), Vol. 1, No. 1, 1962.

[65] *Christian Science Monitor,* Mar. 1, 1963.

[66] Joseph L. Sterne in Baltimore *Sun,* Apr. 27, 1962.

[67] Johannesburg *Star* (weekly edition), Sept. 29, 1962. Pieter Lessing, writing in the *Christian Science Monitor* (Mar. 19, 1963), put the figure at just 20,000.

CHAPTER TEN

THE POLITICS OF REVOLUTION: SETTLING IN FOR A LONG STRUGGLE

By late 1962 Angolan nationalist politics had become thoroughly complex and violent. Bakongo and Cabindan movements, encouraged by local Congolese forces and Portuguese initiative, were proliferating within the émigré-refugee community in the Congo. The Government in Exile (GRAE) was being strengthened by an infusion of new ethnic leadership from non-Bakongo areas—Mbundu, Ovimbundu, Chokwe—and thus beginning to transcend its Bakongo origins, though the Bakongo-Bazombo community remained its basis of popular support. And the MPLA was continuing to push for a common-action front, while also reorganizing itself and competing with the GRAE-FNLA for revolutionary leadership. Both the MPLA and the GRAE were convinced that Portugal was not going to make any concessions on the real issue—the right to self-determination—and so both set about creating the structure and strategy with which to wage a long and costly struggle for independence.

The Bakongo Moderates

During 1962 the Bakongo community continued to produce and sustain by far the most disparate assortment of political movements. In varying degrees some of these competing groups managed to collaborate among themselves as well as with the Portuguese. Without making the slightest concession concerning the substance of its colonial policy, Lisbon combined short-term bribes and vague promises of long-term political rewards to mold several of them into instruments of its own policy. Thus, whether naive, cynical, weak, or unwitting, Bakongo moderates undertook to spy upon, infiltrate, subvert, or publicly discredit Angolan revolutionary movements. It would seem that their main effectiveness consisted in their ability to confuse and mislead themselves, the Portuguese, other Angolans, and outside observers into overestimating their actual or potential political strength. In this regard the role of the MDIA was illustrative and central.

The MDIA's close cooperation with the Portuguese government bore open dividends for its leaders, a number of whom began the year with a three-week guided tour of such centers as Maquela, Quibocolo, Damba, and São Salvador in northern Angola.[1] In May, Jean Pierre M'Bala, the MDIA's secretary-general, further confirmed the extent of MDIA collaboration with Portugal by announcing at the round table of Angolan parties, assembled in Léopoldville by the Congolese minister of interior Cléophas Kamitatu, that in a few days he would lead an MDIA delegation to Lisbon. Implying that the mission would entail personal risk rather than reward, he rather dramatically asserted that he and his colleagues in the MDIA's two-hundred-man executive committee preferred "to sacrifice" themselves "rather than five million Angolans." At the same time he defended the MDIA policy of "extending a hand to Portugal" and claimed that people suffering inside Angola were now pleading: "Forget about independence if it means leading us to annihilation by the Portuguese." [2] When he returned from Lisbon in June, M'Bala gave a glowing public account of his talks with Portuguese officials, though he produced no tangible evidence of concessions concerning the central issue of self-determination.[3] Then in August MDIA representatives told the United Nations Sub-Committee on the Situation in Angola, then visiting Léopoldville, that they "would shortly leave for Luanda in order to study conditions in Angola and to arrange for the transfer of the headquarters of their organization from Léopoldville to Luanda." They added in all seriousness that they "looked forward to action by the General Assembly and the Security Council that

[1] The tour lasted from December 26, 1961, to January 16, 1962. See MDIA, "Le problème angolais: Textes et documents vus par le Comité Directeur du Mouvement de Défense des Intérêts de l'Angola" (Léopoldville, July 29, 1962, mimeo.).

[2] "Réunion du 10 mai 1962 avec le ministre Kamitatu" (Léopoldville, 1962, mimeo.). Nonviolence and collaboration with Portugal were also defended at this meeting by MDIA spokesmen Augustin Kaziluki, Simon Diallo Mingiedi, and Sumbu Martin.

[3] *L'Homme nouveau,* No. 126, June 10, 1962.

would induce Portugal to transfer political power in a peaceful and orderly manner." [4]

The MDIA undertook to collaborate with other similarly disposed Bakongo moderates. At the end of April it joined Ngwizako in denouncing the recently created Angolan Government in Exile (GRAE) and announced its alliance with the Bakongo royalists in a new two-party "cartel." Then a month later the MDIA's Jean M'Bala sent a petition to the United Nations in which he stated that his party was working hand in hand with MLEC and Nto-Bako, as well as Ngwizako, in the search for a nonviolent solution to the Angolan problem.[5]

One indication that the MDIA did some independent if fanciful thinking came in November 1962 in the form of a proposal submitted to the Fourth Committee of the General Assembly by Augustin Kaziluki (vice-president) and Jean M'Bala. For international consideration they offered an elaborate constitutional reform which, in the spirit of their party's ethnic particularism, called for transforming Angola into a loose federation of six states.[6]

During the year the MDIA's cartel partner Ngwizako was rent by the sort of internal dissensions commonly associated with failure.[7] Far from successful at São Salvador in pushing his candidacy for the vacant Kongo throne, party president José Kasakanga finally provoked irritated Portuguese authorities into restricting his agitating to the confines of a Luanda prison. Under the circumstances, one group under the leadership of Emmanuel Loureiro and Antoine Menga in Léopoldville preferred to limit itself to exile opera-

[4] United Nations, General Assembly, *Report of the Sub-Committee on the Situation in Angola,* Document A/5286 (Nov. 14, 1962), p. 23 (hereafter cited as *Report of U.N. Sub-Committee*).

[5] The MDIA-Ngwizako cartel was announced on April 30, 1962; M'Bala's four-page petition to the United Nations Sub-Committee on the Situation in Angola was dated May 28, 1962. See MDIA, "Le problème angolais." In mid-April the MDIA's political director, Simon Diallo Mingiedi, issued a call for round-table discussions with the Portuguese and said that his proposal had the support of both the MLEC and Ngwizako. *L'Homme nouveau,* No. 118, Apr. 15, 1962. On May 10, 1962, the MDIA, Ngwizako, MLEC, and a new group, the *Frente Nacional Angolana* (later MNA—see below), submitted a joint proposal for an Angolan front to Congolese minister of interior Cléophas Kamitatu. See "Réunion du 10 mai."

[6] As proposed, the six units with their capitals were Cabinda (Cabinda), Kongo (Carmona), Malange (Malange), Benguela (Benguela), Bié (Silva Porto), and Huila (Sá da Bandeira). From an eight-page petition (Léopoldville, Nov. 28, 1962, mimeo.).

[7] *Report of U.N. Sub-Committee.*

tions until conditions in Angola became more hospitable. Another faction of Ngwizako, known as the *Wene wa Kongo* (Authority of the Kongo) and led by Manuel Ndimba, who had been with Eduardo Pinock in the king palaver of 1955, and by José Milton Putuilu, favored maintaining an Ngwizako presence within Angola. In June five advocates of close, on-the-spot cooperation with the Portuguese picked up Portuguese passports in Brazzaville and flew to Luanda to put the kingship issue before the governor-general. There they were allowed to visit Kasakanga and were given some good meals and a tour of the capital, but little more. Reportedly even their request for a typewriter with which to prepare their case was put off with the response that "they could borrow one when they got to São Salvador." [8]

Unable to persuade the administration to release Kasakanga from prison, let alone to accept him as king, the Ngwizako delegation finally hit upon a formula that the Portuguese were prepared to accept. The royalists proposed naming a weak figurehead as king, who, they reasoned, could be made into their own spokesman. Thus they put forth and the administration accepted the name of Pedro Mansala, an octogenarian from Zamba on the São Salvador-Cuimba road, who could not read, write, or speak Portuguese. On September 9, 1962, Mansala was crowned as Dom Pedro VIII in ceremonies at the Catholic Church of São Salvador, following which the assemblage moved outside to the church steps to pay the customary homage and make speeches. When it was time for the king to reply to the ritual praise, however, a local Portuguese merchant named Bastos stepped forward and made the king's statement for him.

This usurpation of the role that Ngwizako had wanted for itself was too much for one of its representatives, Kiangala Monteiro, who himself had apparently expected to translate the king's speech into Portuguese. Reportedly Kiangala, who had been one of those imprisoned in 1956 as a result of the king palaver, interrupted Bastos to say that only Ngwizako could speak for the king. The Portuguese military commander told him to be quiet. He refused. The commander then "hit him hard on the head and dragged him away," leaving the ceremonies to conclude as planned. The unhappy Ngwizako delegation next asked for permission to go to Luanda to complain to the governor-general. Instead the government flew

[8] Grenfell, *Notes* (Kibentele), No. 46, Oct. 19, 1962.

them to Santo António do Zaire, put them on a river boat to Noqui, and then transported them across the Congo frontier to Matadi. The whole misadventure ended in an anticlimax a few weeks later in late October, when Dom Pedro VIII died and left the hapless Kongo royalists once again with only Queen Regent Isabel and the bitter aftertaste of a round with the colonial administration.[9]

In a memorandum addressed to the president of the United Nations General Assembly in November 1962, Ngwizako nonetheless took credit for having "been able to elect and enthrone H. M. Pedro VIII . . . with the full agreement and cooperation of the Portuguese government." It went on to warn the General Assembly, however, that there was no political solution "other than the transfer to Him [the king] of the full powers which the first European citizens found in our Kongolese homeland at the time of its discovery in 1482." The memorandum then proceeded to charge that during the past eighteen months Portuguese authorities had employed "fraudulent manoeuvres" and "continuous sabotage" so as to prevent Ngwizako from assuming "Executive Power" in the Kongo kingdom.[10]

Nto-Bako, the third of the triumvirate of seasoned Bakongo moderates (the PDA was of course now solidly in the revolutionary column), had a similarly frustrating year in spite of flamboyant leadership. Angelino Alberto, who ranked among the most unabashedly pro-Portuguese of the Bakongo collaborators, proposed to Ngwizako that it join forces with Nto-Bako in campaigning for an "independent" government to consist of eight Portuguese and eight Africans, four each from Nto-Bako and Ngwizako. Ngwizako refused.[11] In solo performances in 1962 that suggested that he had no need for allies, Alberto boasted to the United Nations Sub-Committee on Angola that his organization enjoyed the confidence of Portuguese authorities[12] and told the Fourth Committee of the General Assembly in New York that Nto-Bako had attained a

[9] *Ibid.* For a Portuguese account of these events, see Artur Maciel, *Angola Heróica* (Lisbon: Livraria Bertrand, 1963), pp. 61–62.

[10] Dated Nov. 27, 1962, the memorandum was signed by Edouard Kanga, general secretary, Victor Grevy Lusawovana, political secretary and chairman of Standing Committee, and José Milton Putuilo, second vice-president. United Nations, Special Committee on the Situation with Regard to the Implementation of the Declaration on the Granting of Independence to Colonial Countries and Peoples, A/AC. 109/Pet. 58, Mar. 8, 1963 (hereafter cited as Special Committee on Independence).

[11] Grenfell, *Notes.*

[12] *Report of U.N. Sub-Committee.*

membership of 900,000—quite an achievement since the prerebellion population of the Bakongo region, from which his movement drew all the support it had, was probably not much over 500,000.[13] Under sharp and hostile questioning from members of the Fourth Committee, however, Alberto was forced to admit that his movement, like Ngwizako, had fallen prey to internal quarreling. In brief, as general chairman of Nto-Bako Alberto stated that he had expelled two of the party's founding members, Messrs. Lozinga Lukoki and François Lele, "for failing to obey his instructions." These two men, still identifying themselves as Nto-Bako leaders—indeed as party "founder" and "general secretary," respectively—had themselves written to the secretary-general of the United Nations. They had asked the world body to "intervene with the Portuguese authorities with a view to the liberation of [Nto-Bako] party members [arrested] in Luanda," where some of them (including one Jacques Zimene, who Alberto maintained was living unharmed at the Hotel Paris in Luanda) had already been reported killed.[14] Responding to the picture that emerged from Angelino Alberto's revealing but clumsy performance before the Fourth Committee, Ambassador Achkar Marof of Guinea said that he "pitied the petitioner, who had chosen a road full of pitfalls." [15] The Ministry of Information in Lisbon thought more highly of Alberto's presentation, however, and reproduced portions of it as an article entitled "I Was Taken in by Anti-Portuguese Propagandists." [16]

Multiplying Moderates

During 1962 three parties and two labor unions were added to the list of Angolan exile and émigré groups based in Léopoldville. With the backing of President Youlou of Congo-Brazzaville, a Bazombo youth movement, the *Front Commun de la Jeunesse Nationaliste de l'Angola,* allowed its ambitions to surpass the scope of youth activities and converted itself into a purportedly more mature and overtly political *Alliance des Jeunes Angolais pour la Liberté,*

[13] Alberto also claimed that, as Portuguese troops restored order and conditions returned to normal in Angola, some 200,000 Africans went back to their villages and that "some 80,000 who had fled to the Congo had returned" to the country. United Nations, General Assembly, Fourth Committee, 1408 meeting, Dec. 4, 1962.

[14] Those reported killed included a Sr. da Cruz, François Mbaninu, and André Mazoa. *Ibid.*

[15] *Ibid.*

[16] In *Portugal: An Informative Review,* Vol. 6, No. 1 (Mar. 1963), p. 27.

or Ajeunal.[17] Taking themselves and their bid for political power with the utmost seriousness, Ajeunal's young politicos, following in the footsteps of Kassanga, Kassinda, and others, set out on a wide-ranging tour of Africa in search of support to compensate for what they could not muster locally. Thus Ajeunal's president Alphonse Matondo and secretary-general Edouard Makumbi traveled about West Africa during the summer of 1962, taking the Angolan cause as far afield as Ouagadougou and Abidjan. Claiming to speak for a major nationalist movement, they were received by responsible officials in several UAM states where they were accorded interviews by the local press.[18]

In November the UPA's youth organization JUPA published a critique of Ajeunal's tactics. According to JUPA, its rivals had recently sent a letter to the GRAE requesting admission to that organization and suggesting a list of Ajeunal candidates for ministerial posts. Soon afterward Ajeunal leaders had held a press conference and argued for the idea of a common front. Reflecting the attitude of its parent organization, JUPA rather contemptuously suggested that Ajeunal members ought to join the ranks of regular party youth groups (JUPA, JPDA, JMPLA) so as not to confuse the Angolan political scene further. Ajeunal, said the JUPA's bulletin, was nothing but an overly ambitious "executive committee" with no following.[19] Nonetheless, relishing their new-found executive status, Ajeunal's young leaders continued for some years to present themselves as representative spokesmen of Angolan nationalism.

Another entry into the 1962 muster of northern Angolan parties was an ethnic group known first as the *Frente Nacional Angolana* (FNA) and then as the *Movimento Nacional Angolano* (MNA). It was formed by exiles and émigrés coming from the region along Angola's northern coast extending from Santo António do Zaire at the mouth of the Congo river down to Ambriz, a coffee port a hundred miles to the south. This area formed what had constituted the Sonyo province of the old Kongo kingdom. Lacking a king or a prophet around whom to rally, the Bakongo people inhabiting the area, some 35,000 Sorongo (or Solongo), had not earlier been an important separate force within northern Angolan nationalism. On the contrary, some had helped to found the UPNA and to organize

[17] *Courrier d'Afrique*, Feb. 12, 1962.
[18] For example, *Abidjan Matin*, Aug. 25, 1962.
[19] JUPA, *Juventude revolucionária* (Léopoldville), No. 7 (Nov. 15, 1962), p. 21.

the UPA. One of the most prominent was Luis Inglês, a former tailor from Santo António do Zaire (born circa 1927), who served successively as a UPA party organizer as far south as Luanda, as a guerrilla leader in the Zaire area (1961), and as head of the UPA's strategic branch office at Matadi.[20]

The Sorongo had, however, formed a mutual-aid society as early as 1942. With headquarters at Boma across the Congo River from Angolan territory, the *Associação dos Mussorongos* had begun to assume a political character only after Congolese independence in 1960. The earliest date given for the creation of the Sorongo's full-fledged political movement—the MNA—is also 1960.[21] The movement had a slow beginning, however, and failed to develop a very significant following among Sorongo refugees arriving in the Congo. Some local African observers speculated that this failure was due in part to the inadequate credentials of the MNA's leaders, i.e., as president, António Monteiro who was a mulatto, and as vice-president and principal organizer, José Tito who was born and raised in the Congo. In May 1962 the MNA joined with fellow Bakongo moderates of the MDIA, Ngwizako, and MLEC in calling for a new Angolan front.[22] Then in August it revealed a deep traditionalist bias when, in its debut before the United Nations Subcommittee on Angola then visiting Léopoldville, it "advocated a meeting of all regional and other [Angolan] chiefs with a view to setting up a liberation front, with the cooperation of political

[20] See Richard Mathews, "A Visit to the Rebels of Angola," *The Reporter*, Sept. 28, 1961, p. 42.

[21] See Maciel, *Angola Heróica*, pp. 121 and 128. According to the "Report of the WAY Mission on Angola," Document No. 1984 (Brussels, June 1962, mimeo.), "The FNA (MNA) was established as recently as early May [1962], and it was the opinion of all observers in the Congo, that the organization, to this point, has little or no popular support, either among the refugee population or among peoples still in Angola" (p. 27). The founding date of 1960 is given in Special Committee on Independence, A/AC. 109/Pet. 149, Aug. 8, 1963.

According to Marcos Kassanga (interview with author, Sept. 3, 1968), Tomas Ferreira, who was living at the Léopoldville home of the MNA's president António Monteiro in early 1961, led a group of seven MNA rebels in organizing a short-lived military campaign inside Angola near the Sorongo town of Tombôco in April of that year. Then upon his return to the Congo, again according to Kassanga, Ferreira persuaded Monteiro to merge the MNA with the MPLA—a union that lasted for some months only—and prepared to lead his own ill-fated October 1961 mission to Nambuangongo. See pp. 213–214.

[22] A proposal submitted to Congolese minister of interior Cléophas Kamitatu. See "Réunion du 10 mai."

parties, or without them, if the latter did not wish to promote political unity." [23]

Presumably the MNA had in mind working with another small Bakongo separatist group known as the *Rassemblement des Chefs Coutumiers du Kongo Portugais* (RCCKP). Though this Rally of Customary Chiefs was a rather obscure organization of exiled, predominantly Catholic, Bakongo chiefs centered in Léopoldville, it seemed to retain some contact with chiefly counterparts still inside Angola. In May 1962 the RCCKP joined with Antoine Menga of Ngwizako at Kamitatu's round-table discussions in stressing and defending the distinction between Angola and the Portuguese Kongo, which, it said, "has its own institutions different from those of Angola." The RCCKP's representative, Antoine Lino, told the gathering that though his movement was "apolitical" it was nonetheless working for the independence of the Kongo and then revealed that in the pursuit of this goal he, like others, had "had occasion to go to Luanda" since the outbreak of the war.[24]

On August 18, 1962, a new, predominantly Bakongo-Bazombo Angolan labor union, the *Confédération Générale des Travailleurs de l'Angola* (CGTA), announced its entry on the scene in a petition submitted to the United Nations Sub-Committee on Angola.[25] Enjoying the support of the Congo's well-organized Catholic *Union des Travailleurs Congolais* (UTC), the CGTA presented itself as a politically unaffiliated trade union guided by the principles of "Christian social doctrine." [26] Led initially by Antoine Luzemo, president, and Pedro Makumbi-Marques, secretary-general, the new labor organization gained admittance to the African regional division of the international Christian labor movement, the *Union Panafricaine et Malgache des Travailleurs Croyants* (UPMTC), whose secretary-general was the Congo's (UTC) leading union personality, André Boboliko. The CGTA set out to organize and educate Angolans working in the Congo in the expressed hope that they would in turn introduce Christian trade unionism into Angola after independence. It was soon competing, principally with the LGTA, for adherents among émigrés and refugees, to

[23] *Report of U.N. Sub-Committee.*

[24] "Réunion du 10 mai."

[25] *Report of U.N. Sub-Committee*, p. 6.

[26] CGTA, "Statuts" (Léopoldville, Mar. 19, 1966, mimeo.), Arts. 4 and 5. For a discussion of the UTC-CGTA relationship, see the CGTA organ *A Esperança* (Léopoldville), No. 2 (Mar.-May 1965), p. 2.

whom it offered the alternative of a politically and militarily disengaged organization, as against the LGTA and UNTA, which were committed to revolution.

Establishing new "nationalist" movements had by now become a prestige-building pastime for ambitious young Angolans living in Léopoldville. Since two of the Congo's three major labor organizations—the FGTK and UTC—were now patronizing Angolan affiliates, the LGTA and CGTA, respectively, it was only logical that the third do likewise. In a move that skeptics refused to take very seriously, the *Confédération des Syndicats Libres du Congo* (CSLC) sponsored the creation of Angola's fifth labor movement in exile to compete with the UNTA (pro-MPLA), LGTA (UPA), UGTA (Kassinda), and CGTA (Catholic). Founded on September 1, 1962, the *Confédération des Syndicats Libres Angolais* (CSLA) received some financial aid and technical help from its Congolese backers.[27] Led by Gracia Kiala, president, and André Kiazindika, secretary-general, the CSLA declared itself in favor of (1) building an Angolan "economic democracy" that would assure everyone a share of the national wealth in proportion to his work and needs and (2) pursuing "nonpolitical" trade unionism in conformity with the principles of the ICFTU, in which it sought membership. For the sake of effectiveness, however, the ICFTU adhered to a policy of concentrating its support on only one Angolan labor movement, namely, the LGTA, which it had already admitted to membership the year previous.[28]

Labor unions had been permitted to organize in the Congo in advance of political parties and had therefore, prior to independence, developed broader national structures than had Congolese parties. As rather artificial projections of this Congolese experience, however, Angolan exile labor unions—in particular, those like the CGTA and CSLA that were not linked to political movements—constituted little more than large executive committees tolerated by the Congolese unions precisely because they did not represent serious competition. Their effective membership was limited to the small proportion of Angolan Bakongo émigrés and

[27] Article 15 of the CSLA Constitution (Sept. 1961) stated that the organization would enjoy the protection of the CSLC. Three CSLA members participated in a CSLC seminar on workers' education during November and December 1962.

[28] According to some generally well-informed observers in Léopoldville, A. Kithima, leader of the CSLC, first advised those who formed the CSLA to join the ranks of the LGTA which enjoyed ICFTU support. In view of LGTA ties with a CSLC rival, FGTK, however, this advice may have been *pro forma*.

refugees holding wage-earning jobs, though their educational function in spreading the concept of trade unionism and collective bargaining was potentially of broader and more lasting significance.

Micronationalism for Cabinda

The year 1962 also produced new political developments concerning the enclave of Cabinda. Earlier, in November 1961, the *Mouvement de Libération de l'Enclave de Cabinda* (MLEC) had fired one of its central committeemen, Nzita Henriques Tiago.[29] Tiago had then formed a rival *Comité d'Action d'Union Nationale des Cabindais* (CAUNC) and in its competition with the MLEC, which enjoyed the benevolent good will of the Brazzaville government, the CAUNC turned toward Léopoldville. In June with apparent openmindedness the CAUNC proposed a referendum to determine which of the Congos Cabinda should join.[30] In August its president Nzita Tiago described Cabinda—by virtue of its customs, culture, language, and history—as an integral part of the Congo-Léopoldville,[31] and by that autumn the CAUNC was arguing for Cabinda's entry into the Léopoldville republic.[32]

The MLEC, on the other hand, became the champion of Cabindan independence. In September 1962 at Libreville, Gabon, during a meeting of the French-speaking states of the *Union Africaine et Malgache* (UAM), MLEC president Louis Franque boasted that Cabinda was nearly three times the size of Luxembourg, and its population was nearly twice the official figure of 60,000 if one counted the thousands of Cabindans living in exile. Though Portugal had violated its obligations under the Treaty of Simulambuco (1885) by destroying rather than protecting Cabinda's traditional sociopolitical institutions, he said, the enclave remained a distinct unit that deserved its own independent destiny. In response to Lisbon's argument that Cabinda had been absorbed into the Portuguese nation, Franque asked: "Would Portugal accept that it be made an integral part of Cabinda?" [33]

Competition between the two Cabindan movements assumed the

[29] *L'Homme nouveau,* No. 100, Dec. 10, 1961.
[30] *Courrier d'Afrique,* June 24–25, 1962.
[31] *Ibid.,* Aug. 29, 1962.
[32] *Ibid.,* Oct. 22, 1962.
[33] *L'Homme nouveau,* No. 143, Oct. 7, 1962; see also *Courrier d'Afrique,* Nov. 1–2, 1962.

form of a press war. The CAUNC managed to get good newspaper coverage in Léopoldville, while the MLEC found space in Abbé Youlou's weekly party organ in Brazzaville. In December, for example, the MLEC used the pages of the Brazzaville paper for a long attack on the CAUNC and its plan to integrate Cabinda into the Congo-Léopoldville and argued that the only proper political course was for Portugal to grant self-determination to the region in consultation with Cabinda's local customary chiefs.[34]

Meanwhile, matters were made more complex during this period by the UPA which, aided by its supporters within the Mayumbe community of the Cabindan interior, continued to conduct military operations within the enclave. In June Mayumbe members of the UPA declared to the press that "Mayumbe-Angola" was "not an integral part of Cabinda, but rather a state apart." As a matter of administrative convenience for the Portuguese, they said, the area had been governed as part of Cabinda, but, they asserted, "The Mayumbe people remain and will always remain an integral part of Angola and absolutely refuse to be colonized again."[35] Dismaying as the proposition might seem to anyone concerned about the future consequences of the balkanization of Africa, the Mayumbe seemed to be arguing that their liberation from the domination of both other Cabindans and the Portuguese could be achieved only by a partition of the Cabinda enclave into a Mayumbe sector to be attached to noncontiguous Angola and a coastal area. That would leave coastal Cabinda to work out its own fate as an "integral part" of its tiny self or of some other country.

Merging Streams

The theatrics of the Bakongo moderates in Léopoldville (or Lisbon) and the miniature-scaled politics of Cabinda were less significant to the long-run development of Angolan politics than a less-noted sequence of Mbundu, Ovimbundu, and Chokwe affiliations or contacts with the UPA-GRAE that took place during 1962. Portuguese press and radio attacks and public demonstrations against the UPA had contributed to that process by making UPA a household word throughout Angola.

Into the JUPA apparatus in Léopoldville came a number of stu-

[34] *L'Homme nouveau,* No. 152, Dec. 9, 1962.

[35] The statement included a pledge "to collaborate in perpetuity" with the central committee of the UPA. *Courrier d'Afrique,* June 6, 1962.

dent refugees from Luanda, including young men such as Leopoldo Trovoada, formerly of the MLA,[36] and Pedro Vaal Hendrik Neto, a former FUJA militant. To New York to open a permanent GRAE office went another Mbundu, Carlos Gonçalves Kambandu, a *liceu* graduate born at Cakumbo near Luanda on November 7, 1926.[37] And to Léopoldville came a delegation of Mbundu chiefs from Kwango and Kasanje, who now in April 1962 sought arms from the UPA in order to pick up where Maria's War had left off and to resume action against the Portuguese. Already in December 1961 a party delegation headed by UPA representative Barros Nascimento had been sent to Kasongo-Lunda and other Kwango-Angolan border areas beyond in order to make contact with and organize among Mbundu refugees and émigrés from Kasanje.

The association of Ovimbundu with the UPA-GRAE also continued to develop during the year. The history of João Chisseva of the *Juventude Cristã de Angola* (JCA) is illustrative. In November 1961 the government education service in Luanda had transferred Chisseva to Cangumbe in the eastern district of Moxico. There he joined with two former members of the *Grupo Avante do Bié* to organize a new campaign to popularize African nationalism. The group soon expanded to some twenty-eight members, though it adopted no name because of an unresolved difference of opinion between some who wished to use the name *Avante* and others, such as Chisseva, who opted for new, more political nomenclature, i.e., the *União das Populações do Sul de Angola* (UPSA). The group managed to persuade one of the more influential *sobas* of the Boma region to permit them to mount a local nationalist campaign. Through him, in January 1962, they made contact with a local Lwena queen (or *nakatolo*) who promised them assistance. By March, however, PIDE had scented their trail. The three founders of the Moxico group fled to avoid arrest, two to Katanga and one to South West Africa. One of the two, Paulo de Cunha Kalei, was arrested in Mutshatsha by the Katangese police.

[36] According to Trovoada, the MLA had sent a roundabout appeal to Roberto following the uprising of March 1961, asking for arms—an appeal that went unfulfilled.

[37] Studying in Portugal at the time the Angolan uprising broke out, Kambandu made his way to England, where he issued a statement denouncing Portuguese policies. "Statement made by Kambandu, African inhabitant of Angola" (London, July 23, 1961, mimeo.), 7 pp.

"A victim of the Tshombe regime," he was returned to Teixeira de Sousa, Angola, on May 5, 1962. Chisseva went on to Léopoldville where he joined the UPA-GRAE.[38]

In Lobito the *Comitê Secreto Revolucionário do Sul de Angola,* which had been formed in May 1961, continued to function on a low key. It established branches or contacts in a number of other urban centers outside Lobito and raised some funds from its supporters which it used to pay sailors shipping in and out of Lobito to carry out letters describing living conditions under Portuguese rule. Such missives went to Ghana and Sierra Leone, and eventually, in October 1962, one got through to Holden Roberto in the Congo. Roberto replied through Luis Inglês at Matadi and via a sailor-courier on the S.S. "Elizabethville." At that time security measures in Lobito were not as stringent as those imposed in Luanda, and thus in late 1962 the Lobito *Comitê* was able to establish and develop a long-distance collaboration with the GRAE, a collaboration further linking Angola's northern Bakongo and central Ovimbundu streams of nationalism.[39] During this period the GRAE produced a number of tracts in Umbundu calling upon the Ovimbundu to take up arms and join the revolution.[40]

The *Ukwashi Wa Chokwe* of Northern Rhodesia also established contact with the GRAE in 1962. Smart Chata made a hazardous two-month long journey to Léopoldville via Tanganyika (avoiding Tshombe's southern Katanga). In the Congolese capital he had new and fruitless discussions with Ambroise Muhunga of ATCAR, whom he found still contemplating the impractical goal of a resurrected Chokwe empire. Then in June he sought out the offices of Léopoldville's Angolan nationalists and met first with Luis de Azevedo, Jr., of the MPLA and then with Holden Roberto. Impressed by Roberto's presentation of the UPA's nationalist doctrine, Chata suggested that Roberto authorize him to organize a UPA branch in Northern Rhodesia. Reflecting an optimism then current among Angolan nationalists, Roberto reportedly expressed the opinion that such an initiative would run too great a

[38] João Chisseva, "Ngau, Ngau, Ngau! O'Sino da Liberdade Tocou" (April 1966, unpublished typescript).

[39] Luciano Kassoma, "The Outbreak of the Angolan Revolution in the South" (Lincoln University, 1965, unpublished typescript).

[40] See, for example, GRAE, "Vangandiange va kua sulu yo Ngola" (Léopoldville, May 19, 1962, mimeo.), signed by J. Maglioni Luvinga, "a son of Southern Angola."

risk of suppression by the white supremacist authorities of the Central African Federation, whereas Angola would probably be free before Northern Rhodesia anyway.[41] Nevertheless, when Chata flew back home in July he introduced the UPA to his colleagues, an initial step toward the eventual creation of a UPA section in Northern Rhodesia. Already during Chata's absence, at a meeting chaired by the society's vice-president, Brown Chipango, the *Ukwashi Wa Chokwe* membership had been advised to join Kenneth Kaunda's United National Independence Party (UNIP). The object was to gain political experience in preparation for the time when one could work freely within an Angolan independence movement.

In the over-all picture, though, the bridge-building and merging that did much to strengthen the UPA-GRAE (the PDA was little affected) during 1962 did nothing to improve MPLA-GRAE relations. On the other hand, it may have contributed to a major review of policy and reorganization of party structure undertaken by the MPLA at the year's end.

The MPLA under New Management

Beginning with the power struggle which ended in the ousting of Viriato da Cruz as secretary-general in May, and continuing with the escape from Portugal and arrival of Dr. Agostinho Neto in Léopoldville to claim his "honorary presidency," the MPLA was kept in a state of organizational flux during much of 1962. The party continued to campaign for a common front, giving wide publicity to a September unity appeal signed by over one hundred Angolans at the MPLA refugee stronghold of Lukala in the Lower Congo.[42] Yet the MPLA was making no perceptible progress toward its common-front goal, a failure that added to intraparty tensions. Graça da Silva Tavares, one of the troika appointed to replace the post of secretary-general held by da Cruz, subsequently resigned from both the secretariat and the executive committee. In November he and da Cruz reportedly launched an appeal to MPLA militia and militants, calling upon them to disavow the party executive committee. In reply, the committee warned party mem-

[41] Interview with Smart Chata, Lusaka, May 12, 1967.

[42] MPLA, "Lettre ouverte adressée au Comité Directeur du MPLA" (Sept. 27, 1962), *Vitória ou Morte* (Léopoldville), No. 7, Oct. 6, 1962; also distributed separately as leaflet entitled "Le Peuple angolais exige l'unité."

bers against the divisive activities of those who had strayed from the party line.[43]

To restore order the MPLA held its First National Conference at Léopoldville during the first three days of December. Viriato da Cruz was named to the preparatory committee that organized the conference.[44] It was attended by seventy voting delegates, who by a vote of thirty-nine to thirty-one elected a new party executive of ten members: (1) Dr. Agostinho Neto, president, (2) Matias Miguéis, first vice-president, (3) Rev. Domingos da Silva, second vice-president, (4) Manuel Lima, war, (5) Mário de Andrade, external affairs, (6) Lucio Lara, organization and cadres,[45] (7) Anibal de Melo (ex-UPA), information,[46] (8) Déolinda Rodrigues de Almeida, social affairs, (9) Desidério da Graça (Dr. Neto's brother-in-law), finance and economy, (10) Henrique Carreira, security. Eight of the thirteen named to the executive the previous May failed to make the new committee of ten.[47]

Under a conference "presidium" representing various branches of the MPLA,[48] the gathering elected a new "honorary president," choosing this time the incarcerated Catholic priest Father Joaquim Pinto de Andrade. Born on July 22, 1926, at Golungo Alto, Father Andrade had attended the Luanda seminary from 1940 to 1948 and then Gregorian University in Rome from 1948 to 1953. He was the former chancellor of the Luanda Archdiocese, and since 1956 had been a member of the Executive Council of the African Society of Culture (SAC), which had its headquarters in Paris. Like the

[43] *Jeune Afrique,* No. 113 (Dec. 17–23, 1962), pp. 14, 19.

[44] MPLA, *First National Conference of the People's Movement for the Liberation of Angola* (pamphlet, December 1962). (Hereafter cited as *First National Conference.*) Members of the preparations committee included Agostinho Neto, Mário de Andrade, Lucio Lara, Eduardo dos Santos, Matias Miguéis, Viriato da Cruz, Gentil Viana, Desidério da Graça, Manuel Videira, Manuel Boal, Domingos dos Santos.

[45] Lara was reputed to have strong Communist sympathies. John K. Cooley, *East Wind over Africa* (New York: Walker and Co., 1965) p. 128.

[46] Former political director of the UPA, who had joined the MPLA at mid-year.

[47] Dropped were Hugo de Menezes, Luis de Azevedo, Jr., Graça da Silva Tavares, José Bernardo Domingos, Georges Manteya Freitas, João Vieira Lopes, João Gonçalves Benedito, and José Miguel.

[48] Madame Guilhermina de Assis of the *Organização das Mulheres de Angola* (OMA), Soba Manuel Miguel representing the "interior" of Angola, Augusto Borges of the JMPLA, Carlo Canoth of the Popular Liberation Army (EPLA), Rev. Domingos da Silva of the MPLA executive committee, Cesário Martins of the MPLA action committee. Chairman: Dr. Neto; rapporteur: Anibal de Melo; secretary: Manuel Rodrigues Boal.

MPLA's previous honorary president, he was shifted back and forth between prison and rustication.[49] In September 1962 he was reportedly shifted from the Benedictine Monastery of Sengeverga near Oporto to Aljube prison in Lisbon. Since it was known that he was seriously ill, it was feared in nationalist circles that he might not survive the reincarceration.[50]

Mário de Andrade, who headed the conference political commission,[51] delivered a speech in which he set forth the need to isolate the Portuguese government from all international support. The new president, Dr. Neto, gave the principal political address. He stressed that the MPLA should overcome its intellectual image and expand its appeal to the peasant class. His central theme, which became the theme of the conference, was that the party ought to give priority to the interior over the exterior, concentrate on programs of political education, military action, and strikes within Angola rather than political action from exile outside. Concerning international relationships, he called for a policy of "nonalignment" patterned on the style of Mali's Modibo Keita. He said that MPLA diplomacy should seek to win new friends and reduce the number of its opponents abroad, and thus enlarge the range of its international action in preparation for a drive to organize an economic and diplomatic boycott of Portugal.[52]

Dr. Neto emerged from the conference with an executive committee and program of his choice. One of the strongest and ablest personalities in the new executive was a young woman. A cousin of Agostinho Neto, she had also come from a Methodist parsonage home at Icolo e Bengo, Catete, where she was born on February 10, 1939, and had attended mission grade schools and completed a course at the Luanda *liceu.* Déolinda Rodrigues Francisco de Almeida had then studied for several years at São Paulo, Brazil, and finally at Drew University in the United States on Methodist scholarships before dropping her studies in order to join the revolution. Intensely loyal to Neto, she organized the MPLA women's section, served as secretary of CVAAR, and worked for Léopoldville's Protestant relief council (CPRA).

[49] See *Courrier d'Afrique,* Jan. 22, 1963.
[50] *Le Monde,* Aug. 12, 1963.
[51] Aided by Américo Boavida, rapporteur, and José Bernardo Domingos, secretary.
[52] *First National Conference,* pp. 9–17.

Viriato da Cruz was pushed farther from the center of power.[53] Yet some characteristics of the party remained unchanged, e.g., a preponderance of Mbundu and mulatto leadership, most of which had lived for some time in or about Luanda, and an intellectual orientation that stressed the importance of party doctrine.

One important change, however, consisted in the addition of a formal military arm to give real muscle to the party's revolutionary structure. Under Andrade's direction young party militants had already been sent to Ghana and Morocco (Algerian bases) for military training. By the end of 1962 they were returning to the Congo, where they formed the nucleus of an armed cadre of 250 to 300 armed men organized within a People's Liberation Army (EPLA). The MPLA was preparing to act on its conclusion that, in view of the intransigence of Portugal, the key to political power lay in military performance.

The GRAE under Roberto

The FNLA-GRAE suffered some setbacks toward the end of 1962. David Livromentos, the young, dedicated, and overworked president of the National Council of the FNLA, collapsed and died on October 14 at the age of twenty-eight.[54] His fellow journalist and another of the PDA's more promising young leaders, Antoine Matumona, had already flown from Léopoldville and active politics to take up a scholarship at the University of Louvain, Belgium. Livromentos was replaced by PDA president André Massaki, who was in turn replaced as minister of education by André M'Vila (PDA), a teacher at the local Salvation Army school. As for Matumona, he was replaced as secretary of state for foreign affairs by another young Bazombo, Pedro Gadimpovi (PDA), and as second vice-president of the PDA by a local business contractor and GRAE secretary of state for interior, Sanda Martin.

[53] da Cruz was not a member of any of the key conference commissions, which, in addition to Mário de Andrade's political commission, included (1) a Commission on Program Action: Lucio Lara (president), Anibal de Melo, Déolinda Rodrigues de Almeida, Desidério Graça, and (2) a Commission on Reorganization of Party Structure: Gentil Viana (president), Manuel Lima, and Vieira Lopes.

[54] See (1) "Information Générale" on memorial services held at Salvation Army Church in the presence of FNLA, MPLA, MDIA, and other Angolan delegations; and (2) "Discours lors de l'Inhumation de M. David Livromentos" by Holden Roberto and André Massaki in PDA, N/REF, SEC/896/62/DF/SM (Léopoldville, Oct. 22, 1962, mimeo.).

Livromentos had tackled his job as president of the FNLA National Council with great energy, but after his death the post became largely honorific. The government (GRAE), not the front (FNLA), became the main organ of the UPA-PDA coalition. On the other hand, the two parties maintained separate headquarters several miles apart, and in the absence of any joint FNLA-GRAE offices the UPA's set of bungalows astride a pot-holed dirt alley in downtown Léopoldville doubled as government headquarters. PDA ministers were not provided with separate GRAE offices at the crowded UPA complex. And since the UPA headquarters had no telephone, communications between it and the PDA were physically difficult. As junior partner and a more-or-less middle-class movement that laid stress upon organization and collegiate decision making, the PDA was unhappy that it was unable to carry its full weight in the government in exile. Most of the important FNLA-GRAE decisions and actions were, in fact, initiated by the more centralized leadership of the UPA and its war-toughened, strong-willed president, Holden Roberto.

Illustrative of the continuing tendency for the UPA to act alone was the journey of the party vice-president, Rosário Neto, to Rome in November 1962. Seeking a new source of leverage against Portugal, the former seminarian presented a memorandum to the Ecumenical Council and discussed the Angolan issue with Vatican officials—all in the name of the UPA, not the GRAE.[55] (Also alert to the potential value of sympathy at the Vatican and the latter's possible influence on Lisbon, the MPLA too sent a message to the Council.)[56]

Nonetheless, GRAE vice-president Emmanuel Kunzika and his PDA colleague, Ferdinand Dombele (minister for social affairs) did join Roberto in his annual pilgrimage to the United Nations during November and December,[57] where they represented the FNLA at the American Negro Leadership Conference on Africa at Harriman, New York, and pressured Roberto for a fuller integra-

[55] "Memorandum Apresentado ao Concílio Ecumênico, Vaticano II Pela Delegação da União das Populações de Angola (UPA)" (Nov. 1, 1962, mimeo.). Rosário Neto had preceded this action by presenting a memorandum on Feb. 13, 1962, to the Papal Observer at the United Nations, New York.

[56] Mário de Andrade and Agostinho Neto, "Message au Concile Oecuménique" (Léopoldville, Oct. 2, 1962, mimeo.).

[57] See "Declaration de Monsieur Emmanuel Kunzika à New York" (Dec. 13, 1962, mimeo.).

tion of their two parties in external as well as internal activities of the FNLA-GRAE. Indeed, Carlos Gonçalves Kambandu, who had set up the UPA's permanent Angola Office in New York at the beginning of the year, was already representing the front, not just his party, in lobbying and informational activities at the United Nations.

Sharing Kunzika's concern over what many considered to be an overcentralization of authority in one person's hands, Jonas Savimbi and other UPA officials joined the PDA leaders in urging Roberto to devolve more internal political responsibility on his associates. The time had passed when a security-minded UPA president could —as he is said to have done—take the key to his (and the party's) post office box with him whenever he left Léopoldville. The capacity of the new government in exile to provide successful revolutionary leadership was clearly tied to its ability to develop an increasingly well-structured and multifaceted organization within which responsibilities were clearly defined and activities well coordinated.

The effectiveness of functional organizations that clustered around the UPA and then, at least technically, the GRAE was also important for success. These groups continued to expand in the number and scope of their activities. The LGTA trade union survived the Kassanga-Kassinda drama of February with no appreciable loss in its membership, which was probably considerably larger than that of any of the other Angolan exile labor movements. The LGTA also conserved its exclusive association with the ICFTU, dating from November 1961, and its new leadership, headed by secretary-general Pedro Barreiro Lulendo, was recognized by the general council of the African Trade Union Confederation (ATUC) meeting at Tunis in December 1962. A younger brother of the Matadi royalist and one-time secretary of the UPNA, Borralho Lulendo, the new LGTA secretary-general Pedro Lulendo, together with his chief deputy Pedro Rana and the executive committee, continued officially to accept the principle of "independent trade unionism," free from government control, even while they tempered it with an acceptance of the primacy of politics during revolution and worked in tandem with the UPA-GRAE.

The LGTA expanded its activities and announced the opening of a center for studies in trade unionism and "general culture," named after the martyred Tunisian nationalist and labor leader,

Ferhat Hached.[58] It also set up a branch in Pointe Noire (unauthorized by the Youlou government) and created a section for the Cabinda enclave.[59] It organized simulated local affiliates inside rebel-held territory[60] and made an abortive effort to reach and organize workers at the diamond mines north of Henrique de Carvalho. With regard to other rebel labor movements, it formally allied itself with a Dakar-based labor union in exile from Guinea-Bissau,[61] co-operated in an unsuccessful effort to create an exile South West African labor union,[62] and rejected proposals for merger submitted to it by the rival UNTA. By the end of the year it was making ambitious plans for 1963 during which it planned to hold its first national congress.

The GRAE maintained a more direct political control over another associate, the army (ELNA), and its training and command base at Kinkuzu. On the other hand, the SARA organization for refugee assistance enjoyed a nominal independence in its relief work. In reality, however, the ability of either SARA (GRAE) or CVAAR (MPLA) to provide tens of thousands of refugees with medicine, food, and clothing inevitably affected political loyalties, and competition between them was intense. As of late 1962 the CVAAR was better staffed and supplied than SARA. Furthermore, GRAE efforts to bar the CVAAR from penetrating and undermin-

58 The Cercle d'Études Syndicales "Ferhat Hached" was said to be in possession of a "vast literature" dealing with labor matters provided by the ICFTU and its Brazilian affiliates. LGTA, "Communiqué" (Léopoldville, Apr. 16, 1962, mimeo.).

59 The *Fédération Régionale de District de Cabinda,* headed by Alexandre Pemo.

60 The function of these groups was to popularize the concept of trade unionism among former farm laborers and other workers through local committees, using mimeographed material sent inside from LGTA headquarters in Léopoldville.

61 Alliance with the *União Geral dos Trabalhadores da Guiné* (UGTG), led by Bartolomeu de Carvalho (secretary-general), signed June 4, 1962. de Carvalho visited Léopoldville and conferred with LGTA officials in July 1962. LGTA, "Press Review" (Léopoldville, Aug. 6, 1962, mimeo.).

62 On July 17, 1962, at the LGTA headquarters in Léopoldville, Jacob Kuhangua announced the forthcoming creation of a South West Africa Trade Union League (SWATUL) in Dar es Salaam. The projected league was to be organized among South West Africans working in Bechuanaland, the Central African Federation, and Tanganyika, and clandestinely within South West Africa itself. The LGTA offered to sponsor the new group for membership in the ICFTU and ATUC—but in spite of a subsequent announcement of its creation in Dar es Salaam and the election of a secretary-general, Paul Helmuth, SWATUL never became more than announced intention. See LGTA, "Communiqués" (Léopoldville, July 17, 1962, and Aug. 18, 1962, mimeo.); and *Contact* (Cape Town), Vol. 5, No. 16, Aug. 9, 1962.

ing UPA-PDA strongholds boomeranged politically when SARA was not able to provide equivalent services.

A new GRAE associate entered the scene in March when a group of nineteen Angolan students, meeting at Lucerne, Switzerland, under the leadership of Jonas Savimbi, formed a *União Nacional dos Estudantes Angolanos* (UNEA). The students involved were all UPA supporters. They met under the auspices of the Swiss Friends of Angola which was directed by a young Swiss-German journalist, Walter Artho, and established a national student union to compete with the interterritorial, MPLA-oriented *União Geral dos Estudantes da Africa Negra sob Dominação Colónial Portuguêsa* (UGEAN). UNEA immediately took steps to request membership in the International Student Conference (COSEC) headquartered at Leiden, The Netherlands; UGEAN was already a member of the International Student Union (UIE) located in Prague, Czechoslovakia.[63] UNEA elected a slate of officers composed of Angolan students in Western Europe and the United States, headed by Pedro Filipe from Luanda, who was then studying at the University of Paris, France.[64] UNEA, like UGEAN, was conceived as a mechanism for mobilizing support within student and other youthful sectors of international public opinion. Whereas UGEAN presented the revolution as viewed by the MPLA, UNEA presented it as perceived by the UPA-GRAE.

Though the GRAE-FNLA and associates had been able to maintain and even modestly to escalate their revolutionary activity dur-

[63] A UNEA delegate, Jorge Valentim, attended the Tenth International Student Conference (CIE/COSEC) at Québec (June 27 to July 8, 1962), independently of the UGEAN delegation headed by Desidério da Graça and José Fret, thus raising a challenge to UGEAN's claim to represent all students from the Portuguese colonies. See UGEAN, "Communicado" (Rabat, July 20, 1962, mimeo.); and UNEA, *A Voz do Estudante Angolano* (Philadelphia), No. 1, Nov. 1962. Valentim also attended the Eleventh Annual Convention of the Organization of Arab Students in the USA (OAS), held at Michigan State University in August 1962. The Convention passed a resolution calling for "closer cooperation with UNEA" and declared its support for the "massive revolution of March 15, 1961," organized by Roberto. See the Organization of Arab Students in the U.S.A., *Newsletter* (New York), Vol. IX, No. 2 (Winter 1963), pp. 22, 44.

[64] General vice-president, Rev. Zacarias Cardoso (Methodist) at Lincoln University, Pa.; first vice-president for international affairs, Jorge Valentim, Lincoln University, Pa.; second vice-president for international affairs, Eduardo Webber, University of Vienna; secretary-general, Mateus Neto, Zurich; treasurer, Calvino Carvalho, Lausanne; information and propaganda, Pedro Sobrinho, University of Montpelier, France, and Alphonse Videira, Redlands University, California; cultural and social affairs, Samuel Albrigado, Germany, Jeronimo Wanga, Lausanne, and Jeronimo d'Almeida, Lincoln University, Pa.

ing 1962, it was essentially a transitional year for them. No government had yet recognized the GRAE; the MPLA was still contesting control of the revolution; Congolese governmental assistance was limited because of a desire not to provoke increased Portuguese assistance to Katangese secessionists; and external criticism of Angolan disunity in the face of Portuguese cohesion and determination was resulting in continued pressure on the UPA and PDA to accept a common front with the MPLA. Such pressures were by no means all from African or Communist sources. In September, for instance, the western-oriented World Assembly of Youth (WAY) announced its support for the creation of an Angolan front based upon a three-party council with decisions to be arrived at by unanimous vote. Its recommendations were similar to MPLA proposals for a United Angolan National Front.[65]

Some of the sharpest criticism on this point came from Britain, which Roberto had curiously excluded from his frequent travels in search of external support. The well-known author and journalist, Basil Davidson, wrote an article in *West Africa* blaming Roberto for Angolan disunity which, he said, "had done a great deal to undermine and confuse the Angolan cause up and down the world." He condemned Roberto's allegedly "steady refusal of all working cooperation with the MPLA," charging that his demands that MPLA members should join the UPA as "mere individuals" looked "remarkably like a device to alienate all those who might contest his own personal leadership of the war." Terming the formation of a government in exile "inappropriate at this stage," he concluded: "No national liberation struggle has ever prospered under an exile leadership which laid premature claim to a monopoly of decision and control. One has the impression, in short, that Mr. Holden is trying to cut up his elephant before shooting it." [66] After a London visit by MPLA president Agostinho Neto, Robert Kershaw's influential and "confidential" *Africa 1963* also blamed Roberto's intransigence for blocking unity moves. It further implied that American suspicions of the MPLA's intellectual, left-wing image and American partiality toward what the editors considered to be the less mature or cultured mass movement of the GRAE helped to account for continued division. Most notably the United States was encour-

[65] World Assembly of Youth, "Report of the WAY Mission on Angola," Document No. 1984 (Brussels, June 1962, mimeo.), pp. 47, 93.

[66] Basil Davidson, "Phase Two in Angola," *West Africa*, No. 2382 (Jan. 26, 1963), p. 87.

aging the pro-GRAE attitude of the Angolan exiles' host government of the Congo.[67]

Some evidence for the idea that the Congolese government did consider the MPLA to be what *Africa 1963* concluded that it was not, i.e., Communist-oriented, could be found in a September article appearing in the Léopoldville weekly *Présence Congolaise.* The article, which was reproduced and circulated by the GRAE ministry of information, said: "Our government has resolutely taken a stand for the Provisional Government of Angola in spite of the outcries of the Portuguese Communist party, Angolan section, camouflaged for imbeciles under the title MPLA." Lest such views be taken as reflecting an undue respect for American bias, however, the article went on to suggest that the Congolese government "ought to study the proposition made by the Brazzaville labor leader [Gilbert] Pongault, proposing that all the States of Central Africa constitute an aid fund to permit the Provisional Government of Angola to live without having to depend on American or other aid." This, the *Présence Congolaise* argument continued, was "the only way for Africa to escape from imperialisms and neocolonialisms [*sic*]." [68]

Concerning the merits and demerits of intellectual leadership and common-front policies, issues that separated the GRAE from the MPLA, Roberto consistently articulated a position similar to that later argued by Régis Debray, interpreter-advocate of Fidel Castro's revolutionary thought and experience. For example, in a speech before a gathering of African students in New York on December 30, Roberto warned against being "seduced by the rank verbiage of a kind of anticolonialist in lounging robes, the kind who makes his appearance in a capital often far from his native land and puts forth beautiful anticolonialist theories inspired by ideas which are completely un-African, the kind who calls himself progressive and proclaims himself the great revolutionary, but never takes off his lounging slippers." [69] Debray was equally harsh and more specific in his criticism of revolutionary intellectuals. Physically weak and unsuited to rural life, he said, "the intellectual will try to grasp the present through preconceived ideological constructs and live it through books." He is less able "to invent, improvise,

[67] *Africa 1963* (London), No. 3, Feb. 1, 1963.

[68] *Présence Congolaise* (Léopoldville), Sept. 15, 1962; GRAE, "Revue de Presse," No. 18 (Léopoldville, Sept. 15, 1962, mimeo.).

[69] Speech published in *A Voz do Estudante Angolano* (Philadelphia), No. 2, Dec. 1962–Jan. 1963; and OAS *Newsletter, op. cit.,* pp. 23–26.

make do with available resources, [or] decide instantly on bold moves when in a tight spot. . . . Thinking that he already knows," continued Debray who was himself widely acclaimed as a brilliant young intellectual, "he will learn more slowly, display less flexibility." [70]

On the intensely disputed issue of the common front, Roberto continued to argue that meaningful unity depended upon a real consensus of political views and held that Angolan unity was "total so far as all elements of the population on the field of battle [were] concerned." "There is," he said, "no other kind of unity." [71] Debray subsequently argued similarly that, "A national front, heterogeneous in nature, is the scene of political wrangling, debates, endless deliberations, and temporary compromises; it can unite and exist only under conditions of imminent danger and in confrontation with an enemy." Real unity, he said, came only as the guerrilla army "created unity within itself around the most urgent military tasks," which as liberation proceeds become political tasks as well. According to the Debray-Castro thesis, the army, centralized, skilled, and sharing "identical class interests, will absorb and unite all revolutionaries as it fights. Thus it will become the "party." [72] While attaching great importance to and exercising personal control over the army, Roberto (in contrast with the Cuban example of total reliance on the army) continued to rely on his party (UPA), its affiliates (LGTA, SARA, UNEA), the PDA (FNLA), and certain pan-African relationships as composite, diversified, and somewhat loosely coordinated bases of political power.

Pan-African Perspectives

At the interterritorial level the GRAE made only one short-lived effort in 1962 to gather around it a group of Portuguese African parties and to form a *lusophone* (Portuguese-speaking) alliance to compete with that of the CONCP. On January 27 representatives of the UPA joined with a Portuguese Guinean and Cape Verdian exile group at Dakar to forge a paper alliance. The UPA thus combined with the *Mouvement de Libération de la Guinée et des Îles du Cap Vert* (MLGC) to establish a *Front Africain contre le Colo-*

[70] Régis Debray, "Revolution in a Revolution?" *Monthly Review* (New York), Special issue, Vol. 19, No. 3 (July-Aug. 1967), p. 21.

[71] *A Voz do Estudante Angolano,* No. 2.

[72] Debray, "Revolution in a Revolution?" pp. 86, 105.

nialisme Portugais (FACCP). Roberto had already made contact with MLGC leaders while he and they were lobbying at the United Nations in New York. The FACCP alliance was logical, given the previous commitment of Guinea-Bissau's stronger PAIGC to the MPLA within CONCP, yet the ephemeral FACCP agreement was negotiated and signed by the trade unionist André Kassinda (LGTA), shortly before his defection, in the name of the UPA without Roberto's authorization. While attending the founding conference of ATUC at Dakar, Kassinda initiated discussions with the MLGC's general secretary Henry Labery, and the two announced the creation of the FACCP and expressed the hope that movements from Mozambique and São Tomé-Principe would presently join it.[73]

The FACCP agreement embodied a promise that Roberto had already extended to the MLGC, namely, help with guerrilla training and arms. In substance this meant a UPA pledge to share with its chosen allies military aid being received from Algeria and Tunisia. Though never disavowed, the FACCP accord was never implemented beyond a communiqué nor revised so as to take into account the formation of the FNLA-GRAE.

The other equally transitory alliance contracted by the GRAE during 1962 was negotiated by Roberto himself with the secretary-general of the South West Africa People's Organization (SWAPO), Jacob Kuhangua. It was viewed by South Africa's liberal weekly, *Contact,* as "a most significant development in the freedom movement in southern Africa." [74] The GRAE's alliance with a movement whose leadership and following came primarily from the Ovambo (Cuanhama-speaking) people straddling the mid-section of the long Angola-South West Africa border prompted speculation that Roberto might thereby gain "firm supporters" in the extreme south of Angola.[75] In reality, the Cuanhama region of Angola was too remote, sparsely populated, and untouched by modern education and economics to offer any immediate potential for nationalist action. Perhaps the alliance's main significance lay in the optimistic

[73] "Déclaration Commune des Représentants de l'Union des Populations de l'Angola (UPA) et du Mouvement de Libération de la Guinée et des Îles du Cap Vert (MLGC)" (Dakar, Jan. 17, 1962, mimeo.). The MLGC's earlier membership in CONCP had lapsed as its rival, the PAIGC, assumed a preeminent role within that interterritorial grouping.

[74] *Contact,* Vol. 5, No. 16, Aug. 9, 1962; see also Angola Information Office, *Free Angola* (New York), Sept. 1962, p. 5.

[75] *West Africa,* No. 2359 (Aug. 18, 1962), p. 899.

assumption of its signers that Angolan nationalists would be extending their action southward. In the short run, the GRAE-SWAPO agreement gained some favorable publicity, gave an illusory sense of accomplishment, and offered added incentive for Luso-South African cooperation in repressing any signs of nationalism along their six hundred miles of common frontier.

By comparison with these two moves to form interterritorial alliances, the GRAE-UPA's efforts on the pan-African level were more impressive. In September 1958, at the initiative of Tom Mboya and Julius Nyerere, a regional organization had been founded to promote and concert programs for early independence in East and Central Africa. PAFMECA, the Pan-African Freedom Movement for East and Central Africa, was viewed in part as a forum and mechanism through which East African leaders could promote federal union along with independence for their countries. At its fourth conference, held at Addis Ababa in February 1962, PAFMECA extended its membership to include nationalist parties of southern Africa and added an "S" for Southern to become PAFMECSA.[76] A jump ahead of its rivals, the UPA sent a delegation to the meeting and became the sole Angolan movement to belong to the expanded organization.

The PAFMECSA conference was marked by a confident if unrealistic optimism, characteristic of the times. The delegates listened to the Pan-Africanist Congress (PAC) representative from South Africa talk of "lunging into the last phase of the liberation struggle,"[77] agreed that a constitution for an East African Federation should provide for the adherence of central and southern African countries when they attained independence, and asked PAFMECSA's Coordinating Freedom Council and its small secretariat under Dr. Mibiyu Koinange to expand assistance to southern liberation movements.[78] PAFMESCA's apparent vitality caused *The Economist* of London to conclude that these advocates of regional unity represented a growing challenge to those like Nkrumah who held that continental unity should come first. This divergence of view, it

[76] See Richard Cox, *Pan Africanism in Practice: PAFMECSA, 1958–1964* (London: Oxford University Press, 1964).

[77] Peter Molotsi, as quoted in *The Economist,* Feb. 10, 1962, p. 537.

[78] Cox, *Pan Africanism in Practice;* and British Information Services (London), *Pan Africanism,* No. R 5512/64, pp. 8–9.

concluded, might prove "a more important division than any that sets the Monrovia group apart from the Casablanca powers." [79]

PAFMECSA reached the crest of its ambitions and activity some months later in a December (28–31) conference at Léopoldville. The meeting was attended by a UPA delegation, which saw to it that interlopers from the MDIA and Ngwizako were expelled from the hall.[80] Besides giving political support to Cyrille Adoula's central government in its efforts to end the secession of Katanga, nationalist leaders from East and Central Africa made a series of formal, public promises to the representatives of southern liberation movements. The conference adopted resolutions urging all African states "to regard countries which continue to supply arms to South Africa and maintain trade and State relations [as] unfriendly and hostile." It called upon African governments and liberation movements to take vigorous steps to see that their nationals withdraw from South African mines and farms so as to deprive them of cheap labor, and called for PAFMECSA states to apply economic sanctions against Portugal, expel its nationals from their territories, and give "financial and material" help to freedom fighters and refugees from Portuguese territories. The conference went on to resolve that, if Portugal did not grant independence to its African territories before the end of 1963, "PAFMECSA and other brother states should intervene." [81]

There was little readiness on the part of African Commonwealth countries to "regard" and presumably treat Great Britain as "unfriendly and hostile," on the part of Basutoland and Malawi to recall thousands of wage earners from the Republic of South Africa to stagnate in unemployment at home, or on the part of African states to impose sanctions against Portugal or to extend significant help to liberation movements, let alone to "intervene" in the Portuguese colonies. Concretely, PAFMECSA could offer parties like the UPA little more than the use of a few typewriters, a mimeograph machine, and office space in Dar es Salaam. Beyond this it could provide only small subsidies from a Freedom Fund to which member governments of the several independent or self-governing countries belonging to the organization were reportedly obligated to con-

[79] *The Economist*, see ftn. 77.
[80] JUPA, *Juventude revolucionária* (Léopoldville), No. 10 (Jan. 11, 1963), p. 8.
[81] Resolutions published in *Tanganyika Standard* (Dar es Salaam), Jan. 3, 1963.

tribute 2800 dollars annually.[82] It would soon become apparent that much more than this would be required if Africans were to make any real dent in Portugal's resolve and ability to hold on to its "overseas province" of Angola.

[82] Cox, *Pan Africanism in Practice,* p. 55; see also Harvey Glickman, "Where Exiles Plan and Wait," *Africa Report,* Vol. VIII, No. 7 (July 1963), p. 3.

A CONCLUDING NOTE

The Angolan explosion of 1961, long in genesis behind a screen of censorship and repression, suddenly rendered Portuguese political psychology a matter of world-wide concern. Contrary to most expectations the rebellion did not force Portugal to make major concessions to African nationalism. Unlike the British, French, and Belgians before them, the Portuguese did not find the human and financial cost of holding onto a colonial empire too high.

Certainly the carefully publicized myth of racial harmony and cultural assimilation in Angola had been bloodied in the agony of flaying machetes and searing napalm. Yet official explanations assigning blame to Communist invaders, Afro-Asian agitators, and Protestant intruders constituted both a stubborn denial of reality and an exercise in self-absolution designed to leave Portugal free to pursue an unaltered African "mission." It was a mistake to assume, as many Americans and even some African nationalists did, that Portugal's own fervently nationalist leadership would accommodate its African counterparts. Just how illusory such expectations were had become apparent by the end of 1962.

The man whose common sense and relative liberalism were thought most likely to start Portugal down the road of colonial reform—a young intellectual who had been named as overseas minister by Premier António Salazar in March 1961, Dr. Adriano Alves Moreira—was fired in December 1962.[1] In a cabinet shuffle widely viewed as having strengthened the power of the military at the expense of more liberal civilian elements, naval Commander António Augusto Peixota Correira was appointed overseas minister.

After nearly two years of a rebellion that had given rise to economic and educational efforts reminiscent of De Gaulle's ill-fated Constantine Plan (1958)—a plan that had failed to stem the tide of Algerian nationalism—hopes that Portugal might seek a solution through political liberalization shriveled. With Moreira's departure it became clear that Lisbon was determined to maintain the political

[1] *The New York Times,* Dec. 4, 1962; and *Washington Post,* Dec. 23, 1962. Moreira's views were set forth in a series of speeches published as *Portugal's Stand in Africa* (New York: University Publishers, 1962).

status quo and to suppress Angolan nationalism wherever and in whatever form it appeared, no matter how high the price.

Moreover, international pressure to induce Portuguese colonial reform peaked in mid-1961 and subsided by late 1962. United Nations resolutions of 1961 condemning Portuguese policy failed to influence that policy; and when a majority of the world organization's members next sought to back up moral censure with material sanctions, e.g., an arms embargo, Portugal's powerful NATO allies balked. In particular, after startling Portuguese and Africans alike by breaking NATO ranks and voting against Portugal at the United Nations, President Kennedy and his new administration edged back into the NATO fold. Lisbon had successfully set such a policy retreat as its price for continued American use of the strategic Azores bases. As was to be the case with other southern African issues, once United Nations resolutions moved beyond the level of lamentation toward collective action and thus threatened to bring retaliation against American military or economic interests, the United States drew back from the confrontation.[2]

By December 1962 the idealism of petitioners who just five years before had asked that Angola be placed under a United Nations administered by the United States was shaken. The expectations of those who had hailed the Kennedy administration's dramatic support for self-determination in Portuguese Africa were already degenerating into a confused and reluctant disillusionment. Washington had indulged itself in an interlude of idealistic but hopefully inexpensive anticolonialism and cold-war strategy calculated both to outpace Communist moves and to win Afro-Asian approval. Its retreat made prophets of critics such as British Baptist Len Addicott, who wrote in 1962: "Only if the United States, the leading nation of NATO, and England, the traditional defender of Portugal, can force Dr. Salazar to change his policy, will they not be seen by the Africans as the accomplices of Portugal." [3]

Events in Brazil compounded the effect of the American shift back to "normalcy." By late 1962 prospects of important, if discreet, diplomatic support for the African cause from the giant of the

[2] A notable exception to this rule has been American compliance with a United Nations-sponsored arms embargo against South Africa. France's defiance of this boycott has brought it lucrative arms sales to South Africa. In the event of an arms boycott against Portugal, the De Gaulle government would most certainly have profited again.

[3] Len Addicott, *Cry Angola!* (London: SCM Press, 1962), p. 93.

Portuguese-speaking world dissolved, just as had the presidency of Jânio Quadros and the political authority of his successor, João Goulart.

On the one hand, the western friends of Portugal were unable or unwilling to dissuade it from pursuing its unreconstructed "mission" in Africa. On the other, the eastern and African friends of the Angolan nationalists were not prepared or able to intervene decisively in their favor. Support for the Angolans was limited to press endorsements and diplomatic rhetoric at the United Nations, some modest financial and material aid, and military training for a few hundred guerrillas. Also the danger of relying unduly upon outside assistance was demonstrated to Angolan nationalists in December 1961 by the case of Goa. Indians who had earlier sought cooperation with African nationalists in the name of Afro-Asian solidarity promptly lost interest in Angola and Mozambique after occupying Goa in military action that had been in no way coordinated with African plans.[4]

PAFMECSA, by establishing the principle of pan-African responsibility for help to southern African territories seeking to liberate themselves from European rule, laid the foundations for a much more ambitious pan-African intervention into Angolan affairs. This collective responsibility was later assumed by the Organization of African Unity created in 1963.

By providing a sanctuary and channel through which the rebels could nourish their revolt, the Congo-Léopoldville became the one truly indispensable source of external aid. It exercised a strong influence on Angolan movements whose headquarters were in its territory. The Congolese projected their own political style, rivalries, and interests into Angolan exile politics. Their imprint extended to the creation of party subsidiaries (Nto-Bako, UCLA) and labor affiliates (LGTA, CGTA, CSLA). The central government granted military facilities, border access, and political favors to one

[4] The Indonesian government under President Sukarno laid claim to west New Guinea (West Irian), Sarawak, and Sabah and prompted international crises and military confrontations in the process. Yet in spite of the "Bandung spirit," Jakarta never served African nationalists by making claims and massing troops in a campaign to annex Portuguese Timor, for which Indonesia could make a much better geographic and ethnic case. Moreover there was no apparent effort made by African nationalists to persuade the Indonesians to mount a diversionary military action—preferably a prolonged feint—in order to force Lisbon to divert troops, transport, and funds from the counterinsurgency and police action in its African territories.

of Angola's two principal revolutionary movements, the GRAE, and thus gave it an advantage over its major rival, the MPLA.

Angolan rebels gradually accepted that they would have to rely primarily on themselves in the fight for independence. But they tended to overrate their own military capacity and to underrate that of their adversary. As of mid-1962 confident insurgents inside northern Angola judged that their rebellion was about to enter a new phase. Whereas they had been fighting in the countryside, they expected that newly acquired stocks of *plastiques* and land mines would now enable them to extend their destructive impact along the roads and into the towns, where the bulk of Angola's Portuguese population lived.[5]

These expectations were, however, to prove wrong. They were as inaccurate as Portuguese claims that the insurrection had already been stamped out, or UPA claims that ethnically diverse Angolans were achieving political unity on the battlefield. In fact, the Angolan rebellion continued, but it was localized within the green, rural north of the country. Furthermore it remained subject to considerable ethnic division, as evidenced in the bitter GRAE-MPLA competition and in the Kassanga-Kassinda affair.

The rebellion itself had not been accurately foreseen by those who had done the most to start it. Plans for limited violence, synchronized with diplomatic action at the United Nations, had not been expected to lead to a general explosion. Yet a sharp deterioration in socioeconomic conditions—lower earnings for already exploited African contract laborers due to a fall in prices for coffee and cotton, coupled with a sharp rise in political tensions, police arrests, and repression coinciding with Congolese independence—had produced unsuspected volatility. Just such an abrupt and radical break in continuity had presented what Harvard professor Barrington Moore has identified as the sort of situation most likely to jar peasants into revolt.[6]

Following the outbreak of fighting, Angolan nationalism had continued as before to develop in a multitude of forms and movements grouped within three major streams. These in turn congregated within two major exile movements that competed for revolutionary leadership. Exiled leaders of two loosely allied parties

[5] Arthur Herzog in *The Observer* (London), Apr. 29, 1962.

[6] See Barrington Moore, *Social Origins of Dictatorship and Democracy: Lord and Peasant in the Making of the Modern World* (Boston: Beacon Press, 1966), p. 474.

(UPA and PDA) within the northern Bakongo stream of nationalism formed a Government in Exile (GRAE). The GRAE was then strengthened as a number of nationalists from the central Ovimbundu and eastern Chokwe stream, as well as a few from the Luanda-Mbundu stream (notably Mbundu from Kasanje) joined one of its constituent parties, the UPA. At the leadership level, though not yet at the base, the political process of knitting national unity appeared to have begun. Furthermore the creation of a host of auxiliary organs, an army (ELNA), health-refugee service (SARA), student union (UNEA), and labor organization (LGTA) presented the image of a revolution concerned not only with winning power but also with improving the health, education, and welfare of its people. The GRAE seemed thereby to be intent upon developing itself as a credible alternative to the colonial administration.

Failure to integrate the PDA into the decision-making processes of the GRAE, however, reflected a weakness in that organization. Most of the important decisions were made personally and exclusively by Holden Roberto, acting through the UPA but in the name of the GRAE, and on the advice of a small and fluctuating number of Angolan associates (e.g., Eduardo Pinock, José Peterson, Jonas Savimbi, Rosário Neto) and Congolese mentors (Patrice Lumumba, Cyrille Adoula, and Justin Bomboko). As of late 1962, after nine months of existence, the GRAE as an organization still lacked the system and structure needed for responsible, complex, and efficient action. It was still young, however, and with much support in the large émigré-refugee population in the Lower Congo and a privileged access to the Angolan border, it was conducting continuous if small-scale guerrilla operations over a widespread area of northern Angola.

The GRAE was also clashing militarily with its principal rival, the MPLA. The MPLA, a product of the urban, multiracial Luanda-Mbundu stream of Angolan nationalism, sought alternately to displace the GRAE's military force inside the country and to persuade the GRAE two-party coalition (FNLA) to join it in a three-party common-action front. The MPLA's well-educated, largely Marxist and mulatto leadership also developed an army (EPLA), health-refugee service (CVAAR), student union (UGEAN), and a loosely related labor organization (UNTA). Yet despite all the efforts of its leaders, Mário de Andrade, Viriato da Cruz, and Agostinho Neto, to identify with Angola's peasants, the MPLA was unable to displace or to merge with the GRAE and thus assure itself the leadership of the rural rebellion.

By late 1962 both the GRAE and the MPLA had come to accept the inevitability and necessity of a protracted guerrilla war for independence. On this there was a consensus. Differences were more a matter of ethnicity, history, ideology, personality, and style. A French journalist defined the dichotomy as stylistic, a contrast between the "rigorous dialectic" of Andrade and the "romantic realism" of Roberto.[7]

In spite of these complicating cleavages, Angolan nationalism had taken root, and all the weed killers in Portugal's greenhouse were probably not enough to eradicate it or to prevent it from choking that fragile European transplant known as lusotropicalism or assimilation. The battle lines had been drawn and the conflict between European and African for political control of Angola—and increasingly of Guinea-Bissau and Mozambique—was due to continue on for many painful years to come.

[7] Dominique Descanti in *L'Express* (Paris), Oct. 31, 1963.

APPENDIX A

PROTESTANTS AND REBELS

According to Portuguese explanations and analyses of the Angolan uprising of 1961, its causes were all external. Of these, one was western. It was the uninvited and mischievous intrusion of Protestant missionaries, who acted to undermine Portuguese authority and encourage the growth of African nationalism.

The two previously unpublished documents that follow cast some light upon the problems faced and posed by the presence of American, British, and Canadian Protestants in Portuguese Africa. The first is a letter from Rev. Joseph S. Bowskill (1872–1938) to a Portuguese colonial official, explaining and defending his role in the events surrounding the revolt led by Chief Buta in 1913–14. The rambling letter reveals how distrust between Portuguese Catholics and Anglo-Saxon Protestants often ended up by turning the Protestants into defenders of African interests.

The second document is written by the Methodist Bishop of Central Africa, Ralph E. Dodge, who spent fourteen years in the Mbundu region of Angola. A biographic note on Dr. Agostinho Neto, it reveals both an empathy for African aspirations and an innocence of the Machiavellian maneuvers that have been ascribed to Bishop Dodge and other Protestant missionaries by Portuguese officials.

1. Letter from Rev. J. S. Bowskill

B.M.S.
São Salvador do Congo.
Aug. 10, 1914.

To His Excellency
Lt. Col. José E. de Carvalho Crates.
Chief of the Cabinet of the Minister for the Colonies.

Your Excellency,

You have asked me to write a defence of the charges brought against me. I note your assurance that this is not for judicial purposes, for were that the reason, I would be compelled to dismiss the matter in a single sentence by stating simply and truly that the whole was a concoction of absurd falsehoods born of religious jealousy—but as it is desired for the information of His Excellency the Secretary for Foreign Affairs, I have great pleasure in narrating fully and frankly my whole connection with this unhappy insurrection.

When I returned to Congo in June 1913, after a furlough in England, my heart was deeply pained at the unsettled state of the country. During the greater part of my 15 years of life here I had witnessed the beneficient and kindly rule of Gen. Faria Leal. I had seen the people progressing in civilization, dwelling in peace and security, and confident in the knowledge that in their ruler, justice and mercy were equally blended.

But now there was a great change; people lived in fear and trembling; the men were being carried off by force to work on the plantations; towns were being looted and burnt; people tied up and cruelly thrashed; women ravished; robbery and extortion rampant; and all this was being done by Government emissaries. Violence had usurped the throne of Peace and Justice had fled the country.

Again and again I was tempted to write directly to the Governor and inform him of the state of affairs, but I felt very diffident about doing so for I remembered that we were foreigners here and I did not wish it to be thought that we were interfering in matters political. Knowing however that my former colleague, the Rev. T. Lewis of Quibocolo, knew the Governor personally, I wrote begging him to take the first opportunity of privately informing the Governor of these things. Unfortunately, he was unable to find a favourable opportunity. Meanwhile chiefs were continually coming to me concerning the demands made on them for labourers for Cabinda, and in every case I strongly urged them to do their best to supply them, for as there they would be under the eye of the Governor himself, they could appeal direct to him should they be ill treated. But matters culminated when Snr. Paulo Moreira sought to force labourers for São Tomé. This coming on top of all the other demands was more than the people could bear, and when the King Kiditu, after strongly urging the chiefs to resist with all their power, himself gave men, the anger of the chiefs was raised to boiling point. They said that he had betrayed them; sold their country for gold and was no longer worthy of the position he held.

Rumours reached me of important discussions being held in different parts of the country and I became apprehensive of serious developments. The gravest news came from the district south of São Salvador. This is mainly Catholic in religion and it was a Catholic chief Tulante Buta, who had raised the standard of revolt. The whole country side was flocked to him; an ultimatum was prepared and sent to the King informing him that if he did not at once reform his ways they would come up and punish him together with all the other native officials who had wrought such havoc in the country.

The town was immediately in great ferment. The King bought gunpowder and distributed it to all who had guns; night after night men patrolled the streets to defend their houses. It was now that the first appeal was made to me to try and preserve peace. A man who was a perfect stranger to me, called to see me. He gave the name of Mfutila, chief of Zamba. He briefly narrated the whole matter and stated that as he was equally related to both Buta and the King, he had been striving his hardest to make peace. But his efforts had been fruitless; the King had loaded him with insults and so he had come to me to ask for my assistance. I told him that it was contrary to our policy to interfere in the politics of the country; we were foreigners here and our work was simply that of teaching, but still seeing that the Gospel we preach is "Peace on earth, Good will among men," if there was anything I could do to preserve peace, I would gladly do it. I further advised him that it would be far wiser, if instead of fighting, Buta got all his grievances written down and sent them by special men to Cabinda. For I was certain that the Governor knew nothing of these evil deeds and would remedy them at once when told of them. Mfutila thanked me for my promise and advice, and said he would report it to Buta.

On Tuesday Dec. 9th, we heard that the insurgents were on their way to the town, and it would be attacked at once. Immediately the people began to flock into the station for shelter. Being afraid lest Buta would not keep to his promise, but would destroy the righteous with the wicked, they brought all their valuables with them and I was busy until near midnight arranging places of safety for goods and people. Then I retired to seek a little rest, but within an hour I was aroused by a number of people coming to visit me. These were the King, his counsellors, Mfutila, and other head men. The King was trembling so that he could hardly speak. He said most piteously "I implore you, do help me; If not we are all dead men." He then stated that Buta had arrived outside the town and might attack at any moment; that the Padres had been out to see him but he had refused to discuss matters with them unless other witnesses were present, and had asked that I be sent for to act in that capacity. But the priests had reported "Mr. Bowskill is only a foreigner here, and he has no right to appear in the country's palaver." To this Buta replied that he had nothing more to say to them. So the King had come to me that I would do something to help. If only I would go out and persuade Buta to hold back his men, come up to São Salvador and properly talk the palaver, then war might be avoided. I replied that Buta was a perfect stranger to me, I did not ever remember once having seen him, that his followers were mainly Catholics or heathen and so I could not expect to have much influence with them, still, if I could be of any service in preserving peace, I was ready to do my best. I would go to Buta at once, but on one condition: "If I am to ask him to come up here I must have a written guarantee from Snr. Paulo Moreira, that he can come and depart in peace," and I drafted out a paper which I asked might be put into Portuguese and signed by Snr. Paulo Moreira.

The King thanked me and all went off, but I heard later that the Padres refused to allow Snr. Paulo to give me the guarantee and so through their action, the war, which might have been stopped, broke out. Early next morning the attack was made. All the men from the Protestant side of the town took their guns and stood on guard around our station, for even then nobody could be sure as to whether the whole town would be destroyed.

At about 9:30 A.M. we were informed that a man was lying terribly wounded in the centre of the town, so Dr. Gilmore, Nurse Bell and I ran around to render assistance. While on our way, a man came running up to me. "Please Sir," said he, "Snr. Paulo begs you to go out and ask Buta to stop this fighting." We went on to help the wounded man and found he had been carried into the Padre's compound. Snr. Paulo was there and he at once came up to me and repeated the request of his messenger. I told him that I did not think I could do anything; I might have succeeded over night, but was afraid it was now too late. Still if he would write out the guarantee I had previously asked for, I would do my best to send it to Buta. While he was writing it we attended to the wounded man.

I brought the paper to our station and called all the men together. I showed it to them and asked for volunteers to go out with it. But no one would take the risk; it was too dangerous. I pleaded with them, but they shook their heads. Then Miguel Nekaka said "If you will go I will go with you." But I did not want to go; I did not think that the attacking party knew my face well enough; they might take me for somebody else, I did not want to be shot. But I soon discovered that if I did not go to Buta, nobody would go, so I consented. All my colleagues wished to accompany me, but we thought it wisest that some should remain with the people, so Dr. Gilmore and I started off together with three natives, Miguel Nekaka, Mantu Parkinson, and Daniel Ngyuvula, the latter carrying a white flag. It is not necessary to detail the incidents of that journey. We met Buta, told him our errand and he told us the grievances of the country. He assured us that he had not risen up against the Government, but against the King and his evil associates, but seeing that Paulo had broken his promise and brought out soldiers who had shot one of his men, he and his men had determined to attack the Residency that night and kill Snr. Paulo. But now that I had gone to him with that guarantee of safe conduct he would come up to São Salvador and publicly state his grievances. As a proof that he would meanwhile keep the peace he gave me the Congo sign—a charge of powder and bullets. (During my absence at Zamba, Mr. Claridge had been called out by Snr. Paulo and the Padres to go stop a threatened attack on the East side of town.)

On our arrival back I found that Snr. Paulo Moreira with Snr. Matos, had sought refuge in my sitting room, where they had been alternately sleeping and waking for nearly 6 hours. I reported to Snr. Paulo the success of our mission and he hesitatingly left the station with his companion.

On Thursday Dec. 11th, Buta and his men came up to state their grievances. Snr. Paulo Moreira sent in a message to us to say they were ready and awaiting our coming. As the full report of everything said and done there has been sent to the Governor by us and by the Padres, I only wish to emphasize here one fact. At the very outset I especially asked Padre Rebello to state in his report that the B.M.S. representatives were present as witnesses, at the request of Buta and his party, and that they take no part in the political affairs of the country. Subsequently I found that this clause had been omitted in the Padre's report. I reported this omission in our letter to the Governor. I did not think it necessary to accompany the Padres when they took their report to Cabinda. I considered that they sincerely loved the people, they would do their best for their welfare. It was because the people heard I was not going, that Buta himself came up here to ask the reason, and I might state here, that this was the only time he set foot on this station.

While the Padres were away at Noqui, I was shown a letter written by a native living in that locality to a relative here. Its substance was that in Noqui people were stating that the English Missionaries were behind this war, and their wisdom was directing it. As the Padres were the bearers of the news of the war, and were staying at Noqui, we could only come to one conclusion as to who were the authors of this outrageous story; and we deeply regretted this additional manifestation of religious jealousy.

This was the first hint we got of the policy of Snr. Paulo and his friends, —to seek to save themselves, by putting the whole blame on us and pretending that it was a "political" affair.

As these various developments had taken place, I had reported them to the British Consul at Luanda, and to our Headquarters in London. But I was so anxious not to bring any shame on the Portuguese Republic, that I strictly enjoined our London Secretary to keep everything private;— "For," I said, "the Governor can know nothing of the evil deeds done here, and it would not be right to allow him to be publicly blamed for deeds of which he had no knowledge. Give him fair play and let him have a chance of remedying these evils."

But the first plain indication of the policy of Moreira and his friends happened on the morning after the arrival back here of the two Padres. Four of the leading Protestant men were arrested and taken off to prison; then the houses of all the others were raided and guns confiscated. Only one conclusion could be drawn from this—all Protestants were to be treated as suspects and might at any time be hauled off to prison. Many of them, seeing this, decided that the further they got away from São Salvador the safer they would be, so they began to leave the town.

As for the insurgents, when they heard of the arrest of these men, and saw soldiers sent out to Mbanza Mputu and Zamba, they gave up all hope of seeing justice done, and prepared for war.

Meanwhile I had seen a translation of the Governor's letter—his reply to the report. We were all delighted at the wise and gracious tone, and I asked the Padres for a number of copies to send to our outstations. I sent copies also to various head chiefs begging them to believe the Governor, refrain from fighting and await his arrival, when all would be settled properly. But it was soon evident, that the action of Moreira and the Alferes [ensign] had ruined completely any chance of peace.

Towards evening on the 19th of January, Moreira and the Alferes came hastily into our station saying that the town was being invested on all sides and everybody must go to the *fortalesa* for safety. I told him that the best plan would be to go out and meet the insurgents and get them to turn back. He replied that this would be foolish as it was useless, and he repeated his demand that we should go to the *fortalesa.* I urged my plan, and sent a native (André Lokwa) to the Padres asking them to go out Zamba way, Dr. Gilmore and I would take the Mbanza Mputu road, and I got some natives to go Lungezi way. Dr. Gilmore and I started off in the dark and after crossing the Luegi River, fell into an ambush. We were surrounded by armed natives; we told them our mission and begged them to send around and stop the attack. After long discussion they agreed to do so and we returned to São Salvador. We called at the Residency to report our success to Snr. Paulo Moreira, and he and the Alferes treated us so insolently that we had hard work to keep our tempers.

On Thursday Jan. 22nd, we heard that the insurgents were collecting in full force at Mbanza Mputu, so I at once went to confer with the Padres about going over and meeting them. We arranged to all start in the early afternoon. We were Pd. Rebello, Pd. Salvador, Dr. Gilmore, Mr. Lambourne and myself. We found Mbanzu Mputu full up with the insurgents—Buta in command. Pd. Rebello brought out the Governor's reply which was read in the ears of all. In the discussion that followed I stood up and begged Buta and his followers to accept the reply, for it was good. They said they would think over it and report later.

Now during our absence, Snr. Paulo Moreira and the Alferes had come over to the station and very curtly ordered our ladies to go at once to the fortress on the supposition that as we had not yet returned, Buta had tied us up. The ladies firmly and politely refused to obey this order. In the afternoon, the Alferes sent for me and my colleagues to meet him at the fortress. On arrival, the Alferes subjected us to a long harangue, wherein he stormed at us, brow-beat us and generally treated us like dogs. Then he said that all of us and our people were to immediately come to the fortress for security. I thanked him for his "kind offer" but said that it was impossible. We were 6 white people, we had almost 70 station children and as many patients in our hospital. Even to remove some of these patients would be to endanger their lives. Further there was no accomodation at the fortress and for so many people to herd together in so confined a space would spell disease and death. Then he said I must send all the townfolk out of our station and order them to the fortress; that Dr. Gilmore and Mr. Lambourne could take back the order, but I must remain at the fortress until the townsfolk arrived. I at once protested against this imprisonment and warned him that if he confined me he would have to answer for it. I told him further that I would go back to the station, and tell the people that "the Alferes had ordered that all should go to the fortress"—but I would not undertake the responsibility of forcibly turning them out of our station. We were permitted to return home and I told the people the Alferes' order. A large number of them when they heard this, at once packed up their things and cleared out of the town.

Late that evening we and the Padres went over to the fortress; we were all told by the Alferes that we must have no further communication with Buta, save that we were to write him a letter telling him to come up and see the Alferes. We and the Padres wrote this letter next morning and it was sent off at once.

The day following—Jan 24th the Priests came in to us with a letter from Buta, in reply to the one we sent him. They and we, unitedly drew up a reply to this, again urging peace, although we knew from the tone of Buta's letter, that peace was now impossible.

That afternoon, as war seemed imminent, we barricaded the backs of our houses, wired up the whole of our station fence and blocked all entrances.

On Jan. 25th, the second outbreak began, all the station staff came to my house seeing it was furthest from the scene of the conflict, and we all remained within its four walls while the fighting lasted. Indeed it was highly dangerous for anybody to leave shelter, for bullets were flying about in all directions.

During the previous week I had written my former colleague Rev. T. Lewis of Quibocolo asking whether he could come along and use his influence for peace. On the third day of the fighting he arrived and we immediately began to discuss the situation. We heard rumours that the fortress was surrounded and the situation there was most serious. So we decided that I should try and get through to the coast, inform the Governor of the serious situation and try and persuade him to come up at once and restore the confidence of the people. Mr. Lewis wrote a letter to the Governor which I took with me. I left here at about 9:00 A.M. on the 30th and slept at Nsamo; the next day at Soko and next afternoon Feb. 1st got to Songololo, the next evening I arrived at Matadi, I immediately drafted out a long telegram to the Governor, telling him of my arrival, that I came with very serious news and begging to see him at once.

I waited the whole of that week and had no reply to that telegram. On Sat. Feb. 7th I heard that the Governor had just arrived at Matadi, so Mr. Phillips (our Congo Secretary) and I went across to see him. Then we heard with regret that the Governor I had expected to see (Governor Cardoso) had gone to Europe ill, and Acting Governor Moraes was in his place. To him I stated my errand, and to him I handed Mr. Lewis' letter.

On Feb. 19th, almost a week after I had returned to São Salvador, a sergeant and file of soldiers came armed to our station—Divengele was with them as translator. The sergeant informed me that I was required at the fortress to act as a witness to the depositions of a native, that it would not take long; I would be back in the station within an hour. I went with the sergeant, Dr. Gilmore accompanying me. We were conducted to a grass shelter in the fortress; there were present, the Alferes, Snr. Moreira; the Padres, and some other white men; Divengele and Tangi acted as translators. The Alferes began to read contracts from a file of blue foolscap before him. He said I had been accused of very grave offences, I had fomented this war; kept it going; assisted the rebels; allowed them to come on our station to fire on the soldiers. He showed me a sharp pointed nickel bullet which he said had been picked up outside our station fence, and therefore we must have dropped it there. Then he referred to the fact that we had been unharmed by the insurgents. Our messengers could go freely through the country, but theirs could not. We could travel where we liked, and he instanced the fact that Mr. Lewis had come through from Zombo and had safely gone back again, and I myself had been able to journey down to Matadi—All these things proved, said he, that we were in league with the insurgents. I then asked him where the man was whose deposition I was to bear witness. He replied that his evidence was being taken and he would shortly appear. Then we saw the man coming: his name was Sandaba. He reeled along in a dazed kind of way as though his legs could not carry him. Dr. Gilmore and I both remarked on his strange condition. The man flopped down on the ground while Snr. Paulo read his evidence—It deposed that I had been over to Mbanza Mputu and told the people there to keep on fighting. I instantly stopped the reading and asked Snr. Paulo Moreira, the priests and all who understood the Congo language to pay close attention to the question I was about to ask the man and to his reply. I asked him "You mean to say that I myself went over to Mbanza Mputu and said these things?" He answered "I do." I inquired again "Do you refer to the time when I and my colleagues went over there and read the Governor's letter?" He answered "No." "So you mean that I went over there myself?" "Yes" said he. Then I turned to them all and said—"Please keep this answer in mind." The white folk all looked at each other inquiringly. Then Padre Rebello said to the man—"Perhaps you meant to say that Mr. Bowskill did not go himself, but sent a letter?" The man was quick to take the hint, for he said "Yes, that is what I mean, he wrote a letter." I retorted to him, "But you said plainly enough that I went myself, and now you alter it." I then asked him whether he saw the letter and he answered "No." Then I asked him how he knew about it and he answered that he had been told so. Finally Divengele asked the man whether he had made the statements of his own free will; whether he had been beaten or forced to say them, and the man made haste to answer that he had not been coerced or beaten. At this Dr. Gilmore and I both smiled, for we had noticed the man's condition as he reeled across to us. Subsequently Pd. Rebello remarked that this was a religious war [with] Protestants fighting against Catholics. I saw the insinuation in his words, so I asked him whether or not Buta and the main body of his men were Catholics. The Padre did not reply to the question. I saw it was useless to argue further with them so I waited to see the next move of the Alferes and Snr. P. Moreira—This was that I must consider myself under arrest, and a prisoner in the fortress.

I was there for almost a week until His Exc. Governor Moraes arrived. He came to see me at once. I told him that the charges against me were utterly false and perfectly absurd. I asked to be allowed to write him a statement of my actions during the whole affair. He gave me permission and that night I wrote fully concerning all that I had done. Knowing that he was entirely new to the work of the district and especially to São Salvador matters, I thought it wise to include in my statement a word of caution—This was to the effect that he would be surrounded by a large number of persons who were from motives of spite or religious jealousy, not over friendly to us. I begged him therefore to hear both sides before coming to any decision. On the following day I was released on parole.

The foregoing is a perfectly true summary of my whole connection with this unhappy affair, [and] I now wish to append to it a few observations.

a. Both Mfutila chief of Zamba and Tulante Buta were perfect strangers to me; I had never spoken to them previous to the time mentioned in the report.

b. The entire district wherein the insurrection first started was unknown country to me, as it was mainly Catholic in religion. I had never until I went to Zamba set foot in it during my whole life here. For it has ever been my policy that a man's religion is his own concern, and it is not my business to seek to make proselytes. My duty is to go to those who have no religion.

c. During the period immediately preceding the first outbreak, both Protestant and Catholics in São Salvador spent the night patrolling the town to guard their houses in case of attack. The Protestants also, in their fear, stored all their goods on our station premises and sought shelter there themselves.

d. Only certain houses in the town were destroyed:—those of the men and their friends who had been guilty of the outrages in the country; these all happened to be Catholics. It was not because of their religion, but because of their deeds, that they were punished.

e. Because no Protestant suffered loss during the first outbreak, it was sought to prove that therefore they were in league with the insurgents, and that the rising was a religious affair. The truth is that there were no Protestants amongst the men who committed outrages, and so there was no reason for a Protestant to be punished.

f. When we sent our full report of the Palaver to Governor Cardoso, we also sent with it a letter explaining our connection with the affair, and entreating His Exc. to come up quickly and see justice done.

g. When the trouble got worse I wrote Mr. Lewis at Quibocolo urging him to come and use his influence to preserve peace.

h. When we saw the grave condition of those sheltering in the fortress I myself journeyed to Matadi to personally interview the Governor and show him the serious state of affairs. I took with me a letter from Mr. Lewis emphasising the necessity of the immediate coming of the Governor. While I was away the Alferes sent soldiers to our station commanding Dr. Gilmore or Mr. Lambourne to take a sealed letter at once to Noqui to inform the Governor of the very fact I had (on our own initiative) gone to communicate.

i. In the matter of Sandaba's evidence—That he had been badly coerced was most apparent and was noted by both Dr. Gilmore and me. As I have narrated, he directly altered his sworn statement—Pd. Rebello and Pd. Salvador, Divengele and Tangi—as well as Dr. Gilmore, can bear witness to this.

I may say that during this year I have never been to Mbanza Mputu save when we all went together, nor sent a letter to Mbanza Mputu, nor have I done anything that would even give the slightest colour to the statement made by Sandaba. His statement is a fabrication of lies from beginning to end.

In conclusion, we are perfectly aware that these charges have been made against us out of spite and religious jealousy. We have been unharmed by the insurgents; we Protestant Missionaries have been free to travel through the country. This has been looked upon as a grave crime.

For 36 years our Mission has been working here; we have succored the poor, supported the weak, helped the oppressed. We have denounced wickedness and preached righteousness. We have never to our knowledge wronged a person. We have sought to educate and civilize the people, and give them the benefits of Christianity. We have taught the youths trades and handcrafts that they might become industrious upright members of society. In our hospital and dispensaries we have ministered to the sick and never asked whether the patients were Protestant, Catholic or heathen.

This is our record, and our reward is that the people trust and love us; believing truly that we are here entirely for their good.

If, on the contrary, they had sought to harm us, treated us with suspicion and made us fear to go amongst them, then we would have concluded that all our years of work were wasted and our hearts would be filled with regret.

During all the time we have been here, we have always been delighted to do everything in our power for the assistance of Government officials and traders in this town.

We have certainly felt exceedingly grieved to think that these wicked charges have been made against us, notwithstanding our past record. We would have thought that the first to repudiate them would have been the white officials themselves. But instead of doing so, they have put upon me the horrible indignity of imprisonment, they have publicly held up me and my colleagues to accusations; they have imprisoned our leading native assistants and bitterly persecuted our native adherents to such an extent that most of them have fled away for safety. Everything that could be done they have done to lower us in the eyes of the people. During the past few months we have been subjected to annoyance after annoyance; our liberties have been infringed, our correspondence seized and we have been forbidden to keep open the avenues of communication with our Colleagues at other stations. The aim has been to isolate us entirely.

To us, when we think of everything, this treatment savours of something worse than ingratitude. Dr. Gilmore and I with three natives risked our lives at the request of Paulo Moreira, and thereby we saved his life and the Government building. In return, I have been thrown into prison: two of those brave natives who went with us—Nekaka and Mantu—are in prison to this day—they have spent 8 dreary months there for no crime whatsoever, save that of being our leading helpers. Dr. Gilmore and I at another time voluntarily put our lives in great jeopardy by going at night to meet a threatened attack on this town. We succeeded in turning the insurgents back on that occasion. And since then, an absurd puerile charge has been made against Dr. Gilmore and an attempt made to bring him to trial in secret.

Our station children when going to the spring for water, are not allowed to go without a military escort—and this not to protect them, but to over awe them. All this was exceedingly hard to bear, but we bore it with patience, for we felt that the officials were acting in ignorance; for seeing they looked for guidance to the very native officials who had been the cause of all this unrest, they could not be expected to know the true facts of the situation.

And so it is with unfeigned satisfaction and pleasure that we see at last the opportunity provided for a full, free and impartial inquiry into everything connected with the insurrection, and we feel sure that now the truth is being brought to light the only result that can follow will be that justice will be done.

And may I add a word expressing our hearty thanks to the Portuguese Ministry for sending His Excellency out here, and to yourself for consenting to come. It has meant a trying journey and a difficult task, but the work of fighting wrong, executing justice, and making peace is divine, and brings with it its own reward.

And this further,—the Portuguese Republic has never had more sincere well wishers nor more loyal supporters, than we of the B.M.S. Our prayers are for its prosperity in the highest and best sense. We trust that these prayers may be answered.

With the deepest respect.

I am your Excellency's obedient servant.

J. S. Bowskill

2. *"António Agostinho Neto," some biographic notes by Bishop Ralph E. Dodge, Kitwe, Zambia, June 14, 1967.*

I first knew António as a small boy when his father was the pastor of the large Methodist Church in the center of Luanda. Our missionary residence was not more than twenty yards from the corrugated iron siding and roof house built on concrete pillars in which the Neto family lived. António was the second boy—second child, when I came to know the family. He had four or five younger brothers and sisters. As I recall, António was already in a government school in Luanda when we arrived there in December of 1936.

Rev. Agostinho Pedro Neto, António's father, was a very highly respected pastor. At one time I was associated with him in the church in Luanda and later I became his superior as a District Superintendent.

During those days I did not know António and his older brother Pedro too well. They were school boys and I would see them going in the morning and returning in the afternoons. They were both very serious minded as was their father. As I reflect back, there was a brief period of close personal relationship when Neto, as a boy in Luanda, helped in my office as my secretary in Portuguese. Even as a boy, Neto was quiet, reserved, a bit shy but always correct and businesslike. I never noted any racial antagonism in him.

António always got good marks in school and progressed from one grade to the next with yearly regularity. He caught up with Pedro and passed him. António was one of the few African (Black) students in the *Liceu* (High School) especially in the upper *Ciclo*. The pattern of the Portuguese was to admit the African students in the same school with the Europeans but thin them out especially in the upper grades. António was one of the few who was able to complete his education in Angola up to the university level.

The Methodist Church gave António a Crusade Scholarship, one of the first granted in Africa, to take medical studies in Portugal. There he began to run into difficulties and it is my impression that due to two or three prison sentences of considerable duration, he was in his studies for about seven or eight years. He studied in the University of Lisbon, University of Coimbra, and finally took his medical degree from the University of Porto in the north of Portugal. During this time I had limited contacts with Dr. Neto when I passed through Portugal or in correspondence. It is my impression that his political consciousness grew with his training and wider experiences. He, like his father before him, has had a strong sense of solidarity with his people.

He was imprisoned in Portugal during his medical studies on charges of Communism or Communistic activities, charges which were never sustained. It was undoubtedly during his university years in Portugal that his political philosophy developed, especially during the long years of his imprisonment.

The next direct personal contact I had with Dr. Neto was after his graduation from medical school when he was practicing in Angola. Although I did not know anything about his political activities during these years it was assumed that he was involved in the rising disaffection taking place among the *assimilados*. Often his name would be mentioned in some indirect reference to Angolan independence. However, I never pressed these matters when talking with Christians of Angola. There was a common understanding that it would happen one day but that day was in God's hands and those of the people of Angola, and I never was interested in inquiring about the progress of independence thinking in the minds of the Africans with whom I associated.

It was during 1959 and 1960 that on periodic visits to Angola one would hear considerable talk about UPA. Whether or not Dr. Neto was at one time associated with UPA I cannot say. At that time I heard more references about UPA than MPLA.

It was on a visit in February 1961 that I sensed a drastic political development since my last visit to Angola six months previous. Nobre Pereira Dias, Gaspar Domingos and others had been imprisoned. As I recall, Neto had also been taken at this time but his wife and children were still in Luanda. I was told that people in rural areas were hoarding salt. When I inquired why salt, I was told that it was needed more than anything else in any kind of long revolutionary seige. I was so concerned that I spoke to the American consul, a Mr. Gibson, about the political situation but he assured me that the Portuguese had everything in hand.

Almost immediately thereafter there was the MPLA inspired raid on the Luanda prison and the massacres of mid-March in the north, usually attributed to UPA.

For me, the development of persons such as Dr. Neto into political leaders has been a gradual and natural process. As education has become more general there has come a self-consciousness and with that a sense of identification with their own people and a desire to do something about it. In other words, in my view there has been a hidden religious motivation of service to their own people as part of the whole nationalist drive as I have observed it at close hand.

I do not wish to say that I approve of everything the nationalists do. They, like me, get caught in cross currents of conflicting pressures. But as I know [Dr. Neto, Rev. Domingos da Silva (MPLA vice-president), Déolinda de Almeida (cousin of Dr. Neto and leader of MPLA women), and Dr. Eduardo Mondlane (Mozambique)—all Methodist educated], they are a group of sincere, hard-working, idealistic young people (and not so young any more) seeking the spiritual and material heritage for themselves and their people which they think is God given.

APPENDIX B

TWO PORTUGUESE DOCUMENTS

Portuguese contentions that African nationalism and violence in Angola could be attributed to foreign interference—Protestant and Communist—were based partly on fear, imagination, and insecurity. Illuminating in this regard is what might be called the Montero-Scheinman affair of early 1960.

Frank Montero, a former Urban League executive, and William X. Scheinman, a New Jersey businessman, both members of the American Committee on Africa, arrived in Luanda by plane on February 6, 1960, from São Salvador. They had driven to the old Kongo capital from Léopoldville where they met with Barros Necaca of the UPA. The two made numerous contacts during their brief stay at Luanda (February 6–10). Upon their return to New York they called a news conference (March 7), presented the two documents below (which Scheinman had carried out in his left shoe), and stated that they had concluded from their trip that only pressure from the United States and other world powers might persuade Portugal to start moving Angola and its other colonies toward independence soon enough to ward off widespread violence.[1]

On March 23, the Ministry of National Defense in Lisbon announced that investigations showed that the two documents presented at the press conference were "nothing more than two themes of a tactical problem elaborated for the final exercises of the [army] Recruit School in 1958." The documents, it said, were not classified as "top secret," though an investigation would be made to discover how they had come into the visitors' hands. Reference in them to light atomic weapons supposedly imported by submarine, the ministry statement continued, was in itself proof that they were "fic-

[1] See *The New York Times,* Mar. 8, 1960; *Christian Science Monitor,* Mar. 8, 1960; *Chicago Daily News,* Mar. 18, 1960; *Africa Today,* Vol. VII, No. 2 (Apr. 1960), p. 11; *Africa Weekly,* Vol. VII, No. 11 (Mar. 11, 1960).

titious documents" used simply for training purposes. It went on to suggest that the presentation of these documents as descriptions of real events constituted "evidence of the plot against the peace and sovereignty of the Portuguese Overseas Territories organized by foreign professional agitators interested, so it [seemed], in fomenting disturbances and campaigns to discredit." [2]

The fact that the chairman of the American Committee on Africa to which the two Americans belonged was a Protestant pastor, Rev. Donald Harrington (Unitarian), apparently helped Portuguese officials conclude that this incident proved the correctness of their conspiratorial view of history and Protestantism. This outrageous affair, they reasoned, confirmed the observations of "those who saw, among the representatives of certain foreign religious sects, agents of opposition to Portuguese sovereignty." [3]

For their part, Montero and Scheinman argued that the Portuguese assertion that the two documents were instructional themes was "impossible to substantiate . . . because they [gave] specific dates, times and places of various guerrilla attacks, all of these dates being in late 1959." [4] In Angola, PIDE pushed its investigation concerning the purloined documents. A trusted civil servant and Catholic journalist, Rosário Neto, who later acknowledged that he had passed the documents on to local priests, fled to Cabinda and from there to the Congo.[5] The police then began cracking down on the clergy. On June 25 Father Pinto de Andrade, Chancellor of Luanda, who had protested against the arrest earlier that month of Agostinho Neto, was arrested and sent to Aljube prison in Portugal. From that time on, he alternated between prison and house arrest. According to an MPLA communiqué, it was a letter to his brother Mário in Europe (in which he wrote of the Luanda arrests of 1959–60 and a meeting he had had with Agostinho Neto on the same subject) that prompted his own imprisonment.[6] The affair of the two documents may have been a factor as well.

As for the military documents, even though they most probably were, as Lisbon stated, only descriptions of hypothetical events used for training purposes, they gave some insight into the thoughts,

[2] *Noticias de Portugal, Boletim Semanal do Secretariado Nacional da Informação* (Lisbon), Vol. XIII, No. 673 (Mar. 26, 1960), p. 2.
[3] *Ibid.*, p. 3.
[4] *The New York Times*, Apr. 8, 1960.
[5] See p. 137.
[6] *Courrier d'Afrique*, July 16–17, 1960.

fears, and tensions then existing within the colonial administration. They revealed serious doubts about African loyalties. And their descriptions of submarines, atomic weapons, infiltration, and propaganda suggested an underlying assumption that there really was a giant international conspiracy against Portugal's civilizing "mission" in Africa.

1. A Situation Paper: Scenario from the Military Command of Angola

C.M.A. [Military Command of Angola]
Q.G. [General Headquarters]
E.N.-2ª Rep. [National Army, 2nd Division]

Annex I.

(Extract from Perintrep No. 10 of 25 October 1959)
Circular No. 20,954

I. General Situation

1. In concrete ways the policy of infiltration that is being carried out in Africa by power blocs of Eastern Europe and North Africa and Asia Minor has become evident in the last few months. It is marked by an intense and shameful propaganda on the part of those same blocs, whether through the radio or the press, or at International Conferences. Its aim is to provoke an uprising by the African people of the [Portuguese] Overseas Provinces and territories of Western European powers.

At the same time, throughout Africa there has been a systematic infiltration by individuals, as many whites as blacks, who are specially trained to spread subversive ideas, agitate the working masses, and prepare and foment acts of sabotage and terrorism!

2. Add to these acts a clandestine inflow of small groups of men and large quantities of light atomic weapons by surface means and powerful submarines, the arrival of large supplies of munitions smuggled through the coasts of Angola, and an infiltration by air and across land borders to the East where strongly armed groups of men are gathering. Especially noticeable in the large urban centers of the Province [of Angola], a swift and strong agitation among the native populations is tending toward insurrection and revolt.

3. As a consequence, acts of terrorism are now taking place in the regions of Nova Lisboa, Luanda, Sá da Bandeira, Malange, Silva Porto, Santo [António] do Zaire, and Lobito, especially attacks on motor vehicles in the streets along with robberies and assassinations.

Every attempt has been made to spot these armed groups. But so far nothing has been accomplished beyond confirming their existence as a result of the above-mentioned acts. They are using perfect guerrilla tactics. They enjoy the connivance of the majority of the native populations who have responded to their political doctrines and have received in return intense instruction in the art of fighting and the use of arms.

4. It is known that about five days ago subgroups of 20 to 30 natives were being organized in the regions of Sá da Bandeira, Nova Lisboa, and Luanda. These were in turn regrouped in clusters of 4 or 5 groups, company pattern, all led by the foreign agitators mentioned above. Beyond this, references have been made to radio stations broadcasting in Arabic and native languages in the region of Nova Lisboa, Sá da Bandeira, and Luanda. In addition, during the past three days new disembarkations of small groups of men and arms have been reported in the regions of Santo António do Zaire, Luanda (North), and Lobito.

II. What the Natives May Do

In view of the intensity of the propaganda efforts being made by the Eastern European and North African and Asia Minor blocs in favor of the liberation of African peoples, the infiltration of agitators into Angola during the last few months, and the advanced operations carried out by them, it is possible that the following may happen:

1. Immediate attacks by clandestine groups of insurrectionists organized in the most populous centers with the connivance of the native population.

2. An uprising of the indigenous masses in the regions of Luanda, Nova Lisboa, Sá da Bandeira, Santo António do Zaire, Malange, Lobito, Silva Porto, and Fort Roçadas, aimed at trying to exterminate the civilized population.

3. Acts of sabotage and terrorism carried out by isolated groups using guerrilla tactics.

The degree of probability of the above possibilities is as follows:

It is considered that possibility No. 1 combined, or not, with No. 3 is most consonant with the objectives of the natives and the techniques used in North Africa.

N.B. This Situation [as just presented] should never be divulged in any form, directly or indirectly, to the troops [largely African] lest a suspicion be created that we consider the native peoples as our enemies. Soldiers should be presented with a clear and concrete situation in which they are shown where the native stands and the dangers that they may face, but should not be presented with such specifics as are given here. This Situation is designed exclusively to create an atmosphere within which the command and staff may be able to enliven the final military exercises of the E.R.I. during the current year.

General Headquarters in Luanda
Chief of the Department

Manuel dos Santos Moreira
Captain of the C.E.M.

2. *Confidential Report from Commandant of Fort Roçadas (December 1959)*

The Commander of Fort Roçadas to his superiors:

In the areas of Cuamato and Cuanhama there are many firearms in the hands of the natives. It was certain that these were not being used until about a month ago. But beginning in October incidents began taking place in widely separated areas, while giving the impression that these isolated actions were centrally coordinated.

Specifically, there were assaults on cattle owned by Europeans and an ostentatious shooting and bearing of arms by natives, contrary to custom.

On October 5 at about the same time, 9:00 P.M., several homes of European shopkeepers were burned down in Evale, Pereira de Eça, and Namacunde, without the use of firearms.

On October 10 at 8:00 P.M. a white woman in Môngua was assaulted by a group of natives, after she had been kidnapped from her home, and she reported that they all had rifles.

On the 20th of October at 6:00 P.M. in Môngua a shopkeeper, suspecting that there was a plot against him, fired upon a group of armed natives who were approaching his residence. There were no casualties, but a few natives were injured in the fray.

In mid-morning on October 25, with a semblance of coordination and organization, several attacks took place simultaneously at Cafu, the military and population center of Cuamato, and Naulila, with casualties on both sides. Some whites were made prisoner.

According to their orders, the Comp. F.R. [regular forces] sent discreetly disguised Cuanhama soldiers to the rebel area in order to collect information on the spot. These soldiers did not come forth with identical findings.

(a) Some affirm that the rebellious natives wish solely to create a panic in the region of the Lower Cunene River in order to force the evacuation of the area by Europeans.
(b) Others contend that the aim is to destroy all vestiges of European settlement in that area, to occupy Fort Roçadas before the coming of the first rains, and then to defend this point from any attack against the region.

On October 30 the Fathers of the Catholic Mission of Cuamato, who spent five days as prisoners of the rebels, were liberated, mainly owing to their prestige. They managed to reach Fort Roçadas, informing it that the aim of the rebels is to force Europeans to evacuate the Lower Cunene and beyond that to occupy Fort Roçadas in order that during the rains they may be able to defend the whole region.

These rebels do not have atomic arms, but most have military rifles.

The aim of the chief of the rebel forces, an African named Cauita, in advancing in the direction of Roçadas, is to gather together behind him all the forces—about 2000 men—in the Cuamato region. Engaged in operations of devastation and terror, they are currently widely dispersed.

It is known that many resident whites in the Lower Cunene (beyond

Roçadas) have been captured and others killed while still others abandoned the region, crossing the river to Naulila.

The Company at Fort Roçadas has been under orders from the R.I.S.B. for some days to wipe out the rebellion and destroy the revolutionary forces. Having learned that since the evening of the 4th of November the rebels have been marching toward Fort Roçadas, the Fort Roçadas Company has been on the march since 4 A.M. of the 5th seeking to engage them, thus complying with the mission with which it has been charged.

APPENDIX C

REBELS AND THE KONGOLESE THRONE

The relationship between prenationalist protest such as the revolt led by Chief Buta in 1913–14 and contemporary Angolan nationalism is patent. The first of the following documents represents one effort by a group of Bakongo modernists to depose a puppet king, Dom António III, and to replace him with an educated man who might use the institution of kingship to work for social and economic reform. The failure of this effort led eventually to the creation of the UPNA (later UPA) and to the uprising of March 1961.

Even after the rebellion had begun, a group of Bakongo royalists organized within Ngwizako continued to seek political power through the Kongolese kingship. The difficulties that they encountered in efforts to persuade the Portuguese to fill the vacant throne with a man of their choice, in spite of their condemnation of the UPA-led rebellion, are laid out in the second document. It is a confidential letter sent to the Baptist mission at São Salvador (translated from Kikongo by Rev. James Grenfell).

Unwilling to allow the throne to be occupied by other than aging, illiterate puppets or their widows, the Portuguese administration found the kingship useful for its own purposes. In early 1962 Portuguese aircraft dropped a leaflet over rebel-held territory. It was signed by the queen widow, Dona Isabel. Reproduced below as the third document (translated from Portuguese), it illustrates how the remnants of Kongolese kingship had become an instrument of Portuguese authority.

1. Destitution Proclamation of December 27, 1955, São Salvador [translated from Kikongo notes of Eduardo Pinock]

First, since you were never chosen nor loved by the people, facts of which you must be aware, as from this date you are no longer our king.

Second, we no longer wish to live under the rule of the Kivuzi clan, which enslaves us by its deeds and misrepresents us before the Portuguese government.
This is the solemn will of the people, those living in the Kongo as well as those abroad.

Gama's Vices:

(1) He is the cause of all religious antagonism in the Kongo for he asserts that he can never work with Protestants.
(2) He is a coward and a puppet of bandits and wicked people.
(3) He is a liar, lacks candor, and spreads false reports about others.
(4) He has turned over our kingdom's prerogatives to the Catholic mission.
(5) When the people came to greet him, he raised up his sword, thus saying, they are all my slaves, slaves of my clan.

Vices of the Whole Kivuzi Clan:

(1) It makes slaves of the people by saying that only the Kivuzi have the right to sit on the throne of Nekongo—that even if it should happen that there were no more Kivuzi men a Kivuzi woman should ascend the throne. This shows that all other clans are considered but slaves of the Kivuzi, when in fact the Nekongo throne is for all the twelve clans of the Kongo.
(2) All the people are convinced that it is since the Kivuzi came to power that our kingdom has been enslaved. This is evident in words and deeds. Furthermore, the Kivuzi has sought to create an atmosphere of hostility between the people of the Kongo and the Portuguese government.

2. *Confidential Letter from Ngwizako*

"Ngwizako."

Associação dos Conguenses de expressão Portuguêsa:
São Salvador de Congo, 23 de Julho, 1961:

The Directors of the Protestant Mission,

Greetings:

We have been here four months, but have not had the opportunity of coming to talk with you about the things that are happening in our country, nor of showing what our thoughts are.

We know very well that the English and Portuguese are old friends but at this time we are following on the radio the news of what is happening here in our country. We have seen that you English missionaries are giving evidence of the truth in the things that are happening in our country. You are showing your real concern for us. Because of this we have had courage to write this letter to give you our very sincere thanks. We know very well that the white Portuguese have treated you badly, therefore, we have written this letter secretly and beg that you will go on showing your real concern for us in whatever way you can.

As you know the U.P.A. party and that of Ngwizako were made up of the children of the Kongo people. These parties are not concerned with either Catholics or Protestants. The difference between us is that our brothers of U.P.A., since they realized that the Portuguese had interfered in the matter of our Kongo throne, and were always lying to us, felt that they must first get rid of the Portuguese from our country—then we would appoint the King.

But we in Ngwizako felt that to get rid of the Portuguese from our country would be a very big and costly matter, for there would be war and many would die, for we have no weapons. So we must go slowly and come to terms with the Portuguese so that they will let us choose a person whom the people want [love] to rule on our throne. He must be a wise person. When we have appointed him he will deal with all the matters we want. As for any condemnation it is only the king who can do that for if the Portuguese are in this country it is the king who called them and he who took the responsibility for their being here at the Conference of Berlin of 1885. The declaration was made by the Padre António Barroso and signed by the King of Kongo Dom Pedro V, on the 16th of June 1884. A copy of the letter was also given to Stanley. This is important evidence for us.

But sad to say, the U.P.A. group was larger and the Ngwizako one too small, and so we were not able to prevent the danger in which we are now.

We agree, it is a serious thing that our brothers have done in beginning to kill the white people, for we know that by talking and agreement the affairs of the country are dealt with.

Nevertheless, Senhores, in all that is happening, we of Ngwizako keep our own point of view. We are waiting permission of the Portuguese Government so that we may appoint a King, or a Regent, since the people are scattered. Since there is nobody on the throne, there is no one who can speak in the name of the Kongo people. We are here as messengers of the people who are in the Congo Republic in order to deal with the matter of the appointing of the King of Kongo, according to the copy of the declaration we have cited. Now very many of those who fled are behind us at this time, for they feel that we must appoint a King in order to bring peace to our country. This too is the right thing.

We ask you then, in the name of God, to help us in whatever way you can in making known to the world how the Portuguese are holding on to our kingdom. That is the way to bring peace to this Kongo of ours.

The Portuguese say that the English missionaries are involved in this war. They are not prepared to see that they, the Portuguese themselves, are the cause, because they interfered with our black kingship. Now they are afraid that in allowing a king they will be chased out, since all Africa now has been enlightened. But now there is nothing we can say except this, help us if you can, so that we may appoint a Regent on the throne.

We know that the King of Kongo received both Catholic and English [Protestant] in our country, for Padre Barroso arrived in our country 13/2/1881 and Snrs. Thomas Comber and George Grenfell on 7/8/1878.

In closing, we tell you again that the Portuguese have interfered with our throne, divided us and brought enmity between Catholic and Protestant. It is this division between the people of one country which has brought all this trouble.

If possible make these things known to Mr. Parsons, for we have already written to him.

Our thanks for everything you can do to help us, for we hope that many foreigners will come to our land of Portuguese Kongo in order to know the real truth of affairs.

Private Secretary:—GARCIA MONTEIRO H. KIASUKA

President:—JOSÉ DOS SANTOS KASAKANGA

3. Letter from Queen Regent

São Salvador

To My Dear Children, Men and Women

Boys and Girls

First of all, I send you my greetings. Secondly, I resolved to write to you to ask you to listen to and accept my plea.

All of you who fled from the towns into the bush where you are living in hiding and where you are being bitten by mosquitoes and sleeping sickness, flies, suffering from hunger, thirst, and all of you who have crossed the border into ex-Belgian Congo where suffering is not wanting.

Come back, NO ONE WILL HARM YOU; DON'T BE AFRAID. Band together in groups, each from his section, that is, the group from Maquela with a white flag, the group from Luvo with their white flag, and the group from Madimba also with their white flag. Come, all of you and present yourself to our authorities. They will receive you with love and happiness; the soldiers will not harm you.

Come with peace and happiness and you will be amongst peace and happiness so that we can all live in peace as we formerly lived.

I speak to you with truth, that this my plea is not intended to call you to suffer; no, no one is going to harm you.

I speak to you with truth, before resolving to write this letter to you, I spoke first with my Portuguese friend, our Authority; we reached an accord on everything that I am telling you in this letter. I repeat, come, don't be afraid, no one will harm you; come show yourselves to the Authorities; I myself can accompany you.

Don't prolong living in this way, in the bush battling a thousand difficulties. If you heed this my plea, I shall be very pleased with you; also my happiness will be more than yours.

I assure you that our Authorities will also be pleased with you.

I am waiting for you here during this month.

Your mother and queen of the Congo ends this message here.

DONA ISABEL M. DA GAMA

APPENDIX D

A FORGERY, AN UNPUBLISHED LETTER, AND A LEAFLET

Portuguese response to the Angolan rebellion included a variety of efforts to discredit African nationalists as Communist puppets, racists, and exploiters. A clumsily forged "secret" letter that was circulated internationally portrayed the rebellion and its leaders as pro-Communist. This letter appears below translated from the French as it appeared in *Carrefour* (Nov. 15, 1961).

The Portuguese public relations effort succeeded in placing articles in massively read publications such as the *Reader's Digest,* i.e., articles by Max Yergan and General Howley. The *Reader's Digest,* moreover, refused to publish a presentation of the African side such as a letter from Holden Roberto, excerpts of which are reproduced as the second document below.

Meanwhile, inside Angola in an effort to destroy the UPA's following, the Portuguese air force dropped leaflets, such as the third document, over the densely forested rebel zones of the north. In condescending language (Portuguese and Kikongo), these red-colored leaflets appealed to personal self-interest and suggested that corruption within the UPA constituted a moral justification for nationalist sympathizers to opt out of the rebellion.

1. Forged "Secret Letter"

Union des Populations d'Angola-UPA
Coin Avenue Mahenge-Plateau
Léopoldville

Strictly secret

Dear Angolan Compatriots,

You must contribute a great deal of money in order to support our friend Patrice Lumumba, whom the tribalists would like to drown. Messrs.

Nkwame N'Krumah and Sékou Touré, our ardent protectors, are at our sides in the struggle against narrow minded men. We have already given M. Lumumba five million [CF] which will undoubtedly enable him to procure the means necessary to regain power and to liberate Angola.

We must also fight against those who wish to form a bloc with outdated tribalists. It is a question of the Azommbo [*sic*] and the Cabinda: they would appear to want to unite with the Congolese. Our faithful collaborator, Alexandre Pedro Claver Tati, thanks to his Cabindan origins, has already daringly launched himself on a campaign to recapture the influence that Abako partisans have been able to establish in the country.

Here in a few words is our future plan: Sékou Touré must rule in the northern part of Africa, Comrade N'Krumah in the center, and your servant Holden Roberto in the south. Just among us, we hope that our distinguished comrade, "The Devil," will help us realize our destiny. Do not believe gossip: Communism is not a bad thing. During our stay in Moscow, we were able to see many magnificent things that Westerners will never have. Inside Angola, arrest the Azommbo who would engage in politics because they are dangerous rivals of ours. Others must understand that Kon Diatontila was by no means any place other than at São Salvador. Why should they, favored by events, assume supremacy. No, no, and no!

Courage! Courage! Money, money and more money! First Lumumba and then us. Comrade "Devil" is here, his eye vigilant. Long live Communism. Down with egocentric tribalism.

Director for Propaganda,
ROSARIO NETO

Head of the East-West Liason Mission,
ALEXANDRE PEDRO CLAVER TATI

President General,
HOLDEN ROBERTO

2. *Extracts from unpublished letter by Holden Roberto to the Reader's Digest*

December 8, 1961

Sir:

A large number of reprints of last month's *Reader's Digest* article "Behind the Terror in African Angola" by Brigadier General Howley are being distributed in the United States. The article attempts to make the point that the Angolans are savages directed by Communist Russia in a diabolical scheme to bring the communists to power in Angola . . . .

General Howley's one correct statement was to the effect that UPA is the leading organization in the effort to liberate Angola and was formed in 1954. Its membership is exclusively Angolan. As of February 1961 it had some forty thousand members in Angola each of whom paid some $0.50 per month as dues. These financed the UPA's operation. After the outbreak of hostilities it was no longer possible to rely on dues of Party members and some aid was obtained from other African countries. We have never had any aid from any communist country and there are no communists among us. I have made many public statements to this effect and a recent investigation carried out by a United Nations sub-committee corroborated this fact. . . .

[Whereas] our resources are modest . . . the Overseas Companies of Portugal . . . have hired a well-known public relations firm, Selvage & Lee, in Washington to engage in propaganda against us. According to *The New York Times* of May 17, 1961, they have raised more then $1,000,000 for this campaign. It is well known that Selvage & Lee have been able to arrange for the travel of American writers and others to Angola where, with Portuguese assistance, they get a guided tour. I suggest that it is no accident that articles which men such as General Howley write, favorable to the Portuguese regime in Angola, are placed in widely read magazines and newspapers. After all, that is the function of a public relations firm.

The George Peabody Agency in New York City has been engaged officially by the Portuguese Government to carry out their propaganda campaign. In addition, the Portuguese have their embassy and consulates, their mission to the United Nations, many private businessmen and a large number of Americans of Portuguese descent all of whom are doing their utmost to present the Portuguese case. When, in addition, they are able to have at their disposal the pages of a widely-read magazine such as yours, it is indeed overwhelming.

General Howley has also been showing to the press a letter praising communism which he alleges I wrote to my compatriots from Moscow. It is a very transparent forgery, it does not bear my signature, and its contents are ridiculous. It is undated as well, perhaps as a defense against confirmatory exposure. I can account for all of my time and I have never been to Moscow or, in fact, to any Eastern country except Belgrade where I participated in a conference of neutral nations. . . .

You have gratuitously done us irreparable damage. I wonder if you would care to rehabilitate your pages by publishing either a statement from me, a piece written by anyone willing to do so presenting the other side of the coin, or even perhaps a precis of the report of the United Nations Sub-Committee whose members, not one of whom is suspected of being a communist, made it very clear that their investigation refutes General Howley in every detail and emphasizes the fact that our fighting force is composed of Angolans, is directed by Angolans, and is inspired by our will to liberate our homeland.

HOLDEN ROBERTO
President
Union of the Populations of Angola

3. Portuguese Leaflet Dropped by Air over Nationalist Territory, January 1962

When you are in the bush fleeing, hungry, cold and sick, when you think a little about the life you are leading, you can't continue to believe in those people who went to beg your money.

Can't you see the women and children starving and dying in pain?

The U.P.A. is lying to you. Your money was taken by the people in U.P.A. who live well and are abandoning you. The U.P.A. is lying and taking you off to war to die.

When there was no confusion, all of you worked in the coffee fields. You went to the store to sell it and you had money with which to purchase cloth, shoes, jackets, shirts, food and wine.

Don't make war anymore. The coffee must be picked in order to have money and food and clothing.

The whites know that the blacks were deceived.

The whites continue to be your friend and are forgiving when the blacks come back to their jobs and take care of the fields.

Coffee brings in money.

If you approach the troops or a post and say that you want to be good again, everything will work out happily. The troops will not harm you and will help you against the U.P.A.

The Army will defend you if you do not want war any longer. The authority will not punish if the black returns to his senses.

APPENDIX E

A PARTIAL LIST OF ANGOLAN NATIONALIST MOVEMENTS – 1944-1962

I. *Luanda-Mbundu*

AN	Angola Negra
CLA	Conselho de Libertação de Angola
CLJCIA	Comissão de Luta das Juventudes contra o Imperialismo Colónial em Angola
CFA-PCA	Comitê Federal Angolano do Partido Communista Português
CVAAR	Corpo Voluntário Angolano de Assistência dos Refugiados
DA	Democratas de Angola
FUJA	Frente Unida de Juventude de Angola
MAJE	Movimento Angolano de Juventude Estudante
MINA	Movimento de Independência Nacional de Angola
MLA	Movimento de Libertação de Angola
MPIA (or MIA)	Movimento para a Independência de Angola
MPLA	Movimento Popular de Libertação de Angola
PLUA	Partido da Luta dos Africanos de Angola
PCA	Partido Communista de Angola

II. *Bakongo*

AJEUNAL	Alliance Jeunes Angolais pour la Liberté
ALIAZO	Alliance des Ressortissants de Zombo
ASSOMIZO	Association Mutuelle des Ressortissants de Zombo
FNLA	Frente Nacional de Libertação de Angola
GRAE	Govêrno Revolucionário de Angola no Exílio
MDIA	Mouvement de Défense des Intérêts de l'Angola
MNA	Movimento Nacional Angolano
NGWIZAKO	Ngwizani a Kongo
—	Nkutu a Nsimbani
—	Nto-Bako Angola

PDA	Partido Democrático de Angola
RCCKP	Rassemblement des Chefs Coutumiers du Kongo Portugais
SARA	Serviço de Assistência aos Refugiados de Angola
UCLA	Union Congolaise pour la Libération de l'Angola
UNEA	União Nacional dos Estudantes Angolanos
UPA	União das Populações de Angola
UPNA	União das Populações do Norte de Angola

III. *Ovimbundu, Chokwe, etc.*

ATCAR	Association des Tshokwe du Congo de l'Angola et de la Rhodésie
—	Chijilochalimbo
CSRSA	Comitê Secreto Revolucionário do Sul de Angola
—	Grupo Avante—Bié
FUA	Frente de Unidade Angolana
JCA	Juventude Cristã de Angola
OCA	Organização Cultural dos Angolanos
SWAPO	South West Africa Peoples' Organization
—	Ukwashi Wa Chokwe
UNATA	União dos Naturais de Angola
—	Vilinga Va Kambungo

IV. *Common Fronts*

FCPPA	Front Commun des Partis Politiques de l'Angola
RDJA	Rassemblement Démocratique de la Jeunesse Angolaise

V. *Cabinda*

AREC	Association des Ressortissants de l'Enclave de Cabinda
CAUNC	Comité d'Action d'Union Nationale des Cabindais
MLEC	Mouvement de Libération de l'Enclave de Cabinda

VI. *Labor Movements*

CGTA	Confédération Générale des Travailleurs de l'Angola
CSLA	Confédération des Syndicats Libres Angolais
LGTA	Liga Geral dos Trabalhadores de Angola
UGTA	Union Générale des Travailleurs de l'Angola
UNTA	União Nacional dos Trabalhadores de Angola

VII. *Guinea-Bissau*

FUL	Front Uni de Libération de Guinée et du Cap Vert
MLG	Mouvement de Libération de la Guinée dite Portugaise
PAIGC	Partido Africano da Independência da Guiné e Cabo Verde

VIII. *Mozambique*

—	Associação dos Naturais de Moçambique
FRELIMO	Frente de Libertação de Moçambique
MANU	Mozambique African National Union
MDM	Movimento Democrático de Moçambique
UDENAMO	União Democrática Nacional de Moçambique
UNAMI	União Nacional Africana de Moçambique Independente

IX. *Interterritorial*

CONCP	Conferência das Organizações Nacionalistas das Colónias Portuguêsas
FACCP	Front Africain contre le Colonialisme Portugais
FRAIN	Frente Revolucionária Africana para a Independência Nacional
MAC	Movimento Anti-Colonialista
UGEAN	União Geral dos Estudantes da Africa Negra sob Dominação Colónial Portuguêsa

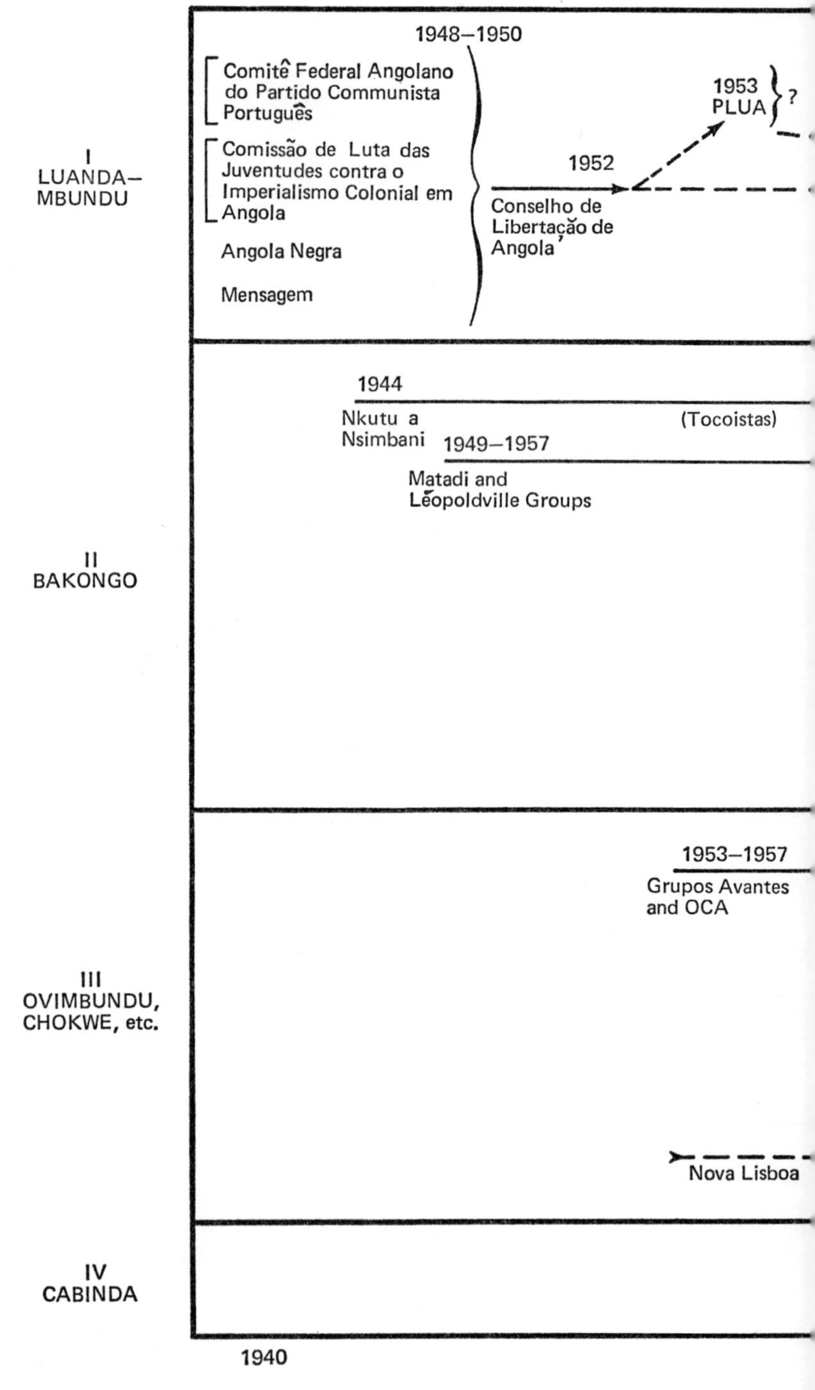

ANGOLAN NATIONALIST
1948–1950
Comitê Federal Angolano do Partido Communista Português
Comissão de Luta das Juventudes contra o Imperialismo Colonial em Angola
Angola Negra
Mensagem
1952
Conselho de Libertação de Angola
1953
PLUA
?
I
LUANDA–MBUNDU
1944
Nkutu a Nsimbani
(Tocoistas)
1949–1957
Matadi and Léopoldville Groups
II
BAKONGO
1953–1957
Grupos Avantes and OCA
III
OVIMBUNDU, CHOKWE, etc.
Nova Lisboa
IV
CABINDA
1940

MOVEMENTS AND ANTECEDENTS

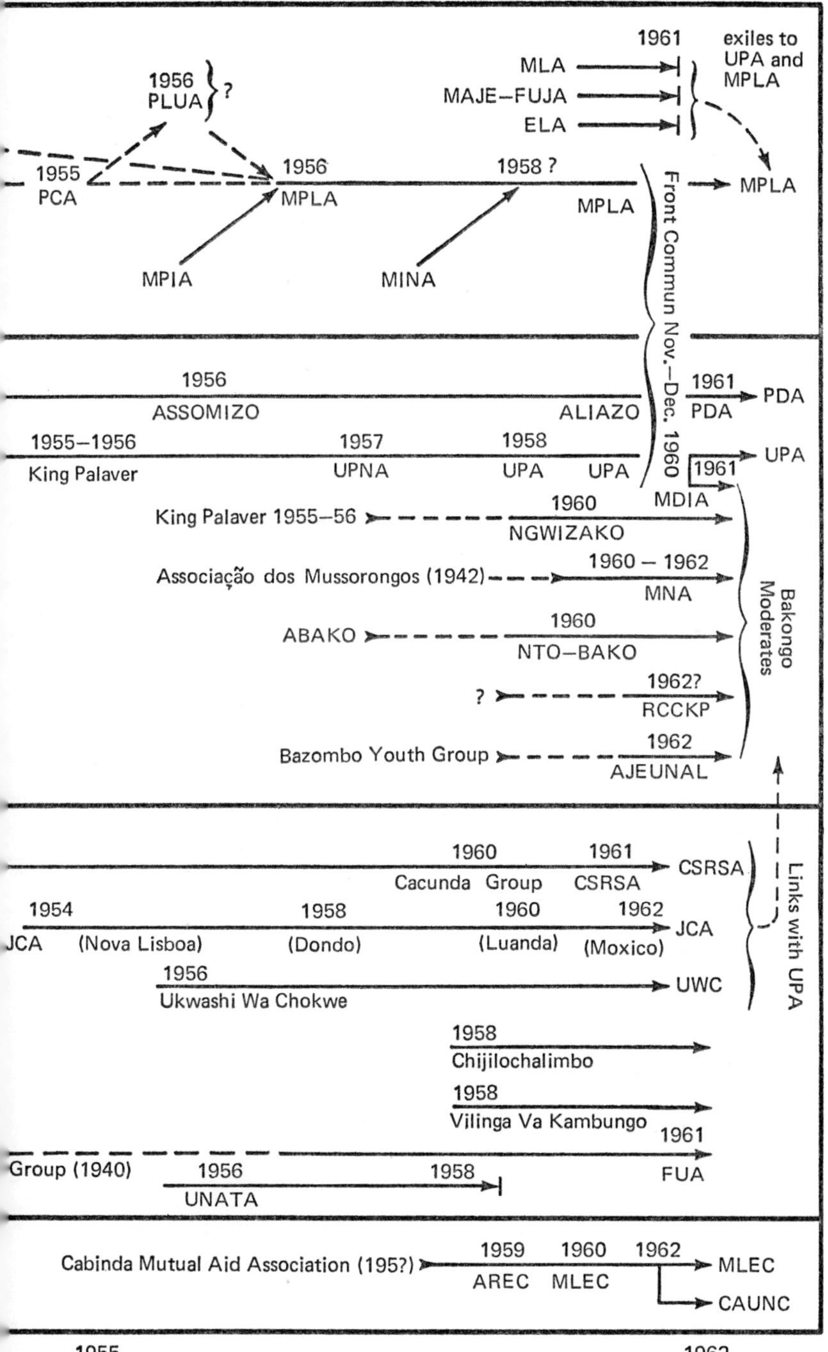

NAME INDEX

Acheson, Dean, 272
Addicott, Len, 55n, 104n, 315
Adoula, Cyrille, 65, 143n, 177, 180, 218, 259, 260, 261n, 312, 318
Afonso I, King, 1, 2
Afonso, Julio, 108, 109
Africano, Francisco José Pereira, 33n
Aguiar, Jordão, d', 94n
Aires, Higino, 33n, *see also* Sousa, Higino
Alberto, Angelino, 93, 221, 234, 235, 289, 290
Albrigado, Samuel, 306n
Allen, George V., 56n, 59n, 62
Almeida, Cândido António Mendes de, 189
Almeida, Déolinda Rodrigues de, 254n, 300, 301, 302n, 332
Almeida, Gaspar de, 110n
Almeida, Jeronimo d', 306n
Almeida, Mateus de, 151
Alvaro d'Aqua Rosada, Dom, 51
Alvaro Nezingu, Dom, 51, 54
Alves, Fernando, 137
Ameal, Jorge, 5n
Anderson, Perry, 140n
Andrade, Joaquim Pinto de, 35, 137n, 201n, 300, 334
Andrade, Mário de, 27–46 *passim,* 93, 94, 126n, 130n, 159n, 160, 162, 163, 193, 203–224 *passim,* 236, 246–276 *passim,* 300–302, 318, 319, 334
André, Manuel, 153n
Antas, Alfredo Furtado, 96n
António III, Dom, 51, 57–59, 63, 91, 168, 339
António, Mário, 18
António, Vasco José, 245n
Arinos, Afonso, 189
Artho, Walter, 306
Assis, Guilhermina de, 300n
Axel, Louis, 188n
Azevedo, Luis de, Jr., 161, 237, 254n, 264, 298, 300n

Balewa, Sir Abubakar Tafawa, 256
Ball, David, 42n
Bangura, Alfredo, 161n
Barata, Óscar Soares, 18n
Barboza, Raphael, 282
Barroso, António, 52, 62, 341
Bastide, Roger, 40
Batista, João, 114n, 135–147 *passim,* 157, 158, 210, 213, 228–243 *passim,* 259
Belo, Octavio, 139n
Ben Bella, Mohamed, 247, 264
Benedito, João Gonçalves, 215–217, 254n, 300n
Benenson, Peter, 38n
Benga, Alfredo, 109n
Benge, António Pedro, 128
Benn, Anthony Wedgewood, 202
Benson, Wilfrid, 65
Bingham, Jonathan B., 275
Birmingham, David, 13n
Blake, C. Melvin, 271
Blakebrough, Eric L., 7n, 148
Boal, Manuel, 300n
Boavida, Américo, 45, 163, 206, 301n
Boboliko, André, 293
Boganda, Barthélémy, 73n, 75
Bomboco, Ferraz, 212, 214, 215, 217
Bomboko, Justin, 179, 259, 318
Bonga, Maurice Kiala, 92, 93
Bongo, Sebastien, 206
Borges, Augusto, 300n

Bourguiba, Habib, 70, 138, 258
Bowskill, J. S., 52, 53, 56, 148, 320–330
Boxer, C. R., 1n
Brancel, Fred, 151n
Brandão, Pais, 47
Brockway, Fenner, 202n
Buta, Alvaro, 52–54, 148, 321–328 *passim*, 339

Cabral, Amilcar, 41, 43, 193, 194, 266
Cabral, João, 54, 161n
Cacunda, Julio Chinovola, 111, 154–156
Cadornega, António de Oliveira, 18
Camacho, Martin T., 132n, 185–187, 276
Campos, David, 58
Canguia [pseudonym for Cardoso, Joaquim]
Canoth, Carlo, 300n
Cão, Diogo, 1, 8
Capinala, Nóe Adolfo, 156n
Cardoso, Joaquim Filipe, 47
Cardoso, Zacarias, 306n
Carneiro, Edison, 202n
Carreira, Henrique, 300
Carrero, Luis Porto, 281n
Carter, Gwendolen M., 5n
Carvalho, Bartolomeu de, 305n
Carvalho, Calvino, 306n
Castelbranca, Hemenio, 47n
Castro, Carlos Gacel, *see* Kassel, Carlos
Castro, Josue de, 202n
Cazuangongo, Dembo, 16
Cemp, Lwiji, 156, 157
César, Amândio, 26n
Chagong'a, José Baltazar da Costa, 198, 288
Chaliand, Gérard, 30n, 193n
Chata, Smart, 118, 119, 156, 157n, 298, 299
Chicusse, Zimtambira, 199
Chilcote, Ronald H., 24n, 102n
Childs, Gladwyn M., 102n
Chilembe, Mayele, 119
Chimbalanga, Maurice, 117n
Chinhundo, Jeremias Cussia Arão, 156n
Chinyama, Osseia Oliveira, 156
Chipango, Brown, 299
Chipenda, José Belo, 108
Chisseva, João, 105n, 106, 107, 129, 297, 298
Chitunda, Jeremias K., 111n
Clemente, Gil, 138
Comber, Thomas, 51, 341
Cooley, John K., 42n
Correira, António Augusto Peixota, 314
Correia, Carlos, 204n
Couderc, Yves, 65, 82
Cox, Richard, 197n
Crates, José E. de Carvalho, 53n, 320
Cruz, Viriato da, 24–26, 32n, 36–46 *passim*, 70, 80, 94, 120, 163, 207, 213n, 252, 254, 266, 280, 299, 300, 302, 318
Cunga, Arão, 111, 155
Cunha, Silva, 79n

Dadet, Emmanuel, 219
Dáskalos, Alexandre, 280
Dáskalos, Socrates, 281
Davezies, Robert, 30n, 128n, 152, 266n
Davidson, Basil, 7n, 202n, 307
Debray, Régis, 308, 309
de Gaulle, Charles, 188, 264, 314
Delgado, Bernardo, 273
Delgado, Humberto, 32, 127, 138, 252
Delgado, Ralph, 103n
Descanti, Dominique, 319n
Deslandes, Augusto Venâncio, 169, 227, 277
Deves (Eduardo) Frederico, 139n, 141, 228, 230n
Dias, Carlos Vieira, 33n
Diasuka, Garcia Monteiro H., 164n, 165n, 167, 168n
Diop, Majhemout, 68
Dirksen, Everett, 182, 183
Diwani, Kibiriti, 198
Djassi, Abel [pseudonym for Cabral, Amilcar]
Djermakoye, I. S., 26n
Dodd, Thomas J., 271
Dodge, Ralph E., 37, 150, 151n, 202, 320, 330–332
Dombele, Bernard, 176, 242
Dombele, Ferdinand, 85, 88, 89, 93n, 171n, 236, 245n, 248, 265, 303
Domingos, José Bernardo, 93, 2[illegible], 212, 235n, 254n, 264, 300n, 301n
Dontoni, Lulukilavo Antoine, 245n
DuBois, W. E. B., 22
Duffy, James, 2n, 112, 127n, 144
Duignan, Peter, 133
Dunbar, Ernest, 187n

Eduardo [Edouard], Johnny, 56n, 87, 134, 139n, 205, 206n, 245n, 248, 264

Edwards, Adrian C., 102n
Ehnmark, Anders, 211
Eisenhower, Dwight, 181
Ekuikui II, King, 103, 107
Estermann, Carlos, 76n, 112

Fage, J. D., 1n
Falçao, Fernando, 281
Fanon, Frantz, 67, 68, 70, 96n, 135, 140, 222
Fanon, Josie, 140
Fele, Buanga [pseudonym for Andrade, Mário de], 40
Felgas, Hélio, 50n, 96, 129n, 143n, 152n, 227
Fellette, Joaquim de, 57
Fernandes, António, 215
Fernandes, Florestan, 202n
Ferreira, Tomas Francisco, 211, 213, 214, 218, 238, 292n
Ferronha, António, 155
Figueiredo, António de, 252
Figueiredo, Elisio, 263
Filipe, Pedro, 306
Franque, Louis Ranke, 174, 295
Fredericks, J. Wayne, 271
Freitas, Georges [Jorge] M., 57n, 94, 206, 254n, 300n
Fret, José, 204n, 306n
Freyre, Gilberto, 40n
Friedenberg, Daniel M., 131n

Gabriel, António, 238,
Gadimpovi, Pedro, 262n, 302
Gallagher, W. J., 188n
Galvão, Henrique, 126, 127, 136
Gama, António José da, 56, 57
Gama, Isabel da, *see* Isabel M. da Gama, Dona
Gann, Lewis, 133
Gayet, George, 188n
Gbenye, Christophe, 207
Gilchrist, Ian, 155n
Gilmore, Haldane C., 52, 65n, 323–330 *passim*
Gilmore, José [pseudonym for Roberto, Holden], 63n, 67, 84n, 97n, 138n
Ginga, Rosa, 59
Gizenga, Antoine, 214n, 261n
Glickman, Harvey, 313n
Goheen, Robert F., 188n
Golden, Wendell Lee, 151n
Goulart, João, 270, 316
Gourjel, Fernando Pio Amaral, 153, 244, 245n, 248, 264

Graça, Desidério da, 204, 254, 300, 302n, 306n
Graham, R. H. Carson, 52n, 53–55, 64–65
Grenfell, F. James, 59, 60n, 143n, 150, 165
Grenfell, George, 51, 341
Grenfell, James, 166n, 339
Grenfell, W. David, 53n, 65n, 76–78, 80, 126n, 144, 148, 166n, 234, 238
Grey, Sir Edward, 4
Gumane, Paulo José, 197, 198
Gwambe [Gwambi], (Hlomulo Chitofo) Adelino, 196, 197, 283

Habsburg, Otto von, 133
Hached, Ferhat, 304
Hagalhãos, Pedro Saldanha, 177
Halleck, Charles, 182
Hammarskjöld, Dag, 43
Harriman, W. Averell, 94
Harrington, Donald, 334
Hassan II, King, 161
Helmuth, Paul, 305n
Henrique Neteyekenge, Dom, 51
Herzog, Arthur, 231n, 234n
Heuval, William J. van den, 261
Hodgkin, Thomas, 8
Holando, Buarque de, 202n
Houser, George M., 55n, 62n, 63n, 64, 67, 132, 153n, 202, 228, 232, 239
Howley, Frank L., 185, 343–345
Huxley, Sir Julian, 202n

Inglês, Guilherme Pereira, 150–151, 153n
Inglês, Luis, 108n, 139n, 292, 298
Inonü, Ismet, 210
Isabel M. da Gama, Dona, 51, 59, 91, 167, 233, 234, 289, 339, 342

Jacinto, António, 24
Jack, Homer A., 55n
Jayle, Christian, 73
João II, King of Portugal, 1
Josias, António Jabes, 93, 94, 100, 171, 235n, 246n

Kajila, John, 116, 117
Kalada [pseudonym for Kassanga, Marcos], 241
Kalei, Gunda C., 243n
Kalei, Paulo da Cunha, 297
Kalundungo, José, 259

Kalutheho, João da Cruz Chisseva, *see* Chisseva, João
Kambandu, Carlos Gonçalves, 297, 304
Kamitatu, Cléophas, 253, 286, 287n, 292n, 293
Kamutuke, Issaias, 109n
Kanga, Edouard, 289n
Kanza, Philippe, 87n
Kapilango, Adão José Domingos, 156
Kasakanga, José dos Santos, 90, 91, 164–168 *passim*, 287, 288, 342
Kasavubu, Joseph, 71, 72, 92, 96, 107 179
Kasdan, A. R., 192n
Kassanga, Marcos, 113n, 114, 135n, 157, 158, 213–216, 237–25 *passim*, 259, 291, 292n, 304, 317
Kassel, Carlos, 176, 177
Kassela, 115
Kassinda, André, 177, 214n, 239–251 *passim*, 291, 304, 310, 317
Kassoma, Luciano, 109n, 111, 156
Kaunda, Kenneth, 67, 299
Kaw, Kenny, 63n
Kayaya, Abreu Moises, 111, 156n
Kaziluki, Augustin, 286n, 287
Keita, Modibo, 301
Kennedy, John F., 94, 182, 186, 187, 189, 202, 222, 232n, 270, 271, 276, 315
Kenyatta, Jomo, 264
Kershaw, Robert, 307
Khamba, J. M. A., 198n
Khatib, Abdelkrim, 209
Khrushchev, Nikita, 130n, 200
Kiala, Gracia, 294
Kiatalua, Norbert, 245n, 248
Kiazindika, André, 294
Kiditu, Dom Manuel, *see* Manuel Kiditu, Dom
Kiditu, Manuel, 56, 57, 59
Kiela, Jacinto Isaias, 259n
Kilouba [pseudonym for Kassinda, André], 241
Kimbangu, Simon, 54
Kingotolo, Antoine, 92
Kitumbi, José, 125n
Koinange, Mibiyu, 311
Kuhangua, Jacob, 305n, 310
Kukia, André, 206n
Kula-Xingu, 125
Kumpesa, Simon, 245n
Kunzika, Emmanuel, 77n, 78n, 83–98 *passim*, 161, 170, 171, 219, 220, 235, 236, 245n, 246, 251, 265, 276, 303, 304
Kuyena, Isaie, 179

Labery, Henry, 310
Lameira, Manuel da Silva, 47
Lange, Halvard, 183
Lara, Lucio, 42, 43, 70, 201, 266, 300, 302n
Lara, Sousa, 42
Larafilho, Ernesto, 281n
Larner, Jeremy, 42n
Lele, François, 290
Lello, Figueira, 59
LeMaster, E. Edwin, 47, 124n, 149, 151n, 191
LeMay, Curtis E., 273
Lemos, Virgilio de, 25n
Lengo [Lengho], João, 54, 55; *see also* Pedro VII, Dom
Leon, Ithiel, 267n
Lessing, Pieter, 130, 131
Lewis, T., 326, 327
Liahuca, José, 178, 232n, 245n, 248
Lie, Trygve, 65
Lijimu, Lackson, 117n
Lima, Manuel, 300, 302n
Lino, Antoine, 293
Lippmann, Walter, 182
Livromentos, David, 171n, 236, 245, 262, 302, 303
Lopes, Craveiro, 105
Lopes, João Vieira, 206, 254, 300n, 302n
Lopes, Zian [pseudonym for Barboza, Raphael]
Loureiro, Emmanuel, 287
Lubaki, Sebastien, 245n
Lubota, Félix, 177
Lubota, Francisco Xavier, 173n
Luiz, Dom, 52
Lukoki, Lozinga, 290
Lulendo, (Francisco) Borralho, 56, 57, 63, 72n, 136, 139n, 304
Lulendo, Pedro Barreiro, 139n, 177n, 304
Lumumba, Patrice, 65, 67, 70, 86, 96, 97, 107, 110, 125, 135n, 147, 318, 343, 344
Lusawovana, Victor Grevy, 289n
Luvinga, J. Maglioni, 298n
Luvuala, Pascal, 176
Luwau, Michel, 95n

Luyanzi, Norman Ambrosio, 59
Luzemo, Antoine, 293

Mabunda, David J. M., 196, 284n
McCormack, John W., 272
Machado, Ilidio Tomé Alves, 33n, 36, 129
Maciel, Arthur, 28n, 32n, 80n
Macmillan, Harold, 188n
McNamara, Robert, 273
McVeigh, Malcolm, 124, 154
Magalhães, 125n
Maholos, Kizamba dos, 48
Mahoungou, Dieudonné, 173n
Major, António Calvino Manuel, 174
Makina, Pedro, 117n
Makonda, Simon, 206n
Makumbi, Edouard, 291
Makumbi-Marques, Pedro, 293
Mansala, Pedro, 288; *see also* Pedro VIII, Dom
Mansianga, Georges, 92, 93
Manuel Kiditu, Dom, 51, 52, 54, 56, 60, 321
Marcum, John, 228n, 232n
Margarido, Alfredo, 25, 82
Maria [pseudonym for Mariano, António]
Maria, Adolfo Rodrigues, 281n
Mariano, António, 48, 124–126, 154, 297
Marof, Achkar, 290
Martelli, George, 134n
Marti, Roland, 72n
Martin, Joseph W., 272
Martin, Sanda, 245n, 248, 302
Martin, Sumbu, 286n
Martins, Cesário, 300n
Martins, Manuel, 56–58
Massaki, André, 83–89 *passim*, 171n, 219, 236, 248, 251, 302
Mathews, Richard, 227n, 234
Matondo, Alphonse, 291
Matos, Norton de, 5, 22
Matumona, Antoine, 77n, 90n, 93, 98n, 170n, 171n, 236, 238n, 248, 250, 251, 254, 262n, 264, 302
Matundu, Albert, 98, 139, 170
Matvin, Feld, 29
Maugis, Marie-Thérèse, 280n
Mazoa, André, 290n
M'Bala, Jean Pierre, 98, 139, 169, 170, 286, 287
Mbande, Nzinga [Njinga Pande], 14, 15
Mbaninu, François, 290n
Mbidi, Emile, 176n
Mboya, Tom, 67, 245, 311
Mbwangungu, Carlos, 113n,
Megalhães, 22
Mekuiza [Mekwyza], José César Correira, 108n, 137n, 178
Melady, Thomas Patrick, 188n
Melo, Anibal de, 87, 137, 139n, 162, 163, 216, 300, 302n
Menderes, Adnan, 210
Mendes, João, 281n
Menezes, Hugo de, 99, 163, 213n, 240n, 254n, 300n
Menga, Antoine, 287, 293
Mengame, Diniz, 197n
Mfutila, 322, 328
Middleton, Drew, 18
Midtsev, V., 253n
Miguéis, Matias, 207, 213n, 215, 216, 254, 300
Miguel, Domingos, 215
Miguel, José, 254n, 300n
Miguel, Soba Manuel, 300n
Milcent, Ernest, 200n
Milks, Harold K., 273n
Millinga, Lawrence M., 197
Mingas, André, 33n
Mingiedi, Simon Diallo, 98, 286n
Mmole, Matthew, 196, 283
Moanda, Faustin Vital, 179
Mobutu, Joseph, 96
Mondlane, Eduardo, 195, 198, 276n, 283, 284, 332
Monteiro, António, 292
Monteiro, Kiangala, 288
Montero, Frank, 132n, 333, 334
Moore, Barrington, 317
Morais, Albert, 281n
Morais, Carlos, 281n
Moreira, Adriano Alves, 166, 191, 260, 314
Moreira, Paulo, 321–329 *passim*
Morgenthau, Ruth Schachter, 27n
Moser, Gerald M., 18n
Moser, Pierre A., 65n
Mouzinho, Antoine, 262n
Muhunga, Ambroise, 117, 118, 156, 298
Mukuma, Dickson, 119
Mulopo, Floricent, 73n
Muntu, Mbutu, 152, 212, 218n
Mussadi, Pedro, 215
Muste, A. J., 65
Mutu-ya-Kevela, King, 103

Muwema, James, 119
M'Vila, André, 171n, 245n, 262n, 302

Nascimento, Barros, 297
Nascimento, Manuel Pereira de, 96n
Ndala, Paulo, 156
Ndimba, Manuel, 288
Ndombe, Francois, 139
Ndombele, Ferdinand, *see* Dombele, Ferdinand
Necaca, António, 56n
Necaca (Manuel) Barros, 56n, 60–98 *passim*, 178, 333
Necaca [Nekaka], Miguel, 52–54, 60 65, 323, 329
Nefwane, Liborio, 59
Nehru, Jawaharlal, 186n
Neto, (António) Agostinho, 35, 37–40, 136, 202, 217, 249, 263–267, 299–301, 307, 318–334 *passim*
Neto, Agostinho Pedro, 330
Neto, João Baptista Nunes Pereira, 28n, 32n, 126n
Neto, Mateus, 306n
Neto, Pedro Vaal Hendrik, 31n, 297, 330, 331
Neto, Rosário, 47n, 48n, 84, 93, 136, 137, 139n, 214, 215, 238–250 *passim* 262, 303, 318, 334, 344
Neves, Daniel, 204n
Neves, Manuel Mendes das, 137n, 248
Ngadimpovi, Pedro, 206
Ngalula, Joseph, 71n
Ngyuvula, Daniel, 323
Nhantumbo, Tomas Betulane, 197n
Nicolas, Prince of the Kongo, 21, 50
Niebuhr, Reinhold, 187
Njapayu, Bennet, 117n
Nkanu, Pierre, 73n
Nkrumah, Kwame, 64, 67, 70, 96, 130, 261, 262, 283, 311, 344
Nogueira, Alberto Franco, 169, 183
Nujoma, Sam, 115
Nyerere, Julius, 311
Nzau, Emmanuel, 73n
Nzinga a Nkuwu, King, 1

Odru, Louis, 29n
Okuma, Thomas, 6n, 155n, 203n
Oliver, Roland, 1n

Padmore, George, 22, 66-68
Padua, Mário Moutinho de, 153
Paiva, Angelino de Castro, 96n
Paka, Francisco, 245n
Parkinson, Mantu, 323, 329
Parsons, Clifford J., 21n, 124n, 140, 141, 143, 146, 150
Passos, Alberto, 204n
Pecado, André, 165n, 168n
Pedro V, Dom, 21, 49-52, 62, 341
Pedro VI, Dom, 51
Pedro VII, Dom, 51, 54–61 *passim*, 65, 164
see also Lengo, João
Pedro VIII, Dom, 51, 288, 289
Pedro, Manuel Bernardo, 141
Peitel, Jacob L., 4
Pélissier, René, 22n
Pereira, Eduardo Vitório, 113
Pereira, João Batista [Baptista] Traves, *see* Batista, João
Pereira, José de Fontes, 19n, 20
Pereira, Pedro Theotónio, 192
Peterson, José Kiasonga Manuel, 85, 86, 139n, 214, 230, 234n. 318
Philip, Dom, 14
Pinheiro, Patricia McGowan, 23n, 29
Pinock, Johnny, *see* Eduardo, Johnny
Pinock, (José) Eduardo, 56–61, 63n, 67, 71, 83n, 85, 87, 89, 107, 108, 125, 136, 211, 218n, 228, 245n, 248, 259, 288, 318, 339
Pio, Eduardo Matoso, 91, 92n, 164, 165
Pires, Alberto, 259n
Pitt, Thomas Fox, 202
Plummer, Sir Leslie, 202
Pongault, Gilbert, 260, 308
Potekhin, Ivan I., 28n
Prado, Caio, Jr., 202n
Putuilu, José Milton, 288, 289n

Quadros, Jânio, 189, 270, 316

Rafael, Luis, 33n
Ramos, José Candide, 174
Rana, Pedro, 139n, 177, 304
Randolph, A. Philip, 188n
Redinha, José, 20n
Roberto, Eduardo, 56n, 72n
Roberto, Holden (Alvaro), 64ff., and *passim*
Robeson, Mrs. Paul, 78
Roosevelt, Eleanor, 131n, 187
Rowe, David Nelson, 278n
Rusk, Dean, 273

Sadi, Pedro, 171
Saitala, Muchima, 116n

Sakaimbo, Kaimbo, 116n
Salamanca, Carlos, 221n
Salavu, F., 243n
Salazar, António, 5, 8, 22, 23, 86, 105, 126, 127, 146, 148, 153, 171, 181, 190, 231, 270–279 *passim,* 314, 315
Sankumbi, 117
Santos, Domingos dos, 300n
Santos, Eduardo dos, 99, 163, 240n, 249, 250, 256, 300n
Santos, Marcelino dos, 161, 197, 213n
Santos, Pedro, 141
Savimbi, Jonas Malheiro, 112, 115, 138, 214n, 221, 244, 245, 248, 258, 264, 304, 306, 318
Savimbi, Lot [Loth] Malheiro, 244
Sayaya, Matos [pseudonym for Savimbi, Jonas]
Scheinman, William X., 132n, 137, 333, 334
Schlesinger, Arthur M., Jr., 187
Segal, Aaron, 39n
Segal, Ronald, 24n
Sengele, Norbert, 259n
Senghor, Léopold Sédar, 203
Sequeira, Loureiro João, 109n
Sequeira, Luis Lopes de, 14
Severino, David Chambassuko, 110
Sidenko, V., 27n, 28n
Silva, António Burity da, 106, 110
Silva, António Simão da, 216
Silva, Christovão da, 151
Silva, Domingos Francisco da, 127, 151, 152, 212, 214, 218, 224, 264, 300, 332
Silva, Samuel, 171n
Simango, Uria T., 284n
Skillen, Edward, 188n
Slim, Taieb, 67
Sobrinho, Pedro, 306n
Soromenho, Fernando Castro, 33n
Sousa, Abilio da, 46
Sousa, André Franco de, 33n
Sousa, Higino Aires Alves de, 33n
Souza, Raoul da, 170n
Stephens, Charles, 232n
Stevenson, Adlai, 181n

Tadeu, Castro, 156n
Taty [Tati] Alexandre, 137, 139n, 174, 243n, 245n, 248, 250, 259, 344
Tavares, Graça da Silva, 254, 299, 300n
Tchiyuka, King of Bié, 103
Teixeira, Bernardo, 144n
Teixeira, Rui, 178
Tevoedjre, Albert, 256, 257
Thomas, George, 7n, 148
Thomaz, Américo, 32, 187
Tiago, Nzita Henriques, 295
Tito, José, 292
Tlili, Ahmed, 176, 258
Toco, Simão Gonçalves, 76–89 *passim,* 107, 279
Toivo, Toivo Hermann ja, 115
Touré, Ismael, 69
Touré, Sékou, 43, 67, 344
Traves, João Baptista, *see* Batista, João
Trovoada, Leopoldo, 31n, 128n, 297
Tshombe, Moise, 119, 298
Tubman, William S., 69
Tucker, John T., 102n
Tucker, Theodore, L., 187n

Valentim, Jorge, 207n, 306n
Van-Dúnem, Carlos Alberto Pereira dos Santos, 33n
Vansina, Jan M., 102
Vasconcelos, Anibal, 281n
Ventura, Rui [pesudonym for Roberto, Holden]
Vetokele, Domingos, 237n, 245n
Viana, Gentil, 300n, 302n
Videira, Alphonse, 306n
Videira, Manuel, 300n
Vieira, Nicholas, 262n
Vos, Pierre de, 179n

Wachuku, Jaja, 256
Wallerstein, Immanuel, 220
Wanga, Jeronimo, 306n
Waring, Ronald, 131n, 144n, 212n
Way, Marion, 151n
Webba, Julião, 152, 153
Webber, Eduardo, 306n
Welles, Benjamin, 190, 270
Westwood, Andrew F., 44n
Wheeler, Douglas L., 1n, 3, 19, 21, 22n
White, C. M. N., 118n
Williams, G. Mennen, 271
Wohlgemuth, Patricia, 276n

Yangha, Thomas, 67n
Yergan, Max, 185, 186, 343
Yevsyukov, P., 253n
Youlou, Fulbert, 73–75, 163, 169, 174, 260, 290, 296, 305
Young, Crawford, 73n

Young, Gavin, 147
Young, Robert, 227n

Zala, Pedro, 237n, 242n
Zangwill, Israel, 3n
Zantura, O. J. [pseudonym for
Roberto, Holden], 68
Zartman, William, 193n
Ziki, Emmanuel, 171n, 248, 264
Zimene, Jacques, 290

SUBJECT INDEX

Abako (*Association pour le maintien, l'unité et l'expansion de la langue Kikongo*), 32, 71–76, 92–93, 100, 164, 178–180, 234, 258, 344
Accra, 64, 67–69, 96–97, 197, 261
  Conference, 42, 64, 67–68, 70
Addis Ababa, 84, 257, 311
African National Congress (ANC), 197
African Service Institute, 261
African Trade Union Confederation (ATUC), 239, 258, 260, 304, 305n, 310
Afro-Americans, 47, 185, 210, 275–276, 303
Afro-Asian Peoples' Solidarity Conference, 160
Afro-Asian Solidarity Conference (Conakry, 1960), 44
Afro-Asian states, 86–87, 163, 181n, 183, 201–202, 209–210, 261, 269–270, 275n, 314–316
  and Portugal, 147
  solidarity of, 224
Afro-Asian University (Tel Aviv), 176n
Afro-Asian Writers' Conference (Tashkent, 1958), 42
Afro-Brazilian Movement for the Liberation of Angola (MABLA), 202
Ajeunal, 290–291, 347
Algeria, 183, 189, 247, 255–256, 258–259, 264, 284, 310
  liberation army, 46, 158, 302
  liberation front (FLN), 70, 158, 175, 241, 247, 258
  provisional government (GPRA), 247, 255, 259n
  workers' union (UGTA), 256
Algerian revolution, 68, 147, 188, 247, 255
Aliazo, 88–89, 161–162, 170–172, 219–220, 347
  and Abako, 92
  and Bakongo bloc, 170–171, 174
  and Belgium and Britain, 219
  and common-front negotiations, 90, 94–96, 99–100, 161–162, 171, 174, 236
  and Congo-Brazzaville, 219
  federalist, 89, 100
  formation, 88–89
  on Kongo kingdom, 89
  and MPLA, 99–100, 161–162, 170–171, 204–205
  and Ngwizako, 90
  nonviolence, 89, 100, 164, 170, 172, 219
  at U.N., 219–220
  and UPA, 88, 99n, 170–171, 235–236
  see also Assomizo; *Partido Democrático de Angola*
Aljube prison, 203, 301, 334
All African Conference, 208–210, 220
All-African Peoples' Conferences, 70, 96, 160, 209, 262
  first (Accra, 1958), 42, 64, 67–68, 70
  second (Tunis, 1960), 43, 70
  third (Cairo, 1961), 160
All-African Trade Union Federation (AATUF), 176, 258n
All-China Federation of Trade Unions, 176
Alliance des Jeunes Angolais pour la Liberté, *see* Ajeunal
Ambaca (M'Baka), 16, 144, 151n
Ambo, 144, 278n
Ambundu, *see* Mbundu
American Committee on Africa (ACOA), 63–64, 69, 132–133, 187, 202, 228, 232n, 239–240, 250, 261, 274n, 333–334
  see also Montero-Scheinman affair
American Negro Leadership Conference on Africa, 275–276, 303

American Negroes, *see* Afro-Americans
Anangola, 22, 24
Andulo, 155, 244
Angola, origins of name, 14
Angola Negra, 26
Angola Office (New York), 304
Angolan Government in Exile, see *Govêrno Revolucionário de Angola no Exílio*
Angolan Liberation Front, see *Front de Libération de l'Angola* (FLA)
Angolan National Liberation Army, see *Exército de Libertação Nacional de* Angola (ELNA)
Angolan nationalist movements
  antecedents, 8–10, 16–27, 46–48, 51–60, 76–83, 105–119 *passim*
  clandestinity of, 10, 23, 31–32, 60, 106–107, 111, 129, 156
Angolan Patriotic Front, 242
Angolan People's Liberation Army (EPLA), 300n, 302, 318
Anti-Americanism
  Angolan 42n, 277
  Fanon, 222n
  Ghanaian, 96
  MPLA, 201
  Portuguese, 110, 155, 183
Anticolonialism, 147, 163, 188, 274, 315
Anti-Salazarists, *see* Democratic opposition (Portuguese)
Anti-Slavery Society, 202
Antonian heresy, 79
Apartheid, 70
O'Apostolado, 137
Arabs, 261
AREC, 90, 95, 99n, 173, 348
Arms, nationalist, nature and source of, 126, 128, 141, 143, 145–147, 161, 179, 211, 217, 222, 229, 233, 258, 261, 277–278, 317
Arms embargo
  against Portugal, 221–222, 224, 268, 271, 315
  against South Africa, 315n
Article 73e of U.N. Charter, 45, 69, 95, 123, 182
Assimilados, 5, 21, 23–24, 26 33n 37–38, 85, 104, 109, 135, 152–153, 170, 192, 195, 218, 331
Assimilation
  British policy *re,* 6
  education for, 20–21, 104
  French policy of, 5, 192
  Portuguese policy of, 2, 4–6, 16, 18, 192
  Protestant missions and, 6, 55
Associação Africana do Sul de Angola (AASA), 106, 109, 113
Associação dos Conguenses de Expressão Portuguêsa, see Ngwizako
Associação dos Mussorongos, 292
Associação Nacional Africana de Moçambique, 198
Associação dos Naturais de Moçambique, 195
Associação Regional dos Naturais de Angola (Anangola), 22, 24
Association des Ressortissants de l'Enclave de Cabinda (AREC), 90, 95, 99n, 173, 348
Association des Tshokwe du Congo, de l'Angola et de la Rhodésie (ATCAR), 117–119, 156, 298
Assomizo (*Association Mutuelle des Ressortissants de Zombo*), 76, 82–85, 88, 98, 170
  see also Aliazo; *Partido Democrático de Angola*
ATCAR, 117–119, 156, 298, 348
Azores Islands, U.S. bases on, 184, 186, 272–274, 276–277, 315
"Azommbo," 344

Baha, 47
Baía dos Elefantes, 156
Bailundu, 102n, 103, 105–108, 259
  area, 155
  campaign (1904), 103
  kingdom, 103
  as pro-Portuguese, 103, 154–155
Baixa de Cassange, 46
  see also Kasanje
Bakongo
  area 1, 33, 102
  in Congo-Léopoldville, 43, 50, 54, 70–76, 84, and *passim*
  ethnic subgroups of, 50–51, 291
Bakongo moderates, 89–94, 98, 139, 164–172, 233–236, 285–295, and *passim*
Bakongo nationalism
  rural peasant orientation, 10, 49, 157
  ties with Mbundu and Ovimbundu streams, 296–298, 318
Bakongo royalists, *see* Matadi Group; Ngwizako

Balari (Lari), 73n
Balombo (Vila Norton de Matos), 111, 155
Bandung, 160
  spirit of, 316
Bangui, 256
Baoio (Oyo), 173
Baptist Missionary Society (BMS), 51–56, 76–80
  African Baptists, 52, 59, 84, 171, 238
  and British policy, 148, 188, 315
  and Buta affair, 320–330
  missionaries, 51–55, 59, 64–65, 104, 124n, 140–150 *passim*, 165–167, 234, 238, 315, 320–330, 339
  Portuguese action against, 53–54, 148, and *passim*
  schools, 53–54, 56, 60, 76–78, 82
  and Tocoism, 76, 81
Baptist Union Assembly, 149n
Barué, Moz., 194
Basutoland, 312
Bavili, 172–173
Bazombo
  area and people, 50, 76–83, 144, 170, 219–220, 235, 285
  "Azommbo," 344
  émigrés in Congo, 82–83, 88–89, 98, 138–139, 170
Bechuanaland, 198, 305n
Beira, Moz., 199
Beja, abortive coup, 277
Bela Vista, 104
Belgian Congo
  Angolan nationalist activity in, 61–66, 70, 72, 82–83
  ban on African activities, 61, 63–64, 66, 78
  education, 20–21, 169
  expulsion of Angolans from, 71
  flight of Belgians from, 123, 133, 146
  involuntary exile of Angolans in, 59
  officials of and Angolans, 58, 63, 71–72, 83
  political activity authorized, 70, 75
  rioting at Léopoldville, 71
  see also Congo-Léopoldville
Belgium
  and Aliazo-PDA, 219, 302
  and Angola, 71–72
  colonial policy of, 8, 61, 63–64, 66, 78
    changes in 70, 75, 82
  and Katanga, 188, 271
  votes at U.N., 189
  see also Brussels
Belgrade, 180, 204, 221, 260, 345
Bembe, 52, 77, 80, 124n, 157, 229, 237–238
Bengo, 37, 39
Benguela, 3, 9, 18, 31n, 102–104, 107, 113, 178, 280, 287n
Benguela railroad, *see* Railroads
Berlin Conference, 1884–85, 3, 52, 74, 167, 341
Berlin crisis, 1961, 184
Bié, 9, 101, 102n, 103–104, 244, 287n
Bocoio (Vila Sousa Lara), 154–155
Boer trekkers, 112
Bolivia, 192n
Boma (Congo), 91, 164, 292
Boma (Moxico), 297
Bourguibism, 146, 219
Brazil
  and Angolan (white) autonomist sentiment, 17
  asylum in, 153
  early influence on Luanda, 21
  as model society, 40
  and MPLA, 189, 201–202, 301
  policy *re* Angola, 189, 201–202, 270, 315–316
  publications from, 23, 78, 108, 305n
  and "Santa Maria," 127
  and slave trade, 2
Brazilian Institute of Afro-Asian Studies, 189
Brazzaville, 66, 70, 73, 86, 98n, 169, 172, 260, 288, 295–296, 308
  Radio, 109, 137
  see also Congo-Brazzaville
Britain, Great, 8, 131n, 197n, 219, 252, 261, 271, 282, 297n, 307, 312
  and Buta affair (1913), 53, 324
  Labour opposition, 188
  and Portugal, 148–149, 163, 188–189, 202, 210, 315
  votes at U.N., 181, 182n, 184n, 188–189
British Cameroons, 66
British observers, 147–149, 212n, 245n, 307–308
  see also Baptist Missionary Society
British Parliament, 149n
Brotherhood of Sleeping Car Porters, 276n
Brussels, 94, 178, 189, 232n
Buela, 229

Bulawayo, S.R., 196
Bunda, 118
Bureau of Educational and Cultural Affairs (U.S.), 184
Buta affair (1913–1915), 52–56, 148, 320–330, 339

Cabinda, 137, 172–175, 287n, 334, 344
 émigrés in Congo-Brazzaville, 172–173
 and forced labor, 52, 321–322
 history and people, 172–174
 and Kongo kingdom, 73
 plantations, 52, 172
 political movements, 90, 173–175, 285, 295–296, 305
Cacongo, 173
Cacunda group (Lobito), 111, 154–155
Cairo, 42, 197
Caluca, 213
Cambo River, 14, 125
Cameroon, 66, 74n
Campanha Nativista, 47
Canada, 155n, 187
Canadian Council of Churches, 188n
 see also Missionaries, Canadian
Cangumbe, 297
Canhangulos, 125, 145
Cape Town, 114, 197
Cape Verde Islands, 36, 40–41, 193, 195, 202–203
Cape Verdians, 194, 309
Carmona (Uige), 9, 82, 141, 287n
Carpio Mission to South West Africa, 269
"Cartel," MDIA-Ngwizako, 287
Casablanca, 160, 176, 258n
Casablanca Charter, 209
Casablanca powers, 160, 203, 254–255, 256n, 258n, 261, 312
 style of, 209
Casas dos Estudantes do Império, 37, 245
Cassange, 15, 124n
 see also Kasanje
Castroists, 219
Catanas, 125, 134, 141, 145, 153
Catete, 15, 28, 37, 39, 264
Catholic Association for International Peace, 187
Catholic Church (Portuguese) in Angola
 action against Protestants, 56–57, 151, 244, 327–329
 in Ambaca region, 16
 attacked by nationalist insurgents, 125, 149
 favors reform, 191
 priests, 1, 35, 49, 52, 57, 106, 137, 149n, 300
  non-Portuguese, 149
Cattier, Congo-L., 63
CAUNC, 295–296, 348
Central African Federation, 299, 305n
Central African Republic, 74n
Centro dos Estudos Africanos, 37
Cercle d'Études Syndicales "Ferhat Hached," 305n
Cercle des Évolués (Stanleyville), 65
Chamber of Deputies, Portuguese, 4
Chetniks, 210, 218
Chicago, conference of African students, 263
Chijilochalimbo, 118–119
Chile, vote at U.N., 181, 201
China (Communist), 44, 176, 189
 see also Peking
China (Nationalist), 278–279
 vote at U.N., 181, 201
Chinese Peoples' Institute of Foreign Affairs, 44
Chinese settlement scheme, 278–279
Chingola, N.R., 116–117
Chitembo, 104
Chokwe, 10, 101, 107, 115–120, 156–157, 285, 296, 298–299
 Angolan-Chokwe nationalism, 117
 emigration to Congo and Northern Rhodesia, 116
 see also ATCAR
"Civilizing mission" (Portuguese), 5, 7–9
 Christian conversion, 40
 conspiracy against, 335
 moral goal of, 131
 persistence despite rebellion, 314
 see also Assimilation
Class conflict, 5–6, 10, 16n, 18–21, 23, 26–27, 36–38, 49, 89, 104, 106, 150, 193, 208, 301, and *passim*
Cocoa, 40, 52, 172
Coffee
 disturbances in region, 35, 134, 141
 exports, 7
 fazendas, 7n, 24, 71, 134, 141, 157, 172, 231
 growers
  African, 141, 216

European, 82, 134
mulatto, 87
port, 291
recession, 123–124, 317
U.S. purchases of, 273
Coimbra, University of, 37–38, 331
Cold war, 10–11, 183, 254–255, 260n, 277, 315
Collaborators, *see* Police informers and collaborators
Colua, 212–214
Columbia University, Andrade lecture, 220
Comcabi, 32n
Comgéral Purigina, 233n
Comissão de Luta das Juventudes contra o Imperialismo Colónial em Angola, 26
Comissão da Revolução Nacional, 136, 146
Comité d'Action d'Union Nationale des Cabindais (CAUNC), 295–296, 348
Comitê Federal Angolano do Partido Communista Português, 26
Comitê de Libertação de São Tomé e Principe (CLSTP), 160n
Comitê da Revolução Nacional de Angola, 237
Comitê Secreto Revolucionário do Sul de Angola (CSRSA), 155–156, 298, 348
Comité de Soutien à l'Angola et aux Peuples des Colonies Portugaises (Paris), 200, 201n
Commission for Technical Cooperation in Africa South of the Sahara (CCTA), conference (Luanda, 1957), 109n
Common front, 95–100, 206, 309–310
initiatives by
Aliazo-PDA, 90, 94, 171, 240, 246, 253–254
Bakongo, 292
Congolese, 253–254
FUA, 281–282
MPLA, 29–31, 43–46, 94–100, 161–163, 174, 203n, 204–206, 220–221, 236, 240, 242n, 249, 253, 263–267, 285, 318
UGEAN, 203–204
UNTA, 176, 242–243
WAY, 307
opposition from
Debray, 309
U.S., 250, 307–308
West, 94–95
policy of UPA-GRAE/FNLA, 43, 70, 94–99, 160, 162–163, 174, 205, 221, 240n, 242–243, 250, 253, 263, 307–310
support from
Congo-Brazzaville, 163
Ghana, 70, 94, 261–263
Guinea, 94
Soviet Union, 253
West, 307
Communist conspiracy or penetration, 26–30, 62, 68, 129–135, 147–148, 165, 185–186, 190, 212n, 231, 232n, 272, 274, 314, 333, 335–336, 343–344
People's Socialist Republic of Nambuangongo, 212n
UPA/Roberto as non-Communist, 68, 97, 231, 344–345
UPA/Roberto as pro-Communist, 96–97, 99, 130–132, 179, 272n, 343–344
and U.S., 182, 190, 250, 307–308
Communists
Angolan, 26–30, 131n, 133
Chinese, 42, 44, 176
French, 27–29, 42, 255
Portuguese, 17, 20, 23, 46, 68
Russian, 29, 42, 252
see also Partido Communista de Angola
CONAKAT, 119
Conakry, 43–44, 46, 69, 93, 96n, 99–100, 159, 161, 194, 205, 220, 235, 262, 264
see also Guinea
CONCP, 160–161, 197, 202–203, 209, 224, 245, 283, 309–310, 349
Confédération des Syndicats Libres Angolais (CSLA), 294, 316
Confédération des Syndicats Libres du Congo (CSLC), 294
Confédération Générale des Travailleurs de l'Angola (CGTA), 293–294, 316
Conferences
African Freedom Fighters (Winneba, 1962), 262, 283
Heads of African and Malagasy States (Monrovia, 1961), 162

Conferences (continued)
Independent African States (Second, Addis Ababa, 1960), 84
Nationalist Leaders from Portuguese Colonies, 45, 196n
Non-Aligned States, First, 180, 204, 211, 260
Conferência das Organizações Nacionalistas das Colónias Portuguêsas (CONCP), 160–161, 197, 202–203, 209, 224, 245, 283, 309–310
Congo-Brazzaville, 1, 162–163, 219, 236, 257, 290
and Cabinda, 172–173
see also Brazzaville
Congo Central (province), 179
Congo-Léopoldville (Kinshasa)
base for Angolan nationalists, 72, 133, 179–180, 233, 258–260, 316–318, and *passim*
and Cabinda, 172–175, 295–296
impact of independence on Angolans, 43, 70–76, 83–87, 109–110, 159
impact of political crises on Angolans, 96, 142–143
political awakening of, 32, 70
and Portugal, 259–260
see also Léopoldville; Léopoldville Group; MPLA; UPA
"Congolans," 139
Congress of Racial Equality (CORE), 276n
Conscience Africaine, 32
Conscript labor, *see* Labor, contract and forced
Conselho de Libertação de Angola, 29
Conservative government (British), 188
Constantine Plan (Algeria), 314
Constitution, Portuguese, 5–8
Contratados, 7, 25, 111, 142, 157, 229
see also Labor, contract and forced
Corpo Voluntário Angolano de Assistência dos Refugiados (CVAAR), 206–207, 301, 305–306, 318
COSEC, 306
Cotton
growing in Kansanje-Malange, 46–49
recession and strike, 124–126, 154, 317
see also Maria's War
Cottonag, 47
Council for Freedom in Portugal and Colonies, 202
Courrier d'Afrique, 236n, 250
Coutinho, Vila, 199
CSRSA, 155–156, 298, 348
Cuamato, 114, 337
Cuanhama people, 4, 101, 114–115, 119, 135, 157, 240, 310, 337
Cuba, 261, 267
Cultura, 33, 280
Cultural organizations, 23–26, 33, 37, 62, 72–73, 108
Curie Institute (Dondi), 60, 105, 110, 178
CVAAR, 206–207, 301, 305–306, 318, 347
Czechoslovakia, 176, 252, 306

Dahomey, 192n, 256
Dakar, 194, 203, 239, 258, 260n, 305, 309–310
Damba, 93, 169, 286
Dange, 141, 143n, 151, 215
Dar es Salaam, 196–198, 283–284, 305n, 312
Declaration of Human Rights, Universal (U.N.), 106, 246
Dembo, 15, 215
Dembos, 15–16, 40, 49, 126n, 130, 145, 149, 151–152, 212, 215, 218
Democratas de Angola, 17, 34n, 35
Democratic opposition (Portuguese), 17, 32, 127
in Angola, 280–281
and MPLA, 208, 252, 281
and UPA, 138, 208
see also "Santa Maria"
Diamang, 150, 233n
Diamonds, 7, 9, 106, 115, 150, 305
Direco, 32n
Diretório Revolucionário de Libertação (DRIL), 129
Disunity, Angolan nationalist, factors in
class and education, 10, 19
cold war, 10–11
ethnicity, 10–11, 19, 86, 119, 210–219, 223, 231, 317
ideology, 11, 242, 252, 263
imperialism, 160
Portuguese policy, 154–155
Dondi, 60, 105, 110, 155, 178
Dondi Institute, 110n, 111, 244
Dondo, 15, 144
Douala, 66
Dragoẽs de Angola, 155
Dundo, 9, 106–107, 115

Dutch occupation of Luanda, 14

East African Federation, 311
East African Goan League, 196
Eastern Europe, 162, 176, 335
École Pratique des Hautes Études, Paris, 40
Economy, Angolan
  development of, 8, 278
  Portuguese asset, 7–9, 20, 24, 47
Ecuador, vote at U.N., 181, 201
Ecumenical Council (Rome, 1962), 303
Education
  for acculturation, 20–21
  areas relatively deprived of, 112–114, 119–120
  Bazombo concern for, 78, 83, 89
  Catholic missions and, 7, 54
  higher, 21
  impact on African society, 8
  initial Portuguese effort, 1
  popular, 105–106, 108–109
  in Portuguese Kongo, 54, 60, 63
  qualification for leadership, 20–21
  reaction of whites to educated African, 150, 153
  reform of, 191
  school population, 5–6
  social stratification by, 19
  use of vernacular in, 54
Egypt, 203, 255, 261
Elite
  black (African), 20–21, 26, 104, 110, 168–169, 263
  évolués of Congo, 32, 65–66
  leadership of, 10, 23, 32, 111, 205, 207–208, 236, 308–309
  mulatto, 20, 23, 26, 41, 106, 263
  white (European), 10, 18, 23, 26, 32
Elizabethville, 84, 117, 156
"Elizabethville," S.S., 298
Emergency Relief for Angola (ERA), 232n, 261
Envol, 236n, 246
Escola de Aplicação Militar de Angola, 213, 240n
Estado Novo, 5, 22–23, 26
Ethiopia, 257
European Angolans
  arrests of, 33–34
  casualties in 1961 uprising, 143, 150
  of central and southern Angola, 17, 103–104, 110
  counterterrorism of, 144–145, 149
  of Luanda, 16–18
  psychology of, 149, 153
  vigilantes, 6, 129, 153, 155
European autonomy, movement for, 17, 280
Evolués (Congolese elite), 32, 65–66
Exército de Libertação Angola (ELA), 32, 129
Exército de Libertação Nacional de Angola (ELNA), 157–158, 175, 216, 237–241, 243, 259, 305, 318
Exile politics, 10–11, 263, 301

FACCP, 309–310
Fascism, 23, 252
Fazendas, 141, 217
  see also Coffee
Federalists
  Aliazo, 89
  MDIA, 287
Fédération Générale du Travail du Kongo (FGTK), 177, 294
Fellowship of Reconciliation, 65
Ferreira affair, 210–219
Fez, Morocco, 161
Finland, 192n
Fishing, 113, 124
Force Publique (Congo), 133
Foreign Ministers' Conference of Independent African States (Monrovia, 1959), 69
Formosa, 278
  see also China (Nationalist)
Fort Roçadas, 336–338
Fourth International, 63n, 218, 261
France
  Angolan students in, 306
  assimilation effort in Africa, 5
  asylum in, 41, 193, 281
  broadcasts by, 109
  colonial policy, 8, 138, 146, 183, 188, 192, 282
  votes at U.N., 181, 182n, 184, 189, 200, 268, 271, 315n
Free world, 182, 224
French Communists, 27–29, 42, 255
French Congo (*Moyen Congo*), 73
  see also Congo-Brazzaville
French Equatorial Africa, 27, 74n, 75
French language, 136, 139, 168–169, 236
French-speaking Africa, 170, 203, 256, 295
French West Africa, 27

French writers, 30, 152, 188
Frente Angolana de Libertação Nacional (FALA), 241n
Frente de Libertação de Moçambique (FRELIMO), 284
Frente Libertadora Moçambicana, 283n
Frente Nacional Angolana (FNA), 253n, 287n, 291
Frente Nacional de Libertação de Angola (FNLA), 245–246, 251–254, 262–267, 302–303, 309, 318
  see also Govêrno Revolucionário de Angola no Exílio (GRAE)
Frente Revolucionária Africana para a Independência Nacional (FRAIN), 34n, 43, 46, 160, 194
Frente Unida de Juventude de Angola (FUJA), 31, 129, 297
Frente Unida para a Libertação de Angola (FULA), 32n
Frente de Unidade Angolana (FUA), 31n, 280–282
Fribourg, University of, 138, 245
Front Africain contre le Colonialisme Portugais (FACCP), 309–310
Front Commun de la Jeunesse Nationaliste de l'Angola, 290–291
Front Commun des Partis Politiques de l'Angola (FCPPA), 95–100
Front de Libération de l'Angola (FLA), 161–162, 204–205, 220, 249, 253
Front de Libération Nationale de l'Angola (FLNA), 238
Front Uni de Libération de la Guinée et du Cap Vert (FUL), 194
Fuesse, 213, 227–230

Gabon, 295
Ganguela (Nganguela), 101, 114, 118–120, 157, 240n
  see also Lwena; Luchazi
Genocide, 72, 87, 249
Georgetown University, Roberto speech, 222
Germany, East, 201
Germany, West, 7, 94, 163, 258
Germany and South West Africa, 3–4, 54, 114
Ghana, 42, 66–70, 96, 108, 255, 256n, 257, 261–263, 298
  Bureau of African Affairs, 68
  and common front, 70, 94, 261–263
  Freedom Fighters Conference, 262, 283
  Positive Action Conference, 70
  Radio, 247
  and Roberto, 130, 261–262
  Roberto-UPNA mission to, 64, 66–69, 83, 135, 171
Ghanaians, 109, 111
Ghardimaou, Tunisia, 175
Goa, 113, 209–210, 224, 271, 316
Goan League, 45, 196
Goan movements, 160n, 197
Golungo Alto, 15, 144, 154n, 300
Govêrno Revolucionário de Angola no Exílio (GRAE), 243–249, 255–263, 296–299, 302–313, 318
  and Abako, 258–259
  and Algeria, 247, 255–256
  and Britain (Roberto avoids), 307
  and Congo-Léopoldville, 258–260
  and Ethiopia, 257
  and French OAS, 258–259
  and Ghana, 261–262
  and Israel, 261
  and Liberia, 257
  and Nigeria, 256
  seeks recognition, 248, 307
  and Sudan, 258
  and Tunisia, 258
  and UAM, 256–257
  and U.S., 258, 267, 269, 307–308, 333, 343–345
Grande Vanguardo-Commando, 240n
Grêmio Africano, 22
Groupes d'Études Communistes (GEC), 27
Grupo avante, 108, 111, 297
Grupo Ohio, 108
Guinea, Portuguese (Guinea-Bissau), 3, 41, 43, 161n, 193–194, 203, 209, 239, 276, 282–284, 305, 309–310, 319
  see also Partido Africano da Independência da Guiné e Cabo Verde
Guinea, Republic of (Guinea-Conakry)
  at Accra Conference (1958), 67
  aid to liberation movements, 255, 257
  and common front, 94
  delegation at U.N., 69, 290
  MPLA headquarters in, 43, 46, 93, 99, 159, 161, 200, 204, 220, 235
  support for MPLA, 203
  and UPA (Roberto), 69, 130, 171
  see also Conakry

Harriman, New York, 275, 303
Health conditions in Angola
 lack of doctors, 38
 nationalist criticism of, 63
Henrique de Carvalho (Saurimo), 119, 305
Houser mission, 228–233
Huambo (Wambo), 101, 102n, 103
Huila plateau, 9, 112, 114, 287n

Iberian Revolutionary Directorate, 127
Icolo, 39, 301
Idealism, 11, 72, 146, 153, 155, 224, 231, 315
Ideology
 Andrade on, 255
 cause of division among Angolans, 11, 242, 252, 263
 Debray on, 308
 Fascism, 23, 252
 lusotropicalism, 40
 Marxism, 18, 20, 27–29, 42n, 44n
 MPLA program, 203, 220–221, 301
 Roberto on, 224
 UPA-GRAE program, 223–224, 248
Imbangala, armies of, 14, 102
Immigration into Angola
 Cape Verdian, 278
 Chinese, 278–279
 Jewish, 4
 Portuguese, 4, 6, 17, 19, 103–104, 112
Imperialists, 160, 203–204, 267, 308
India, 210, 224, 271
Indian Council for Africa, 209
Indigenas, 5, 170, 191–192
Indonesia, 316n
Informers, *see* Police informers and collaborators
Inga hydroelectric project, 73
Inhambane, Moz., 195, 196n, 197
Institut d'Études Politiques, Léopoldville, 88
Intellectuals and protest 13, 20, 22, 24–31, 37, 41–42, 202, 207–208, 302, 308–309
International Commission of Jurists, 34–35
Internationial Confederation of Free Trade Unions (ICFTU), 177–178, 239, 241, 294, 304, 305n
International Congress of Negro Writers and Artists (Second, 1959), 42
International Labor Organization, 36
International Rescue Committee, 261
International Student Conference (COSEC), 306
International Student Union, 306
Iron ore, 7
Israel, 176, 261
Italy, 200
 see also Rome
Ivory, 103, 115

Jabako, 92
J-Aliazo, 205–206
Jeune Afrique, 210
Jewish Territorial Organization (ITO), 3–4, 104n
Jingas, 15
JMPLA, 205–206, 291, 292n
Joint African High Command, 209
Johannesburg, 197n, 232, 284
JPDA, 291
Junta Patriótica Nacional Revolucionária, 210
JUPA, 99n, 136, 205–206, 230, 291, 296–297
Juventude Cristã de Angola (JCA), 105–108, 111, 129, 297–298

Kakonda kingdom, 102n
Kampala, Uganda, conference (1961), 245
Kansuswa (Mufulira), 117–118
Kasai, 14, 15, 106–107, 115
Kasanje
 cotton and prenationalist protest, 46–48
 kingdom, 15, 46
 Maria's War of 124–126, 145, 154
 region, 115, 297, 318
Kasongo-Lunda, 297
Kasonzola, 47–48
Kassanga-Kassinda affair, 236–251 *passim,* 304, 317
Katanga, 104, 113, 115, 117–119, 271, 297–298
 lobby in U.S., 271
 secession, 84, 259, 271, 307, 312
Kenya, 197, 254, 264
Khartoum, 258
Khatib Plan, 208–210, 220
Kidista, 79
Kikongo language, 1, 56, 62, 78, 80, 84, 89, 136, 139, 168, 230, 231n, 339, 343
Kikongo-speaking people, 49–50, 214

Kimbanguists,
in Angola and the Congo, 54, 78
influence on Tocoism, 80–81
Kimbundu language, 26, 40, 62, 80, 84, 230
Kimbundu-speaking people, 13, 16, 66, 214
Kimpwanza, 231
"King palaver" (1955–56), 56–60, 66, 90, 140, 288, 339–340
Kinkuzu, 259–260, 279
Kinshasa (Léopoldville), 50
Kishikongo, 50
see also Bakongo
Kitwe, N. R., 88, 117, 119
Kivuzi clan
Aliazo challenges, 90
destitution of, 58–59, 340
kings, 51, 52n, 56
and Ngwizako, 89, 164
Kizamba, 48, 126
Kongo dia Ngunga (São Salvador), 51
Kongo kingdom
efforts to restore, 8, 56–64, 67, 72–75, 89–92, 164–169, 259n, 287–289, 339–342
history, 1–2, 14–15, 49–63, 320–330
independence of, 21, 50, 61–62, 166
Kwame Nkrumah Institute for Ideological Training (Winneba), 262
Kwango province, 126, 297
Kwango River, 15, 46, 125

Labor, contract and forced, 7–8, 24–25, 36–52 *passim*, 60, 63, 71n, 104–126 *passim*, 141–142, 195, 280, 321
Labor organizations (nationalist), 175–178, 242–243, 293–295, 304–305, 316
Labour party, British, 188
Lagos, 66, 256
Lajes (air base), 273
Land reform, 223
Latin-American states, 87, 269
Laundry and Dry Cleaner Workers' Union (Cape Town), 197
Lausanne, 221
University of, 245
League of Nations, 47
Léopoldville,
Foncobel quartier, 88
Kalina quartier, 78
province, 74, 235
Radio, 86, 207
riots of 1959, 71, 75, 107
Zoo Restaurant, 237, 246n
Léopoldville Group, 60–64
Leua, 116, 156
Liberation Committee for Africa, 210
Liberia, 69, 138, 184, 257
Libreville, Gabon, 295
Liceu Salvador Correia (Luanda), 37, 77
Liga Africana, 22
Liga Angolana, 19, 22
Liga Geral dos Trabalhadores de Angola (LGTA), 177–178, 230, 258, 293–294, 304–305, 316
alliance with Guinea-Bissau union, 305n
and UPA, 177, 239, 240n, 241, 309–310, 318
western orientation, 177, 304
Liga Nacional Africana (LNA), 22–24, 36, 96n, 195, 207
Liga Ultramarina (1910), 22n
Lisbon, *passim*
Radio, 233, 242n, 252–253
University, 38, 40, 178, 331
Loango kingdom, 172
Lobito, 86, 104, 107–109, 111–112, 154–156, 174, 280–281, 298, 335–336
London, 3, 45–46, 51, 189, 202, 206n, 210
MPLA office at, 45, 96n
Lourenço Marques, 195, 196n
Lower Congo, 50, 62, 72–73, 75, 78, 84, 92, 103, 178–179, 207, 219, 228, 235, 247–248, 299, 318, and *passim*
Luanda
Dutch occupation of, 14
ethnic communities of, 16–22, 46
February 1961 uprising, 46, 126–130, 138, 145, 212, 332
"Free press" of, 4–5, 19–20, 22
intellectual-Marxist protest in, 13, 24–37
Methodists at, 149, 330–332
and railroad link to interior, 15–16
and slave trade, 2, 13
tocoistas at, 80–81
Luanda-Mbundu nationalism
conflict with Bakongo, 200–224 and *passim*
core area, 15–16
ties with Bakongo and Ovimbundu, 214, 296–298, 318

urban, elite leadership, 10, 318
Lucerne, 306
Luchazi, 118–119
Lucunga, 227
Lui River, 125
Luimbale, 105
Lukala, 299
Lumumbist cults, 110n
Lumumbist nationalism, 208
Lunda
district, 115, 125, 156
empire, 14–15, 115, 118
politics (CONAKAT), 119
Luremo, 125
Lusaka, N. R., 116
Luso-American, 186–187
see also Portuguese-American
"Lusotropicology," 40, 113, 319
Luso, Vila, 104, 154, 156
Luvale, 119
see also Lwena
Luvo, 91, 92n, 150, 342
Lwena (Luena), 101, 115, 118–119, 297

MABLA, 202
Maconde, 96, 198
Madeira Islands, 112, 164, 185
Madimba, 52, 93, 134
Malange, 15, 28, 46–49, 84, 93, 124–126, 136, 149, 287n, 335–336
Malawi, 199, 312
see also Nyasaland
Malaya, 192n
Mali, 203, 255, 301
"Mamã Negra," 25
Maquela (do Zombo), 50–51, 76, 80, 88, 169, 286
"Maria" movement, 48, 124–126
Maria's War, 124–126, 154, 297
Marimba a Tembo, 125n, 126
Marxists, 18, 68, 263
African, 263, 318
European at Luanda, 17, 20, 23, 26–30, 33
in Portugal, 17
and tocoistas, 80
see also Communists; Ideology
Matadi, 51, 56–60, 62–64, 71, 84–85, 88–89, 91–92, 136–137, 228, 289, 292, 298, 304, 326–328
Matadi Group, 56–63
Matamba kingdom, 14–15
Mayumbe (Maiombe), 86, 173–174, 296
M'Baka, 13n, 16
Mbanza Kongo, 1, 91
see also São Salvador
Mbanza M'Pangu, 229
Mbanza Mputu, 324–325, 327–328
M'Bochi, 73–74
M'Bridge River, 157, 213, 229
Mbundu,
area, 62, 102, 144, 212–219, 285, 320
kingdoms, 2, 13–15, 49
people, 4, 10, 13–16, 102n, 130
refugees, 84, 93, 136, 249, 297
Mbwila (Ambuila), 49
Melègue, 175
Mensagem, 24–26, 33, 41, 280
Mestiços, see Mulattoes
Methodists, 149–153, 320, 330–332
African pastors, 37, 149–153, 218, 330
Portuguese bar, 271
on reforms, 191–192
scholarships, 38–39, 263, 301, 331
schools, 23, 149
witnesses to Kasanje uprising, 47–48, 124–126
witnesses to Luanda uprising, 129
witnesses to northern uprising, 144, 148–153
Miscegination
as conscious policy of, 18–19, 40, 185
as European sexual privilege, 18
see also Assimilation
Missionaries
American, 6, 47, 55, 110n, 126, 151, 155, 192
see also Methodists
British, *see* Baptist Missionary Society
Canadian, 110n, 155
MLGC, 160n, 194, 309, 349
Moçâmedes, 9, 113
Moise Noir, 47
Mombaka prison (Lobito), 155
Mombasa, Kenya, 197
"Monangamba," 24–25
Mondo, 171
Môngua, 337
Monrovia, 69, 161–162
see also Liberia
Monrovia states, 255–260, 312
Montero-Scheinman affair, 35, 132n–133n, 137, 333–338
Morocco, 138, 146, 160–161, 203, 209, 255, 259, 263, 302
see also Casablanca

Moscow, 131, 176, 252, 255, 257, 345
  see also Soviet Union
Mouvement de Défense des Intérêts de l'Angola (MDIA)
  and Aliazo, 98n
  and Bakongo bloc projects, 170, 174, 287
  nonviolence, 138–139, 169–170
  origins and leadership, 98, 138–139
  and PAFMECSA, 312
  and Portuguese, 98, 139, 164, 169–170, 286–287
  and unity talks, 253n, 292
Mouvement de Libération de l'Enclave de Cabinda (MLEC), 95n, 173–175, 295–296
  and Bakongo unity, 170, 287
  and common front, 99n, 161–162, 171, 174, 253n, 292
Mouvement de Libération de la Guinée dite Portugaise (MLG), same as enlarged *Mouvement de Libération de la Guinée et des îles du Cap Vert* (MLGC), 160n, 194, 309
Mouvement National Algérien (MNA), 247
Mouvement National Congolaise (MNC), 96n
Mouvement de Regroupement des Populations Congolaises (MRPC) 73–74
Mouvement de Résistance Bakongo, 74
Movement for Colonial Freedom, 45
Movimento Angolano de Juventude Estudante (MAJE), 31
Movimento Anti-Colonialista (MAC), 41–43, 160, 193–194, 266
Movimento Democrático de Moçambique (MDM), 199
Movimento para a Independência de Angola (MIA or MPIA), 29
Movimento de Independência Nacional de Angola (MINA), 30–31
Movimento de Libertação de Angola (MLA), 30–31, 87n, 128–129, 297
Movimento Nacional Angolano (MNA), 291–293
  and common front, 292
  merger with MPLA, 292n
Movimento Nacional de Libertação de Angola (MLNA), 32n
Movimento dos Novos Intellectuais de Angola, 24n
Movimento Popular de Libertação de Angola (MPLA)
  and Abako, 207
  and Algeria, 255–256
  and Aliazo-PDA, 99–100, 161–162, 170–171, 204–205, 236–237, 240
  and anti-Salazarists, 127, 208, 252, 281
  army (EPLA), 300n, 302
  and Brazil, 189, 190n, 201–202
  and Britain, 45, 202
  and Casablanca states, 203, 254
  and common front, 29–31, 43–46, 94–100, 161–163, 174, 203n, 204–206, 220–221, 236, 240, 242n, 249, 253, 263–267, 285, 318
  and Congo-Léopoldville, 159, 207, 252, 308
  European and socialist orientation, 45, 252, 253
  early exile organization, 37–46
  First National Conference (1962), 43n, 300–302
  on forced labor, 36
  and France, 130, 200
  and Germany, 94, 201
  "honorary president," 40, 263–264, 299–301
  Léopoldville committee, 57n, 93–94, 99, 100n, 161, 235n
  Léopoldville headquarters, 200, 204, 207, 220
  and Luanda uprising, 127–130
  Manifesto, 30, 43–44
  membership, 45, 254
  and MLEC, 171
  and Morocco, 161
  mulatto leadership, 208, 236, 302, 318
  nonaligned, 208, 254–255, 301
  non-Communist, 220, 252, 307
  and northern uprising, 152
  origins, 28–30
  program, 203, 220–221, 301
  and "progressive forces" of world, 203
  and Senegal, 203
  and Soviet Union, 130n, 200, 252–253
  steering committee, 39, 45, 204–205, 207, 240n, 249, 251, 254, 300
  and UPA/GRAE, 43, 70, 94–100, 159–164, 162, 200, 205–208, 210–219, 236–238, 240, 247, 249–252, 262–267, 285, 308, 318, and *passim*

and U.S., 94, 201–202, 220–221
and Western Europe, 200
women's organization (OMA), 300n
see also Communist conspiracy or penetration; CONCP; CVAAR
Movimento de Unidade Democrática-Juvenil (MUDJ), 38
Moyen Congo, 73, 172
see also Congo-Brazzaville
Moxico, 104, 115–116, 156, 244, 297
Mozambique, 3, 32, 41–42, 69, 109, 127, 137, 146, 193–199, 203, 209, 269, 271, 274, 276, 282–284, 310, 316, 319, 332
Mozambique African National Union (MANU), 196–197, 283
M'Pangala, 229, 231
MPLA, *see Movimento Popular de Libertação de Angola*
Muceques, 26, 33, 37, 129
Muchikongo, *see* Bakongo
Mucondo, 152–153
Mueda, 198
Mufulira, Kansuswa African Township, 117–118
Mulattoes, 1, 4, 18–20, 22–24, 26, 33, 37, 41, 47, 106, 113, 137, 153, 172–173, 193, 204n, 208, 236, 302, 318, and *passim*
Multiracialism, 6, 18–19, 40, 45, 186, 195, 281
see also Assimilation; "Civilizing mission"
Municipal councils made elective, 192
Mussuco, 125

Nambuangongo, 66, 141, 143n, 145, 151–153, 210–219
Napalm, 224, 229, 230n
National Association for the Advancement of Colored People (NAACP), 276n
National Broadcasting Company, 227–228
National Council of Churches, Africa Committee, 187, 188n
National Editorial Association, 272
National Urban League, 276n, 333
Nationalist movements, Angolan
antecedents, 8–10, 16–27, 46–48, 51–60, 76–83, 105–119 *passim*
clandestine nature, 10–23, 31–32, 60, 106–107, 111, 129, 156
Ndongo kingdom, 2, 13–15, 49
Ndulu kingdom, 102n
Negage air base, 277
Negroes, American, *see* Afro-Americans
Neocolonialism, 160, 203, 267, 308
Néo-Destour, 138
Netherlands, 200, 306
New Delhi, 209, 224
New England, 185–186
New Guinea, 316n
New York, 69, 95, 97, 132, 137, 185, 210, 219–221, 228n, 232n, 237, 241, 261, 274, 297, 304, 308, 345
Ngola, 14, 62
Ngolo Ritmo, 33n, 207
"Ngolas," 15
N'Gunda, 229
Ngwizako (*Ngwizani a Kongo*)
and Abako, 92
and Aliazo, 90
and Bakongo bloc, 170, 174, 287
and common front, 94, 99n, 253n, 292
and negotiations for Kongo kingdom, 90–92, 100, 164–168, 287–289, 293, 339–342
and Nto-Bako, 289
origins, 90
and PAFMECSA, 312
and UPA, 92, 233, 287, 341
Nhaneka-Humbe, 112–114, 119
Nigeria, 66, 256
Nkutu a Nsimbani (*Solidarité*), 78
Nogueira Co., 64–66
Nonalignment, 180, 204, 208, 223, 246, 254–256, 301
Nonviolence,
Aliazo, 89, 100, 164, 170, 172, 219
MDIA, 98, 138–139, 287
Ngwizako, 166
UPA, 87, 100, 139
Noqui, 79, 136, 289, 324, 328
North Africa, 158, 175, 282, 335–336
North Atlantic Treaty Organization (NATO)
and Algerian war, 183
allies and Portugal, 148, 188–189, 201, 204, 224, 268–269, 274, 276, 315
arms in Angola, 144, 183–185, 201, 232n, 275, 277n
and Khatib plan, 208–210
meeting of, 183
re Portugal and Angola, 132, 188
Portuguese membership in, 148, 188
see also Azores Islands

North versus south in Angola, 236, 245, 256
Northern Rhodesia, 104, 116–120, 298–299
  Angolan education in, 10, 88, 116n
  education in, 6
  see also Ukwashi Wa Chokwe
Norway, 183
Nova Caipemba, 141, 152–153, 218
Nova Lisboa, 60, 104–107, 109–112, 135, 154–155, 157, 177, 213, 229, 240n, 280, 335–336
Novo Redondo, 156, 174, 207
Nto-Bako Angola, 92–94, 99n, 100, 164, 169–170, 221, 234–235, 289–290, 316
Nyasaland, 198, 284
N'zassi, 174

Ochimbundu, *see* Ovimbundu
Office of Munitions Control, U.S., 184
Olongende, 108
Onjiva (Vila Pereira de Eca), 115, 337
Oporto, 191, 301
  University of, 331
Organização Cultural dos Angolanos (OCA), 108–109
Organização das Mulheres de Angola (OMA), 300n
Organization of African Unity (OAU), 96n, 316
Organization of Arab Students in the USA, 11th convention, 306n
Ovambo, 114, 310
  see also Cuanhama people
Ovamboland, 114–115
Ovamboland People's Organization (OPO), 114
Overseas Companies of Portugal, 185n, 186, 345
Overseas Territories, Portugal, 5
Ovimbundu, 138, 154–156, 178, 221, 248
  area 104, 285
  kingdoms, 101–103
  people, 4, 10, 62, 101–112, 178, 244, 296
  traders, 104, 115
Ovimbundu-Chokwe nationalism
  sources, 10
  ties with Bakongo, 244, 296–298, 318

Pan-African Congress, Third (Lisbon), 22
Pan-African Freedom Movement for East, Central and Southern Africa (PAFMECSA), 311–313, 316
Pan-Africanism, 73, 209, 309–313, 316
  and Ghana, 64, 67–69
Pan-Africanist Congress (PAC), 197, 311
Panzi district, 126
Paris
  correspondence courses from, 88–89
  FUA exiles in, 281
  MPLA leaders and, 41–42, 94, 96n, 111, 194, 200, 300
  University of, 306
  see also France
Partido Africano de Independência (PAI), same as enlarged *Partido Africano de Independência da Guiné e Cabo Verde* (PAIGC), 46, 160, 193–194, 282–283, 310
  see also Guinea, Portuguese
Partido Communista de Angola (PCA), 27–30, 40n
Partido Democrático de Angola (PDA)
  and common front, 236, 240, 246n, 253–254
  creation of, 235
  and FUA, 281n
  in GRAE/FNLA, 302–304, 318
  middle-class movement, 303
  and MPLA, 236–237, 240, 246n, 265–266
  and Simão Toco, 279
  and UPA, 235–236, 245–246, 248, 250
Partido de Libertação de Moçambique, 197n
Partido da Luta dos Africanos de Angola (PLUA), 28–30
Partido Nacional Africano (PNA), 21–22
Pastoral letter, Catholic hierarchy of Angola, 191
Peking, 252, 257
  Radio, 44
  see also China (Communist)
Pende, 14
Pennsylvania, University of, Roberto speech, 222
Pereira de Eça, Vila (Onjiva), 115, 337
Petitions to the United Nations, 24n, 26, 43, 45, 61–63, 65, 69, 87, 95, 99, 138, 143, 151, 173–174, 254–255, 277, 281, 287, 289

Petroleum, 7
Pigiguiti Quay, massacre of, 193
Poets and protest, 24–26, 38–40, 280
Pointe Noire, 66, 73n, 162, 172, 207, 305
Police
  African, 104
  Belgian, 63n
  Congolese, 234n
  Katangese, 297
  Portuguese, 10, 27, 31–33, 39, 59, 83, 110–111, 128–129, 140, 149, 155, 169, 173–174, 202, 245, 282, 317
  South African, 115, 197n
Police informers and collaborators, 10, 93, 107, 170, 196n, 245, 285–286, 289
Polícia International de Defesa de Estado (PIDE), 31n, 33, 36, 41, 96n, 107, 109, 115, 120, 138, 154–155, 164–165, 173, 194, 196n, 266n, 280–281, 297, 334
Ponta Albina lighthouse, 80
Population of
  Angola, 5, 10
  Bailundu, 103
  Bakongo, 50, 290
    émigrés in Congo-Léopoldville, 72
  Bazombo, 76
  Bembe, 77n
  Cabinda, 172, 295
  Chokwe émigrés in Northern Rhodesia, 116
  Chokwe in Angola, 115
  Cuanhama, 115
  eastern Angola, 4
  Ganguela, 118
  Kongo kingdom, 1
  Luanda, 20
  Lwena and Luchazi in Northern Rhodesia, 118
  Mbundu, 16
  Mozambique, 195
  mulatto, 18
  Nhaneka-Humbe, 112
  Ovambo, 114
  Ovimbundu, 62, 101, 105, 178
  Portugal, 4–5
  Portuguese in Angola, 6, 17
  Portuguese Guinea, 193
  Protestants, 55, 76, 105
  Quibocolo, 76
  refugees in Congo, 227
  Sá da Bandeira, 113
  São Salvador, 51
  Sorongo, 291
Porto Alexandre, 80, 156
Porto Amboim, 102
Porto Amélia, Moz., 198
Portugal
  air force, 35, 144–145, 152–153, 227, 229–231, 235, 273, 277, 343, 345–346
  democratic republic, 4, 17, 21–22
  economic relationship with Angola, 7–9
  Estado Novo, 5, 23, 146, 153
  illiteracy in, 5
  National Assembly, 110, 190n, 192
  nationalism, 3, 5, 9, 127, 149, 190, 314
  navy, 35
  population of, 4–5
  public relations, 185–187, 272, 276, 345
Portuguese-American Committee on Foreign Affairs, 132, 185–187, 221, 272, 276
Portuguese-Americans, 185–186, 345
Portuguese Angolans, *see* European Angolans; Portuguese settlers
Portuguese army, 16, 18–19, 35, 39, 44, 86, 125, 194, 199, 282, 284, 333–338, 346
  African soldiers
    defecting, 111, 135–136, 142, 157, 174, 198, 229, 240n, 259
    loyal, 151n, 155
  brutalized by war, 153
  counterinsurgency (1962), 229–230, 277–279
  psychosocial campaign, 279
  Recruit School, 333
  suppresses 1961 rebellion, 144–145, 153, 192–193, 210, 212, 227
  training documents of, 35, 333–338
Portuguese colonialism
  expansion, 2–4, 13–16, 19, 49–50, 102–103, 112, 115–116
  policy, 5–10, 18–19, 48, 51–60, 70, 103–104, 110, 112–114, 150, 186, 220, 278–279, 314–315, and *passim*
Portuguese cultural impact
  on Bakongo, 1–2, 50
  on Luanda, 16–18
  on southerners, 112, 236
Portuguese immigration, *see* Immigration into Angola

Portuguese language, 21, 54, 65, 230–231, 343
Portuguese settlers, 6, 9, 17, 24, 86, 103–104, 112–113, 129, 153, 155, 172, 195, 278
  see also European Angolans; Immigration into Angola
Portuguese students, 37, 68
Positive Action Conference for Peace and Security in Africa (Accra), 70
Potemkin villages, 230
Prague, 176, 252
Présence Africaine, 42, 203
Press
  absence of free, 7, 129, 143, 154
  Angolan nationalist, 87, 171, 207
  censorship of, 5, 22, 126, 129
  foreign in Angola 127, 129–134, 272
  "free press" of Luanda, 4–5, 19–20, 22
  mulatto protest journalism, 19–20
Press, world, and African nationalists
  American, 45, 129n, 185–187, 227
  Brazilian, 189n–190n
  British, 147, 220, 245n, 307
  Congo-Brazzaville, 174, 295
  Congo-Léopoldville, 71n, 296
  Communist, 28, 42n, 255
  French, 28n, 30n, 130, 179, 200, 215–216, 255, 319
  Ghanaian, 68
  Luandan, 33n–34n, 87
  Protestant and Catholic, 83, 88, 236n, 250
  South African, 199, 310
  Soviet, 28n, 42, 176
Primavera farm, 134, 141
Prophet sects, *see* Syncretic religions
Protestants
  African attitudes toward, 55, 146
  barred from Cuanhama region, 114
  decline in missionary personnel, 6, 271
  Portuguese harrassment of, 6, 53–55, 147–154, 155n, 271
  schools, 23, 53–54, 60, 65, 76–77, 82, 88–89, 105, 108, 110–111, 149, 178, 244, and *passim*
  see also Baptist Missionary Society; Methodists; Missionaries; United Church of Christ
Provisional Government (of Angola), 243–244, 247–248
  see also Govêrno Revolucionário de Angola no Exílio (GRAE)
Puri, 141

Quanza Norte, 126n, 151
Quanza Sul, 126n
Quela, 125n
Quessua, 23, 124, 149
Quibocolo (Kibokolo), 52, 76–77, 79, 144, 145n, 148, 169, 171, 286, 321, 326–328
  Protestant Choir of, 77
Quicabo, 141
Quicuzo, 141
Quimbumbe, 141
Quioco, *see* Chokwe
Quitexe, 141, 143n, 152, 212

Rabat, 161, 197, 203, 209n, 220, 264, 283
Racial attitudes, 5–6, 20, 26, 40, 45, 55, 81, 106, 144, 185, 187, 208, 249, 265, 343, 345–346
Radio Free Europe, 186
Railroads
  Benguela, 104, 106, 116n, 188, 207, 244
  Léopoldville-Matadi, 56, 88
  Luanda-Malange, 15–16, 28
  Pointe Noire-Brazzaville, 172
Rassemblement des Chefs Coutumiers du Kongo Portugais (RCCKP), 253n, 293
Rassemblement Démocratique de la Jeunesse Angolaise (RDJA), 206
Reader's Digest, 185–186, 343–344
"Realization," by A. Neto, 39
Rebellion of 1961, 123–158, 210–219
  atrocities, 143–145, 150, 174, 201, 220
  casualties, 150, 222
  guerrilla phase, end of 1961, 222, 227–233
  long-term causes, 5–8, 25–26, 43–44, 54, 60–61, 110, 140, 142, 148, 280
  short-term causes, 48, 59–60, 71, 123–124, 317
  see also Uprising of March 1961
Red Cross, 206n, 232
Reforms (colonial)
  advocates of, 17, 22–23, 56–60, 113–114, 187, 190–191, 223, 268, 271, 315
  failure to effect, 27, 192, 314–315
  opposition to, 6, 190, 314–315
  Portuguese, 190–193, 279–280

Refugees, 145, 227–228, 232–233, 279, 290n, 342
Cabindan, 174
inside Angola, 228, 232
relief programs for, 178, 206–207, 232, 261, 301, 305–306
Religion, *see* Catholic Church; Missionaries; Protestants; Syncretic religions
Religious protest, *see* Syncretic religions
Réunion de Consultation et d'Étude pour le développement de la lutte des Peuples des Colonies Portugaises (1957), 41n
Revolt of Chief Buta, *see* Buta affair
Revolution, study of, 37, 282n
Revolutionary Government of Angola in Exile, see *Govêrno Revolucionário de Angola no Exílio* (GRAE)
Rhodesia, 251
Rio de Janeiro, 96n, 189
Rome, 138, 300, 303
Rosicrucians, 82, 89
Rubber, 103, 115

Sá de Bandeira (Lubango), 107, 111–114, 135, 154, 157, 244, 287n, 335–336
Salazarist regime, 5, 17
Salisbury, S. R., 117, 198
Salvation Army School, Léopoldville, 82, 88, 246, 302
"Santa Maria," 126–127, 136, 198
Santa Maria Island, 273
Santo António do Zaire, 289, 291–292, 335–336
São Paulo, Brazil, 96n, 202, 301
São Salvador, 1–2, 49–65, 76, 80, 84–85, 91–93, 140–141, 150, 164–169, 213–214, 229, 230n, 239, 249, 286, 288, 320–330, 333, 344
São Tomé, 1, 19, 40–41, 52, 60, 280, 321
São Tomé and Principe, 22, 52, 203, 204n, 310
Saurimo (Henrique de Carvalho), 118
Scandinavia, 189, 200
Sele, 103, 177
Self-determination, 6, 44, 69, 75, 138, 166, 171, 188, 190, 221, 236, 260, 271, 279, 285, 315
Selvage and Lee, 185, 272, 274n, 345
Seminar on the Problems of Portuguese Colonies (New Delhi), 209, 224
Senegal, 189, 194, 203
Serviço de Assistência aos Refugiados de Angola (SARA), 178, 206, 230, 232n, 248, 261, 305–306, 309, 318
Sharpeville, 198
Sikama, 83, 88
Silva Porto (Bié), 104, 108, 155, 244, 287n, 335–336
Silver, Portuguese search for, 13
Simulambuco, Treaty of, 174, 295
Slave trade, 1–2, 13–14, 19, 49, 102–103, 115, 172, 195
Sociedade Cultural de Angola, 33
Solidariedade Africana para a Independência de Angola (SAIA), 32n
Songo, 141
Songololo, 58, 211, 326
Sons of Angola, 17
Sorongo (Solongo), 291–292
"So Santo," 25
Sousa Lara, Vila (Bocoio), 154–155
South Africa, Republic of, 70, 112, 114–116, 120, 192, 195–198, 262, 274, 278, 310–312, 315n
South African mines, 195–196, 197n, 312
South West Africa, 3–4, 35, 114–115, 263, 269, 278n, 297, 305n, 310–311
South West Africa National Union (SWANU), 263n
South West Africa People's Organization (SWAPO), 114–115, 263n, 278n, 310–311
South West Africa Trade Union League (SWATUL), 305n
Southern Africa, 209, 256, 268
Southern Christian Leadership Conference, 276n
Southern Rhodesia, 116–117, 196–198
Southerners (Angolan), 236–237, 259
Soviet Union, 23, 133, 176, 182–183, 186, 189, 200, 252, 270–271, 276
agent, 29
writers, 27n, 28
see also Submarines, Russian
Spain, 189, 192, 206n, 258, 268, 274
Student Non-Violent Coordinating Committee, 276n
Students, Angolan
Luandan, 31, 128n, 296–297
organizations of, 203–204, 306

Students, Angolan (continued)
Ovimbundu, 101, 108–112, 138, 178, 245
in Paris, 42n, 306
in Portugal, 37, 184, 293, 245
in United States, 184, 263, 306, 308
Submarines, Russian, 202, 333, 335–336
Sudan, 192n, 258
Sugar, 41
Swedish writers, 211
Swiss Friends of Angola, 306
Switzerland, Angolans in, 138, 306
Syncretic religions
at Bela Vista, 104
Kasonzola, 47–48
Kidista, 79
Kimbanguism, 54
Lumumbist cults, 110n
Maria, 48, 124–126
repression of, 48
Tocoism, 79–82

Tanganyika, 196–198, 284, 305n
Tanganyika Africa National Union (TANU), 196, 197n, 283–284
Tanganyika Mozambique Makonde Union (TMMU), 196
Tchintanzi, 174
Tchiyaka kingdom, 102n
Terceira Island, 273
Thysville, 66, 86, 88, 132, 259
Timor, 47, 316n
Tocoism, 79–82
Tocoistas, 80–82, 107, 279
Tombôco, 152n, 210, 213, 292n
Torre de Vigia, see Watch Tower movement
Trial of Fifty, 34–35
Tribalism, 45, 67, 131, 144–145, 218, 221, 231, 237, 242n, 249, 265, 344
Tripolarity in Angolan nationalism, 10
Trotskyite, 63n, 218
Tunis, 43, 70, 94, 96n, 97, 138, 140, 143, 158, 194, 258, 304
Tunisia
embassy at Léopoldville 96, 136, 138
relations with UPA/Roberto, 70, 96, 136, 138, 143, 161, 176–178, 182n, 229, 241, 247, 258–259, 310
at U.N., 138, 146
Turkey, 181, 210

Ubangi-Shari, 73, 74n, 75
Ucua, 141, 144, 152, 210, 215, 217, 229
Ukwashi Wa Chokwe, 116–119, 156–157, 298–299
Umbundu, 84, 191, 102n, 104, 154–155, 174, 298
region, 111–112
União Democrática Nacional de Moçambique (UDENAMO), 160n, 196–198, 283
União Geral dos Estudantes da Africa Negra sob Dominação Colónial Portuguêsa (UGEAN), 203–204, 306, 318
União Geral dos Trabalhadores da Guiné (UGTG), 305n
União Nacional Africana de Moçambique Independente (UNAMI), 198, 283
União Nacional dos Estudantes Angolanos (UNEA), 108n, 128n, 306, 309, 318
União Nacional para a Independência Total de Angola (UNITA), 112n, 115
União Nacional dos Trabalhadores de Angola (UNTA), 160n, 175–176
and common front, 176, 205, 242–243, 253n, 294, 305, 318
and Communist ties, 176
and MPLA, 160n, 176, 242
União dos Naturais de Angola (UNATA), 113–114, 135, 157
União das Populações de Angola (UPA)
and Abako, 72–76, 92, 178–180, 344
and Algeria, 70, 158, 175, 241, 310
and Aliazo/PDA, 84–85, 88, 170–171, 235–236, 245–246, 248, 250, 318
in Angola, 83–84, 97, 227–233, 331, 343
and anti-Salazar democrats, 86, 138, 208
and *assimilados,* 152, 218
and Brazil, 189n
and Britain, 182n, 307
and Catholics, 55, 62, 249, 265
and common front, 43, 70, 94–99, 160, 162–163, 174, 205, 221, 240n, 242–243, 250, 253, 263, 307–310
and CONCP, 160
and Congo-Léopoldville, 71–76, 83–87, 96–97, 133, 142–143, 159, 178–180, 233, 258–259, 307–308, and *passim*
early organization, 83–88, 96–100
and FACCP, 309–310

and France, 182n
in Luanda, 64, 68, 108, 135, 137, 145
and March 1961 uprising, 130–147
and Mbundu, 48, 93, 145, 244, 297
and MDIA, 98–99, 138–139
membership, 97n, 142, 344–345
and MLA, 297
and MPLA, 43, 70, 94–100, 159–164, 200, 205–208, 210–219, 236–238, 240, 247, 249–252, 262–267, 285, 308, 318, and *passim*
and mulattoes, 137, 152–153, 218, 249
Necaca's leadership, 96–98, 139n, 333
and Ngwizako, 92, 233, 340
and nonalignment, 223, 246
and nonviolence, 68, 87, 100, 135, 138–140, 145–146
and Ovimbundu, 138, 157, 244, 297–298
peasant rural orientation, 152, 245
program, 223–224, 248
relations with Communists, 68, 96, 99, 167, 179, 231–232, 343–345
Roberto's leadership, 84–87, 94, 97–99, 179, 182–183, 186, 189n, 223, 238, 242, 249, 272n, 318, 343–345
and Soviet Union, 253, 344–345
steering committee, 85, 87, 97, 213
and SWAPO, 115, 310–311
and Tunisia, *see* Tunisia
and *Ukwashi Wa Chokwe*, 298
and U.S., 61–62, 69–70, 72, 94–96, 142, 182–183, 186, 201, 212, 221–222, 224, 231, 249–251, 267, 269, 307–308, 333, 343–345
see also Govêrno Revolucionário de Angola no Exílio (GRAE); *Frente Nacional de Libertação de Angola* (FNLA)
União das Populações do Norte de Angola (UPNA), 63–67, 75, 83, 85, 89, 107, 178, 292, 339
UNICEF, 72
Unidade Angolana, 207
Union Africaine et Malgache (UAM), 256–257, 291, 295
Union Congolaise pour la Libération de l'Angola (UCLA), 235, 316
Union de Défense des Intérêts Africains (UDDIA), 73–74, 98n
Union Générale des Travailleurs Angolais (UGTA), 241, 294
Union Générale Tunisienne du Travail (UGTT), 176–178, 241, 258
Union Panafricaine et Malgache des Travailleurs Croyants (UPMTC), 293
Union des Populations Camerounaises (UPC), 66
Union des Républiques de l'Afrique Centrale (URAC), 75
Union des Travailleurs Congolais (UTC), 293–294
Unitarians, 55n, 334
United Arab Republic, 203, 255, 261
United Church of Canada, 105
United Church of Christ, 105, 178, 245
United National Independence Party (UNIP), 299
United Nations
Angolan expectations of, 231
Congo operations, 229, 272
General Assembly
Fourteenth, 69, 86
Fifteenth, 45, 87–88, 97, 123, 181
Sixteenth, 184, 219, 268
Seventeenth, 184, 268–269
Eighteenth, 270
Fourth Committee of, 45, 69, 184, 275, 287, 289–290
Special Committee on Territories under Portuguese Administration, 245, 275, 279
Sub-Committee on the Situation in Angola, 192, 221, 281, 286, 289, 292–293, 345
lobbying at, 63, 68–69, 95, 237, 303–304, 310
Secretary-General, 63, 65, 87
Security Council, 130, 138, 140, 142, 181–183, 201, 268n
trusteeship for Angola, 61–62, 72
see also Article 73e; Petitions to the United Nations
United States of America
Air Force, 229, 230, 273
ally of Portugal, 163, 181–182, 184–186, 188–190, 232n, 269, 272–274
Angolans lobbying in, 63, 69, 142–143, 219–224, 237
Defense Department, 273
Department of State, 56, 62, 184, 186, 271, 274
Kennedy administration, 181–182, 186, 189, 222, 270–272
military aid to Portugal, 184, 201, 273

United States of America (continued)
policy toward colonial and nonwestern areas, 42n, 181–182, 201
pressure on Portugal, 183, 185, 190, 192–193, 270–271, 274
response to Angolan uprising, 181–187, 209–210, 232, 261, 268–277, 315
votes at U.N., 181–184, 186, 201, 268–269, 274, 276
see also American Committee on Africa; American Negro Leadership Conference on Africa; Anti-Americanism; Azores Islands
United States of Latin Africa, 74n
UPA, *see União das Populações de Angola*
Uprising of March 1961, 130–135
eruption of fighting, 142–143
nationalist military strategy, 145–147
Portuguese response to, 144–145
preparations for, 140-142
see also Rebellion of 1961

Vatican, 57, 303
Vigilantes (white), 6, 129, 153, 155
Vilinga Va Kambungo, 119
Viragem, 33n
A Voz da Nação Angolana, 87, 108

War on Want, 206n
Washington, 182–185, 195, 201, 209–210, 220, 271
Watch Tower movement, 78, 80–81
Wax, 103, 115
Wene wa Kongo, 288
West
aid to Portugal, 276–277
Angolan disillusionment with, 72, 146, 212, 315
influence on Angolan nationalists, 94–95
response to Angolan issue, 181–189, 200–203, 209–210, 271, 276
West Irian, 316n
"Western Civilization," by A. Neto, 38
Western Europe, 306, 335
Winneba, Ghana, 262, 283
World Assembly of Youth (WAY), 206n, 307
World Congress for General Disarmament and Peace (Moscow), 255
World Federation of Trade Unions (WFTU), 176
World Health Organization (WHO), 72

Xandel, 125n

Yugoslavia, 180
see also Belgrade

Zaire district, 164, 167–168, 292
Zamba, 288, 322–325, 328
Zambia, 116n
see also Northern Rhodesia
Zanzibar, 197
Zombo, 50–51, 95n, 327
see also Bazombo